EDUCATING
DEXTER

EDUCATING DEXTER

Dexter Manley AND Tom Friend

RUTLEDGE HILL PRESS
NASHVILLE, TENNESSEE

To life
starting over at thirty-one
—T. F.

Published in Nashville, Tennessee, by Rutledge Hill Press, 513 Third Avenue South, Nashville, Tennessee 37210. Distributed in Canada by H. B. Fenn and Company Ltd., Mississauga, Ontario.

Typography by D&T/Bailey, Nashville, Tennessee

Library of Congress Cataloging-in-Publication Data

Manley, Dexter, 1959–
    Educating Dexter / Dexter Manley and Tom Friend.
      p.   cm.
    ISBN 1-55853-194-7
    1. Manley, Dexter, 1959–   . 2. Football players—United States—Biography.   I. Friend, Tom. II. Title.
    GV939.M288A3   1992
    796.332'092—dc20
    [B]   92-27364
                                    CIP

Printed in the United States of America
1 2 3 4 5 6 7 8 — 98 97 96 95 94 93 92

Contents

Preface

THE BEST PART OF DEXTER MANLEY'S RETIREMENT speech was that he *read* it.

If only he could read his own psyche. In the year he and I spent on his autobiography, a year when he unconsciously gravitated toward cocaine, Dexter would speak desperately of overcoming his illiteracy and drug addiction and of sacking the hell out of NFL quarterbacks, but he would sometimes—in mid-sentence—inexplicably stop, pick up the telephone, and dial whomever.

In a restaurant once a total stranger walked by us palming a cellular phone, and Dexter asked if he could borrow it for a local call.

Put it this way: Dexter doesn't focus as well as Minolta. But you can't fault him. His intentions are admirable. An illiterate for two-thirds of his life, Dexter always had to have a pocket dictionary handy, regularly quizzed me on the meaning of words, and kept *Fortune* magazine on his coffee table rather than coffee. He negotiated his 1991 football contract for himself over—what else?—the telephone, but he'd consult his Verbal Advantage word source book during all the negotiating. He even sprang one of his new words on the Phoenix Cardinals general manager, Larry Wilson: *foil.*

He said, "Larry, I'm going to foil you."

Early in the 1991 football season, Dexter would drink Perrier in a wine glass. We would attend an Alcoholics Anonymous meeting one day, and then he'd browse a liquor store for champagne the next. He'd say, "Hey look!" I'd turn to find him chugging a bottle of wine, and I'd be about to call him a name when he'd show me he'd never popped the cork. He'd done it just to get a torrid reaction out of me.

His behavior put me in a peculiar quandary. I was no substance abuse doctor, but should I have threatened him not to step foot in the liquor store or else? Should I have body-blocked this 260-pound defensive end when I weigh precisely 140 pounds soaked with Evian? Should I have simply stayed in the car to protest his going inside the liquor store? But if I stayed in the car, what if he actually drank a quick Bloody Mary inside? Sometimes I felt I needed to baby-sit him.

Yet, through it all, Dexter remained this devoted father who'd order his three children to say "Yes, sir" and "No, sir." On a three-way telephone hookup one day with Dexter, me, and his then six-year-old son, Dexter Manley II, he told Little Dexter to hang up. Little Dexter said, "All right," and slammed the phone. Then he realized he hadn't tagged a "sir" to the end of his statement, so Little Dex politely picked up the telephone again and said, "All right . . . sir!"

I've been inside their home. A family portrait hangs well displayed on their living room wall. It didn't strike me much until Dexter's wife, Glinda, alerted me that Dexter posed for the shot with a cocaine hangover. At closer glance, you could notice his reddened, tired eyes.

Dexter—one of the greatest pass rushers the NFL has ever seen, primarily during his days with the Washington Redskins—knew all along what was at stake, and still he drifted toward cocaine. What was on the line for him? To name a few material things: a $600,000 salary and a fancy-schmancy car. To name a few nonmaterial things: his wife and kids.

He'd often say, "I have this good computer and this bad computer in my brain." No wonder he could never focus.

Finally, using cocaine like nasal spray in November 1991, he flunked an NFL drug test for the fourth time and had no choice but to retire before his time. Depressed, he then watched the Redskins win Super Bowl XXVI, just days after he'd begged out of a drug treatment center in Arizona. "The Redskins did it without me," he moaned. "Those boys are getting another ring and won't give me one."

More than anything, I'll never forget the traumatic days leading up to his retirement speech. He was in such denial that he told me: "Hey, I can get pedicures now. I never wanted to get pedicures while I was playing football 'cause I wanted to keep my feet rough. But now I can get a pedicure. Isn't that great?"

Educating Dexter, then, is all about his awakening to see there's more to life than perfect toenails.

—Tom Friend, January 1992

Acknowledgments

THIS BOOK WAS INITIALLY BRAINSTORMED IN THE spring of 1988 after Dexter admitted in a U.S. Senate hearing that he had steamrollered through high school and college on no further than a second grade reading level.

He was seeing a private tutor at the time but had slapped the following bumper sticker on his Ford Bronco: "It Is Better to Build Children Than to Repair Adults."

I told him he had a book in him, although he maintained he had sacks in him. He suggested we wait.

About a year later, we agreed to take his story to a book agent.

If it were all that simple in between, I'd stop here. But it wasn't. I will thank my former editor Frank Deford, who sponsored me to Sterling Lord Literistic long before the *National* folded, and Stuart Krichevsky of Sterling Lord, who pulled the rabbit out of the hat— twice.

I will thank Ben Bradlee, Len Downie, and George Solomon for letting me borrow the Redskin beat at *The Washington Post* for three seasons. Otherwise I never would have met Dexter.

I will thank the Phoenix Cardinals and Tampa Bay Buccaneers for access the Washington Redskins never would have granted a biographer.

I will thank my buddy Glinda Manley and her prolific children who don't have to call me Mr. Friend anymore: Dexter II and Dalis ("Sissy").

I will thank Dexter's other son, Derrick Manley, my roomie.

I will thank the staff of Sierra Tucson Treatment Center for making me understand I'm as much a patient as Dexter is.

I will thank everyone who spoke candidly about Dexter and his life in these pages, especially his sweet sister, Cynthia, his aunts

Monneola and Joycee, and his uncle Wilbur, all of whom painted a great verbal portrait of his childhood. And Dexter's high school wife, Stephanye, who could've been bitter and said no comment but did the opposite.

I will thank Darryl Grant, Dexter's closest friend on the Redskins all those years.

And the others I am indebted to for speaking from their hearts about Dexter are Pham Chopra, Dale Roark, Pat Jones, Bobby Beathard, Wayne Sevier, Neal Olkewicz, Bobby Mitchell, Bubba Tyer, Joe Theismann, Dan Riley, Darrell Green, Rick Walker, R. C. Thielemann, Gerald Franklin, Cathy Jones, James Wanser, Luther Booker, Maurice McGowen, and Larry Marshall.

I will thank the best newspaper editor I've ever come across, Emilo Garcia-Ruiz, who proved he wouldn't make a bad book editor.

I will thank the best book editor I've ever come across, Ron Pitkin of intelligent Rutledge Hill Press.

I will thank Lisa Lang and her family for making the Houston portion of the book comfortable and informative.

I will thank Charlie Dayton and the Redskins public relations office; Aaron Ogata of Radio Shack-Marina del Rey for solving all my technical and printing queries; and H. I. T. Secretarial Services of Santa Monica for transcribing four-months worth of tape, even the loud stuff from Houston's Restaurant.

I will thank my close friends—Diane Murray, Kathy Wetherell, Lori Jackson, Tom Wald—for injecting me with sanity, not to mention my soul mate Patricia M. Friend, who just so happens to be my mom.

Plus, the rest of the Friend family who, for some reason, refuse to lose faith in me.

Last and *definitely* not least, I bow to Dexter, my confidant.

—Tom Friend, July 1992

Prologue

FIRST THINGS FIRST: I CAN READ MY OWN BOOK. The mere size of it intimidates me because I've always been scared stiff of long books, but I can pronounce every word in here.

I thought you should know that. I have been tested and dissected by many teachers with thick bifocals, and they have informed me that I teeter on a ninth-grade reading level.

I only backtrack to a kindergarten level when I am on cocaine. Some say cocaine is performance-enhancing, but, hell, it ain't reading-enhancing.

I am not sure if there was a single incident that saved me from being obliterated by drugs; probably, there were a few. But I can tell you that eight months ago—free from Paul Tagliabue's Dixie cup and tempted to pour cocaine even on my eggs—two things occurred to lead me one last time into drug rehabilitation.

This may have saved me from becoming past tense.

It was January of 1992, not long after I'd been forced to retire from the National Football League for having cocaine in my pores. I was about to leave my house to use drugs again when my seven-year-old son asked, "Daddy, are you going out to do drugs?"

I said, "Nooooooo."

I lied.

I don't know what's worse, lying to the kid who looks like you, talks like you, and has your same first and last name, or not being able to read Dr. Seuss to him.

When I got back from using cocaine again, my son and my five-year-old daughter both asked me to read them a bedtime story, and I couldn't complete three syllables. I could not read. I couldn't stay focused, probably from being under the influence, and I saw myself slipping into my old, wrong, lazy, grammar-school ways. I saw the word *his,* and I said something not even close. It doesn't take a rocket scientist to read *his,* but it was hard for me to even look at the word.

So my son and daughter went and fetched their mom.

"Mommy, can you read to us?" they asked. "Daddy can't."

You may have heard of me, Dexter Manley. You *should* have heard of me. I am the large football player who stayed eligible for high school and college football as an illiterate. I am the large football player who tried conning every drug counselor I ever met. I am the large football player who was asked on national TV if I was on drugs and answered, "I'll take a leak for you right here." I am the large football player who, at age thirty, sneaked into school with ten-year-olds to relearn the English language. I am the large football player who testified to the U.S. Senate regarding my learning disability and—for reasons I can't comprehend—became a folk hero over it. I am the large football player you frequently see crying on TV. I am the large football player who set the NFL record for drug tests flunked—four.

After my fourth flubbed test—during the 1991 season—my marriage barely was held together by a thread, and my wife was ready to snip it clean. Glinda already had made an appointment with her divorce attorney, and she already had banished me to sleep in the basement, not with her, because of my propensity to do coke and hang on the telephone with other women.

So, I woke up on February 14, 1992, and wrote her a note. It was no valentine.

Here I was, banned from football and unable to read a three-letter word to my son, Dexter II, and my daughter, Dalis. Here I was, so out of whack I was fibbing to my kids. I knew I had no choice but to break my link with drugs. My note to Glinda said I was checking into rehab—for a *fifth* time—in Tucson.

*D*exter's note was in broken English. I could hardly make it out.
    All I know is Little Dexter's kindergarten teacher called me later to say, "Mrs. Manley, Little Dexter was a wreck in school this morning." Apparently, Little Dexter kept saying to the teacher, "My daddy told me this morning he's leaving. I need to say goodbye to my daddy."
    Then the teacher said, "Please tell Big Dexter that if he leaves to come say goodbye to his son."

But next time I heard from Big Dexter was at 4:00 P.M. from an airplane phone.

Now let me tell you about my son, Dexter. He's a real suburb guy. I was a city slicker growing up, but Little Dexter gets to hang out on cul-de-sacs. Little Dexter's got eyes the size of the moon, and he tells total strangers, "My daddy did crack." He walks up to these people, tugs on their sleeves, and breaks the news as if he's Peter Jennings. Well, I never did do crack—I snorted regular old cocaine—buy my son has heard of crack and has an imagination.

Little Dexter also saw my retirement speech on TV. He saw me read my goodbye—I read unbelievably well that day—and he also saw me break down and bawl my eyes out in the process. I do not know what that does to a seven-year-old, but I do know one of the first people to call our house that evening happened to get Little Dexter on the telephone.

Little Dexter casually asked him, "Do you know my daddy's not playing football anymore?"

He tries to act unaffected by it all, but his seven-year-oldness eventually comes out. The night I left for Tucson, Glinda had to field his thirty questions. Little Dexter's repeated remark to her was, "Do you know where Daddy is? Do you know where Daddy is?"

Later that evening, Glinda was on the telephone during dinner and told a friend, "I just hope Big Dexter doesn't end up in J-A-I-L."

Little Dexter, my first grader, shouted with his half-dollar-sized eyes: "Jail! That spells jail . . . Is *that* where Daddy is?"

He spells pretty good, huh?

To be honest, rehab ain't a lot different from jail. I mean, when you get arrested, at least you get one phone call. But, hell, when I checked into the Sierra Tucson treatment center last February, I wasn't even allowed to call Information.

I had to tiptoe in the middle of the night to use the phone. I learned later this was all part of my impulsiveness, of my disease. It is just so hard for me to follow rules.

I have had car phones, portable phones, cellular phones, phones practically attached to my ear, but I never, ever considered that as a disease. Are there TA meetings? Telephones Anonymous? I had always felt like, This is nothing. This is just the phone. I checked with a lot of drug counselors, and I realized I was not willing to give up my relationship with Ma Bell. Bottom line was, I had a hang-up with phones: I couldn't hang up.

Until now—and this is a miracle—I never, ever believed I was an alcoholic or addict. Of course, for years I lied and said I believed it. I lied, went to practically every drug treatment center in America, and memorized the Alcoholics Anonymous steps, but it was all for show, all to get my ass back into football. I'm one hell of an actor. I'm a survivor. As a member of the Washington Redskins, I had my own TV show and didn't even know how to read flip cards. I ordered from the menu at the Palm Restaurant not knowing how to read the Soup of the Day; I was on drugs from 1985 on and kept the Redskins in the dark about it. They might have stayed in the pitch black, too, if my wife hadn't snitched to the coach, Joe Gibbs. I tell you, I can put on some Boy George makeup.

I used to sign autographs like this: "Dexter Manley—Say No To Drugs (?)."

Think they took my question mark seriously?

I played around a lot, but deep inside now, I'd like to stay cleaner than the pope. Actually, I'd like a lot of things:

1. I'd like my daughter to walk without pain.
2. I'd like to read *War and Peace*, without underlining every word with my finger.
3. I'd like to redo elementary school, with competent teachers.
4. I'd like the big contract I screwed myself out of.
5. I'd like my daddy to come back from the dead, even though he used to lock me in a closet.
6. I'd like my brother and momma back, too.
7. I'd like my other brother to quit stealing.
8. I'd like my sister to remain off crack, or I'll cut out sending her checks.
9. I'd like to lose my own drug pusher's phone number.
10. I'd like to ring Joe Montana's clock. Oh, that's right, I've said that before.

At this point, I'll have to settle for Doug Flutie, who is no Montana. I am playing in Canada now for the Ottawa Roughriders, exiled from U.S. football like some sixties draft dodger. But I've come to the realization that my big problem is I've denied I am an addict. In *my* mind, an addict is down and out and scrounging through trash cans for Spam. I never considered myself down and out. I mean, I own a Rolls-Royce.

I never believed I was an addict, yet from 1987 on, I kept a daily calendar of when I did drugs. That way, I knew how many days I had from the time I did coke until the time I had to take a urine test. I kept a calendar for cocaine that exact same way a woman keeps a calendar for her menstrual cycle.

I never believed I was an addict, although some people saw through my bullshit. I snuck into the Hazelden Foundation in January 1986 under an assumed name—merely to keep my marriage afloat— and Redd Foxx's nephew, who was in there with me, told me right then, "You'll be back."

He also said, "If you don't stop doing drugs, it's going to get worse every year."

Five years later, as a member of the 1991 Tampa Bay Buccaneers, I snuck one more hit of cocaine twelve weeks into the season and committed my football suicide. I had to retire from the NFL. An old timer at an AA meeting told me right then, "You don't fucking believe AA son. I don't believe you fucking believe it."

I better believe it now.

I have learned that three things can happen to you if you stay on cocaine: You'll get locked up in jail, be covered up with a white sheet, or end up in the loony bin.

I vote for none of the above.

You know, I have never had to function without football before. Growing up, I could not read dictionaries, but I could read offenses. Football got me C & R suits in high school, a hot rod car in college, and Luis Vuitton bags as a pro. I know nothing else besides football. So do I have the toughness to provide for my family now? Do I have what it takes? I don't know that I do.

I'm real sensitive. I cry at movies; I cry for the homeless. People say they like me because I am a particularly muscular man who is able to weep in public. That doesn't mean I'm weak or strong; but what I'm wondering is, when the tough times really begin, am I gonna bawl in the corner or what?

I believe a lot of that has to do with . . . I guess I want to blame my daddy.

But I won't blame my daddy. I've learned not to. Nor will I make excuses for my behavior. I'm pointing the finger right here—*at myself.* I am the one who couldn't read or write. I faced up to it, and now I am actually writing a column for an Ottawa, Canada, newspaper. Not long ago, I couldn't even write a memo.

I repeat, I am pointing the finger right here. I mean, I was the reason Little Dexter has such fear. The whole family flew up to Ottawa for my Roughrider press conference in June, and somebody told Little Dexter that Ottawa has only four or five murders a year. And Little Dexter, who's used to a murder a day in Washington and wonders if I'm going to be the next to die, delightfully shrieked, "Oh, yeah!"

I'm blaming everything on *me*. I am the one who put that crap up my nose; no one stood over me like a Los Angeles cop making me do it. I am responsible for my actions. People look at me goofy-eyed and say, "How could you throw away a career and a $700,000 salary by using drugs?" Well, all I can do is help you understand.

AN IDLE THOUGHT

The whole reason I laid out $105,000 cash for that Rolls-Royce of mine—as if I had Mafia money or something—was because I thought it would steer me away from drugs.

This was after the Washington Redskins and I won the Super Bowl XXII in San Diego in January 1988. I took an innocent drive one day to scope out some cars, and the computer in my brain said, "Gimme that Rolls."

Glinda flipped, and I had to rationalize to her why it was great to have $100,000 less in the bank. I told her the Rolls would start making me feel like a respectable man and that it would slow my butt down. I told her no dope addicts tool around in Rolls-Royces.

I bought that car for image, man. I figured people would say, "Boy, that Manley . . ."

It all boiled down to false pride. Everything about me was fake and unreal, and that's because of my low self-esteem. I simply wanted to make people think, Boy, that Manley is a nice guy. Look at him. He's a very respectable man, a young guy driving a Rolls. Boy, he must have some money somewhere. He's not spending it all on drugs.

But after about a month, I lost the thrill of that car. It didn't make me respectable. Hell, I only drove it on Sundays, and I kept it locked up in storage the rest of the time. I don't think it's got even four thousand miles on it today.

I need to sell that sucker right now so I can pay off my second mortgage. Personally, I think it should go for a price in the $80,000-

$90,000 range. I mean, it's Dexter Manley's Rolls-Royce. That's like somebody buying Liberace's Rolls-Royce.

Of course, the way the economy's going, it might not be easy. Hell, they're not even buying Donald Trump's crap right now.

Time to sell the Rolls-Royce.

CHAPTER 1

A Lousy
Twenty Bucks' Worth

I WAS THE TURKEY LAST THANKSGIVING. THANKS-giving eve I was shaving in the locker room at One Buccaneer Place, and the Tampa Bay trainer tapped me on the shoulder, almost making me drop my can of Foamy.

He said, "Hey Dexter, Dr. Brown wants to talk to you."

Doc Brown is the National Football League's drug advisor. I had met him exactly one year earlier when I was begging back into football. I had just finished a year's suspension for cocaine snorting, and it was Doc Brown and Commissioner Paul Tagliabue who reinstated me. I sort of liked Doc Brown. He was more responsible than his predecessor, Dr. Forrest Tennant, who actually came out to Redskin Park once in the early 1980s and gave our team a lecture on how to beat a drug test.

I thought Tennant's job was to catch us *on* drugs. But that day, Tennant alerted us to the dangers and side effects of drugs and how you can sweat them out of your system. He said, "Drink a lot of water, which will flush 'em out of you, or sit in a sauna."

Our coach, Joe Gibbs, blurted, "Hey, don't tell them how to beat it!"

But after that, boy, I used to wear out that sauna at the Regency Club in Virginia.

Anyway, when I got on the phone with Doc Brown on Thanks-giving eve, he said, "Dexter, get to a pay phone and call me back."

My heart palpitated. I phoned him back from my cellular phone in my truck, and he said, "Dexter, we have a positive test."

I put on my Boy George makeup. I told Doc Brown I didn't do cocaine. I guess he wanted me to confess, but I kept lying up a storm. Right then, one of my Tampa teammates saw me talking on the phone in my truck and started banging on my window. He wanted to use my apartment to be with some freaky woman he'd lined up. I could hear him yelling, "Come on. I got to go to the freak. The freak's gonna meet me."

His freaks may have been coming, but my career was going. Ignoring him, I told Doc Brown someone must've framed me, someone must've put cocaine in my drink. I was getting tested three times a week—Mondays, Thursdays, and Fridays—and Doc Brown said there were 1,332 nanograms in my system from the previous Thursday's urine test. That's a boatload. And he said there were 582 nanograms from the next day's test, that Friday.

I was trying to con Doc Brown. I was in such denial, I said, "Doc Brown, I would not do drugs on a Wednesday night and then walk in on a Thursday of my own free will with a boatload of coke in me, and take a drug test. I'm from the ghetto of Houston. I got street sense. I'm not someone from skid row who just doesn't care and just walks in for a drug test."

He just answered, "We have a positive test."

I asked, "Am I out of football?"

"I don't know," he replied.

When he asked me what I did the Tuesday night before the positive Thursday drug test, I told him the truth: I went to a strip bar. He asked me what I ate, and I told him I ate a sub sandwich, ate it in my truck. I went inside the bar, sat there by myself, had a Coca-Cola, and went home by myself.

Well, that was almost the truth.

I hung up with Doc Brown and drove home. My son Derrick, who was fourteen, was visiting me from Houston. And at first, I did not tell Derrick what was brewing.

I never tell Derrick what's brewing. I didn't tell Derrick I was checking into drug rehab in the spring of 1987, and Derrick found out about it from a teacher in elementary school. I mean, my first wife, Stephanye, almost fought that teacher. Derrick hears a lot of things about me at school. Kids say, "Dumb Dexter" to him and things like, "I was smoking crack with your dad."

Derrick thinks they say these things because they're jealous of him, and he says he ignores them and walks away. I don't know how long he'll be able to keep that up.

Derrick's mother even suggested last year that Derrick tell no one in school who his father was. So he denied my existence. How do you like that?

Well, on Thanksgiving eve, Derrick and I were on our way to Champions to eat, and he was the first person I lied to. I was a wreck, as he could see. So I slammed the brake and told him the league had a positive test on me. But I also swore to him that I didn't use drugs. I swore their test was inaccurate.

My old ghetto tricks were coming out. I wanted to see if Doc Brown would let it slide. If he did, I wouldn't have to tell *anyone* the truth.

When I told Derrick my lie, he clammed up like Harpo Marx. All Manleys have the gift of gab, but he muted on me.

I said, "Are you mad and angry? Are you scared?"

We arrived at Champions, and Derrick still was handing out the silent treatment. Eventually, he bummed a quarter off me to play a video game. That's what he wanted to do now—play Nintendo.

I later told him, "Derrick, don't go this way. Let my life be a lesson to you." If my son doesn't learn from this, there's something the hell wrong with him.

The next morning, I woke up sad and melodramatic. The instant my eyelids opened, I thought of the tragedy. I did that every morning for a week. I'd awaken thinking I'd had a nasty dream, hoping it wasn't real. I thought, Why do I have to learn the hard way? Why do I have to cost myself my family?

Sure enough, Glinda asked me for a separation a month and a half after my relapse, which was no shocker. She had threatened to do so many times.

If he goes back on drugs, I'm not going back with my husband. Print that in his book! It hurts me because his kids love him more than anything. I mean, Dalis sometimes sits in the car staring into space, and I say, "Dalis, what are you thinking about?"

She answers, "My daddy."

She does it once or twice a day. Every day.

At the dinner table one day, I was talking about Thanksgiving and she said, "I'm sitting next to my daddy on Thanksgiving."

"Daddy's not going to be here for Thanksgiving," I replied. "He'll be in Tampa playing football."

She stopped eating and looked down at the floor. I tried soothing her, "Christmas is real quick after Thanksgiving, and he'll be home then." But it was like the wind had been knocked out of her.

If I leave him, my kids will hate me. I'll be the culprit. But I'll tell them

*the truth. I'll tell them it's hard to live with their daddy when he's on drugs.
And Dexter and I will part as friends. But my kids will have anger. They'll
think, Mommy broke it up.*

But I will not go through it again.

I returned to practice after Thanksgiving, still waiting to
hear how Doc Brown was going to sentence me. Since it would be my
fourth positive test, he had the option of booting me out. It hadn't
really sunk in that I could be through with football forever. It was still a
secret and hadn't been leaked to the media. And I'm used to secrets.
Of course, they tell you in Alcoholics Anonymous, "Your best secrets
will get you drunk and high again."

I'd almost made it through the season clean, but I was on my own
in Tampa. My family was in D.C., and I was lonely. There was a
topless bar a half mile from my Tampa apartment, and I could never
drive by that strip bar without looking at it out of the corner of my eye.

With me, it was always cocaine luring me to women, women
luring me to coke. It's happened that way every time, and my wife
knows it. The average Joe Blow can go into those strip bars with no
problems, so I used to wonder, why can't I? But it's simply another form
of addiction. The Sierra Tucson drug rehab center even told me in
1989 if I don't get my sex addiction straightened out, something bad
will keep happening. Just like Gary Hart.

See, going into those strip bars got my mind on coke. In the old
days I used to purchase coke in women's restrooms in strip bars.

So, here's how I relapsed: On Tuesday, November 19, 1991, after
hanging out at the strip bar, I had the opportunity to buy coke. I figured
I'd purchase it for a friend but wouldn't touch it. *Would not touch it!*

Immediately, though—probably from the fear of knowing I was
about to have cocaine in my presence again—I sweated through my
Ralph Lauren shirt.

In reality, my real relapse had begun a month earlier when I
started loitering in liquor stores, buying champagne for friends. I had
no business buying anyone alcohol, but it was my disease owning me.
Then, one night, I took a tiny sip of champagne. Pretty soon came my
tiny hit of coke.

I'll show you how confused I was. The night I used coke, I thought
of FBI agents on TV. There, the agents always taste the cocaine when
they arrest drug dealers to see if it's authentic. They never get high off
of that, right? So, my thinking was I'd just test the coke as an FBI
agent would. That way, it'd never show up in my system. I took a taste

from my finger tip, and then I put a little coke in each nostril—sniff, sniff. That was it. No more than twenty dollars' worth. Paranoid, I flushed the rest down the toilet.

As little as I'd snorted, I thought it would be out of my system by my next drug test in two days, November 21. I did my usual six-pack of Evian to flush it out as Forrest Tennant had suggested.

Unbelievably, my test showed those 1,332 nanograms. I asked a guy from a drug lab how in the world that much could register, and he said the coke must have been very pure, right off the boat from South America.

When Doc Brown busted me on Thanksgiving eve, I flashed back to my childhood and the lousy neighborhood I'd grown up in in Houston, Texas. I said to myself, Will I have to live there again? I can't do that to my kids.

My kids need good schools. Both my little boy and my little girl have been diagnosed with the learning disabilities I have.

I'd have to be stingy with my money. Because I'm a shopaholic, it'd strangle me some. Glinda buys sales; I don't. I never thought Paul Tagliabue could suspend me for overdosing on shoes, so I used to live in Florsheim stores. But no more. I'd have to cut the lavish spending. Everything would go to my kids' schooling.

Fortunately, about $300,000 of my $650,000 contract in 1991 was deferred until 1992, so I could rest easy and know I'd have money coming in initially. I'd just be smart with my money.

Well, after that "FBI snort" of mine on November 19, I suited up for three more NFL games. I didn't stop using drugs, either. Cocaine looks like snow, and it has a snowball effect, too. After I sniffed that one measly amount on November 19, the cycle started again. I had two or three more relapses. The league only knew about the first relapse, and I held out hope they'd let me off the hook.

They didn't catch me. Like I said, I played three more games after my original relapse. One was in Miami. I wasn't sure at the time if it would be my last; so I played like a rookie. I cherished every moment. At times I'd be overcome with sadness. I'd look at the highlight scoreboard and get teary-eyed. Mark Duper ran in front of me once, and I thought, Damn, he'll play two or three more years. I looked at all these average players and thought, Damn, they'll make $500,000 or $600,000 next year.

I appreciated the blue skies and the national anthem like never before. I mean, when I was a Redskin, I never stood still during the anthem. The team would get nasty letters about me because I'd be pacing the bench as soon as the "Oh, say can you see . . ." started. But I stood still as a rock for the Miami anthem.

That morning, I had sniffed around the team to see if anyone knew of my relapse. I saw the Tampa Bay owner, Hugh Culverhouse, and the team doctor, Doc Diaco, in the cafeteria. Mr. C just said, "Hi Dexter!" He didn't know diddly.

I was still in denial. I kept telling my attorney, Bob Woolf, I'd take a lie detector test, insisting that I hadn't done drugs.

I was hoping to sack Dan Marino's butt in that game, but he has the quick release of a baseball pitching machine and escaped. But it felt good afterward when Don Shula approached me beside our team bus and said, "You looked good out there, Dexter."

Unfortunately, Doc Brown couldn't keep my secret forever. He sent my original positive drug test back to the lab to be double-checked, and it came back positive again. A lousy twenty bucks' worth of coke was going to cost me my livelihood. Pretty soon, Doc Diaco knew, Mr. Culverhouse knew, and I even got a phone call one night from a *Tampa Tribune* newspaper reporter who knew. I simply talked him out of printing the story. I didn't deny it; I just made him feel guilty by saying, "How can you come to me with something like this that can destroy my family?" He bought it.

I hoped the league would let me finish the season and then quietly retire. My relapse wouldn't have to be released to the public. But one of the league officials said that would set a bad precedent.

I desperately wanted Mr. Culverhouse to ask Paul Tagliabue to have mercy on me. I wanted to be dressed nice and conservative and approach Mr. C and come clean to him with my feelings. I wanted to tell Mr. C, "Sir, I've been clean two years, and I don't want this to come out. It could be devastating to my family, so I'd just like to retire and save face. Can you tell this to Commissioner Tagliabue?"

Mr. C liked me. Everyone in Tampa liked me. They liked my energy and the way I played football. I wanted to tell Mr. C I'd made a grave mistake and that if the NFL could just let me retire, I'd have an easier chance of finding a job after football. I hoped he'd be sympathetic. If they would let me finish the season, I'd even donate my last game check to drug prevention in the Tampa area. I'd rather do that and save my name.

I figured Mr. C had voted for Tagliabue back when Tagliabue had been elected commissioner and maybe he could pull if off.

Well, I never had the guts to ask him. I pulled Mr. C aside at the pregame meal before my last game against Minnesota on December 8. I began, "Mr. C . . . "

Then I looked at him dead in the face, man to man, and said, "Mr. C, I'm sorry. Thanks for the opportunity."

He said, "Of all the people around here, I was pulling for you, Dexter . . . I frankly don't understand why you did it, but it's in the league's hands now."

It just wasn't in my gut to ask him to go to Tagliabue for mercy.

Of course, then Mr. C came up to me before kickoff and said, "I want three sacks, Dexter, and that's that."

I started to say, "If I do, will you . . . " I came so close, but I didn't ask him.

During that game, which turned out to be my very last, I contemplated so many things. I even considered faking an injury. That way, they'd have to pay me past my retirement. But that wasn't in my gut either. Guess what I did do, though? I got a sack.

The following week, we decided it was best that I admit my relapse at a news conference and retire. The whole day, I thought of my kids.

For instance, Glinda and I had had an argument that summer in front of them in a Phoenix hotel room. While we argued, little Dexter sneaked to the hotel room door and latched the chain.

He didn't want his daddy to leave.

I know where he's coming from on that one.

An Idle Thought

You know, there's one other drug I took before football games, and I used to swallow it right in front of Joe Gibbs.

The NFL has outlawed this drug, although I'll have you know my six-year-old son can buy it—no questions asked—at any 7-Eleven convenience store.

I'm talking about Sudafed.

It never showed up in my urine, so I'd sometimes take ten Sudafeds a game.

I would never have known to try it, but the league's assistant director of security, Charles Jackson, lectured our Redskins team during the 1987 training camp, warning us not to use certain drugs. He listed marijuana, and then Sudafed.

I turned to my teammate Darryl Grant and said, "What's Sudafed?"

Darryl told me he popped Sudafeds himself. I called Thomas ("Hollywood") Henderson, who told me Sudafed was a stimulant. It may be a cold pill to you and your grandmother, but to NFL players it dries you up and—for some reason—enhances your performance.

I walked out of that meeting with Charles Jackson with a new trick up my sleeve.

His marijuana speech had been enlightening, too. He told us that smoking marijuana dilates your eyes and ruins your concentration and causes receivers to drop the football. So, I left that meeting ready with new ammunition. I'd start telling running back Kelvin Bryant, "Hey, you better catch that ball, KB, or else it's that marijuana."

And whenever KB would drop one, I'd go, "Hey, stop smoking that weed, KB. Stop smoking that dope. If you don't stop dropping 'em, the coaches are gonna know."

Meantime, I tested the Sudafed before a game at Buffalo in 1987. I took five tablets before kickoff and five more at halftime. I was foaming at the mouth I was so loaded. I went off in the locker room, tearing up chairs and coffeepots and sweating profusely. Our trainer, Bubba Tyer, and doctor, Doc Knowlan, thought I was on coke and made me take a drug test the next day.

By the way, I sacked Jim Kelly's ass twice.

CHAPTER 2
You're Calling Me Dumb?

YOU'RE PROBABLY CALLING ME STUPID FOR snorting coke instead of Neo-Synephrine.

Glinda did. After I informed her I'd slipped up again—for a fourth time—she said to a friend of ours, "Dexter's either mentally retarded or sick. He's probably both. A mentally retarded person does this. The man has a personality defect."

Everyone believes I'm dumb. Jack Kent Cooke, the Redskins owner, called me a "bloody idiot" on TV after I'd relapsed in 1989. He was terrible to me on the air. He said, in that Hepburn voice of his, "How can Dexter be so stuuuupid?"

He then called me the next day and said something like, "Hi Dexteeeeeer." I started conning him and denying to him that I had done drugs, telling him the Redskins were wrong and that he and Joe Gibbs already had convicted me.

But he had called me to tell me to watch the TV news.

"You watch halftime of the Penn State-Maryland game," Cooke had said. "I've gone on TV talking sweeeeeell about you."

So I watched, and he said on TV he'd take me back when my drug suspension was up. All that bullshit.

The next morning, he called again. I said, "Good morning, Mr. Cooke," and he said, "I don't want to heeeeeear that shit, Dexter. You owe me an apooooooology for your comments to me yesterday, saying I was convicting you. Did you hear what I said on TV about you?"

It was as if Mr. Cooke was trying to deny he ever called me stupid. He said, "You always trust the media, Dexter. Joe Gibbs and I always tried to tell you: Don't trust the media!"

Hell, the only reason he'd telephoned me was he wanted me to tell the media he'd supported me. It was nothing but a con. He wanted good PR after he'd originally called me stupid. I never obliged him.

Cooke wanted a good image, but he ended up catching a lot of heat for saying I was stupid. He's supposed to be an upstanding citizen and very responsible man, but how can he get on me when he has a four-year-old daughter he's seen only once?

How can he get on me when his current wife, Marlene Ramallo Chalmers, served three and one-half months in the joint for conspiring to import less than a kilogram of cocaine? Hell, maybe I snorted some of the coke she imported.

Listen, it's nothing about being stupid! I didn't want to go back on coke.

Why did I relapse? No one can answer that. No doctor, no psychologist. The only one who can answer that is me.

I've been to drug treatment more than I've been to the bank. The counselors in there are always delving into my past, into my childhood. They want to blame my addiction on my parents, and I don't buy it.

They want to say I grew up in a dysfunctional home, but I tell you I had great parents. They gave me morals, took me to church, made me try and study after school.

When I did something wrong, I caught a whupping. Today, they call that child abuse, but that's discipline, man. I understood that.

Dysfunctional? It's not like my daddy came in the house like an alcoholic beating up my momma. These other patients I've been with in rehab centers have major crap from their pasts to deal with. They whine about child abuse and sexual and mental abuse and incest. I didn't have any of that crap growing up.

I can say the one awful thing from my childhood was my lack of education. My daddy called me dumb, and it created low self-esteem. If I want to be angry today, it would be because my daddy didn't have the money to get me the right education, but that's all.

These drug counselors always want to dissect my siblings and my origins to look for clues on why I'm an addict. So let's dissect me.

AN IDLE THOUGHT

People often ask me if I have a role model.

Well, since my daddy couldn't be a role model from his casket, I had to find somebody else.

That's why I've sort of anointed Fred Ford, who for several years was the man the NFL put in charge of giving me a urinalysis cup to pee in.

You'd think a drug tester/drug testee relationship would be adversarial, but I can smooth things over with most anyone. Mr. Ford is an older black man, with morals and character and intelligence. I admired that. The first time I met him was in the office of Redskins team doctor Donald Knowlan, and Mr. Ford was strictly business.

But I loosened ole Fred up. I said, "Mr. Ford, these white folks have you and me fighting one another. Mr. Ford, how can you and I fight each other, man?"

From them on, Fred Ford and I were closer than a toe to a toenail.

CHAPTER 3

Body Double

NEVER UNDERESTIMATE THE IMPACT OF A DADDY. So let me bring you up to date about mine.

My daddy went by several different aliases. Carl was his real name, but my granddaddy—Arthur Manley—nicknamed him Mike. I don't know why. My daddy also nicknamed himself Doc. So that's three names he had.

I asked my daddy's sisters—Aunt Monneola and Aunt Joycee—how my daddy met my momma, and Aunt Monneola answered. "He told her a lie."

"A lie?" I questioned.

Aunt Monneola said, "Yes sir. He told your momma he was a doctor."

I imagine that's why he called himself "Doc" or "Dr. Carl." He was a limo driver for Tenneco Oil Company in Houston, wore a uniform on the job, and Aunt Monneola says, "Every time your daddy went out, you didn't know whether he was going to work. That's because he would dress like he was a doctor."

So I suppose my daddy was a con man just like me. I asked Aunt Monneola why he never was in the military, and she answered, "Probably told a lie to get out."

Sounds as if my daddy and I are body doubles. He was dark skinned, and I'm dark skinned. He was about six-foot-three, as I am now; he dressed spiffy, just as I do; and he liked foot-long cigars, just as I do.

The Redskins used to think I had a big mouth, but my relatives say my daddy could "talk the ears off a jack rabbit."

When I was a boy, he never went anywhere without a hat or shined shoes. He had more alligator and crocodile skin in his closet than a real alligator or crocodile has on its carcass.

I'm told he'd drive to Houston from his hometown of Sealy, Texas, when he was younger and order a tailor-made suit. But he'd only have a "quarter" to pay for it. "Your daddy would have the suit sent to Sealy, C.O.D.," Aunt Monneola remembers, "and everybody would have to hustle to help him pay for it."

Somebody asked Aunt Monneola if Daddy was a womanizer, and she answered, "He thought he was. He thought he was cute, and he knowed he was the best-dressed man in Sealy. He didn't have no girlfriend, but he knew he was the best dressed. Mike liked Mike. He was in love with Mike."

I've been accused of the same thing.

A lot of what I know about my daddy is from Aunt Monneola and Aunt Joycce because he died when I was just seventeen. In fact, he died with me having told him—guess what?—a lie.

An Idle Thought

What, me lie?

I imagine it's possible. I mean, my attorney Richard Bennett and I once told the Redskins a little white lie to get a new contract out of them in 1983.

What we did was tell the Redskins I had a three-year, $1 million offer from the Chicago Blitz of the U.S.F.L.

That was a lie.

What we did arrange for was Blitz general manager Bruce Allen— son of the late George Allen—to go along with our fib. Bruce, whose dad had been fired by the Redskins in 1977 and had a score to settle, leaked it to the Chicago papers that the Blitz were aggressively pursuing me, and the Redskins got all hyper about it.

Jack Kent Cooke and Bobby Beathard called me in for a meeting at our training camp in Carlisle, Pennsylvania, and Mr. Cooke said, "Dexteeeeeer, I'll give you $100,000 cash on the side if you accept our contract offer to stay."

"Mr. Cooke, I just want what's fair."

"Dexteeeeer, what is fair? What do you want?"

Mr. Cooke thought he could bribe me with the $100,000, but I hedged, "I have a representative, Richard Bennett, and I shouldn't accept anything without him being here."

Mr. Cooke answered, "Bobby, God darnit, trade that guy! I want you to trade him to New Orleans."

Well, knowing how the Dallas Cowboys were our rivals and everything, I replied, "Mr. Cooke, better yet I'd appreciate it if you'd trade me to the Cowboys."

"The Cowboys wouldn't take a guy like yoooooou. Too much money! Get out of my office right now!" he demanded.

Joe Gibbs walked up to me later and said, "Dexter, you shouldn't disrespect the grandfather."

Well, the next day in the papers, the Redskins had leaked it out that I might get traded to the New Orleans Saints. John Riggins was walking around the locker room spouting, "Dexter's gonna be traded, Dexter's gonna be traded."

It was sort of hilarious. Tim Brant, one of the Washington sportscasters, gave me a red Chicago Blitz cap, and I wore it all over Carlisle. The Redskins thought I was serious. We were about to play the Bengals in an exhibition game on a Friday night, August 12, and I told Gibbs I was going to Chicago to speak seriously to the Blitz on Saturday.

Which was a lie.

Gibbs suggested that was the wrong thing to do. That Friday, the Redskins signed me.

CHAPTER 4

"Manley Blood"

LIKE I'VE SAID, MY REHAB COUNSELORS WANT TO blame my drug addiction on my upbringing. I don't think they know as much as they think they know, but maybe it's worth looking at my childhood.

I can't say I ever slept past 8:00 A.M. growing up. I still never do. It was my daddy's rule that we had to be up with the roosters, like we were farmers or something, and no naps were allowed afterward. He was a human alarm clock, shouting, "Up time! Up time! Up time!"

Saturday mornings, I'd want to get my butt out of the house before my daddy assigned the chores. Otherwise, I'd have to wax the floors or mow the yard or scrub.

If his limo was in the driveway when I came home from school, I hated it and would hang around outside until nightfall. If I went inside, it meant I'd have to stay busy and couldn't watch "Leave It to Beaver" on our Zenith.

I liked that show. See, I was just like the Beav.

I was always mischievous. I used to put on P. F. Flyers and actually think I could fly. I didn't jump out of a window to test them out, but I would sprint down the street, hopping in the air. I also thought if I chewed a Lifesaver, I was gonna live longer. So I started sucking on a pack a day.

I remember fiddling with an electrical box outside our house, receiving an electrical jolt and flying backward twenty feet like a paper airplane. Now, that's a Beav for you.

My sister Cynthia can vouch for me:

Our mom and daddy were hard workers, so we kids were on our own a lot. We'd want to go to the park or to the movies, and our folks didn't really have the time to take us. That let Dexter run on the loose.

23

Dexter would terrorize the monkeys at the zoo and get tossed out of the place. He'd hurl sticks, anything he could toss at them. One monkey—and I don't know where the monkey learned this—gave Dexter the finger.

We were at a wishing well once, and Dexter and some other guys attempted to steal coins out of the well. I was so embarrassed, I walked off.

There was this train you could ride through the park, but instead of dishing out a quarter to ride it, Dexter would stand by the track and hop it for free.

We went horseback riding on Sundays, but Dexter would incite the horses. He'd make his horse bite or kick another horse because there might have been some young lady on it. In fact, I remember Dexter caused one girl named Sherri's horse to charge off, and it galloped right in the middle of traffic.

The park people wouldn't let us ride horses there after that because Dexter was always racing the horses. He would take off his belt and beat the horses to go Kentucky Derby speed. He wanted to see them buck and kick up their hind legs.

Our parents took us to ride horses one day, and the park people wouldn't let us near the stables. My daddy said, "What did ya'll do?" and we said they must've had us mixed up with some other kids. We talked our way out of a whupping.

Dexter sucked his thumb in those days and—matter of fact—still does. Another one of his habits was to take a down pillow and rub it against the corner of his eye. One morning, we woke up to find goose feathers everywhere. Dexter got a whupping for that. Dexter did so much.

He'd watch "The Three Stooges" on TV and then act like a stooge around the house. One summer day, my momma was in the kitchen when Dexter came in the house hollering.

"I can't see, Momma! I can't see! Please, Momma, I can't see!"

Momma threw down her pots and spoons and was about to have an angina attack. "Dexter, Dexter," she screamed. "Tell Momma what's wrong!"

Dexter yelled, "My eyes are closed! My eyes are closed!"

He'd seen Curly do this to Moe on "The Three Stooges."

I think that's why Daddy didn't want us watching TV.

Dexter was just so hyper as a kid. Daddy would say, "If you don't shut up, Dexter, you're going to bed." Dexter would just talk, talk, talk, talk. He'd get on all our nerves. He'd keep yapping because he knew he was agitating his daddy.

We'd be trying to sleep at night—we all slept in the same room—and Dexter'd make us laugh. Daddy would charge in threatening, "If you don't go to sleep, you're gonna get a whupping." And it wouldn't be just Dexter. All of us would get a whupping.

Dexter and our brother Reginald were like twins, only Dexter was a year younger and smaller. Dexter would say, "I want to get big so I don't have to wear Reginald's hand-me-downs."

That's why Dexter ate everything in sight. He ate so much Daddy took everything off the table before dinner, put two pitchers of water on the table instead, and ordered Dexter to drink two large glasses. That way, Dexter'd be half full before dinner even started and wouldn't pig out on so much food.

That boy was a trip.

Our house, on 2910½ Page Street in the Third Ward of Houston, sat on cement blocks. It was a rented, one-story, wood-frame home painted Dentyne white, though it's deteriorated and faded now. I'd say we had the nicest furniture on the block.

But Eric Herring, one of my classmates, lived in a brick house. I always wished for a brick house, and when I was recruited by colleges, I'd fool the scouts into believing I lived in a brown brick house across from mine on the corner of Tuam and Page. It was a lovely big, brown, brick house.

It may be coincidence, but my house today in northern Virginia is brown brick.

I must say, I was proud of our Zenith television and our stereo and our furniture. That was a damn good job Daddy had—limo driver for the Tenneco Oil Company. He chauffeured the company presidents around. He worked there for twenty-eight years, while my momma worked seventeen years as a nurse's aide at Methodist Hospital.

Daddy was on call twenty-four hours a day. He chauffeured the Isley Brothers when they were in town, but if I was late, he'd run me to school in the limo and let me sit up front with him.

My daddy liked that job. He was a big fella who, from what I understand, didn't like hard labor. He was more into being a sharp guy. You know, "Dr. Manley."

I considered myself a fortunate kid because I had a mother and daddy who weren't divorced, plus I had my sister Cynthia and two brothers, Reginald and Gregory. We weren't poverty in motion or anything. It was a happy childhood, no matter what those drug counselors say.

Being from the Third Ward, we were definitely a class ahead of the sad-sack people in the Fifth Ward, which was called "the Bottom," or "the Nickel." The worst thing people called the Third Ward was

"Dodge City" because I guess you had to dodge or headfake a few stray bullets.

There were four of us in one room: Cynthia, Reginald, Gregory, and myself. That is, if Gregory wasn't locked up somewhere. I always slept on the floor. My drug counselors believe that might have affected my self-esteem.

When I was a baby, I slept in a dresser drawer instead of a crib. Momma pulled out a drawer, lined it with blankets, and stuck me in there fast alseep. My counselors might be interested in that one, too.

I used to sneak out of the house a lot to eat my food alone. Since my daddy didn't appreciate me pigging out, I'd go to Church's Chicken, buy me a bucket of wings and legs, and hide under the cement blocks behind our house to eat.

Of course, my daddy would find out—Cynthia could tattle—and he'd get angry and take that chicken away and hand it to my brothers and sister. I didn't want to share my food, so I had to find other secret eating places, like in our shed or the bushes.

Mostly, though, I was just a scared little kid. I'd see car headlights from the back window of our bedroom, and I would be petrified. I thought I was bad or devious—by the way my daddy treated me—and that people were coming to take me away. My drug counselors might find that interesting, too.

Crazy things happened in my neighborhood. A friend from elementary school, Wendell, was squashed by a truck when he ran across the street. They sent his dead body to the funeral home down the street from us. I was so fascinated by death, I wanted to go inside there.

The garage door of the funeral home usually was open, and we could see them embalming bodies like they were repairing cars in there.

I was drawn to the place, and for a long time I used to go inside that funeral home and kiss dead people.

I'd kiss them on the mouth or on the forehead, or I'd touch them. I'd start feeling their bodies because I couldn't believe death or couldn't fathom it. This was while I was in grammar school. My counselors probably think this has something to do with my drugs, too. They think everything does.

As for my immediate family, there were no early tragedies, except for my brother Gregory getting hauled off to jail and me getting carted to the hospital. I was allergic to seafood, but I kept eating it. It started when Larry Moore's mother made gumbo. I ate it like I ate everything else—slurped it up in a minute. I passed out on the porch, unable to breathe because I was swollen like a Macy's parade balloon. The paramedics tried to give me an injection, but they failed to find the vein. They broke a couple needles trying which is why I'm scared stiff of needles to this day.

After my seafood attack that night, Momma took me to a diagnostic hospital, and the docs found I was allergic to seafood, grass, and dust. They told me I couldn't play football because that would mean rolling around in the grass. I thought to myself, Screw them.

For some reason, I kept eating seafood. I was like the Beav. So as a kid I went for five or six ambulance rides to the hospital.

Aunt Monneola thinks I always wanted people to feel sorry for me, which is why I kept shoving seafood down my mouth:

I think Dexter wants attention because his daddy was always favoring his oldest son, Reginald, and because his momma had that girl of hers, and, Lord, his momma was crazy about Cynthia.

Yep, I was convinced Reginald was Daddy's favorite. My daddy's name was Carl, and Reginald got Carl as his middle name. My daddy seemed to lean toward Reginald because he was smart. He would get in reading contests with my cousin Andre, who was almost a genius.

It made Daddy proud to see Reginald spelling words as accurately as Andre. Reginald didn't do crap in athletics, but he was praised every time we went to Sealy to visit our aunties. I didn't get praised in the least, and I can tell those drug counselors that didn't aid my self-esteem, for sure.

I wasn't the only one who felt second fiddle to Reginald. My other brother, Gregory, who was really our half-brother—Momma had given birth to him long before she'd met Daddy—was also lower than Reginald on Daddy's totem pole.

Reginald could do no wrong in my daddy's eyes. Gregory and I could do only one or two things right.

I'll give my drug counselors an example. Daddy had a car other than his limo—a Pontiac Bonneville—and he'd leave it sitting in the driveway a lot while he was at work. One day Reginald tried driving that Bonneville back and forth in the driveway, except he inadvertently hit the gas when he meant to hit the brake and rammed into our house, which was practically made of balsa wood. We had to repair the house. Even worse, Reginald crushed Daddy's bedroom window.

Hell, if that was Cynthia or me who did that, I think we would've had to leave. But Reginald still got to camp out.

Reginald—we called him Ratchie—was about a year older than me, but he went to two different high schools than I did: Stephen F. Austin and Lamar. I wanted to go to Jack Yates High School because it had a studly football program; he wanted to go to white schools so he could steal their money. They kicked him out of Lamar because he was lifting all the football players' cash. I mean, Ratchie wasn't so much into playing football as he was for making money *off of* football players.

It wasn't him getting spanked left and right; it was me. When I got a whupping, I got it bad. I set our bedroom closet on fire right after Christmas one year. I was poking a pencil into our space heater in our bedroom, and it caught fire. I was sitting there with this red hot pencil when Daddy called me from the other room. He had a voice as deep as Barry White, and I panicked and tossed the pencil into the closet. If we'd have had a smoke detector, it would have gone off in a minute.

As it was, I think one of Cynthia's dresses got burned up. I *know* Daddy tore my ass up. He whipped my butt using an electrical cord. My daddy whupped with much effort. My son, Little Dexter, asks me before I whup him, "Daddy, is this gonna be hard or soft? Daddy, how many more licks? Daddy, why don't you control your temper?"

All good questions, but I tell you my daddy didn't control his.

See, Reginald and Cynthia were smart and excelled in school. Reginald was an A student, but I was an F student. So I acted up. My daddy thought I was a bad-ass kid, which is why he stayed on my case.

I probably deserved it because I even set a neighbor's house on fire. One of our neighbors—Victor—had a stack of newspapers in front of his house, and we were playing with matches. I guess I had pyromaniac tendencies, but so did Victor. As I recall, he poured gasoline all over those newspapers, which will usually do the trick. My daddy stuck me in the closet to punish me.

We didn't burn down the house, but a snippet of it caught fire and burned some of their furniture. Daddy had to buy them a brand-new bedroom suite and lent them our own bedroom furniture in the meantime. I continued sleeping on the floor.

To this day, I feel that Reginald was the apple of my daddy's eye. The rejection still hurts me, but did that drive me to use drugs? It's not like I'm mentally disturbed by it and have problems dealing with it.

It would be different if my daddy had molested me or something.

If he did, then I could say my childhood was messed up, but the worst thing he ever did to me was put me in the closet for setting the neighbor's house on fire. My counselors tell me that's abusive, and I agree. If you love your kid, why would you shove him in a mothball-flavored closet? But did it drive me to drugs? Hell if I know.

I admit my daddy used to pick on me. He would make me wash the dishes and clean the floor, and if I missed a smudge spot, he would make me do it over. If I didn't wash a skillet correctly, he'd walk by and slap me or would fake like he was gonna hit me upside the head. I remember ducking all the time.

Today, sometimes I slap my kids around a little, too. Maybe that's some of the "Manley blood" in me. When I whup little Dexter, sometimes it reminds me of what my daddy did to me. Things like that can be mentally abusive, and I can see little Dexter being scared of me. That's not good. Children shouldn't have fear of their parents, but I had fear of my daddy. I had great fear.

The term *Manley blood* comes up a lot, like when I was in Sealy a couple of summers ago. Aunt Monneola and Aunt Joycee were ragging on me for not calling them more, and I told them I do call them. Aunt Monneola shouted, "Don't lie to me, boy. I got Manley blood."

"What kind of blood is Manley blood?" I asked.

"Kill-you blood," she answered. "Kill-you-if-you-mess-with-me blood."

My daddy had Manley blood, for sure.

My drug counselors seem convinced there must have been other physical abuse in my house when I was growing up, but I only saw Daddy hit Momma once. Reginald, Cynthia, and I were all sitting on the couch when he smacked her. I leaped up and walloped him back. I think I was in junior high at the time.

The drug counselors should also know that we had to say "Yes, sir" and "No, sir" to our daddy. There was no talking back. I do the same with my kids now. That's one thing I can safely say about my upbringing: The Manley kids were respectful children. Everyone said so.

Another of Daddy's rules was if you didn't go to church, you couldn't go out and play. Matter of fact, I wanted to be a minister as a child. Dexter Manley, a minister? Well, I liked the way ministers have power over people, the way they preach.

But, hell, my daddy never went to church himself. Instead, he'd watch wrasslin' on TV.

If my counselors want to say my daddy contributed to my drug use, maybe they can say the same thing about my half-brother Gregory.

Daddy probably never told Gregory he loved him either. Maybe what happened to Gregory can give my counselors clues about me.

See, Gregory was even smart. I used to look up to Gregory. I'd always ask Gregory to stay home, but he was always being carted off to jail.

Gregory had to be Jesse James. He'd break into schools, pick up a typewriter, and go sell it. Or he'd hijack a car. Gregory baffled a lot of us. He just had sticky fingers.

Gregory eventually married a professor at Texas Southern University, a real bright woman, and his in-laws presented them with a home as a wedding gift. He had a decent job at a jewelry store, and he had a nice ride. The story goes that Gregory began stealing diamonds, and they caught him red-handed on camera.

Why didn't I steal? I was afraid of my daddy, that's why. I knew that if I did that, I'd have a big price to pay. That was his way of being a father figure. He'd tell me what's right and wrong.

He told the same things to Gregory, which makes it so hard to figure what happened to him. Gregory was so intelligent. He made bookworm grades in school and was artistic. He could draw whatever you put in front of him. Gregory easily could have been an engineer.

Normally, my daddy was gracious to Gregory, who had been his stepson since he was two years old, but I'm sure not being a true Manley was tough on Gregory. Eventually Daddy booted him out of the house because he wasn't going to school and was doing drugs.

Daddy went to see him in jail every Sunday. I'd say Gregory's been locked up some ten times, though everyone else says seven. Once Gregory was even arrested at our house for stealing school supplies. I mean, Gregory even stole people's dogs. Daddy spent a lot of money trying to bail him out of jail.

When Greg was a kid and we'd go to Sealy, Aunt Monneola and Aunt Joycee would even sew up Gregory's pants pockets so he couldn't load them up with stolen goods.

When I was a little boy, I stole twenty cents from an old man. Twenty cents, and, boy, my grandmother tore my ass up. But we didn't tell my daddy because he would've chain-sawed me in two.

My drug counselors hear all this and seem convinced my daddy ruined me. Well, man, like I said, I don't buy it. It's not like Daddy never did things for me.

I got in a fight once in junior high, for instance. My running mate, Gerald Franklin, and I went to a high school game—Jack Yates

High vs. Worthing High—and we were hot-headed and got into it with some high school kids from Worthing.

There was a big chase, and the guy we were chasing tried escaping by hopping a gate. Gerald used his belt to slap at the boy as he climbed, and the belt buckle—one of those huge Texas Hook-'em Horns types—slashed part of the boy's nose. He fell down, and Gerald and I pounded him. Then Gerald frantically yelled, "Dexter! Police!"

Never looking up, I said, "I'm not scared of no police. I'm not leaving!"

Next thing I knew, some policeman had a gun in my back. I wasn't scared of no police? I immediately whined, "Please Mr. Police, don't shoot. I'll be a goooooood boy."

The car they used for transporting us to the juvenile center was as hot as the Mojave. I was sweating horribly, so I said to Gerald, "Frank, it's hot. They gotta roll the window down."

"Don't worry, Dex," he answered.

But I rammed the car door: "Ehhhhhhh, roll the window down!"

The cop said, "Don't beat on the door."

I went, Bam, bam, bam on the door.

The cop threatened, "Do that again, and I'll beat your ass."

But I was scorching, and I had asthma and all those other allergies. I couldn't breathe, so I rapped on the door again.

The cop clouted me on the hand with a long flashlight, and I thought my hand was broken.

When he asked us how old we were, we said fourteen. But the cop thought we were fibbing because we were large for our age. Gerald said, "Dexter, be quiet. Let me tell 'em."

Clearly, Gerald was more insightful at this point. They got hold of Gerald's sister, and she talked to my daddy. When Daddy arrived, they ushered us inside the police house, and Gerald started telling the police officer the whole story. He said, "There were five of us and ten of them," as if we were poor and defenseless.

Being all riled up and proud that we'd raised some hell, I argued, "Gerald, you're wrong. There were ten of us and five of them, and we beat them up." I thought it was a big deal that we beat them up, and my father—who overheard the whole police interview—was giving me this look like, Shut up, you meathead.

I was glad my daddy was there, and I was puffing my chest out. Here I was getting picked up out of a police house in a white limo, but when I got outside, Daddy said, "Just shut up. You talk too much!

Gerald was talking and had the story going good, and you had to put your two cents in."

"But we beat 'em up, Daddy," I objected.

Right then, he kicked me in the behind and growled, "Shut your damn mouth. The boy had already told it like it was." I almost fell down the police house steps.

But I felt good my daddy had come to get *me*.

Another night, while playing in a high school basketball game, I got elbowed in the eye and started bleeding. Daddy and Mom had to come to the hospital to sign forms so they could stitch up my eye. He said, "You big sissy. There ain't nothin' wrong with you." But I felt good my daddy had come to get *me*.

Another time in high school, I lifted a quick thirty dollars out of some boy's wide-open locker and kept on walking. The boy yelled, "Whoooooa."

I was supposed to be in Spanish class, so I darted in there while the señorita teacher was at the blackboard. I grabbed the map off the wall, then turned and chased that boy back down the hall. I beat him up with part of Asia.

They threatened to suspend me, but, as I recall, my daddy came down and got it straightened out. All I know is I really felt proud. Fathers generally don't come to school. I guess it was the wrong way to get attention, but I was so proud.

My daddy came to get *me*.

Another great time was when he took me to the dentist. I had a cavity, and my daddy took me to get it fixed. I was so glad I hadn't brushed with Crest.

'Cause my daddy brought *me*.

I guess you could say I treasured my daddy's attention. I mean, a cavity is a great moment in life? My drug counselors want to say that's part of my problem, but, hell, I don't believe it. My daddy took me to see Don Drysdale pitch for the Dodgers against the Astros. He took Reginald and me to see the Globetrotters as my birthday present.

He also took us to see James Brown perform, and we went to the rodeo. That was happy stuff, too. Every summer, we drove to Hainsville, Louisiana, to see my momma's family or to Sealy, Texas, to see my daddy's family. And every Fourth of July he barbecued. *Every* Fourth of July.

He would get up with me every morning at 5:00 A.M. to throw the newspapers. I had a paper route, and he drove Reginald and me around in his Bonneville while we tossed papers.

So I don't know if I can blame it on Daddy like my counselors want. The only thing I can say is that he didn't tell me he loved me while he treated Reginald like King Tut.

Maybe that affected my self-esteem. Well, not maybe. It did.

An Idle Thought

I don't know if it's because my daddy drove a limo, but if I won the $100 million lottery, the first thing I'd do is hire a chauffeur.

I'll tell you something I did once that was grand. Glinda and I were in Atlantic City for the Tyson-Spinks fight in June 1988, and our hotel was only a Dan Marino pass from ringside. Instead of walking to the fight via the boardwalk, though, we rented a limo.

We rented it just to take ourselves two doors down to the fight. The Big Wheels were pulling up in limos, and I wanted to be a fat cat, too. Limos represent power and money. So we pulled up, hopped out, and it was like big league. People stared at us like we were Frank Sinatra or something.

Magic Johnson was there that night. So were Michael Jordan and Sugar Ray Leonard. The ring announcer called all of our names before the fight and introduced me as "Dexter Manley of the World Champion Washington Redskins." I pulled in a big ovation. George Steinbrenner, they booed to hell.

CHAPTER 5

The First Secret

HERE'S SOMETHING ELSE THAT MAY HAVE relevance to my drug counselors: I thought I was an ugly kid. I thought I was too dark. Girls used to call me "pretty black," but I didn't believe them.

Today I think I'm handsome, but not then. I wished I was light skinned at times or that I was white.

My nickname was Diebone because of the line down my forehead. I'd have appreciated a name like Franchise instead, but I told people it was my O. J. Simpson look. O. J., if you'll recall, has my same forehead.

So the diebone and my dark complexion made me feel inferior. Other kids would say, "Look at that little black Manley." Stuff like that.

So I guess I needed extra attention from girls. My first real girl-friend—from sixth grade to tenth grade—was Cathy Jones. I didn't earn an allowance from my daddy, but one year he gave me fifty dollars for Christmas and I bought Cathy a thirty-seven-dollar ring. Boy, did he get mad!

I really loved Cathy. She was the girl I was going to marry. High school's a little young to be thinking about marriage, but accidents happen.

Turned out it wasn't Cathy.

I met Stephanye Baker in the hallway my junior year in high school. She was sixteen, and I was seventeen. She was looking for a classroom, and I saw this good-looking girl with long, pretty black hair. I always was a sucker for long hair, so I stopped her.

We began dating, and she liked *me*, diebone and all. I met her momma, Miss Baker, and Stephanye taught me how to drive in Miss Baker's Pinto. My daddy didn't teach me.

I'd catch the bus over to Stephanye's house, and Miss Baker would leave us dangerously alone in the living room. She would stroll through the living room every now and then, but I guess not often enough—because soon Stephanye was pregnant.

At first, I told Miss Baker, "I'm gonna marry Stephanye. I'm gonna marry her." But when I mentioned marriage to my daddy, oh boy! I don't think he was so angry that Stephanye was pregnant, but he was absolutely against us getting married. He was afraid I would ruin my shot at going to college if Stephanye and I tied the knot. In fact, he gave my buddy Gerald a hard time because I'd gotten a girl pregnant and Gerald hadn't. Gerald says my daddy called him a sissy.

I finally brought up the idea of marriage to Daddy—with a lump in my throat—and he flew off the handle. I needed a "Father Knows Best" routine from him, but he just ranted at me instead. He felt I was too young and asked me how I was going to take care of the little rascal. He said I had a chance to go to college—to be somebody—and here was this stumbling block.

Daddy told me, "There are plenty of other girls. You shouldn't be married. You're too young." Just the tone of his voice, you could tell the man was pissed.

I knew to drop it right then. I had to keep secrets.

I didn't ask his opinion on elopement, either.

I agreed Stephanye and I were too young to have a kid, but in February 1977, during my senior year of high school, Miss Baker decided I should marry Stephanye, or else I couldn't see the kid. I guess I was being railroaded.

I didn't want to be married, but I wanted to see Stephanye and the kid. Besides, I figured marriage wouldn't get in the way of football, which was my way out of the Third Ward. Having a kid didn't sound so bad, either. It built my ego. I'd brag, "Hey, I'm gonna have me a son." At the same time, deep down, I was wondering, Who's gonna pay for the kid's Gerbers?

When Miss Baker told me I *had* to marry Stephanye, I said no at first. She was steamed. She wanted a classic wedding in a church, with rice thrown afterwards and everything. And I didn't want an illegitimate kid.

My buddy Gerald said not to get married and my daddy naturally said no, but their votes didn't count. I couldn't be someone who'd turn his back on a kid. I wasn't raised that way.

I talked to Gerald one day by the baseball field at Yates High School, and we both sat there crying with fear. I felt trapped. I didn't want to lose Stephanye or my kid or my daddy.

At about this time, for the one and only time in my life, my daddy was proud of me for football. Oh, there were times when he had praised me (like when Reginald and I did some summer work and I gave my cash to Momma while Reginald kept his; Daddy said I'd turn out to be special some day, and that lifted me ten feet in the air), but praise was minimal from him.

But when I was being recruited to go to college, my daddy was never prouder of me. Hell, white men were showing up at our ole wooden house in limos. My daddy's approval meant so much to me. I'd run a wonderful race for the track team and look up in the sky and think, This is for Daddy.

Not that he said much, but I could tell he was pleased with my football. For the first time, he showed me off to the presidents at Tenneco, the people he chauffeured. Usually, he just showed off Ratchie.

During recruitment, Oklahoma State offered my daddy a job at Conoco, and he even came to some of the games my senior year. Before that, he had to be at the airport with his limo, or else Friday night was Tenneco's bowling league time, or he had other business to attend to. But he showed up for about three or four games my senior year, and I could see those alligator and crocodile shoes up in the stands.

The day Ron Meyer came by from SMU, three or four limos were stretched in front of our little house. All these white guys tried to talk me into enrolling at SMU, and I could see the wonderment on Daddy's face.

All I know is we never had so much company at our house. One day the recruiter from Kansas State came down to wine and dine me, and my mother cooked chitlins. Now, you know white guys don't eat no chitlins, but that Kansas State man sat down and acted like he enjoyed them.

Daddy said, "You don't have to eat those chitlins."

But that guy would just about do anything to get me to sign that letter of intent.

Cynthia can't tell that story with a straight face:

With all these strangers coming, we had to keep the house spotless. You could run a finger across our floor and not get a speck. One recruiter—I believe he was Doug from Kansas State—came over, and we had chitlins and candied yams and cabbage and onions—the whole nine yards. And, you know, chitlins do have a scent. We were used to it, of course, but Doug's nose turned up, and his cheeks started turning red.

See, he and Dexter had just come in after going out to eat, but Dexter's always ready to eat. Dexter announced, "I'll eat again!" So, naturally, Doug said he'd eat, too. He sat at the table and ate chitlins and looked like he'd keel over. He almost choked.

Daddy would cook for the recruiters himself. I mean, we always had to do our house cleaning, but now we had to do extra! Let me just tell you something, when all those men were coming to our house and we were gettin' letters and mail, he was one proud father and he'd show it.

But if he'd seen Dexter in the pros, he'd have been happier than a punk in a pea farm.

Well, while I was debating whether to marry Stephanye, she was plumping up like a ballpark frank. I had no choice. I married her in a hush.

Mr. Baker picked me up in front of Jack Yates High School after school one day, and we went down to the courthouse and Stephanye and I exchanged our vows. I had to steal my own birth certificate out of the house from under my daddy's nose.

I imagine Stephanye was petrified herself:

When I first met Dexter, he seemed real nice. Football recruiters hadn't started hounding him yet. He'd come over to my house after school, and it was real pleasant.

I felt sorry for Dexter. He had a sister and brother, and everybody liked Reginald most. He was a charmer. And, of course, everyone doted on his sister. You'd feel sorry for Dexter.

Reginald used to have the car and everything. But can you imagine Dexter being in the eleventh grade and not knowing how to drive? I hated his father. He was the meanest man, the meanest man alive.

One time we were having a phone conversation, and Dexter got some tuna fish out. I guess they weren't supposed to eat while the daddy wasn't there. He came in and saw the tuna fish Dexter was about to eat and threw it in the toilet.

Let me also say that until Dexter started being recruited, you wouldn't believe how he'd dress. Put it this way: There wasn't much effort on his parents' part toward Dexter, but whatever Dexter wore, he always kept it neat and clean. He was never sloppy.

There was never a doubt I'd have the baby. No abortions. Dexter was *pretty cool through the whole thing, but he basically had a big head going because scouts were on him like white on rice. He began eating very well and getting rent-a-cars every day. Senior year, he had a sweet life.*

He had new clothes, the cars—he was happy. Meantime, I was pregnant. But it was an easy pregnancy; the baby was born two months premature.

I went into labor on Good Friday, and my mother was out of town working at the time. So it was just Dexter and me and his mother.

Dexter dropped me off at the hospital at noon and stayed an hour, then went to get his mother. She sat with me during the labor. I was cursing Dexter, meantime, to get the hell out.

So, Dexter goes to a party and—you know what—gets in a fight!

I liked Dexter's mother being there with me, but I never had a relationship with her after that. She was tough to have a relationship with. One minute, she'd be talking nice and the next minute talking crazy.

I said, "Miss Manley, I'll never do this again!"

She replied, "I know, baby." She was a rock. It was just me and her.

That was in April, and I was able, afterward, to go to Dexter's prom. I never missed anything.

As for Dexter's daddy, I know he eventually held the baby, but I don't think he knew we were married. When we got married, his daddy was really sick. When he wasn't in the hospital he was home in bed. We never thought anything about him finding out, because he was always in bed, always drugged.

But we didn't tell his daddy because he was a mean, mean man. I guess I only saw the bad part of his daddy. I didn't see the happy part.

The night Derrick was born, I did break a few heads at J.B.'s, a place on the corner of Scott and Cleburne. It was a Friday night, and we were all at a dance there. Worthing High School people were there, too, and we were always brawling with those boys. Our quarterback started it when he got into it with a Worthing guy, and I ended up hitting some joker upside the head. I got back to the hospital at 9:58 P.M. and Derrick had joined the world at 9:28. So I missed his birth.

My daddy still didn't know about the marriage. At the hospital, Stephanye was listed under the name Baker because of her daddy's insurance.

Meantime, I naturally wanted to spend nights with my wife, so I had to sneak out of our house most evenings to get over there. Daddy thought the Bakers were trash because I'd be slumber-partying over

there. We were legally married, but he'd say, "Those people are nothin'
but trash for letting that boy spend the night."

I would stay at both places—home and the Bakers—to make it
look good. Knowing how I loved to eat, my daddy thought I was
stealing steaks from his freezer and laying them in Miss Baker's. So he
put a lock on the door to his freezer and refused to part with the key.

Eventually, it leaked to my daddy that I'd gone behind his back to
get married. One night Stephanye and I attended the same party
as, unfortunately, Cynthia and Ratchie. Somehow Stephanye and
Cynthia made their way to a corner and were drinking booze and
talking. I was sort of a square, so I wasn't drinking.

As soon as Stephanye told Cynthia about our secret wedding,
that tattletale Cynthia was out the door like lightning to tell our
father. I heard he almost had a heart attack.

So I knew I had to avoid him, but he was avoiding everyone
himself. Something was peculiar with his health, and we weren't sure
what.

Turns out he'd had colon cancer for four years, but he didn't even
tell Momma.

He led us to believe he was going to the doctor just for checkups.
My checkups were twice a year, so I couldn't understand why his were
twice a week. All he would tell us was, "The doc just wants to do
tests."

We didn't know it was cancer 'til the day he died. Cynthia says
she should have guessed. In the summertime, no less, he would sit in
his overcoat with the heater on, and all his hair fell out.

After he first checked into the hospital, my sneaky Aunt Joycee,
who'd been visiting from Sealy, grabbed Daddy's medical chart and
wrote down every big word she saw. She raced home to Sealy—over an
hour away—whipped out her medical dictionary, and was the first to
realize he had cancer. She confronted Daddy, but he made her promise
not to say a cotton-pickin' word.

By this time, I had to get to college. I had chosen Oklahoma
State, and the coach there, Jim Stanley, wanted me up for early
conditioning. It was June of 1977. I'd been married three months, but
I'd never told Daddy my secret.

When I got to the hospital—Park Plaza Hospital—he was lying
in the bed with an oxygen mask over his face. He asked me if I was
married.

We'd never really discussed it. I mean, he had been sick. I forget
how I responded. I think I just nodded.

Little did we know, he had been told he had only a week to live. The doctors suggested he stay in the hospital, but he decided if all he had was a week, he'd be with his family.

I had just left for Oklahoma when he asked Cynthia to come fetch him. Immediately, he wanted to barbecue. It was difficult for him, but he knew Cynthia and Reginald loved his cooking. He was in the back grilling, trying to put up his indestructible front, when smoke from the charcoal overcame him and he passed out and scared everyone half to death.

There was an oxygen tank in the bedroom, and Cynthia had to roll it through the kitchen to revive him. It was big for her, about four feet tall, and it could have exploded in there with all the cooking going on. It didn't, and Daddy didn't pass away, either.

A day and a half later, he was weak and in bed, and Cynthia figured if she could keep him awake, he wouldn't die. Sound reasoning, huh? She was reading to him, but then she got tired and started to leave. He asked her, "Where are you goin'?"

When he said that, she figured she should stick by his side. Pretty soon she fell asleep. When she woke up, he was sleeping and still breathing, so she went to bed.

The next morning, her little daughter, Qwindella, went to kiss her granddaddy before going to school, as she always did.

"Granddaddy, I'm fixed to go," she said. "Granddaddy? Granddaddy?"

Cynthia called paramedics and the ambulance took Daddy away for good at age 52.

The previous night I had had one last conversation with him from Oklahoma State. His voice was strained, and I was homesick and lonesome. But I was in college, and that was the bottom line for him.

After my daddy hung up with me, he called his best friend, Mr. Irvin, and Mr. Irvin's wife, June, spoke with him. All he said to her was, "Welp, I got Dexter in school and everything." That was his last accomplishment.

AN IDLE THOUGHT

Speaking of death, I've threatened suicide a couple of times.

This was when I was wrapped up in drugs in Washington in 1985. I told Glinda I was gonna kill myself, but it was really a con so she'd forgive me for using cocaine. Otherwise, she'd slam things or throw a vase at me and break picture frames.

So what I'd do is tell her, "I'm gonna kill myself." That way, she'd start hugging and kissing on me.

I went so far as to hop in our bathtub once, without filling it up with water, and laid a gun down next to me. I'd done drugs and had stayed out all night. I knew Glinda was coming home, and I wanted sympathy. When she came in, I said I was gonna blow my brains out, and she got nervous.

It was just my way of manipulating:

I remember that day. When I came home, I couldn't get in the garage door. I couldn't figure out why the door was locked. I started banging and finally barged my way in. I felt something eerie, though. I thought maybe Dexter was dead or that he'd overdosed or something. His car was there, and no one answered my hollering.

I walked in the bathroom, and he was sitting in there with his gun. I got pissed and said, "You stupid idiot. You're really going to kill yourself? You are selfish to leave us like this."

I didn't know it was a gimmick. But I guess he did it because he was scared of me. He's really scared of me, isn't he?

From the bathtub, I called Gerald Franklin, my ole buddy from Yates High School. I told Gerald to come see me, that I was gonna shoot myself. He started bawling on the phone and said he was coming and that I should stay cool:

Man, I used my last dollar to get on that plane.

I got off the flight expecting a guy to be all depressed, but Dexter met me at the airport hopping up and down, "Frank! Frank! Frank!"

I said, "Nothin' wrong with you, boy."

Man, he just wanted attention.

That wasn't my only suicide story. One time in 1986 I was wasted in a Marriott hotel and called my attorney at the time, Richard Bennett. I told Richard I was gonna take a flying leap out the window.

Richard told me to go home. I think he paid no attention.

CHAPTER 6

Mentally Retarded?

IT'S A WONDER I MADE IT TO COLLEGE, NOT knowing how to read or write. We ought to look at that.

I started flunking tests fairly early in life. I accumulated nineteen Fs in second grade at Douglas Elementary and had to repeat the year. I can recall not knowing what the teachers were talking about during class sessions. I wondered, why can't I keep up?

That's when I decided not to trust any teacher. My momma and daddy were called in and told, "Your son is educable mentally retarded," which probably went over real smooth with Daddy. He didn't hear the *educable* part; he just heard the *mentally retarded.* I only heard that part myself.

The teachers suggested I enter a special education program, away from the regular curriculum, and my parents treated the teacher's words as gospel. They believed I was incapable. This is why I felt my daddy loved Reginald and Cynthia more than me: I just couldn't measure up. Daddy flat-out called me a dummy.

He didn't know any better; he was ignorant, too, and frustrated with me. His other kids did all right. I never liked going home after school because we either had to do homework or he'd put me in a spelling or arithmetic contest with my brother or sister. I couldn't even spell *hello.*

He'd get so agitated when I received a bad grade, he'd want to whup me, thinking I wasn't trying.

All we did in my special ed class was play with blocks. I don't remember much else. I remember that our recess time was different from the rest of the school's, and the regular kids pounded on our windows as they came in from playing kickball. They'd chant, "Mentally retarded! Mentally retarded!"

It wasn't until my late twenties that I didn't believe them.

My special ed teacher, Miss Smith, was no taller than a couch. She had a hunched back, so she seemed disabled. Plus, I was in a room with physically disabled kids, too, who foamed at the mouth. I was one pissed-as-hell kid.

I turned over desks. I had an attention deficit disorder, like little Dexter has today, and I probably could have used some Ritalin, which is the hyperactivity medicine Little Dexter takes. I remember ambling over to the pencil sharpener one day, leaving my No. 2 pencil in there long enough to become sharp as a pitchfork, then throwing it at a girl. She was disabled, with a splint or something up her spine, and this pencil stuck like a dart in her neck. I was ushered to the principal's office for a butt-whupping. I was scared of Mr. Marshall, the principal. I wonder if Mr. Marshall was scared of me?

I remember the pencil incident. I came down pretty hard on him so he'd see the severity of it. But if you listened to Dexter long enough, you'd believe he did little wrong. Put it this way: Dexter could sell a tuxedo to a rat.

Dexter was a very likeable kid. I was at Douglas for eight years, and many things occurred to Dexter before I got there. When he was in special ed, it wasn't a program to brag about. I think he's a classic example of where a school didn't respond to a child's needs. Special ed was one of our weakest programs. We mostly had traditional teachers who were totally incapable of making the changes necessary for special education students.

You also must realize Dexter came through a dual system of education. There was no interracial teaching. It was either a black school or a white school. The Supreme Court, in 1954, may have decided on desegregation, but school systems spent twenty years fighting it. I don't think there was a lot of interest in the black student.

Knowing what we know now, I'd say Dexter was learning disabled rather than special ed back then, but he was not being instructed as learning disabled. He was told he was educable mentally retarded, and his parents bought into that stigma. See, the problem was the diagnosis. It was compounded by his being in a black school, which did not have the same learning disabled services available to white schools.

When Dexter was at Douglas, the school had a special ed program and a reading clinic. But what troubles me was why Dexter didn't get referred to that reading clinic. We could've saved Dexter Manley if we'd just gotten him into a reading clinic. The school system has to assume a major responsibility for the uneducation of Dexter.

It's just an example of what happens in a dual system, although I'm not sure if he would've gotten the proper diagnosis at a white school because of the cultural differences. Maybe because he's black they would assume he's slow and always would be.

Why did Dexter's father call him dumb? That's how it was back then. If you weren't able to keep up with your class, you were perceived as dumb.

I can't fault his father when it was common, when I got to Douglas, for special ed kids to be treated as second-class citizens. They were teased during recess because they had a room separate from everyone else. I changed that. I moved them to the main building from a temporary building out on the playground. They had been isolated in a wooden shack, but we moved them inside the main building.

If I had the chance to do it again, I'd take a kid like Dexter Manley and run him through a special program modified to meet his needs and make sure it continued right on through. And I bet he would've outperformed kids who didn't have a learning disability.

It turned out instead that Dexter acted up all the time. But he acted up because of his problems with deciphering the written word. That's difficult for a ten-year-old to take.

I could not read "See Spot run," and I was gonna do my damnedest to make sure nobody knew my secret.

I had some close calls. At Sunday school once, our teacher called on me to read from the Scriptures. I couldn't have read one syllable, so I had to think up a lie.

I patted my pockets and said, "Oh, I forgot my reading glasses." No one suspected I was fibbing. It was common for people to wear reading glasses, so I pretended.

Kids said, "Dexter, I didn't know you wore glasses."

I didn't.

I never returned to Bible study class for fear of being called on again. My parents thought I'd gone, but I'd hang out at the nearby hospital cafeteria. I never wanted to be humiliated like that again.

I never once had homework through sixth grade. But I walked up—cap and gown—with my sixth-grade class at Douglas Elementary and graduated. I was embarrassed to be on the stage with the rest of the students. I didn't belong there.

Of course, they pass you when you're in special ed. They know you're dumb and that there's no cure. I did not wish to walk up and graduate with that class. But, you must understand, the whole thing in my life was to hide and keep secrets.

Cub Scouts was probably the best part of elementary school. I had a uniform and all. We'd go on Friday night trips and stay over the weekend. You'd learn how to build a fire—legally—and learn camping. And you'd do the "James Brown."

I'd even do the dance for money. It's a dance. I'd dance for dollars. When I was a little boy, five or six, I'd dance 'til they threw coins at me.

There was a little sidewalk outside my house, and my audience would be my momma and her sister and this lady who lived across the street. I'd dance, and they'd pitch me quarters and nickels and dimes. I could do all the stuff James Brown used to do—the mashed potato, the split, and all that one-legged stuff, turnin' around.

I did that better than I read.

But once I graduated to Ryan Junior High School, my survival tactics took over. There were no special ed classes at Ryan. At least, no one told me of any. I went straight into their mainstream curriculum—English, math, social studies—and don't ask me how I passed.

If there was one error in my educational evolution, it had to be right there. Someone from Douglas Elementary should've told someone at Ryan Junior High that I'd spent the second through the sixth grades in special ed, playing with building blocks. But not a soul said a word.

After junior high began, my daddy expected me to come straight home and execute my homework assignments. He wouldn't let us kids go outside until we completed them, including Reginald. It was another of his hundred rules. He would say, "No such thing as no homework."

He'd find us *something* to do. He'd find math problems for us to solve or a word problem. On Sundays we had to come in early to do our homework, too. Sundays were busy. We'd have an eleven o'clock service to go to, Bible training—which I'd skip—and church again at night. If we didn't go to church, we couldn't go outside. A lot of kids went to movies on Sundays, but we couldn't go unless we'd gone to church and our daddy had checked our homework.

My plan was to have somebody do my work *for* me. Could I or could I not negotiate at an early age. I'd have some girl in class who liked me do my work for me. Or I had my sister, Cynthia:

At home, I would help Dexter with his homework, but I don't know how he got by in class. Every Friday we used to have what the school district called "sentence dictation." I had it from third to sixth grade. I don't know if Dexter had it, but the teachers would read sentences and you'd write them and punctuate them. They'd give you about ten sentences, and you'd be graded accordingly.

Right after the dictation, you'd have to send your papers up front, so I don't know how Dexter did it.

I was almost three years older than Dexter, and I knew our mom and dad said he was in class for slower students. So, I'd do his homework. I just wanted him to get his grades.

We'd have to sit at the kitchen table after school and do homework, but I'd do mine at school. See, I had choir practice after school and there'd be a thirty-minute gap before it started, so I'd do my homework. When I'd get home, I'd sit in the kitchen and do homework for Dexter and Reginald.

I'm sure Dexter also got passed because he was an excellent athlete. At Ryan the coaching staff was crazy about him, and when I was in school all the athletes seemed to make As and also never seemed to be in class.

Shoot, the football players would get the teacher's edition of the textbook with the answers in it and run off copies. Or the coaches'd give 'em copies of assignments with the answers on them. Been going on for years. At Ryan and at Yates.

Dexter, he'd just hustle to get by. One time he came home with someone else's homework and erased the name and put his own on it.

My mom, she'd say, "Don't call Dexter dumb. He's just a little slower." My father'd say, "I know you can do better, but you don't try hard enough." I mean, Daddy encouraged him. He wouldn't always call him dumb. I mean, he'd say that to any of us who'd come home with a bad grade.

Reginald even made some Fs. But Reginald wasn't slow, he just didn't care. In fact, Reginald sat in Dexter's seat and took tests for him. They looked like twins, and Momma dressed them alike. It happened at Ryan and Yates.

I won't ever forget when Dexter got those nineteen Fs. They knew then he had a problem. People'd say "Retarded," and he used to cry. People'd call him retarded, and he wasn't. He just was a slow learner. Plus, Dexter used to do things just to get attention. He'd cut up in class and act really terrible. One time, he grabbed Miss Smith by the collar and pinned her against the wall. They called our father, and he got a whupping.

Dexter'd cry when that happened. But sometimes you didn't know if it was fake. I'd tell Dexter, he should've been an actor. If he got a whupping, he could fake crying real quick. He can cry as good as he wants to.

I never had to deal with what Cynthia calls "sentence dictation." It wasn't included in special ed, and not in junior high, either.

Besides, I had so many safeguards against failing. Other than Cynthia, one of my neighbors, Champ—Robert Winters was his real name—would cheat and help me with my homework. I think Champ's in prison now.

We'd all gather on my front porch and pass around our home-work. This was our version of a law school study group. Champ was a smart guy. He wanted to be slick and cool when he could've just been smart.

Most guys went out and did drugs and stole. My thing was to make it in football, and to do that I had to cheat in school. There was no other way.

Cynthia definitely cheated for me, and Reginald chipped in, too. Reginald knew his stuff. Hell, that's why I'd have him *take tests* for me.

Being that we were almost twins and he went to another school, it was easy for him to slip in, sit in my seat, and take tests for me. We looked like our daddy, so my teachers were stumped.

I graduated from Ryan, thanks to Reginald and Company, and at Yates High School, Ratchie continued to be my stunt man. In English class he wrote a full paper for me. I've never written one essay paper in my entire life.

It was about that time—in high school—that I changed my birthdate. I was actually born on February 2, 1958, but for my entire college and pro career, I've led people to believe I was born on February 2, 1959. I even told Momma one day that I was born in '59, and she said, "Nah, uh, uh . . . Wait a minute. . . . . you might be right . . . I don't know."

The Tampa Bay Buccaneers thought I was thirty-two years old last season, when I was really an old fogey at thirty-three. If I hadn't had a relapse, I would never be telling you this right now.

I lied about my age because I had to repeat second grade. The rest of my classmates were born in '59, so I wanted my birth year to be '59.

Another reason why teachers passed me was because I showed up in class. You can pass a lot of classes by just saying, "Here!" when they call roll. I dressed nice, and I had almost perfect attendance. On attendance alone, they gave me Cs and Ds.

I also got by because I was an expert at multiple choice. I had good vision! I'd sit in the middle of the room for the view. During tests, I'd never do the essay part, just the multiple choice. I'd get almost all the multiple choice answers right—I knew who the smart suckers were— and then I'd hope that'd be enough to land me a C or a D.

To be honest, it baffles me now how I got by. I know, for sure, I was on the pity-pot a lot, begging and crying. And I know one girl who definitely did my work was Cathy Jones:

I took a couple tests for him. I mean, I was his girlfriend. It was nice going out with him, because everyone was scared of him and no one bothered me.

At Jack Yates High School, I used to write answers on the side wall of the classroom, and I'd make sure Dexter would sit in the same seat I had sat in the previous period. All the answers would be on the wall right next to him. The teachers would always check desks to see if answers were written in pencil there, but teachers never thought about scanning the wall.

I wanted to see him get his grades. Life was hard enough being black; and without an education, that's even worse. A lot of people helped him, though. It wasn't just me.

I knew all along he couldn't read or write. He spelled my name once C-A-T-Y.

But I quit dating him because I wanted a millionaire. I couldn't be with somebody who couldn't read. I wanted to become an engineer myself.

I originally had met Dexter playing volleyball, and I said, "That guy's too black. I can't talk to him." But I liked him because he was nice. He'd walk me home, and I'd walk him home, and I'd say, "Since we're here, let's do homework."

Of course, I'd end up doing all the work. I'd say, "Let's turn to page thirty-seven and read the paragraph." He'd mouth his words as if he was speed-reading, and then he'd say, "I got it. You tell me your answer, and then I'll tell you mine." He always gave the same answer I did, but he still never told anybody he couldn't read.

Even today, there are kids whom teachers feel sorry for, and these kids are given Cs. I call it, "I'll C you through."

At Yates coaches would talk to teachers and say, "He needs to get out of here." Teachers would pass him just to get him into football.

At Ryan he was loud and boisterous. I'd help him with his homework, but I never did his classwork. But he didn't always need me. He had that good vision, as he says.

I remember one day he said, "I didn't take my test today."

"Who did?" I asked.

"Reginald," he said.

Once he had been in a fight or something, and they wouldn't let him come back and take a test. I talked to the teacher or somebody, crying like he was my husband. They had suspended him, but they let him come back and take the test over.

One night a couple of years ago, he called me and said, "Cathy, you didn't want me, and now my wife drives a two-seater Benz, and my dog has a bed, and you're driving an Audi, and you said you'd marry somebody better and richer."

So I knew then that Dexter had learned to count his cash. He couldn't do math, but he could do money.

Let me explain something. The only encouragement I received in my life was from athletics. I mean, how can you expect praise when you're in special ed class? You can't produce. But the next thing you know, you're in athletics and your encouragement finally comes.

So, can't you see why I would do anything to stay eligible for football? Football is when—for the first time—people thought I was special.

Even then, when I stepped on the football field, my inferiority never really left me. I'd feel great for a minute, but when it would come time to talk and communicate with people? As a kid, I never felt I could do that.

I had no choice but to hide behind football.

By my senior year, school counselors were helping me. Why not go to my teachers and beg them to give me Cs and Ds? Here I was trying to get out, and my only way out was football.

A certain Miss Simmons would not cooperate. She was an English teacher, the roughest of all on me. I thought she was going to flunk me from here to Galveston, so I went running to my head coach, Luther Booker:

*A*s Yates' head football coach, I tried to keep tabs on all my boys. I recall when Dexter was a tenth-grade boy, I'd say he was about six-foot-one or six-foot-two, thin, a basketball-looking guy. He weighed 175, 180 pounds probably, and I remember he was walking down the hall, and—as usual—was dressed very neat.

His shoes were shined, he had a T-shirt on and a pair of blue jeans, but the jeans were always starched, steam-pressed, and neat. His hair was very short, because during that time the Ivy League cut was popular, and he had a handful of books. He was one of the most studious-looking boys in school. This was our particular view of Dexter every day. Oh, and he kept a pencil behind his ear.

So I'm walking toward the front door, and I see this boy with big tears rolling down his cheeks. I think, I better get to him.

I say, "What's the matter, boy?"

He's sniffing, and he says, "My teacher says she's gonna flunk me."

I say, "No, boy, it's kind of early in the school year to be flunking."

He says, "No, she's gonna flunk me."

I'm thinking I've gotta get this boy out of the hallway and in the coach's office. So I get him in there, and I say, "It's early in the semester, boy. See if you can do some extra work."

He repeats, "She says she's gonna flunk me."

And then he looks at me with those eyes. "I don't have time to flunk," he says. "I've got to play pro ball."

I ended up with a C in Miss Simmons's English class. That's one of the classes Reginald was my stunt man in.

I do remember crying to Coach Booker. I was afraid I wasn't going to play football.

The way Booker described me is true. I went to school dressed flawlessly. My daddy dressed sharp as a tack, so that was an influence on me. You're an extension of your household. I didn't have to go to school with holes in my drawers and in my pants. I went to school spiffed up. My daddy'd take me to Walter Pye's and buy me clothes. He didn't verbalize his love, but he thought he was showing his love by feeding and clothing us.

I was never ineligible for football in all my high school days, though I never knew how to read or write. I may have flunked a few courses, but I think the administration took care of me behind the scenes.

Drawings on the football chalkboard were no problem for me, but if I had to write or spell things out? No way. That's a major problem. My heart palpitates. I have a tough time writing now at age thirty-four, and I panic whenever I have to spell. So imagine how it was for me at Yates.

Booker must've gone to teachers for me. He has to have that kind of relationship with the faculty. He needs the students and the faculty on his side. Without that, he will not have a football team or a job. Otherwise, who could stay eligible?

I knew Booker would advise me whom to take English class from. It was all hand-me-downs. Miss Simmons didn't listen to Booker, but some of the faculty went along with him, so he'd instruct me to take their classes.

You'd have thought there'd be somebody at Yates High School who could see through my crying and my acting and my cheating and discover I was an illiterate, but no one said a word. I always thought Mr. Melton, the principal, must've known. When I was in the tenth grade, my buddy Gerald and his brother Kenneth messed with a girl. This girl said we raped her. It happened at Gerald's house.

The girl went to Mr. Melton, and he made all of us write down our version of what happened. I'm sure Mr. Melton could not believe the paper I turned in to him.

We had to write it on our own, and I had everything spelled backward and wrong. He must have known I was illiterate from reading that piece of trash paper.

What'd he do? Nothing. The case was over.

An Idle Thought

Some people want to nickname me Xerox, because of the way I copied other people's papers in school.

Howie Long of the Raiders says that when we were together at a scouting combine after our senior year of college, I copied from his paper during an intelligence test and even wrote *his* name down on *my* paper.

He's wrong for saying that. I mean, I was an expert when it came to wandering eyes and copying answers, but I know not to put down "Howie Long" where it says "Your name."

CHAPTER 7

The Two Letters I Understood: X and O

IF IT WEREN'T FOR FOOTBALL, I BELIEVE I'D BE dead right now or in the Hard Time Hotel. Football meant everything to me.

I even sneaked into the Super Bowl in 1974 when it was at Rice Stadium. It was pouring rain, and my friend Jason West and I hopped puddles the whole way from the Third Ward to the stadium. I sneaked in between ticket agents when they were distracted. Jason and I had no seats, but we stood and watched. It was my first NFL game.

I wanted so badly to be a football star. I used to see Bob Hayes and Bob Lilly after games on TV interviews wearing just T-shirts and football pants, and I'd think that was so cool.

I had two goals in life: play pro football and be in the Superstars competition on ABC.

But I don't believe I opened a single college scout's eyes until James Wanser got hold of me in high school. Wanser was Yates's defensive coach, and he taught me how to be a plumb fool on the football field.

The offensive coach, Maurice McGowan, got so sick of my roughhouse tactics, he wouldn't want me to practice. Booker, the head coach, threw me off the team for a day because I murdered our own quarterback, Harold Bailey, in a scrimmage one afternoon:

Wanser had Dexter hitting my quarterback. As head coach, I had to do something. I couldn't let Dexter practice against my varsity offense. Here's my defensive coach prodding him, but I couldn't have my quarterbacks beaten to a pulp. I only put him out a day to teach him a lesson.

See, Dexter wanted to stand up as a defensive end, and with his height

52

and visibility, it was better for him. It was simple for him to get to a ballcarrier when he was running a 4.6 or 4.5 in the 40. He had that basketball body, you see, those long legs that could step over people. He could give an offense headaches. But then we'd run straight at him in the schoolyard to tone him down.

That Dex was a card. During one game, I later learned they were standing behind me on the bench doing a little dance they called the bump. It was an important game, and we were winning and so I guess they were celebrating.

The next day I really laid into Dexter—really all of them. That Dexter, he could fool with you.

I idolized Jack Lambert, the Steelers' middle linebacker. I wore No. 73 through high school, but in college I wore 58 in honor of Lambert. I see highlights of him even today, tapping his feet like a fool before a snap, and I still go, "Whooooooa." I saw how he played the game, and I admired that. I also admired a guy like Ray Nitschke, a tough nut for Green Bay.

I idolized Muhammad Ali, as well. *Idolized* him! He was a big-time hero to me. I just like his crooning style. If I sounded like Ali the way I mouthed off in the pros, it's no coincidence.

But I patterned myself most after two people: Lambert and another linebacker, Dirt Winston of the Steelers. I liked the way Winston looked in his uniform.

I was the backfield coach—I'm Maurice McGowan—and we used to have problems with Dexter. He was wild, just wild, on and off the field. One day he had his helmet on backward. Practice was boring to him, and he just slipped it on backwards. We all laughed, but that boy needed attention.

Was he the best player? No. His junior year, we had at quarterback Harold Bailey, who later played with Dexter at Oklahoma State, and at wide receiver Eric Herring, who played at the University of Houston and briefly with the 49ers. I believe Dexter was jealous of Eric, who had all the attention.

Dexter came back to visit our school after the 49ers won the Super Bowl XVII in January 1983, and he even brought Eric up then. He said, "You happy your boy got his Super Bowl ring? Well, I'll get mine."

Recruiters came after Eric, but also after Dexter. One day a Kansas State guy and another guy got in a fight over him.

Dexter had a way with recruiters. He'd say, "I'm comin' to your school." He told everybody he was coming to their school. He'd say to the scout, "Meet me after school at three o'clock," and then he wouldn't be there. They'd come to us, whining, "Where is he?"

"Probably with someone else," we'd laugh.

And when they were recruiting him, Dexter'd tell the scouts to go see his best friend Gerald. He'd say, "If you take me, you have to take Gerald, too."

That McGowan, hell, he put my buddy Gerald and me down in high school all the time. He told us we'd never amount to anything. He said the only one who'd make it was Eric Herring. I'm supposedly jealous of Eric? Eric was the best man at my first wedding. They're jealous I made it, that I made something of myself.

But Eric was McGowan's boy. Bailey was his boy. That's why they wanted to kick me off the team. They never expected me to make it, not in their wildest dreams. McGowan would say to me, "You'll get kicked out of college for rape or peeking in a girls' bathroom." I had a momma and a daddy who'd beat my ass if I did that. Maybe because I was from the Third Ward, he stereotyped me.

Hell, yeah, scouts were coming after me. Scouts were paying me in high school. Oklahoma State offered me a car; SMU only offered a TV set. That's no big news or anything. Both of those schools have served their probations from that era.

I had my way with college scouts. I'd play one against another. All the Big Eight schools came after me, and I'd play them like a drum. I got money from them. Who needed a job when you could get easy money this way?

My coaches were mad because they weren't part of my success. They wanted cash, too, but I ran my own show. I had my clothes tailored for me when I was in high school, and I could tell my coaches were jealous. I'd flash hundred-dollar bills, four or five hundred at a time.

Booker, my head coach, and I didn't get along. We do now, but I wasn't kissing anybody's ass back then.

When McGowan said I'd get kicked out of college for rape or peeking in a girls' bathroom, what was he trying to do? Motivate me? That's not motivating. It's probably just what he thought of me. I'll never forget that. Never!

My coaches must've thought I was a loose cannon. I wasn't. I was just insecure and scared as hell.

I guess it was hard for me to have friends. I was arrogant, because I had it going on, man. I'd wear my sunglasses at night, and there weren't too many people who wanted to be around a loudmouth joker like me. It was a mask to hide my fear.

I'll never forget our game in the Astrodome my senior year. On one play, I grabbed a running back who already was way out of bounds and javelin-threw him fifteen more yards. Booker and Wanser yanked me out of the game, but that was just the way I played. I don't know what that stems from.

I was so angry at the world I could easily have been wanted by sheriffs instead of Oklahoma State. James Wanser knew this and tried to teach me a lesson.

While we were at a basketball tournament in Huntsville, Texas, Wanser arranged it so our team could tour the Huntsville State Penitentiary. Danny Jackson, Gerald, Marshall Garden, and I all went, and I'll never forget that day. We weren't actually allowed inside the penitentiary, but we were instructed to look around outside. We saw guys in white uniforms and guards on horses.

I thought about how I couldn't read or write and how I could be in one of those cells unable to function. The experience wiped me out. I was afraid to take a wrong step and break the law. I didn't want to be a guy picking cotton, working in the fields, one of those young black men tied to a ball and chain. It looked like slavery to me.

Kids at school were smoking dope and up to no good, so Wanser felt I needed to see those inmates. I was bullheaded. I mean, high school coaches can be like fathers sometimes:

I met Dexter when he was in the seventh grade, and he was something to behold. I said, "Hey, boy, I'm Coach Wanser." I think he already knew who I was.

I was a country boy from seventy-two miles north of Houston. My growing up was totally different from a Houston boy's. Dexter's community was a ghetto.

So I couldn't necessarily relate all the way. But Dexter's daddy, boy, he was a gentleman, and Dexter was his carbon copy, same smile. And Dexter's older sister was the pillar of the neighborhood. She was articulate.

But I'd get hold of Dexter in practice and I'd use my imagination. We didn't use tackling dummies. We used bodies. I'd say, "I want to see pain." With the undisciplined things he did, it was hard to read Dexter. You'd get mixed emotions. He was mischievous, and I understand a mischievous person. As a kid, I was mischievous, which might be why we got along.

He needed that trip to Huntsville. The prison there is the headquarters for the whole state of Texas. It's a prison town with a lot of hardened criminals.

By bringing those boys, I was showing them the ways of this world. I wanted to give an overview of prison time. It ain't no joke being in prison. While we were there, we saw three, four buses of new arrivals, and when Dexter saw that, he changed. There were field hands in the surrounding area, and the boys were listening to what was going on.

I knew the guards, and I had them talk to the new arrivals by the fence so my guys could hear. The new arrival boys were crying. It was no concentration camp, but you could see the effects.

Back at school, meantime, Dexter was trying to impress the college scouts. The recruiters were supposed to sign in with the principal, but some of them didn't. There were a variety of restaurants in the neighborhood where they would meet with kids secretly, or at the Holiday Inn.

Dexter showed up with new cowboy boots and leather jackets, and I said, "Damn, somebody's in your pocket, boy." But I was really happy for the boys, because they didn't have any livelihood.

When I think of Dexter playing high school ball, I think of that game against Furr High School. We played 'em at a new stadium. It was threatening a hurricane, and it was a pigpen out there. It rained, cleared up, and rained some more. And, man, Dexter was in a hurry every play. He was involved in every play. I was thinking, "Dexter's a madman."

We played well under the circumstances, but we lost 30–28 or something. It wasn't Dexter's fault, but he took it hard. They cleared the stadium, but he stayed behind. He was being remorseful. Everyone else was in the field house.

Why was he upset? Well, we'd lost out for the district title, and that was the most distasteful thing. I was down myself, but it was a profound experience for him. I've never seen him react that way, never seen him cry that hard, and I was really down because of him. I was close to crying myself.

Actually, until my senior year, I wasn't convinced I'd be recruited by colleges. I had a calcium deposit in my elbow my junior year, and my arm stuck out as if I was deformed or something.

The summer after my junior year, I knew I had to work my ass off if I was to be recruited. I was feeling insecure. All the other guys from my class were getting letters and brochures from schools, and my mailbox was empty. I felt like I was a better athlete than they were. I had played a lot as a sophomore, and these other guys were waving around letters from Texas or Texas-Arlington. My only letters were my daddy's bills.

I probably had two or three letters, but not enough to put a rubber band around. I wanted to steal my teammates' letters, put my name on them, fill out the questionnaires, and mail them back to the colleges.

I may not have been able to read or write, but I could fill out an application. You just put your address and name. Who can't do that?

It was either go to college or go to hell. By my senior year, I could finally move my elbow better than the Tin Man, and when the season started, Coach Wanser told me to bust some heads in front of those scouts.

I knew I had to be a mad dog when the scouts where there. It's not as if I didn't know who they were. They were the white guys. I mean, who else would they be? It's not as if there'd normally be white guys hanging around Yates, which was 98 percent black and 2 percent Mexican. But during practice you'd see them standing on the sideline, with a pencil and pad. So, homeboy, I'd turn it up. I'd turn it up, jack.

I started cutting people's lights out, and recruiters started recognizing me. Finally, I had enough letters to wrap a rubber band around.

*B*eing Dexter's best friend, Gerald, I know all about him. He'd be dangerous on the football field, but then he'd be a scaredy-cat at night and we'd have to escort him home from parties. Just the littlest thing, and he'd jump behind somebody. But then he'd run to a fight in a minute.

My momma always told me a bad ass is a scared ass. I guess I believed her.

Dexter and I had been together since kindergarten, but I tell you, those recruiters messed up our minds and split us up. We were gonna be a package deal. I should've gone to Oklahoma State with him. We'd been with each other since we were kids. They called us salt and pepper. Everywhere I went, he went. Our girlfriends were best friends—Stephanye Baker and Barbara Bates.

We were very dedicated working out. Dexter and I would train on the railroad tracks in back of my mother's house. We'd run on 'em and make sure to hit each wood panel. We'd go maybe two miles up that track.

When we were coming up, Muslims walked around town selling newspapers. We were into getting noticed, so we cut all our hair off just like them and were baldheaded. These Muslims would wear suits, so for two or three weeks we wore suits, too. We'd go around and eat these Muslim guys' food. But they had fish and bean pie, and Dexter couldn't eat the fish, so that ended that.

Dexter wore his football socks inside out in those days. When they got dirty on the outside, he'd turn them inside out. We didn't wash our football *clothes every day, and we both sweated a lot. So he'd turn his socks inside out to make 'em look clean.*

Then the recruiting started. We kept the money the recruiters gave us. I'd say we got seventy dollars a day.

One of them was from the University of New Mexico, and Dexter told him a real sob story. He said, "My girlfriend's having a baby, and I need $200. If you bring me $200, I'll sign a letter of intent." Dexter got the $200, and we split with the dough to have fun.

We came back by the gym, and there this recruiter was. He was really nervous, and Coach Booker just said, "Dexter swindled another."

Dexter kept the money, all right. Recruiters also let us have their hotel rooms for a few extra days when they'd leave town.

But that McDuffie guy—Oklahoma State's recruiter in town—had one objective: to get Dexter Manley. Dexter took him high and dry. Dexter got promised a Cougar and that they'd pay him every month in school. They've already been on probation for cheating, so this is no revelation.

But Dexter's main ploy with recruiters was playing up his pregnant girl. He used Stephanye being pregnant to capitalize.

We were being wined and dined, but Dexter seemed to be into going to college. He was even starting to study—or getting more and more people to do his work for him—and he'd lift weights. I was working out two times a week, but he was going four times a week.

So, we were at a party—out on the porch—and he says, "Frank, you're not working out like you should. We got to go to college, man." He had tears in his eyes, and he hugged me. He told me to get back in the groove and that he loved me. That meant a whole lot to me.

He did no drugs as a kid. What was on Dexter's mind was to make it to the NFL, and he had to be at his best on the football field. That was his only way out. That's why he didn't do no drugs or drinking. I drank and smoked marijuana myself, but it wasn't a habit because I hung with Dex, and that wasn't his bag.

I can picture that night on the porch with Gerald like a home movie. Gerald had started to smoke dope and booze it up, and I was doing the opposite. He was my best friend, and I saw how he was falling into the drug trap, so I told him to lighten up. I was no party guy. I was dedicated. I knew what I wanted. We ran those train tracks, boy, to get in tip-top condition. You had to hit each wooden panel with quick steps, which helped your calves. Black folks got some of the greatest training theories in the world, huh?

On the other hand, I had zero chats on a porch with my daddy. I mean, I could never have told my daddy how recruiters were dangling cash and how I had tailored suits. I couldn't tell him they were loaning me rent-a-cars. As I've said, my daddy wasn't real approachable.

All this mad recruiting started my senior year. The recruiters would meet me in the hallways at seven in the morning. It was a blast, taking their money and then ditching them. I was taking $500 a pop. I think I'd give Stephanye $25 of it. I'm a stingy guy.

One particular morning, two recruiters—Kansas and Oklahoma State—actually had a brawl over me. Coach Booker says there'd be thirteen, fourteen different scouts in his office sometimes, and this one morning the guys from Kansas and Oklahoma State were in the school building before Coach Booker even arrived, at about 7:30. They'd normally meet him in the hallway most every morning, but this time, they split the hallway and went searching for me, to intercept me before I went to class.

Finally, someone ran in screaming to Coach Booker, "Coach, they fighting! They fighting!"

Coach Booker said, "Who's fighting?"

"The college recruiters, that's who."

Apparently, they were calling each other bad names and making negative comments about each other's schools. Eventually, it came to some roundhouse right hands.

I particularly remember Wayne McDuffie, the recruiter from Oklahoma State. I wanted a suit once, so he splurged for a suit from Walter Pye's. I feel like this is when I began to get spoiled. It's part of getting conditioned to cheating. You're allowed to cheat, and you believe that it's OK to get away with it. Soon I'm thinking these people owe me something, and then I'm conjuring up ways to extract money from all these college scouts.

Your way of life is being formed right then, whether you'll do things the right way or cheat and do them the wrong way. I did them the wrong way. If I'd told my daddy, he would've pulled out the electrical cord and whupped me. You think I'd volunteer myself for that?

I had tailored suits, I was driving dealer cars, and I didn't even have a driver's license. My daddy never knew. I'd park around the corner. If he'd known I had those cars, he'd have had a conniption fit.

Anyway, graduation day came, and out of 502 kids, I ranked 250th! From mentally retarded to 250th! I thought I was a brain.

Daddy couldn't come to my graduation, though, because he was sick. Momma went by herself.

I was happy I was out of school, but at the same time, what was I gonna do? I had scholarships, of course, but I still couldn't read.

So, I got to college, and—as I've said—my daddy died right away. After the funeral, I headed straight back to Oklahoma State. It was still summer, and no one was in school except a few frat boys.

When I returned after the funeral, I was like a zombie. I cried a lot because of my daddy dying and because I was a lonely kid. Man, I was so depressed. I had no transportation, and I sat in the apartment alone all day.

I'd go to church, and every time I'd cry. I'd hear church songs reminding me of home.

I cried during Homecoming that year. I always cried during Homecoming week because everyone else had family members visiting, and I had nobody. My sister would come up and see me, but not during Homecoming or Parents' Day. And Momma, well for her, everything changed for the worse when Daddy passed.

I tell you, there were plenty of times I used to go in my room and cry. I had no family. It was something I would never have again from the day my daddy died. Family was over.

My drug counselors believe that's a clue.

AN IDLE THOUGHT

If you think I negotiated swell deals from those college recruiters, you should've seen me in the NFL.

Against St. Louis in 1985, I tackled Cardinal Stump Mitchell on a running play and said, "Hey, Stump. Fumble the football, and I'll give you five hundred bucks."

The SOB wouldn't fumble. He said, "Five hundred dollars ain't enough."

CHAPTER 8

Family Ties?

MY MOMMA, WHOSE NAME WAS JEWELLEAN, was born in 1932 in Hanesville, Louisiana, one in a family of eight. I think she just about out-survived them all. She was a real introvert who wouldn't spit out her feelings. But if you talk to my aunts and uncles, they'd say she was the sweetest person and the best sister anybody could ever have.

She also—darn it—would never fight back. She was just one of those quiet-as-a-mouse types. Daddy ran the house, and Momma's job was just to take care of us. She was a homemaker for a long while.

When she became pregnant with Gregory from a previous boy-friend, I'm told my grandmother banished her, and my momma had to go live with a schoolteacher. Then she moved to Houston.

She was an athlete, I'm told, and was offered a junior college basketball scholarship. I must've got my athletic ability from her because when it came to sports Daddy was a big, sorry fucker.

Momma showed me love, without a doubt. She was attractive, with brown skin and long hair. Obviously, I got my dark complexion from my daddy. I had a good-looking mom. She would be in the church choir singing, while all the other ladies used to shout. You know how they shout in black churches, in that spiritual way. They go, "Hee Hee Hee" and all this mumbo jumbo. But I never saw my momma do that. I've seen Momma cry in church, but not shout.

I'd feel sad for my momma when she cried in church. I knew it was the spirit in her, but I would feel down because it seemed she wasn't happy. When I see people cry in church, I think, What's wrong? How could they just shout and cry like that? Maybe my momma had some troubling feelings I knew little about.

See, my momma kept things wrapped up inside of her, although I do remember her reacting when Gregory kept getting handcuffed off to jail. Daddy would spend his money bailing Gregory out, and we'd see Momma crying. She could bawl in a minute. She'd cry and break up plates. She'd cry and the next thing you knew, she'd be washing dishes and taking a saucer and slamming it on the back porch.

I'd say, "What's wrong, Momma?" One time she was crying on the bed, and I didn't know whether it was because her sister was sick or what. I remember the song on the radio that day: "Rainy Night in Georgia." Every time I hear that song, I think of Momma.

She whipped me once. It was on a Friday night, and she whipped me just as Daddy did, with a flimsy electrical chord. I'd been at Vacation Bible School with the Choice boys—Henry and Leslie who lived close by on Idaho Street—and they were bored in there like me. It was summertime and it was hot, and what we wished for was some fruit punch.

We broke into the kitchen and guzzled all the punch. The pastor, Reverend Brown, got wind of it, and he saw fit to tell my momma that Friday night.

When she got home, I collected my whupping. At times, she could be a disciplinarian. But if we didn't have a daddy around, I bet we could have run all over her because she was just so nice.

My momma paid me attention, much more so than my daddy. I was in a talent show at Douglas Elementary because she helped me put together a drum set. We got two Folger's coffee cans, tied them together with string and—presto—I was the drummer.

She went to that talent show with me. Having my mother there was the greatest thing in the world. These were the things my daddy would *never* be a part of. I marched proudly down the street with the other little kids, holding my Folger's coffee cans. We were all heading to Douglas for the talent show.

Everything changed when my daddy passed. Momma went downhill like a bobsled, and that tells me *something* was amiss in her before he died.

I was seventeen when I returned to Oklahoma after Daddy's funeral. The next time I laid eyes on my momma was at Christmas, and I saw a lady who had gone from a true believer to a hell raiser. She'd drink all night, sitting outside on the front porch with just her bra on. She'd drink three or four fifths of vodka and a six-pack of malt liquor, and she'd be burning the couch with her cigarettes. She'd walk out the front door leaving the gas stove on.

My drug counselors say my momma must've drunk all her life,

but, Lord no, I do not believe she drank until my daddy passed. You know how people say they're Christians, but they're really not? Well, I know what my momma was like, and she *was* a Christian woman. She was no fake one, drinking beer and cruising out at night. Daddy may have gone out, but Momma stayed put. The only time she went out was with my daddy. She took care of us, cooked our meals, worked her job, and then eventually quit her job to take care of Daddy's house. She was at church as much as the pastor.

But I believe I know what turned my mom into a drunk. What happened is she lost faith. From 1973 to 1977 practically everyone on Momma's side of the family died. First, it was her sister in 1973. Then it was her father in 1974, and her brother was killed in Shreveport in 1975. In 1976 her other brother got rung up with bullets in Houston, right around the corner from our house.

Another of her brothers, my Uncle Hollis, may or may not be dead. Hollis was homeless for more than twenty years—you could call him a derelict—and he refused any charity. My Uncle Wilbur (Hollis's brother) gave him clothes once, but Hollis refused to wear them. He tossed them to some other derelict.

It turned out everyone lost touch with Hollis, and Hollis has never been heard from since. The authorities presume he is dead, but Uncle Wilbur says he very well could be alive because his body's never been identified. This is the kind of baggage my momma was carrying.

Then my daddy died in 1977. So it was just year after year, and when my daddy passed, the screw got loose in my momma's head. She started drinking and stammering. Once when I came home from college and was getting ready to go to a party with Gerald, she sent both of us out in a hurry for a six-pack. She was a Bud woman. But they didn't have Bud at the store and when we came home empty-handed, she ordered, "Just get me any beer."

We got her Schlitz malt liquor, and when I woke up the next morning, she complained, "Long as I live, don't get me the Bull again. The Schlitz malt liquor bull was chasin' me in my dreams. There were bulls everywhere."

Out of the blue, my momma would start fussing about my daddy. These were things I'd never heard before out of her, since she'd always been such a quiet woman. She'd accuse a light-skinned woman who had lived next door to us—Miss White—of having had a fling with my daddy when he was alive. So, I'd play along and say, "That's why Daddy was gonna leave you, to marry Miss White next door." Well, that'd fire her up. She'd pull my hair, just yank as if I wore a wig. Pretty soon, I'd just walk in the door, and she'd just grab my hair immediately.

Maybe she hadn't been appreciated by my daddy, sort of like me, and maybe it was all just pouring out of her. Daddy had been from Texas, and Momma had been from Louisiana, and she'd scream out, "Carl always said I should hush because Texas bought Louisiana, but I'll be goddamned if he bought me!" It sounded to all of us as if she'd been repressed and anger was hissing out of her now.

Other times, you could see the remorse in her, the hurt from my daddy's death. She wanted to give up. She'd say she had no reason to live. They'd been married twenty-six years.

Faith had just been sapped out of her. She'd been this church-going woman, but she wouldn't attend church like she used to. In the summertime, when Houston thermometers would get higher than a pizza oven, she'd shut all the doors and wouldn't dare venture outside. Cynthia would beg her to go to church, but she wouldn't want to see any of her old church friends.

She kept saying, "No reason to live, no reason to live."

The burden fell entirely on Cynthia, who had to live with Momma and also work a job. In one swoop, Cynthia suddenly became the momma of the house. The stress would eventually lead Cynthia to crack cocaine. After the death of Daddy, I'm tellin' you, nothing and nobody was the same.

Reginald lost his senses, too. Cynthia believes, and I kind of agree with her, that Reginald would be alive today if Daddy hadn't passed away so young. If he had stayed alive, there's no way Reginald would've been out on the street dealing drugs, which is how he got his ass shot and killed.

See, when Daddy was living, Ratchie worked. His rule was if you stayed under his roof, you had to work. And if you didn't, you had to enter college or pick up a trade. Daddy always preached college and a trade, college and a trade.

If I hadn't made it in football, my trade was going to be the military. I would've been like Roger Staubach and gone in the navy.

Of course, I knew I was gonna make it in football.

Cynthia, meantime, went to Texas Southern for a while. So did Gregory. They didn't graduate, but at least they attended for about a year or so.

Reginald chose no college and no trade. Instead, he worked in a hospital, and he worked for Gulf Oil. He worked at Tenneco, where my dad was, for a while. He had real good jobs, but his friends in the Third Ward teased him about how many hours he had on his punchcard.

They'd show him wads of hundred-dollar bills and tell him how much cash they'd make in a day versus how much he made in two weeks. They were dealing with drugs, but the money sounded sweet to Reginald and he quite naturally wanted to try it. He began selling drugs, making $700, $800 a pop.

Ratchie submitted to the temptation because he had no daddy to discipline him. No one was around to keep tabs on him any more, certainly not Momma, who was using Daddy's inheritance money for six-packs.

My father had been the foundation. As soon as he died, my brother started hanging with the wrong crowd. He might have been hanging with them before Daddy passed, but he'd have been scared to come home in trouble with Daddy around. So, he'd resist.

It's also possible Daddy wasn't hard enough on Ratchie, which might have started Ratchie on his troubled path. Our daddy sure as hell was hard on me.

Well, it only took about a year after Daddy's death for Reginald to reach the point of no return.

I'm not saying Reginald changed that much. He'd still catch the bus home after he'd made his drug deals, and he gave most of his money to his girlfriend or his little boy, Kindrick. He'd spend all day with her and his son, and catch the bus home by 7:00 P.M. Then he'd shower, put on his blue jeans, and go do what he was doing on the street corner.

Matter of fact, when Ratchie was selling drugs, he'd give guys money if they were hungry. He was kind-hearted.

But other bullshit came with all that moola he carried. I was going into my junior year of college and was home for the summer when I noticed a lot of shooting going on in the neighborhood one day. Two boys were shooting bullets at my brother, and here I was inside the house getting dressed to go out. Reginald dashed in the house, whipped a gun from under the mattress, and split.

My instinct took over. I ran up to this corner, and I'll never forget our neighbor, Butler, flashing out of the blue and saying, "Here, man! Here!" He handed me a gun the way you'd hand a guy a baton in a relay race.

So I dashed to my car and hightailed it up the street. I rolled my window down and started shooting at those two boys who were blasting at Reginald, like I was Wyatt Earp or something.

I'd just panicked, and I shot all over somebody's porch. Somehow, I didn't hit a soul. I gave Butler back his gun.

The next day, I zipped right on back to school. I said, "Man, it ain't worth it being here." I was so scared. I told Ratchie, "Look here, something bad's gonna happen to you."

And you know what else? The next day, the two boys we shot at were walking around the neighborhood with my brother! Here I am, jeopardizing my football future blasting a gun, and the next day they're all bosom buddies! That's how ludicrous it was.

Well, the curtain came down on Reginald that fall. He and his girl were gonna be married in October 1979, but he didn't make it out of September.

The day before it all ended, Reginald seemed to have a premonition. Cynthia says the night before his death, he blurted out, "Momma, can I sleep with you tonight?"

Then he said, "Momma, I don't feel I'll be here long."

And he laid down in bed with her in the same spot Daddy had died in.

Cynthia was an insurance agent, and the next day Reginald asked to use her car. Cynthia said no. He said he wanted to go around the corner, and she just said, "Uh uh." He didn't have a license. To this day she feels if she'd let him borrow the car, he might have gone over to his girlfriend's house and might still be alive.

Reginald said he was going around the corner, car or no car. Momma said, "Reginald, be careful," and he replied, "I'm just going around the corner for a beer, Momma."

Some forty-five minutes later, they heard a gunshot. Cynthia dropped her pencil and said, "I hope Reginald isn't around."

Ten minutes later, there was a rapping on the door. Cynthia says she knew right then.

One of Butler's friends had come to get her. They brought her around the corner, and Reginald was lying in blood on the curb, a crowd around him. Butler was with him, and Reginald was telling Butler, "Don't let Cynthia see me like this. Promise me, don't let her see me like this."

Cynthia stood behind the crowd bawling her eyes out. Ratchie had heard her crying, and as soon as Butler said, "I promise, man, I promise," Ratchie closed his eyes for good.

It was eleven o'clock at night when my sister phoned me at Oklahoma State. My friend Tammy picked up the phone, and as soon as Tammy said, "Hi, Cynthia," then had distress written all over her face, I knew. I just knew. I started hollering in the bed.

Even though it was late, I jumped up, put on my clothes, and went to Iba Hall, which is where my teammates lived on campus. I stood up on Harold Bailey's bed and started to throw a chair outside. They stopped me.

My coach at the time was Jimmy Johnson, who's now head coach of the Dallas Cowboys. He asked me to stay and play in the game that weekend against Wichita State, promising, "I know a sheriff in Texas. Don't worry, we'll catch the guy who shot your brother. We'll solve that problem."

I agreed, and Pat Jones, who's currently the head coach at Oklahoma State and was my defensive line coach back then, gathered all of my buddies together from the Houston area to keep track of me. It was the way of the streets to go avenge your brother's death, and they feared I was gonna head back to the Third Ward with a rifle. Pat Jones told my buddies, "Let him cool down before he ends up in jail." Those boys shadowed me that entire week.

Well, I ended up twisting an ankle against Wichita State, which was a blessing. Maybe it saved my life. I was on crutches, so I couldn't go manhunt the guy who murdered Ratchie. I wanted to, but I'm grateful my ankle swelled up. I was gonna go burn a particular house in the Third Ward. I knew that house had something to do with my brother's murder. I'd probably have set the whole block on fire. You know how I used to play with matches.

But when I finally limped home for Ratchie's funeral, I stayed in the house, other than going over to the Houston Oilers' complex for treatment.

I never did have a complete explanation of what happened to Reginald. I just knew he'd been pulled out of a club, and this guy named Forest, I think, drove by and shot him. It was a setup.

Here was this young guy, Reginald, twenty years old, getting lit up by a gun. It shows you what the hell is going on in the streets. There are so many Reginald Carl Manleys who've wasted their lives. Those people who shoot them up don't respect life.

My brother was involved peddling drugs and probably didn't give some money back to his pusher, perhaps no more than $500. So they whacked him.

One day when I was home from college, I finally saw the guy who supposedly set Ratchie up. Gregory, Tammy, and I were driving down the street, and when I saw him, I stopped the car, and Greg and I chased his ass down. I kicked him with my feet, and the guy kept begging, "Please stop! Please stop!"

I've heard so many theories on what happened the night Ratchie was murdered. Gerald has one, too:

Dex's brother was selling a drug called D's or Lou's on the street. They look like birth control pills. The story is that Ratchie sold these pills to a white guy, but it was supposed to be somebody else's sale and Dexter's brother beat him out of it. Well, the next day the guy who was supposed to get the sale came back and shot Reginald on the curb.

My anger comes and goes on this subject. About a year and a half ago when I was in rehab, I went to Houston's restaurant with a friend from high school, Lisa Carol Lang. That day we had driven by where my daddy worked and also had been by the depressing Third Ward, so I was in a reflective mood when we got to the restaurant. I asked Lisa, "Do you know how my brother died?"

She didn't know. I told her the legend on the street was that Reginald was supposed to deliver drugs but gave them baking soda instead. I told her he'd been killed for nothing and thank God I'd messed my ankle up in that Wichita State game, as I'd made up my mind I was gonna kill the guy who murdered him. God saved my life by injuring my ankle.

As I told her this story, I began sweating and slammed my fist on the restaurant table and nearly broke the damn thing. I knocked the salt and pepper shakers flying and shouted, "They killed my brother for nothin'! I'm gonna kill all those SOBs now!"

Everything got quiet in the restaurant, and people got up to leave. The next thing I knew, three Houston police officers were standing by the bar.

I had to chill out.

The worst thing of all is that Ratchie's death drove my momma further into her booze. It was just another funeral for her to attend. She ran out of the house that night and saw my brother on the curb with a white sheet over him. She and Cynthia wailed like dogs.

If my daddy hadn't died, who knows? All I know is he had bequeathed his favorite ring to Ratchie, and as Ratchie went astray in his final weeks, he pawned that ring for cash.

When I heard he'd pawned it, I drove all the way back from Oklahoma and bought Daddy's ring back—for *me*.

AN IDLE THOUGHT

One of my relatives who is not dead is Eric Dickerson.

Eric, the running back you've all heard of, is my cousin. My grandfather's sister (on my father's side) is Eric's mother. Her name is Aunt Red.

Eric and I confide in each other. When I relapsed in 1989 with the Redskins, I was in denial and felt like lying to the world. I was about to meet with the commissioner, and I called Eric in Indianapolis from my truck at about 7:00 A.M. I woke his butt up.

We talked about how I'd messed up and used drugs, and I asked him, "What should I do?"

See, I wanted to lie to Tagliabue and the media and say I was clean, but Eric suggested I face up to it. I ended up admitting to the cocaine, although my natural instinct was to fib.

Two years later, when I retired from the Buccaneers in tears, Eric and I spoke again. He said, "Man, the two people who are always on TV crying are Jim Bakker and Dexter Manley." And he laughed.

I admit that's pretty accurate.

C H A P T E R 9

Scarred for Life

MY DADDY WAS DEAD AND MY MOMMA WAS inebriated twenty-four hours a day. College got off to a forgettable start.

But it became very livable when my car arrived. Oklahoma State had promised me wheels for signing with them, and I requested a Cougar. I wasn't sure they'd come through, but then they did—on the day Elvis Presley died.

I was coming off the football field my freshman season when some white man waved me over. He walked me around the corner and said, "There's your car, son."

I was a kid on Christmas morning and birthday morning combined. The first car in my life. Every time I hear an Elvis song to this day, I think of that car in front of Gallagher Hall. It had 200 miles on it, and I was the happiest guy on earth.

I had the sharpest ride on campus, a brand smacking new '77 Cougar. It was metallic brown with a glittery paint job and a burnt orange vinyl top. I had strobe lights installed, too.

I put my jersey number on the little windshield bug—No. 58 for Jack Lambert. I put DM 58 across there, too, and then I put my new nickname up there—Hollywood.

I don't know where Hollywood came from. Some guy just started calling me that, because of Hollywood Henderson and the way I dressed. I was flamboyant like my daddy had been. And Hollywood Henderson was a linebacker, and so was I. I was about 225 pounds and could run like Bob Haynes. Of course, you've got to live up to a name like Hollywood.

Oklahoma State has already served its probation for this car they got me, but at the time it was covered up real CIA-like.

I went racing around immediately. I couldn't believe they'd kept their word. Normally when you sign with a school, you'd expect your car right away. But mine wasn't waiting for me on the curb when I arrived, so I doubted it would ever come.

Motivated by my wheels, I started rolling my freshman year. I was so cocky. I had cash, a new car, and clothes, and I lived off campus. My wife, Stephanye, was finishing high school, so I also wasn't tied down.

Academics were a joke. One reason I had chosen Oklahoma State was they told me they had a criminology department and a hotel/ restaurant management class. I wanted to major in criminology and minor in hotels. I wanted to be an FBI agent or run a Ritz Carlton. These were not things I had to be an expert reader for.

But when I arrived for freshman year, they handed me a class schedule and told me my major was business. There was no criminology and no Ritz Carlton training available. They lied. I thought I was going to need books, but instead my first-semester freshman courses were Special Topics (a gimme A), the Economics of Social Issues (which had a lot of multiple choice, so I squeezed out a D), Intercollegiate Football (which gets you an A if you simply show up for football practice), Archery and Riflery (where I eked out a C), Weight Training (my favorite class and I only got a C), and Coaching of Wrestling (another A).

Second semester I aced Intercollegiate Football again, dropped English Composition (I couldn't compose), failed American History, 1492 to 1865 (I couldn't remember back that far), eked out a D in Introduction to Sociology, and managed a strong B in Man and Society (another multiple-choice special).

I went to a summer school workshop to earn three more credits, took a swimming pool management correspondence course, a metric system correspondence course, and a religion course at Southwestern College in Oklahoma City, all to keep me eligible for football heading into my sophomore year. I barely squeaked by with a D in swimming pool management—I didn't like cleaning swimming pools, would you?—and I aced the religion course somehow. Obviously I flunked the metric system course.

I was learning how they played this game. I graded out pretty well in the football games, although I had a difficult time picking up the defensive scheme. I would get things backwards. I was just slow with it.

Since I would sometimes blow assignments, it was up to my pure hustle to overcome it. I had to be reckless out there.

In a game against Florida State or Kansas, Coach Stanley said, "Dexter, I need you to go get the quarterback. I need you to go get me a sack." Well, I went and got that sack—from nose guard. I was just playing out of my mind.

I remember one year playing Oklahoma, and we were winning 21–14 at half behind Terry Miller's great running. I was so excited that as we left the field at halftime I picked up a football and slung it way up in the stands. We just *knew* we were going to crash those Boomer Sooners. Hell, they beat us 63–28.

College was a blast. There were a lot of white guys and some black, but I remember a bunch of us going to one of those frat houses and beating up some frat boys. They ran around in polo shirts and sports cars, and the football players didn't like that.

I guess I made some enemies at Oklahoma State. Once when we came off a road trip, I noticed my gas cap was off and there was sugar everywhere on the street. I called a tow truck. If I had started that car, my engine would've been torn up. I had to put a lock on my gas tank after that.

Another time, I was watching a Martin Luther King TV documentary in the athletic lounge and nearly murdered some white boys. The documentary was showing one of King's protests where policemen sprayed young black kids with water, and one of the white boys made a comment. Man, I lost it. I picked up a chair and ran them all out of the room.

I realized then I had better control myself. In the Third Ward, I wasn't used to hanging around white boys. It's not that I had prejudice—I'd had a white coach in the seventh grade whom I liked—but to see this old white policeman spraying these black kids . . .

Well, my attitude eventually caught up with me and rearranged my face. I have this elongated scar on my left cheek today, and I've got my Cougar to thank for it.

I was at a party at the student union the spring of my freshman season, and when I went to leave with a girl, my Cougar was sandwiched tightly between two cars. Harold Bailey, our quarterback who had attended Yates with me, had his car directly behind mine, and two black boys were sitting in a piece of junk car very close in front of mine. But I had the finest car on campus, and it did not deserve to be cramped.

Well, these two black guys in front of me didn't go to Oklahoma State. They liked to crash parties at school, trying to score with college girls. They probably knew who I was, because I was big time.

So I went up to them and said, "Excuse me, can you guys let me out, please?"

Maybe I wasn't that tactful about it. Actually, I just said, "Let me out."

Their reply was, "You think you're some fucking hotshot freshman, Manley. We ain't lettin' you out."

Coming from the Third Ward, I just hit the roof: "Man, let me out! Look here. I'll move that piece of shit for you." I started talking trash, and these were two big guys.

The party let out, and we were arguing as people trudged by. Bailey finally showed up to back out his car but these two guys and I were still pointing (middle) fingers. Then I hopped in my car right quick, burned rubber, and nearly hit Bailey.

I parked my car, and these two guys were still talking trash. They said, "Look here, we're gonna kick your ass," and I said, "That's OK."

So Billy Wells, one of my teammates, brought me a gun and said, "Shoot 'em, Manley." And another teammate, Worley Taylor, said the same thing.

I said, "Nah, I ain't gonna shoot 'em."

These two bad boys said they were heading to the Alpha House for another party, and I said, "Tell you what, I'm goin' back to Iba Hall, and I'm gonna change clothes and we're gonna fight."

I almost flew to Iba Hall. I put on Bailey's Texas high-school all-star-game jersey—No. 11. I made him let me wear it 'cause that jersey was a big deal. And I put on a pair of jeans and a pair of Converse football shoes with rubber cleats so I'd have good footing when we'd scuffle on the concrete.

Then I walked into the Alpha House party. I saw one of the guys dancing, and I ripped his ass up. I shot-putted him through these swinging saloon-type doors, and he smashed into this girl, Delta, who was walking behind the door just at that moment. Delta lost all five of her front teeth. The whole school hated me for that.

So, anyway, the guy picked himself up and dove out the back door. He kept on running. He was talking like, "Please Mr. Manley, stop." I was kicking some booty.

The other of the two guys tried dashing out the front door, but I collared him, threw him on the concrete, and started soccer-style kicking him and uppercutting him. You know how big frat houses have porches with long staircases down to their front sidewalk? Sort of like plantation mansions? Well, that's where we were. I was standing over this guy in front of this staircase, kicking him like Jan Stenerud, and my teammate Worley Taylor was down there saying, "Dexter, Dexter, he's got something."

So Worley pulled out his gun and was gonna slap this guy upside the head. But Harold Bailey, my homeboy from Yates, caught Worley's hand. I think that freed up the bad guy on the ground.

I was standing up at that moment, and it doesn't seem like the guy could've cut me from the ground. But he did.

James Cowans, a teammate from St. Louis, shouted, "Dexter, Dexter! You're cut!"

I said, "I'm cut?"

He said, "Yeah, you got cut on your face."

The bad guy climbed up from the ground and started to walk away. So Worley gave me the gun, and he said, "Shoot that nigger, Dexter, shoot him." I had the gun in my hand, my finger on the trigger, and I paused, and I said, "Nah, man." I just put the gun down and started feeling for my face. I didn't feel a thing.

I could've shot that guy, and I would have been locked up with my brother Gregory. I pointed that gun, and then I stopped. I think it was Bailey who said, "Dexter, don't do that."

So I handed Worley back his gun and went down to the nurse's room. They laid me on the table, and I still couldn't see my face. I had no mirror. I just wanted to see it, man, but I felt no blood. Then the doctor said, "You don't have a bad cut, but you've got a cut."

He sewed eighteen stitches in my face like I was some sort of afghan. I could not wait to get up off that table and see if I looked like Frankenstein.

When I found a mirror, I still couldn't see it because the doc had gauze over the stitches.

Well, I was the big talk on campus that weekend: Dexter Manley got cut. Dexter Manley got cut.

I wound up playing basketball on the same intramural team as the guy who cut me. Somehow, he'd gotten into school. The only reason I didn't murder him was that I was going to church at the time and had a sense of forgiveness inside.

It was tough restraining myself. You know how janitors have big brooms they sweep a basketball floor with? I was gonna take that broom and pop that guy right in the head during an intramural game. But something told me, Don't do it.

God must've relieved me of the violence to maim that boy, because I was gonna use that broom handle like Willie Mays.

Well, the police got involved, and we had to go speak to them on campus. I had to take a lie detector test because the boys I beat up wanted to file charges. They told police we had a gun. They said he cut me in self-defense.

We lied and said we didn't have a gun, but we also told the police officers he cut me with a razor blade. He'd actually gotten me with a box cutter.

Meantime, I was contemplating plastic surgery. One plastic surgeon in Oklahoma City wanted to shoot me with a medicine that would supposedly reduce the size of the cut. But that meant I'd have to get a shot in the jaw, and I hate shots.

It just wasn't worth it, so I went to other doctors. One doctor told me to put vitamin E on the wound, and it'd smooth out. That's what I've been doing to this day.

That incident changed my life, man. I didn't have to be bad no more. I didn't have to prove a point. I've never had a street fight since then.

Before then, I guess I'd never turned away or backed down. I mean, I didn't have to go back to that Alpha House. I could've gone to Iba Hall and stayed there. The argument was over! But I just had to prove I was bad. And look what happened.

That cut hurt my self-esteem for a long time. My drug counselors probably think it contributed to my drug use. I always thought I was an ugly kid before, but I was *uglier* now with this scar. When I'd go in restaurants, the first thing I'd do was head to the restroom and look at myself in the mirror. I'd ask people, "Does the scar look bad? Does it look bad?"

Sometimes even today when I go to restaurants, I sit on the inside, with the cut next to the wall where nobody can see it. Or on TV interviews, I try to give my other side to the camera, instead of the cut side.

Its size has reduced, and it's smoother. You can hardly tell now. I've rubbed vitamin E on it every day for about five years. I also douse it with cocoa butter to smooth it out.

Another way it hurt my self-esteem is that people saw the scar and figured I grew up in a slum and stereotyped me. The scar added to this aura I seemed to have as a wild man. It seemed to make me more imposing.

Afterward, my whole family back home was pissed. Momma was particularly bothered, and I think it made her drink even more beer than usual.

I don't think it comes up much anymore because I dress and carry myself well. But if I just walked around with no scruples and still acted rough, folks would say more about the scar.

People don't mention the cut much to me today. Maybe they're afraid to ask. Some people think it's a football cut, and sometimes I tell people I got cleated. But I tell 'em the truth eventually.

I also tell them I got the cut at a *white* school.

AN IDLE THOUGHT

Mike Tyson's been in more fights than me, and his face isn't scarred. That's one lucky short guy.

You know, it may sound demented, but Tyson—rape conviction or no rape conviction—also used to motivate me on the football field.

When we played the Giants in 1988, there was an article on Tyson in *The Washington Post* that day. I read it the best I could and athletic-taped it on my locker at RFK Stadium before kickoff.

Just Tyson's killer instinct fired me up. In the article, he'd claimed to be the best in the business, and I pictured myself as the best in my business. So I was gonna go out on the field and be an intimidator, just like Tyson.

By halftime, I hadn't even breathed on Phil Simms. Lawrence Taylor had just come back from a four-week drug suspension that day, and he already had caused a fumble and had a sack.

I was pissed. I came in at halftime, tore Tyson's picture off my locker, and dunked it in the trash can. I shouted, "I don't deserve that picture in my locker, damn it!"

Wouldn't you know it? I carried that anger into the second half and sacked Phil Simms *four* times. After the game, I went scrapping through the trash for the picture like a homeless guy.

CHAPTER 10

Married
. . . With Child

My HIGH SCHOOL MARRIAGE NEVER MADE IT
to a silver anniversary.

I'm not saying I didn't care for Stephanye. I did and still do. But
we were too young to be wed.

Stephanye was going into her senior year at Yates High School
when I left for Oklahoma State, and her mother—Miss Baker—was
the one left with the baby rattle. So Stephanye had as normal a senior
year as you can have. She baby-sat after school like the rest of the girls
in her class, only the baby she sat was hers.

Stephanye is bright and was an Honor Society member, and she
never hid the fact to her classmates there was a Derrick. The summer
after my freshman season, I came home and lived with Stephanye at
Miss Baker's house—like a regular man and wife. I mowed the lawn
and took out the trash, except there was some other trash I had to deal
with, too.

I'd heard Stephanye on the telephone once talking to some guy,
sort of lovey-dovey, and I guess that made me snap. We got into it, and
she stabbed me in the arm with a pair of scissors.

I needed fifteen stitches inside and fifteen outside. There's still a
scar today, but I guess Stephanye had her reasons:

Well, he had confronted me, and I figured I'd better grab some-
thing. We both have a temper. When it came to Dexter, I always felt I had to
protect myself. At that point, yes, he caught the raw end of the deal. We were
too young, and neither one of us was ready. He wasn't through sewing his

77

oats, and I wasn't. I caught him with a pair of twins, myself. After all the things Dexter had done, we promised to stick together.

Well, even after she attacked me like Edward Scissorhands, I still brought Stephanye and one-year-old Derrick up to Oklahoma State with me as I was heading into my sophomore year. The university arranged a scholarship for her, if you know what I mean.

Miss Baker says our first mistake was bringing Derrick with us, but I insisted. I was going to be a responsible daddy. I approached fatherhood a lot differently than my daddy ever did.

True, Stephanye needed to get acclimated to college life, and Derrick might have been an added burden on her:

At school, we had an apartment in the married dorm. It wasn't bad. I mean, I met a few people—football players and their wives. Dexter was a doting father. He had to take Derrick to the doctor once, and he tripped out and didn't know nothing. But Dexter was really good with Derrick; he was really there for Derrick when we started out.

But we lasted one semester. After Tammy, it was splitsville.

I met Tammy in front of Lewis Field as I was going to football practice. She lived in the girls' dorm across the field and would walk near us.

One day L.P. Williams, Ed Smith, and I were dressed for practice early and were people-watching. Tammy walked by and I spoke to her. I learned she was from Houston.

Our QB, Harold Bailey, liked her first, but I saw her again at a party and out of all the guys she liked me. It was my freshman year. Stephanye was still back in Houston in high school, finally taking her ACTs. Tammy and I ended up dancing at this party. Everyone watched us like hawks, because we were both excellent dancers.

When Stephanye came to college the next year, Tammy would come over to the house and eat. Miss Baker says Stephanye thought Tammy was her friend. I personally don't remember these dinners too well, but it's true Tammy had a crush on me. I used to go over to her apartment. Quite frankly, I was a cheating dog:

One night, Dexter told me he was taking a friend to work. But a friend of mine called to say Dexter and this girl Tammy were having a rendezvous at her apartment. Sure enough, his car was there at her place.

I told him to come down, and he wouldn't. I broke the front window, and he wouldn't come down. I kept hitting it, and he still didn't come down.

I had always believed in Dexter because he has this uncanny way of making you believe in him. When we went to college, we were going to let bygones be bygones. I was struggling from day one in school and had a real bad case of tonsilitis. Dexter'd be telling me he'd be studying with a tutor when he'd actually be with Tammy.

I didn't know this until later, but he cheated on me when Tammy rode with us to and from Houston on Thanksgiving break. She, Harold Bailey, Dexter, and I were all in one car. While Harold was driving and I was sleeping in the front seat, Dexter and she were in the back kissing.

I eventually learned all about this hot affair and blew up. It was a Sunday, and I went to visit her. I knocked her down a couple of times and told her next time she's involved with somebody's husband, don't befriend the wife.

It was just so low of her. She rode with us to college, and my mother fixed food and sandwiches for all of us. And she and Dexter would be in the back making out. Wow.

What blew Tammy's and my cover was that one of my teammate's wives told Stephanye how I was messing with Tammy. Lord, Stephanye put on her clothes and hit that door in a minute. Stephanye knocked on her dorm door and as soon as that knob turned open, boy, they were going at it. A catfight. When I came back in the house later and saw Stephanye, she had tossed my clothes outside and said, "Your ass is next."

I hit the door. Next thing I knew, her daddy was there, loading her shit up. He had come for her in a heartbeat. He took all her clothes, all our furniture, her Pinto, my son.

It was a sad day when she split. I went to my teammate Worley Taylor's room and started bawling my eyes out, as usual. Seems like a lot of things in my life end with me bawling my eyes out. But they were leaving, I was lonely, I was young, I'd failed at marriage, and that's why I needed a handkerchief.

I did love Stephanye. She was my first love. And I loved my kid. Next thing I knew, they were leaving like the rest of my family had left me.

I didn't run home begging her to come back. I was going with Tammy now, and she moved right into my apartment.

So I guess my daddy had been right when he advised not to get married. His reason was I might mess up my football future, but I hadn't done that.

AN IDLE THOUGHT

As you can see, I didn't handle my wedding ring too well.

But I'm careful as hell with my Super Bowl rings.

I keep all three of them in a Virginia bank safe-deposit box, although I took them with me to Phoenix in 1990 when I played for the Cardinals.

As soon as I arrived in Phoenix, I put those rings in a bank vault. But when I was leaving the Cardinals for the Tampa Bay Buccaneers, the people at my Phoenix bank didn't want to hand over my rings.

Somebody there asked me why I never wore them, and I said, "I have worn 'em. To hell and back."

C H A P T E R   11

GPA

I MADE IT TO THE NFL BECAUSE OF TAMMY Wilmore. I had entered college with an ACT score of 8 and with the reading level of a second-grader. I had no business staying eligible for tiddlywinks, much less football.

Luther Booker, my high school coach, had suggested I take my ACT test at Oklahoma State rather than at Yates because he figured the college might have some control over my results. So the summer before my freshman year, I brought a No. 2 pencil to the testing room thinking that—poof—the college coaches could make me a scholar.

Well, I can't say I aced the thing. I was able to put my name and address on the test, and that's it. That is it. I could not finish the test. Hell, I couldn't even start it!

I left that place crying my eyes out. I was living in an apartment by my lonesome, and I'll never forget the pain I was in. It reminded me of grammar school; I felt about as smart as a blocking dummy. I panicked that I wouldn't be admitted to college and that I'd have to catch a bus back to the Third Ward and hang out there the rest of my life.

Dale Roark, the athletic department's academic advisor, told me later I had scored an 8 on the ACT. That's when I knew Oklahoma State was covering up for me in school, why they were about to put me in bowling classes. After that ACT test, they knew I was a fool. When I had envisioned college, I'd seen myself taking geology or business classes; but that was just denial on my part. These people at Oklahoma State thought I was a dummy and had me major in physical education. I didn't want to, damn it. Something inside of me wanted to fight them.

Tammy Wilmore fought with me. There were times in college when Tammy begged teachers to let me take my work home. I'd personally cry to these teachers, and Tammy would plead for take-home tests, take-home pop quizzes, take-home essays, you name it.

When she was successful, Tammy would do the work.

I wasn't sure how many teachers she was conning. When Tammy later told me the extent of her begging, I was grateful. She went behind my back, asking these professors for mercy.

Tammy began supervising my schoolwork during my sophomore year. My freshman year, I didn't have her as my right arm, but I got through by cheating and taking courses as easy as ABC. They'd handed me a class schedule simple enough for a fourth-grader.

In my sophomore year, Tammy would write a list of words for me to study, but I couldn't absorb them. I tried to memorize phrases, but I didn't have the ability to sound words out. It was all up to her, not me. Here is my sophomore year, first-semester report card, which I didn't have to take home to get signed, thank God:

1. Education and Vocation Orientation—F
2. Intercollegiate Football—A
3. Biological Sciences—F (Tammy hated science and math, so she was absolutely no help here.)
4. Introduction to Recreation and Leisure—D (We played basketball or racquetball.)
5. Social Recreation—B (It was fairly laid-back.)
6. Introductory Psychology—D

That got me a total of nine credits. Here's the report for my second semester, sophomore year:

1. Economics of Social Issues—B
2. General Geology—D (Is that Rocks for Jocks?)
3. Care and Prevention of Athletic Injuries—C
4. Beginning Golf—Incomplete (I can't remember what happened, but I could hit a ball a long way.)
5. Leadership—A (I've always been a leader.)
6. HPELS Workshops—B
7. R.O.T.C., a summer school correspondence course—B
8. Introduction to the Humanities—C: Tammy and I took humanities together. I would fall asleep and snore in the classroom, and the other students would crack up. I definitely did not do any essay portions of the tests, just the multiple choice. The essays would mean thinking real hard and finding a plot and writing, and I could never do

that. But I still managed a C. That woman teacher was nice. Even though she told Tammy I wouldn't pass unless I did the essay, I think Tammy talked her into letting me take it home to do.

Of course, I didn't know that at the time. Tammy had gone to the instructor and told her I was from a black high school where they just passed me because I was an athlete. She added that in Texas it was just all football. She tried to explain what kind of person I was, that I was a good guy, and the teacher could see I always showed up with a folder, looking responsible. But the teacher still said, "Dexter's not going to pass without the essay part."

Tammy just wouldn't give up. She told her at my high school the rule was No Pass, No Play, that academics were less important than lunch period so they just passed me. She explained that I was just a person who needed more time to do my work. I needed to take home the essays because one class period wasn't enough time for me to finish it. She told her without football, I'd actually lose my mind. I guess the teacher felt sorry.

My credits for that second semester were eighteen, so for the entire school year, I'd gotten twenty-seven credits.

In my junior year, I had a new coach, Jimmy Johnson, who apparently did not wield as much power with the teachers as did my previous head football coach, Jim Stanley.

I hadn't declared a major yet, although I was in pre-business. My first semester, junior year academic record was this:

1. Intercollegiate Football—A (Just for showing up to practice.)
2. Introduction to Economic Analysis—F
3. Physical Geography—Withdrew
4. American History, 1492–1865—D: I tried history again, after flunking it my freshman year and cheated my way through. Multiple choice, you know.

But I would never cheat off Tammy's paper on multiple-choice tests. I wouldn't trust Tammy's decisions. Why? For one thing, Tammy's study habits weren't what they were supposed to be. She had too much going on; she had to work. You think I'd trust her over someone who was just there for college? I mean, she was in college, but she wasn't studying as much as these others. So why look at her paper? Also, she said she didn't like multiple choice.

What I'd generally do is look at white people's answers and then look at hers. If she had a different answer, I'd choose theirs. But when it came to her doing my homework, I had confidence in her.

5. Beginning Tennis and Racketball—C: Tammy thought I should change my major to P.E., and I think she went to my defensive line coach, Pat Jones, to discuss it with him. They became buddy-buddy, and I'm sure she persuaded him to help my cause. I decided against the P.E. major because I thought a major that would link me with every driver's ed teacher in the world was hokey. But I continued to take any course where one of the requirements was wearing short pants.

6. Bowling—C: I could wear long pants for bowling, and it was still easy. Tammy took it too, and we actually had written tests. I only got a C because I didn't always go to class and I'd tend to sleep when the lady was talking. I also got ticked because Tammy was bowling as well as I was. I was a powerhouse bowler, as you can imagine, and my goal was to break pins, but I'd step over the line, and my accuracy came and went.

I finished with eight credits for the first semester and needed to do a little bit more brainstorming in the second semester. My record follows:

1. Intercollegiate Football—A
2. Basic Business Law—C: Don't ask me why I did so well in business law. I don't think Tammy took the course with me, but that doesn't mean she didn't do my work. She was quite busy at the time, working in the engineering department, so she dropped down to only six hours of school herself, and then she worked at Wal-Mart. She also managed to cook dinner and do my homework with neat handwriting.
3. Introduction to Economic Analysis—D (Tammy got a D, too.)
4. Labor Problems—D
5. Marketing—F
6. Sociology of the American Family—B (We took that one together, and I made better grades in the classes she liked.)
7. HPELS Workshop—D

I had needed sixteen second semester credits to stay eligible for my all-important senior season; you need twenty-four credit hours each year to be eligible to play the next season. Obviously, staying eligible for my senior season would give me my only shot at playing pro ball. It was either stay eligible or go back to the Third Ward and maybe a life like Ratchie's.

I passed only fourteen credits in the second semester, which gave me twenty-two for the entire year. I needed two more.

Scared to death, I enrolled in three summer school courses, but I dropped one of them, a communications course. I wasn't confident, either, of passing Voice and Speech Improvement; so I had Tammy take Church Business Management for me at Oklahoma City South-western College. Jimmy Johnson got me in that class.

This is why I say I owe it all to Tammy. She stayed up all night with that religion course, while I slept. I never once looked at the work. To me, it sounded like an easy course, but she'd get mad doing the homework. She said it was the most boring class she ever took, but Tammy came through with an A.

Then, my senior year, the first semester was the last one that ever mattered to me:

1. Intercollegiate Football—A
2. Original Policy Systems—B: The teacher, a lawyer, was a good friend of mine and I conned him for a B. I would ask, "Do you think you can represent me when I turn pro?" Boy, his eyes would light up. I hardly went to that class, and I've honestly forgotten his name.
3. Geography of Music—Withdrew
4. Marketing—C: I passed, while Tammy had to drop it. One night she crammed all night for one of the tests, and I went to bed early. I got a B; she flunked.

How'd I pass? Multiple choice.

She was taking only nine hours, working, getting home at 10:00 P.M., and cooking me dinner. I'd eat, and she'd do my home-work. I guess it was all catching up with her.

There was so much on her mind when she went to take that test, she drew a blank. And marketing is something you need to memorize.

I personally thought it was kind of ironic, considering her major was marketing and she flunked the test.

At nights she would be in bed doing my work, and I would be asleep. She would get mad because she thought I should at least be *awake* while she was doing my work for me. Soon I'd be snoring, and she'd slap me on the forehead.

5. Principles of Office Management—D
6. Coaching of Basketball—Incomplete (Well, I didn't go to class because it was taught by the basketball coach and I figured he'd give me a grade.)

After my senior football season ended, the second-semester classes didn't mean a hill of beans to me. I failed the only two I took: Management and Introduction to Social Psychology.

Academically, I stayed eligible four consecutive seasons, which was the bottom line. I was credited with eighty-nine hours of coursework, leaving me eleven hours short for graduation. Originally, I had wanted to be an FBI agent with a major in criminology and a minor in hotel/restaurant management. As it turned out, my major on the transcript was business, but it really was football. All the cheating and sympathy-getting were for survival.

Tammy couldn't go to *every* instructor and get on the pity-pot for me. Each instructor has his or her own way how to handle people like me. Not every teacher passed me because of who I was. I guess only the athletic department's academic advisor, Dale Roark, knows for certain:

I'm sure we had a hotel and restaurant administration class, so I don't know why Dexter didn't take it. On the other hand, there may not have been an undergrad criminology class. So Dexter would've had to take sociology and then get an advanced degree someplace else or go to a penal institution to learn how to be an FBI agent.

When I hear what his schedule was, I particularly notice those HPELS Workshops. Those probably were some of the courses players take to lift their GPA, like Weight Training and Lifting, or Leadership, or Rappelling.

Of course, he got an A every semester in Intercollegiate Football. Athletes are allowed to take intercollegiate athletics every semester here, and that grade counts toward their GPA (grade point average). It's not great, but at least they got something for the thirty to forty hours they put in each week for football. The band gets two hours' credit, so why shouldn't the players receive credit?

He had to pass twenty-four hours every year—September to September—to stay eligible. Up until sixty hours, he needed a 1.8 to stay eligible, and after sixty hours, he needed a 2.0. That was a Big Eight rule.

What we were trying to do was keep him in school and hope that at some point he'd take off on his own. I was trying to build his GPA so he would be around the next year.

Understand that the philosophy of the university then, and probably now, was until you declared your major, anything you took was counted toward eligibility. So he could get away with Archery and Riflery and Beginning Golf. After he declared his major, he had to pass twenty-four hours in that major, and everyone must declare a major after sixty hours. Dexter may not have reached sixty hours until his senior year.

Anybody who's an athlete can pass tennis and bowling. What knocks them down—and Dexter got a C in bowling—is they don't go to class. That's why they get Cs.

I hear Dexter had a girlfriend helping, and if I were in his shoes, I'd have done it, too. The courses meant nothing to him, other than he needed the grades. If he'd wanted something out of them, he'd have done the work himself.

Once Dexter made it to his senior year, all that was important was that he be eligible going into his first semester. He could simply pass six hours the first semester and stop, which is what he did.

We may not have diagnosed Dexter with a learning disability, but everyone was aware Dexter had learning difficulties. We tried to get tutors to work with him and asked him to go through remedial reading classes, but he wasn't interested.

You wanted to get these players to an eighth- or tenth-grade reading level, because the average reading level among athletes is eighth to twelfth. So you try to get them up there so they won't fall too far behind, and you supplement with a tutor.

But the major point with Dexter was twofold: He was interested in football, and he saw that as his primary source of future income. He didn't show much interest in anything more than staying eligible. He was looking at it from a different pair of glasses. He saw football as the means to an end, and everyone else sees education as a means to an end. Besides, he was too big to threaten.

It took him a long time—to the mid-eighties—to say, "Athletics isn't everything." For a while, he thought he was Superman, but it turned out athletics wasn't a means to an end.

If we keep kids in school long enough and keep preaching, they'll mature. They can see, Wow, something bad can happen to me athletically. Then what do they fall back on? The answer is education.

Dexter never did reach the point in college where he wanted an education badly enough to get it. We'd approach him about remedial reading classes, and he'd say, "Why do I need that when I'll play pro ball?" You'd see him, and you'd think nothing could stop him from reaching his goal.

But if he hadn't made it, he'd have gone back to the streets. And someone might have shot him.

Dexter's one of the fortunate ones who didn't get hurt, and he made a big wad of money. Educationwise, he was a big disappointment, but he's not in jail and not on the streets. He found a vocation for eleven years. I'm proud he did well in the pros, and I just wish more guys had made it.

Now, was his college transcript a typical transcript among athletes? We have a lot of kids that are marginal students who hustle harder than Dexter. We paid forty dollars an hour for remedial reading classes, and he didn't want to take advantage.

Sure, we did all we could to keep him eligible, but we had other athletes who were good athletes whom we worked like hell to keep and they flunked out. So a lot of kids didn't hustle like Dexter did.

The way Dexter hustled was to politic for grades. He was streetwise and did a hell of a job. I mean, we once had a kid whose native language was Spanish, and he made a five-hour F in a beginning Spanish course. He just didn't go.

Dexter hustled for grades. He was in class for the most part. He was out there hustling grades any way he could.

What Dexter didn't do was hustle to learn.

It doesn't surprise me that Dexter's never written an essay or that he got a lot of help in class. I mean, he didn't have a chip on his shoulder, and he sounded intelligent when you talked with him.

We may not be very smart, but we knew he couldn't read a textbook. I'm sure he used it to his advantage and maybe plea-bargained with some of his teachers for a B or C.

Some teachers were sympathetic, and some weren't. Some professors don't like athletes because they miss lots of classes to go to a game; so they grade them low. If I put someone like Dexter in one of those pro-fessors' classes, I'd be remiss in my job. He wouldn't have stood a chance.

So I tried to put him with professors who would help him.

I agree we exploited Dexter for fours years, but he exploited us, too. Coaches further their careers with players like Dexter, and players in turn groom themselves for pro ball.

An athlete like Dexter helps us get grants. The better you do on a football field, the more perhaps a company like General Motors will look at you and award a grant. When we had Barry Sanders here, I'm sure we took those we were trying to get a grant from to a football game. So it was in our best interest to keep players eligible.

Dexter had an advisor when he was in college. The only input I had on his class schedule was to look at it and say, "I'm not sure he's capable of taking that course or this course." I'd say, "You need something lighter the first semester so you're able to have time to play football." Freshmen, *especially, have no conceivable idea how much time football takes from their studies.*

Do coaches go to teachers to fight for a player's grade? Sure. I've done it myself. You plea-bargain for grades. If a kid comes in and says, "I need a C to stay eligible, and I've made a D so far," there's nothing I can do but send him back to his professor. If a kid says he got cheated, that's different. Maybe then I will go to his professor. But we discourage coaches from going to teachers.

Dexter's first coach, Jim Stanley, did go to teachers. But in the long run it really hurt his program. I liked Jim, and, outside of academics, I thought he was a pretty good guy. But he ended up on probation, and when he left, he didn't have many athletes left. When Jimmy Johnson inherited the job, they were down to fifty to sixty football players. They either dropped out, flunked out, or just left.

Now, Jimmy, he wasn't as bad about going to teachers as Stanley was. Of course, all coaches look after number one, and that's not a fault. They'll get fired eventually if they don't consistently win, so you can see their side about going to teachers. If they could get the kind of kids who are ambitious in the classroom, it'd be a piece of cake. But to win, they try to get great athletes and make students out of them.

I'm quite sure that if Dexter started school today, he would never make it. People are so careful now. They don't want that bad publicity, a guy coming back after four years saying he couldn't read. Today teachers think, If I pass a kid who couldn't read, they'll fire me. We're also getting smarter athletes because of Prop 48.

One guy, referring to Dexter, asked me, "How could this have happened, a guy making it through college not knowing how to read or write?"

And I said, "Have you asked his high school principal? Why are you blaming me? They had him for a lot longer than I did. If they had any guts, they'd have said, 'He can't read, no diploma.'" Of course, then they'd have deprived him of about $5 million.

I've worked all my life and won't make $500,000. So, who's worse off?

Well, Dale Roark is right, I was hustling teachers, getting to know them. First, I'd always attend class. Next, I'd cry to teachers. And then I'd beg teachers. It was about being open and telling them my background.

I also bet Jim Stanley did go to teachers for me. Jim Stanley had clout on that campus, boy. And Stanley had a lot of other kids at Oklahoma State who were just like me.

I had some tutoring at Oklahoma State, though not a lot. I had study hall, as well. In my freshman year, I remember sitting in study hall like a statue for maybe an hour or two hours, whatever was required.

But I was like a little kid in there. I would horse around. When I was at Oklahoma State, I felt like I was back in grammar school, at Douglas Elementary with Mr. Marshall.

How could I participate in study hall when I didn't even know what the hell I was studying? I couldn't even read the books so what was I doing there? So I would disturb someone else. If they had had a principal's office in college, I'd have been there.

Hell no, the tutors didn't help me learn to read. What could tutoring help me with? These weren't personal tutors. They were study hall tutors. They'd go around to everybody, checking on work and asking if I needed any help.

I'd tell them I had no work. I couldn't do my work, so I acted up.

'Course, I had Tammy, just the way I'd had Cathy Jones at Yates.

AN IDLE THOUGHT

My most famous football quote was probably in 1986 when I threatened 49ers quarterback Joe Montana before a Monday night game.

I said, "I'm going to ring his clock."

But that ain't what I meant to say.

See, I got it backwards. The correct expression would've been "ring his bell" or "clean his clock." But I got it twisted. It was my learning disability, my dyslexia. But nobody knew about it back then. It was absolutely wrong, and I did not know. I mean, everybody loved that quote. They wanted to know, "Dexter, how do you ring a clock?"

CHAPTER 12

I Fought with Authority and Authority Kicked My Ass

THE DAY AFTER MY FACE HAD BEEN CUT IN THAT campus scuffle, the trainers made me suit up for spring football practice.

Here I was with eighteen stitches in my cheek and a six-inch slash, and I had to slide on a helmet. I immediately got hammered right in the face, in the middle of some macho hitting drills. I just stopped.

One coach went off on me. He screamed, "Don't you quit in drills! Then, you'll quit in the game."

In those days, white coaches didn't know how to identify with black players, but you kowtowed to them anyway if you wanted to stay in college. That was the game. If you didn't cooperate, you were on Amtrak. I was finding this out.

I basically liked my first coach, Jim Stanley, although I remember him almost booting me back to Houston for decking our star running back, Terry Miller, in practice. It was just like high school. In the back of my brain I could hear Coach Wanser saying, "Break some heads," but Stanley wouldn't stand for it.

My teammates thought I had a screw loose. Before a game in Arkansas, I ran into a little wall to get myself fired up. Hey, it takes a certain kind of football player to do that. Others might think it takes a knucklehead, but I was into that sort of bodily harm.

I think Stanley liked me right back. One Sunday after the Colorado game during my sophomore season, Stanley had Don Eckles and me over to his place to ride horses. Stanley—who now coaches the Houston Oilers defensive line—was sort of like a farmer in those days, raising horses on the outskirts of Stillwater, Oklahoma. He had about 200 acres and a bunch of horses that hadn't been tamed.

So Stanley, his wife, his son, Don Eckles, and I were over on his property, and Coach saddled me up on this one horse who'd never been ridden before. They said its name was Nigger.

I was used to riding horses in Houston, and I was a wild rider. So I hopped on this horse, Nigger, and as soon as I landed on his back, he went 200 miles per hour. They all had to hop on their own horses and come get me.

Pretty soon after that, college football started taking me for a ride. During my sophomore season the NCAA began another investigation of Oklahoma State. The school was already on a two-year probation, but a white man called me and said, "Is that your Cougar in the back of Iba Hall?"

He continued, "Is that your car with a dent up front?" I didn't even know there was a dent.

So I went out and looked at the car, and there really was a dent. I told him yes that was my car, and he kept calling me. I went to tell Jim Stanley, and Jim Stanley said don't talk to him, just hang up. So I wouldn't talk to this guy from the NCAA.

I needed to get to my momma before the NCAA did, but they beat me to her. They had been calling her all that week, and they got her while she was under the influence of alcohol, and she started spilling the beans.

By then my momma was a complete alcoholic, and she told the NCAA: "I don't know where that boy got that car from. But he drove up here in that brand-new car. I don't know. That school bought that car for that boy."

I used to say my uncle gave me the car or that I got it from an inheritance. But my coaches were mad the NCAA called Houston, and they were also pissed at Momma. There was a big article in the Tulsa paper about it.

Well, the NCAA tacked on two more years' probation, although it had to do with a lot more than just my Cougar. A few years later, Jimmy Johnson got the school on probation, too. If they go on probation again, they get the death penalty like SMU.

So they're real strict now at Oklahoma State. But, before, how do you think they got Hart Lee Dykes and Barry Sanders and Thurman Thomas and Leslie O'Neal?

Oklahoma State was kicking some butt, man, but I'm told Barry Switzer at Oklahoma turned them in. He had to compete against them.

I used to love going against Switzer because he knew who the best players were in Oklahoma. I used to play great against Switzer. If I played great against Nebraska, Oklahoma, Arkansas, Missouri, even Kansas, Kansas State, and Colorado, then the pro scouts would come to see me, and my stock would go up.

Naturally, when the second probation came down, Jim Stanley was fired. I'd never heard of this Jimmy Johnson guy they hired as Stanley's replacement, other than that he'd come from Pitt and his hair never moved. When he first got there, it was a cold day and we were running sprints in the snow. I was trying to transfer to USC at the time because I was so tied into Jim Stanley.

I called the running back coach at USC. He said he knew who I was and that they'd give me a scholarship. But when I found out I'd have to sit out a year and be a scout team blocking dummy, I decided not to go. I didn't like being called a dummy.

Pretty soon all of my Oklahoma State funds stopped coming in, all my extra benefits courtesy of the previous coaching regime. So I had no money to pay my bills. I mean, I was used to walking around town chest out, shopping in jewelry stores. That's how I bought Stephanye her wedding ring. I'd walk in there and say, "I want to get that fine jewelry; put it on my account." That's how I bought my watch and how I bought everything. There was this clothing store in the student union called Mr. G's, and the guy there would let me have shirts and pants at will.

Where was my money coming from? Well, first, I had cash making its way to me from Tenneco Oil Company, my daddy's employer.

I got a check from them for something like $2,000 in 1978 for school. My daddy had set up a scholarship fund for us, and I was at the right age to collect. Second, I was getting a Social Security child survivor benefit check for like $317 a month. The school paid the rent at married student housing, and the only thing I had to do was come up with about $50. I had it made.

But then this check I was getting from the school stopped finding its way to me. I'd been netting $450 a month from this white guy. He paid me my money every month, but that stopped when we went on probation.

My credit started going bad around town, too. I couldn't pay the jewelry store or this bill or that bill.

Jimmy Johnson, the new coach who today runs the Dallas Cowboys, had calls every other day about me. So he wanted to get rid of me. In fact, when he first saw me, he told me to get rid of the Cougar.

I said, "I'm not getting rid of my car. Are you crazy?" So everyone wanted to know where I got it. I told them my uncle helped me get this car.

Johnson put *me* on probation for a while. He clearly was trying to run me off. It was like he had to clean house—as he later did with the Cowboys—and I was one of Stanley's boys, getting all this money.

I swore to Jimmy Johnson that I had good credit around town, but he put me on probation anyway. He said if I got in any more trouble, I'd have to leave.

As I was heading into my junior year, spring football practice came, and Johnson went on a recruiting trip. He left a guy named Bruce Mays in charge—Bruce is now a go-fer for Jimmy Johnson with the Cowboys—and all the players who remained from Stanley's team had to go through weight training and conditioning.

Johnson had just come from the University of Pittsburgh, where he'd coached Hugh Green, who had been a Heisman candidate as a linebacker. Jimmy was so high on Green it was like he was his godson.

Here I was, playing the same position, only I was bigger than Hugh Green. After we ran the 40-yard dash, it turned out I was faster, too. I ran something like 4.5 with Mays watching.

Man, Jimmy Johnson came off that recruiting trip wanting to know who the hell I was. First thing, he took me off probation. He didn't know anything about me, but all of a sudden he'd discovered another Hugh Green in Dexter Manley. His whole outlook changed. If I hadn't run that good 40 time, I'd have been out of there.

I don't know what happened with the creditors. I think Jimmy Johnson talked to them. I talked to them, too. The Texaco man says I still owe him.

I used to get free gas. I'd just say, "Look here, I'm gettin' gas. Put it on my account." And I'd take off.

But see how it spoiled me? It set me up.

Thing is, once I ran that 40-yard dash and had Jimmy Johnson foaming at the mouth over me, I didn't really need him. I had the leverage. So, I told him, "I'm leaving, man." I said, "Look here, I've got to leave school. I've got to leave 'cause I need more money. I need y'all to take care of me."

Of course, you must understand how I was dressing back then. It was 1979, and I had one of those nice Seiko watches that cost me about $300 or $400. And I had a Hartman bag that was a big-time thing, too. So I was like too sharp.

When I went in there demanding money, Jimmy Johnson was angry. He spouted, "Look at you, you're sharper than I am."

Then he took his watch off and winged it at me. He told me, "You have a nicer watch than I have."

Here I was trying to get some more dough from him, but he wasn't giving up a cent.

He told me to go ahead and leave. But he kept me.

By that time, I had few allies in the athletic department. As Jim Stanley was on his way out in January 1979, about fifteen other guys and I had sued Oklahoma State for stripping us of our Basic Education Opportunity Grants. The school said we couldn't reap BEOGs plus our scholarships.

We'd been receiving this BEOG money every semester, but when the athletic department quit divvying it up to us, Jim Stanley told us to file suit. There were football players, basketball players, and a lot of other athletes, but I guarantee if you go back and look at the press clippings, the headlines said, "Manley and OSU Athletes Sue Oklahoma State." They used my name because it was like I was the ringleader when I really wasn't. I was the youngest one. But, for some unknown reason, my name was in lights.

So I went to court. I guess it's on record that I said the following:

> I am married, and my wife and I have three children. My wife is a homemaker, and therefore provides no income. . . . [My scholarship] does not provide me with any money to use to purchase clothing, pay medical bills, pay for transportation to and from Houston, Texas, for me and my family, cover the cost of purchasing such necessities as deodorant, toothpaste, soap, the cost of washing my and my family's clothes, or the costs of transportation in Stillwater. Further, since I am married and have three children, it is necessary to provide the above necessities for all five of us.

I also said if I wasn't accommodated, I'd have to leave Oklahoma State.

Well, obviously, I'd lied. First, while I was still married to Stephanye, by that time I was not living with her. I was living with Tammy. I didn't tell anybody I had split up with my wife, and I stayed in married-student housing because I did not want to live in a dormitory and because they were funding part of a married student's rent. But I wasn't supposed to be there.

Second, I lied about having three kids. There was a girl from high school who accused me of fathering twins by her, and maybe subconsciously that's why I said I had three kids. I don't know.

This was one time I clearly needed my daddy. Things would've been so much better if I'd had a role model I could confide in and talk to, although he often scared me so much that I couldn't talk to him. But I believe I could've spoken to him about this BEOG thing.

When you're nineteen years old and in college, you don't know whom to turn to. I had coaches, but we'd been getting investigated—which I was a part of—and I didn't know if I could trust the coach.

Coach Stanley didn't want me getting on the stand and telling how I was getting illegal checks from the school, in addition to my BEOG. So here were a white coach and a black ballplayer, and the white coach told me to go lie on the stand.

If Daddy had been around, he wouldn't have allowed that.

Well, in April 1979 I said under oath that I had three kids, and the U.S. district court judge Luther Eubanks ended up dismissing our suit.

That was that. The BEOG stopped, and that's why I was having great pains trying to pay my bills around town.

And then—in February 1980—the roof caved in.

I'd been receiving Social Security benefits ever since my daddy died. Harold Bailey's mother told me I could get Social Security—about 300 bucks a month—but I wasn't sure. So as a freshman, I had gone to the Social Security office and filled out the forms. You couldn't be married and receive these benefits, and, of course, I was married at the time, but Stephanye was in Houston finishing high school and wasn't living with me. So I lied and wrote that I was single.

My way of thinking was: Stephanye and I are not together. She's in Houston. I'm in Oklahoma. In other words, I was greedy and wanted the money.

They initially paid me a lump sum—like $2,000—in 1977. I couldn't even read the check. I thought it said $200, but Harold Bailey read the check to me. I ran to put that money in the bank.

Then, I started getting $317.20 a month.

I got caught when I sued the school for the BEOG grants. In my court statement, I'd said I was married and living in the married student housing. Of course, you couldn't be married and receive the Social Security benefits.

When I'd been on the witness stand for the BEOG grants, I had to list all of my expenses, including rent, and I mentioned married student housing. By doing that, I was saying I was married, but how could you be married and still be getting Social Security checks?

So somebody put two and two together. It was February 1980, and two months earlier I finally had filed for divorce from Stephanye, although the divorce wouldn't become official until May 1980. I was at the athletic dorm when three white guys came up to me in dark suits and dark shades. One of them said, "Are you Dexter Manley? Is your mother Jewellean Manley?"

I said yes.

He continued, "We're from the FBI. We want to talk to you about Social Security."

I immediately started crying—as is my way—and they guided me into the football office. They knew *everything* I'd been doing. They even knew I'd been at the Social Security office in Stillwater the previous week filling out some more forms. It was just like the movies. They'd been spying on me and now were telling me my every move.

I said, "I'm going to prison, aren't I?" I'd been petrified of jail ever since that day in Huntsville when Coach Wanser had us tour the state penitentiary.

They said I was still married, even though I'd filed for divorce, and that lying on Social Security was a felony, and a felony is five to ten years in prison.

I said, "I'm not living with that girl. I have another girl."

I went to the office of one of our assistant coaches, and I was bawling. I'd never really been in such big trouble before. He asked me, "What did you do? Did you kill somebody?"

I just knew I was going to prison.

Well, they didn't book me or anything, and I didn't go to jail right away as I thought I would. First, the school hired me a lawyer. Jimmy Johnson then said, hey, it was no problem, he could get me out of it. I went to Tammy, and I'm crying and telling her to come visit me in jail, but Tammy was more levelheaded than anyone.

First, Tammy explained that Jimmy Johnson was wrong, that there's no way you can just get out of dealing with Social Security. "This is the federal government we're talking about," she warned. Jimmy Johnson was telling me, "Aw, don't worry about it, it's going to be OK," but she was saying this was big.

The headlines in the paper made me feel so horrible. I think from that day on, I started getting a bad rap. From that day on, pro scouts and people in general started questioning my character. It didn't make me look too promising.

I just felt my daddy had worked all his life, so why couldn't I get that money? I was helping Stephanye out some by sending some of the money for Derrick.

But the thought of jail terrified me. Tammy kept repeating, "You've got to get on this. You cannot let this go." She'd ask me, "Have you heard? Have you talked to these people? What's going on? It's not just going to die." She knew how I was. She knew I'd try to avoid the problem and wish it away, which would cause me so many other problems in the years to come.

Tammy was the one who helped me out the most. She kept warning me, "Don't trust Jimmy Johnson. Get on it, Dexter, get on it!" She said even though I was the star athlete, Jimmy Johnson couldn't take care of it. Tammy had a lot of common sense.

So, eventually, I went to court. Again, there was ole Judge Eubanks. He was an old man, and he liked me. He thought I was a good kid, but my lawyer told me I still was close to going to jail.

The president of the school had written a letter on my behalf to the judge. So had Jimmy Johnson. And the lawyer representing me was a big OSU alum. Things started looking up for me.

I remember the morning I was going to court—it was June 1980, prior to my senior season. One of our assistants, Larry Holton, who recently was the defensive back coach at Illinois, took me to the courthouse. I had a suit on, and I put a big handkerchief in my pocket.

Obviously, I had to plead guilty. In his statement, my lawyer said something like, "Everybody has a profession. There are doctors, lawyers, and other kinds of people out there. But Dexter Manley's profession is football. That's all he knows."

Judge Eubanks was downright sympathetic, I guess. He spared me from jail and placed me on three years' probation, ordering me to repay the benefits I'd fraudulently taken—$10,571.20 worth.

I was sentenced under the Youth Corrections Act, so fortunately I was able to clear my record if I stayed clean through my probation. All I really had to do was go to this youth program for a year, my last year of college, plus make restitution. In other words, when I went pro—which I was fully planning on doing—I had to pay the 10,000 bucks back.

It taught me a lesson. I'd always gotten away with things and had started to think it was OK to cheat. I mean, the scouts started giving me money here and there, and I started thinking maybe it was OK.

They *told* me it was OK, and I became conditioned to do the wrong thing. My daddy wasn't around to say, "No, that's wrong," and I needed that.

When the sentence came down and I found out for sure I wouldn't have a ball and chain tied to my ankle in jail, I was singing hallelujah. I was praising the Lord. But I kept thinking about my daddy. I thought, If only he were alive, I wouldn't be goin' through this. His death had made me decide, OK, hey, there's a cheap way out. Here's a way I can get some money and help my family. I mean, we didn't have any money coming in. Momma had some money left to her by Daddy—we all did—but once you get a taste of it, you just get greedy. And I wanted more money.

And the bottom line is that I lied, and I paid a price. On the other hand, I got off easy. I always seemed to get off easy. I always seemed to be bailed out.

My rehab counselors probably think that's why I kept experimenting with drugs. I never thought I'd get caught. Everything in my life was usually made better for me, whether it was with my grades in school or with three FBI guys knocking on my door in dark suits and shades. Somebody always took care of me. I thought I was invincible.

AN IDLE THOUGHT

When I was in the middle of the illegal money scandal at Oklahoma State, a man named Don Breaux was coaching at nearby Arkansas and read all about it.

This same Don Breaux was hired by Joe Gibbs my rookie season.

It was Breaux who told Gibbs about my college escapades. During a meeting my rookie year, Gibbs was addressing the entire Redskins team and said, "Dexter Manley had to take a pay cut just to be here."

C H A P T E R 13

Blackballed?

I TRADED IN MY COUGAR FOR A TEN-SPEED BIKE. Even the Phoenix Cardinals wouldn't make a trade that bad.

As part of my restitution to the federal government for my Social Security fraud, I had to sell my car and turn the cash over to the authorities. Pat Jones, my defensive line coach, was responsible for making sure I did. He marched me to the used car lot.

They handed me $1,800 for the car, and Pat snatched the cash out of my hand. "Pat, at least let me keep $800," I pleaded. "Nope, Dexter," he answered. "We've got to give everything to the government."

Out of sympathy, I guess, he ended up buying me the ten-speed. On the bright side, at least I could get from 0 to 20 mph in fifteen seconds.

I went from the best wheels on campus to two Schwinn wheels. At that point, I had no choice but to change styles. Instead of wearing my slick Hollywood outfits, I got into shorts and tights and bicycle stuff. I figured I'd turn it into a campus fad.

Turning in the Cougar marked the end of my hellraising era. I was used to parking that car wherever I pleased—in the middle of the street, where Jimmy Johnson was supposed to park, wherever.

I had gotten into a heap of trouble over that car. Once Tammy and I were about to take in a movie when a campus policeman tap-tapped me on the shoulder while I was in line and said I had mucho parking tickets and a speeding ticket. He asked me to accompany him to the police station. I wanted to fight him, but Tammy talked me into going downtown quietly. I had to stay overnight until Pat Jones and Jimmy Johnson got me out.

When I had to part with the Cougar, Tammy and I decided that when I got drafted—in the first round, presumably—I'd buy myself a Jaguar to take its place.

I didn't blame Pat Jones at all; he was a good guy. The school had gotten me a job at a construction site the summer after my junior year. The first day on the job, I went to the site all sharp, with a new pair of lizard-skin shoes, the way my daddy would've gone.

I lasted *one* day.

I thought it would be an office job, but they handed me a hard hat and a shovel. I never went back. I guess I was really like my daddy.

But I did get my shoes dirty on the football field. I led the team in minus-yardage tackles my sophomore, junior, and senior seasons, but the best I could ever make was second-team All-Big Eight. I personally think Jimmy Johnson never played me up.

I mean, Pat Jones even started alternating me:

I had recruited Manley when I was at SMU. I wasn't his main recruiter, but I do remember going to watch him play at Yates and visiting with him. Then I went to Pitt with Jimmy, and then I followed Jimmy to Oklahoma State.

We had our ups and downs with Dexter. I mean, we alternated him his senior year, but he was untapped potential. You'd see it in spurts.

We had another pretty good young freshman who deserved some playing time, and Dexter was a guy you had to prod. You wanted to hit his hot button, and maybe by alternating him you would.

He'd been a full-time starter his junior year in '79 when we won seven and Jimmy was coach of the year. But Manley hurt his shoulder his senior year. So it was a combination of things—his being hurt, us getting off to a 0–5–1 start in 1980, and us wanting to see a young kid play.

I talked to some NFL people that year, and they were in the same quandary about Dexter—great talent, but up and down as a player. We were all wondering what we could do to bring him out. We had had Hugh Green at Pitt, and maybe we should've let Manley be more aggressive like we were with Hugh.

As far as his not making All-Big Eight, the guy was up and down enough to keep him from that. He was such a great, great pass rusher. Maybe there were things I could've done to highlight him more. We'd line him up over the tight end or tackle, and we'd stand him up. Normally, great pass rushers are down in that stance, and I don't know if we took full advantage of his pass rushing skills. Jimmy also thought Manley was being distracted by all the extracurricular things going on in his life.

I remember taking him to turn in his Cougar. There's a fine line between giving a kid guidance and delving into his personal life too much. I didn't ask too many questions. I'm not sure, though, if I knew the severity of what was going on with the government.

All I'm saying is, with Manley it was always something. His divorce was one thing, and then when we got there, we heard all about that fight at the student center, and we're wondering, What are we getting into here?

You hear about his debts at the jewelry store. You're inheriting a downtrodden situation, and you're wondering, What are we dealing with?

His schooling was another matter. All I know is when I had him in team meetings, I didn't want to put him in a situation where I'd embarrass him in front of several guys and make him read. I was surprised to a point when I heard he couldn't read, but I knew he had some trouble.

I remember driving to a function when Howard Cosell came on his radio show saying something like, "Here's a guy who graduated from Oklahoma State and couldn't read or write!" First of all, Dexter didn't graduate, and second, the rules are different now with Prop 48 and all.

Dexter couldn't have survived today, but where would he have ended up? He was able to manipulate the system, and now it can't be done with these new rules. But if he hadn't manipulated the system, he might be in a pine box right now in the Third Ward.

Dexter is a classic example of the streetwise youngster. His existence is based on survival skills. The only lifestyle he knows is the way of the street. You do what you can do to survive. He's a victim of his environment, but on the other hand you're talking about a guy who's had his own radio shows. You could hear this guy on the radio and never dream he had a learning disability.

Yeah, they alternated me with a lacrosse player. Some preppy guy. He wasn't worth a nickel. He was an All-American in lacrosse, and they handed him a football scholarship. To wreak as much damage as me, he'd have needed to take his lacrosse stick on the field with him.

This guy was not even six feet tall. Jimmy Johnson was screwing with me for no reason, but he was doing that to a lot of us seniors.

I never really enjoyed playing for Jimmy Johnson, partly because I overheard some Oklahoma State coaches say I'd never amount to nothing. To me it was a form of racism or stupidity, but, boy, I had to prove those people wrong.

What may have influenced the coaches to say that was my problem picking up the defense. I was a little slow, and at the time no one knew of my learning disability.

Criticism from my college coaches made me a worry wart. I was convinced Jimmy Johnson cared more about the Astroturf than me.

Right after the Social Security case I really turned into a Bible-toter. Obviously, I wasn't one of those holy-rolly's when I was with Joe Gibbs, like half the Redskins were, but college was a time I went to church. Tammy would take me. I used to go to church all the time in Stillwater. I was saved.

I carried that Bible around. A minister who was going to school there preached to me and helped me change myself. It was a time in my life when I didn't know what would happen to me, and I turned to the church. Was I sincere about it? For a while. I do believe that if I had been a good reader, my faith would've been stronger. How do you get faith? By reading the Word. And because I couldn't read the Word, I just listened.

But I needed something greater than me in my life. I just felt so sad for myself, so sorry.

I thought I'd be a first-round pick, or *at least* a second-rounder, but then Joe Courrege, my agent, started getting mixed signals. Courrege was from Dallas, and I first met him in a hotel lobby at the Blue-Gray game. He paid me up front, as I recall. He reeled me in with his Bible talk.

Well, one of the things Joe Courrege did for me right away was help me eavesdrop—my favorite pasttime—on general managers. To let me know how they were evaluating me, he'd let me listen in on his phone calls to GMs, and I'd hear them ripping me.

One GM—Tom Braatz from the Atlanta Falcons—said, "Well, that Manley's not very smart." Braatz was most recently running the Green Bay Packers about a year ago. He called me a dummy on the three-way hookup. He said, "Manley's a great athlete, but he's not very smart. I don't think he'll get drafted that high." He didn't know I'd heard every word.

Before then, a lot of scouts who came to Oklahoma State to work me out thought I'd get drafted real high, especially when they saw me run like a mouse from a cat. They had great highlights of me on film, too. In one game, I was at nose tackle, and this big ole fullback from Colorado broke through into the clear. He was twenty-five yards downfield, and guess who caught him? Me. I walked that joker down. That may have been the highlight of my Oklahoma State career. They showed that play at end-of-the-year banquets for a while.

But then when I heard Tom Braatz, I was crushed. I figured, That word is just going to travel. Joe Courrege told me the Social Security deal would also hurt me in the draft, that people would question my character. I mean, I was a black guy who had cheated on Social Security and wasn't bright either! Teams must've said, Let's stay away from him.

And I was sure Jimmy Johnson was trashing me behind my back. Early in my senior season, I was going to church and being very productive on campus. Then after my senior football season, I blew off my classes and started training every day at the campus football facility. I was training for the scouts who'd come around with their stopwatches.

I'd put in my four years at Oklahoma State, and I thought I was entitled to work out on campus. But word leaked out that there'd been some burglaries from players' lockers there. So Jimmy Johnson called me in his office and said, "I don't want you around the facilities."

I told him, "I'm going to use the facilities. I'm still a student here."

Then he accused me of taking the money. I didn't need to take no money, so we started a big argument in his office. I always had my backpack with me, and I'd carry my Bible in there. He was sitting down at his desk, and I placed my Bible down in front of him.

He snapped, "Get that thing off my desk."

I was telling him what kind of person I was and that I don't have to steal.

But he threatened, "You'll never play football in the National Football League if you don't take that Bible off my desk. I'll put the bad word out on you."

"I don't give a . . . I don't care what you say," I chewed him out. Even as a Bible-toter, I cussed him out. I told him to come from behind that desk, and I'll kick his ass. All this with the Bible on the table.

He was lying. He just didn't want ex-players around. Or ex-black players. He didn't want them training to get ready.

I don't know if Jimmy Johnson was literally against me or if it was something that had been eating at him for a while—athletes who'd finished their eligibility causing trouble. But, see, I always spoke up. I always was outspoken. Whatever I wanted to say, I said it, and I said I was gonna kick his ass. That didn't help my case for going high in the draft, either.

Jimmy thought I was a smart ass, I guess. One day we were taking a bus at 10:00 A.M. to play Kansas State, and I woke up with the roosters like I usually do to eat breakfast. But then I went back to my apartment, dozed off, and overslept until ten. I hauled ass over to Iba

Hall, but Johnson had left without me. Hell, I got to fly to Kansas in the school president's jet while the rest of the team had to drive five hours. Jimmy was pissed. He started me but took me out after a quarter. Jimmy was an asshole.

So here I was, practically alienated from my program, with no more cash coming in and with a ten-speed bike for transportation. Fortunately, one of the assistant trainers let me borrow his car. I could get that car whenever I pleased. He always had his radio tuned in to Paul Harvey, which reminded me of my daddy because he listened to Paul Harvey. It was a real struggle for me in those days, but at least I had a car to take Tammy out to McDonald's or Wendy's.

Another godsend was a woman named Nancy, whose husband was a teacher at the university. We'd go to their house, and they used to cook for us. Jimmy Johnson certainly didn't want me around the dining hall. It got to the point where I was low on cash, and Nancy would buy us pork and beans or whatever. Tammy had to quit school, and she found a job at Kmart. Not long before, I'd been the B.M.O.C., charging up a storm at Mr. G's. Now Tammy was supporting me from Kmart.

At about that time, I started traveling to scouting combines, which meant I'd need a lift to the airport in Oklahoma City. Nancy let Tammy use her car.

Finally, Nancy lent us money. I figured I could pay her back in no time because I was gonna get drafted, unless Jimmy Johnson blackballed me.

But I needed Joe Courrege to check it out for me. Well, we heard the Miami Dolphins were interested, though my preferences were the Raiders—for obvious reasons—and Tampa Bay. The Bucs had a raucous defense with the Selmon brothers.

Washington worked me out, too, and the Redskins' general manager Bobby Beathard and his assistant, Mike Almon, told me at a Tampa combine that *they* were gonna pick me. They had an old guy, Coy Bacon, and they thought I could take his job as right defensive end. Beathard said, "I like you." But I didn't necessarily buy Beathard's story:

Oh, Dexter was an incredible athlete when we scouted him. He's a talent. No one would ever question that. He had a bad rap at Oklahoma State, and, in fact, whenever we went back to Oklahoma State to scout after Dexter joined the Redskins, he still was the topic of conversation. He didn't leave there clean and he burned some bridges, but Dexter always has a way to pull himself out of everything because he could charm you to death.

In college he was a linebacker, a tremendously talented athlete. He flew around on the field and played with a lot of enthusiasm. So we were excited to draft the guy, but our feeling was we'd make him into a down lineman. It's hard to find guys with that talent. He had a great knack for rushing the passer—a very strong upper body with all the speed and quickness of a defensive back.

We figured his stock in the draft might fall because people might think he was too small to be a defensive end and he didn't fit the bill as a linebacker. Our feeling was he could get bigger. I've never seen anybody yet who can't gain weight, and he didn't have that far to go.

Yeah, I told him we'd pick him. I've never told that to a guy we didn't pick. In those days, Dallas used to go around telling guys, "We'll pick you in the first round," and then they'd have twelve guys sitting there who'd been told that. I just told Dexter, "Don't say it to anybody, but we're going to take you." I just couldn't tell him where.

Draft day was more tense than Clarence Thomas getting confirmed. This was *my* confirmation.

Tammy and I didn't speak much that day, though I'm the type who can't sit still. Every time the phone rang, I'd be through the roof. My teammate L. P. Williams stopped by, but it was all small talk. The phone rang one time, when my teammate Larry Dokes pretended he was from an NFL team. I could've wrapped the phone chord around his neck. I told him, "Don't call my frickin' house no more."

The first round, second round, third round, fourth round all passed me by. It was about 6:00 P.M., and I was sucking on raw eggs when Beathard finally called in the fifth round. Tammy answered, and he said, "My name is Bobby Beathard, and I'm with the Washington Redskins." I was trying desperately to be calm. But, hell, I should've gone at least in the second round so, actually, I was pissed.

After I hung up with Beathard, Tammy wanted to call him back. She did it, too. She'd seen that the Redskins had traded a couple of future picks in the third round to get the chance to draft me early in the fifth round, and she asked Bobby if—because of that—I would be paid on a third-round level. It was a good question, because we thought they were getting me cheap, but Bobby Beathard said no.

I personally didn't want her to call Beathard back, but I guess that's how my career started with the Washington Redskins. They'd had me for five minutes, and I already wanted to renegotiate.

AN IDLE THOUGHT

As Jimmy Johnson found out, it's not wise to mess with Dexter Manley.

Chicago Bears coach Mike Ditka tried the same thing in 1987, and it got me riled as hell.

Before a playoff game with us that year, Ditka told the media I had the "IQ of a grapefruit." How'd he know? Well, you should've seen what I did the week before *that* game.

We were in a team meeting, and Joe Gibbs was telling us how the Bears had talked badly about our players and how Ditka had talked disrespectfully about me and that a coach shouldn't do that. I was sitting there with the rest of the team, and I just started foaming at the mouth. I mean, I lost it. I picked up my chair and slammed it against the blackboard. I was going, "We've got to kick their ass!"

In all the mayhem, I even slit my forehead open. Gibbs ran out of the way and just looked at me. Man, those coaches and those players loved that crap. It was violent! Gibbs didn't say a word. He didn't say slamming my chair was wrong and he didn't say, "Control yourself, Dexter." Not one player said a negative word to me either. You could've heard a pin drop. All I remember is Joe Bugel just shaking his head. Bugel was getting off on it.

I wasn't doing it for show, either. It was the Wednesday or Thursday before the playoff game, and it was just a matter of my low self-esteem leaking out of me.

The meeting closed down immediately. Gibbs didn't even finish. The players got up and split into their position meetings.

We kicked Ditka and the Bears' ass that Sunday.

CHAPTER 14

(Prized) Bull in a China Shop

I ARRIVED AT DULLES AIRPORT WITH ENOUGH bags to spend six months in Europe. An employee of the Redskins who identified himself as Lego picked me up in a van and made a smart comment about the quantity of my luggage.

"Well, I plan on stayin' a while," I told him.

Lego couldn't understand a fifth-round rookie guaranteeing himself a roster spot, but I knew I was the best thing the Redskins had. I wasn't going anywhere but to the First National Bank.

They may have thought I was Leona Helmsley with those six suitcases of mine, but I wore the same outfit every day for the first month: overalls, Oklahoma State T-shirt, Converse Chuck Taylor hightops, bandanna tied around my neck, and carrying a handgrip.

I was like a guy you'd see in a prison movie, squeezing the handgrip like I was schizo. Otis Wonsley was another rookie whom Lego picked up at Dulles, and I squeezed Otis Wonsley's hand so hard he hollered. Among the rookies, I was the most boastful. I treated minicamp as if it were in Giants Stadium—flying sideline to sideline— and I even volunteered for special teams. I ain't no dummy. I knew the coaches liked it if you were gung-ho for the suicide squad. The special teams coach, Wayne Sevier, was leaving to play golf one day after a minicamp workout, and luckily I caught him with his clubs. I requested to be on every special team. I figured that would show them I'm a bad mother, because I wanted to be on *every* special team unit.

Early in training camp, I took over the show like I was a senior vet. After a hit, I'd jabber about how it measured on the Richter scale, and I talked big about Oklahoma State. However, when the veterans showed up, I kind of went into my own little shell.

Torgy Torgeson, our defensive line coach, lined me up against George Starke, an old-time tackle, and I flipped out. I was petrified because George was a vet. I played cautious, but I stalemated him. I was so freaked out, I ducked my head in a bucket of Gatorade and even peed on myself.

Tight end Donnie Warren used to look like he was laughing at me. He kind of looks like John Elway, with that Mr. Ed look to him. On one scrimmage play, he blocked the crap out of me. I knew he couldn't block me, but he did. So the next play, I took care of business. I retaliated, and I started talking trash to the tight end coach, Rennie Simmons.

Immediately, a tight end, Rick ("Doc") Walker, and a corner-back, Lamar Parish, gave me the nickname Prized Bull. I was there to take the job of the starting right defensive end, Coy Bacon. I knew Bacon was over the hill, and pretty soon there was almost a fight between Lamar and Coy because Lamar had been showing me around. Lamar saw me kicking rear end on the field, so he adopted me, and Coy Bacon naturally thought of me as the enemy.

In the spring when Bobby Beathard had first mentioned Bacon's name to me, I had thought, Who's Coy Bacon? I hadn't heard of any of the Redskins, other than Joe Theismann and Monte Coleman. I knew of Monte because he and I were linebackers in college, and we'd both been compared to Hollywood Henderson. Everybody else was news to me, even John Riggins.

I certainly did not know who this Dave Butz guy was. At first I thought he was just a UPS courier. I saw him in the locker room looking klutzy in his big ole baggy clothes. I didn't think he was a football player at all. I'm serious.

The first time I saw the owner, Jack Kent Cooke, was in April 1981 at minicamp. I thought he was just some old guy sitting in these sideline chairs, trying to take a load off. I had no idea who he was.

All of my rookie negotiations were with Bobby Beathard, who told me I was the highest paid fifth-rounder in the league. He told me I had a great deal.

Guess what he did then? He gave Larry Kubin, a linebacker, who'd been drafted in the *sixth* round, a $100,000 signing bonus! Since Kubin was a medical redshirt, he had the choice of going back to Penn State for one more year and had leverage. But who really had the greeeeat deal?

My base salary was $40,000 and my signing bonus was $25,000. Tammy had to read my contract to me. She didn't like my deal. She said there were too many incentive clauses, too many "If he does this, if he does that," a lot of words she didn't understand. So you can imagine how foreign the language was to me. But believe me, I had the numbers part down pat. I also knew I could wave goodbye to my bonus.

Out of that $25,000 bonus, I'd say I walked away with thirteen grand. After I paid the IRS, it was more like nine grand. Taxes ate me for lunch. I moved into a town house, but I hardly had anything inside it, and everything I did have I rented. Plus, I immediately bought a beat-up Mercedes in Texas—the Jaguar was too expensive—and there was also Social Security to think about. I paid some of the Social Security debt in a lump sum, and the Redskins garnished my wages to pay off the rest of it. After my rookie season, I didn't have any cash flow. It was like, "Where's my money?"

Something always would pop up. Like Texaco. I had a credit card with them during college, and when my Social Security money was pulled, I couldn't pay it off. When I moved to D.C., I forgot about it. But Texaco found me. It was always somebody finding me.

I thought Texaco could afford to let me go. It was just $1,200. I thought, I'm just a little guy, and it's such a small amount of money, and they've got millions of people with credit cards out there, so why do they need my money? I didn't think Texaco would miss $1,200.

That was my way of thinking. That thinking came from people always doing favors for me. Over the years, people just slipped me favors here and there. "Oh, you're Dexter Manley, come on in the movie." That sort of thing. I didn't think Texaco would miss $1,200.

What saved me was I began earning one heap of an incentive check on the field.

It started in the exhibition season, when I had what I believe was my most studly quarterback sack ever. In a game against Baltimore I laid out Bert Jones. Cold. From the blind side, I hammered him.

On the next play, all eleven Baltimore Colts ran the ball right at *me*, and I stuffed the play. I had a great game. As I'd hoped, the Redskins put me at punt protection wideout, and the Colts couldn't stop my release downfield. I'll never forget they double-teamed me on punts, and I destroyed those guys. Destroyed them.

I'd never met this guy Dexter Manley before. I was just Darryl Grant, a measly, quiet ninth-rounder from Rice, and this guy was loud. He carried himself in a way like he was the man.

When we first got to D.C. for minicamp, Mark May, the number-one pick, and I had a rental car, and we were driving to McDonald's one night. Dexter kept saying, "I can't wait! I want me a Jaguar!"

And Mark commanded, "Dex, this is the nation's capital. You've got to buy American."

Dexter kept saying, "I should've gone in the first round. I was gonna go in the first round." The whole time he's squeezing, squeezing that handgrip. He was 100 percent pure football player. He had just one thing on his mind: football. He could not get enough.

He repeated over and over, "There were guys drafted ahead of me who I killed in college. I'm the best. I should've gone in the first round."

Here he was, this big dude, and a lot of vets went wild over him. Like, "Who is this guy?" Doc Walker and Lamar Parish called him the "Prized Bull," and it was kind of their way of welcoming him.

Dexter and Coy Bacon didn't get along. Coy was from the old school, which was intimidating rookies. So Dexter would never come to the dinner room. He didn't want to have to sing his alma mater song. Coy kept looking for him, and he'd see Dexter on the field and say, "You gonna sing, rookie."

When Dexter did go to eat, he'd be squeezing the handgrip in one hand, eating with the other, and sweating something awful.

Dexter'd say to me, "Darryl, you got to get one of these squeezers. You got to get a good grip."

See, he thought it was funny if he squeezed your hand tight like a vice. He thought it was funny when he'd do that to people in the business community. In my opinion, he was trying to impress people by squeezing so tight, but after a while I'd squeeze back, and he'd say, "Ouch, don't do that!"

One night Otis Wonsley, Dexter, and I drove to this bar in Harrisburg, Pennsylvania, on a day off from training camp. Dexter was dressed in jeans, a cowboy hat, and cowboy boots, but when we got there, Dexter didn't want to pay the ten-dollar cover. He wants everything free.

So there was this big guy at the door, and Dexter announced, "I'm not paying ten bucks." Then Dex got smart. He said, "I'm Dexter Manley of the Washington Redskins," and the bouncer stuck his hand out to shake. Dexter squeezed his hand so tightly, the guy was on his knees. He let us all in free.

Inside, Dexter had one glass of white wine. I've never seen a dude get so drunk off one glass. One glass, and he was zonked. He's dancing around with his cowboy boots on, dancing with other guys' girls, squeezing the guys' hands to get 'em away. He'd say, "I want to dance with your woman."

He was all over the floor, kicking his heels up. I told Otis, "We better get him out of here before there's trouble." One glass of wine, and he was lethal.

We left, and when we stopped at a red light, there was this guy on the corner waiting for a bus. Dexter shouted, "I'm gonna get you!" Then he hopped from the car and chased the guy a block. I said, "Otis, what is this?" Otis said, "We better get him back to campus, and if he's not back soon, we're going without him."

Somehow we snagged him back in the car, and his mayhem continued on the field. Coy Bacon and Dexter were the big sideshow. First of all, Coy didn't want to come to minicamp, and Coy and Gibbs had it out. Torgy Torgeson, our defensive line coach, would give instructions, and Coy'd say, "Torgy, I'm as old as you are. Don't talk to me like that."

The vets would have to run to the pay phone to call Coy out of bed for team meetings. Coy was leading the team with six sacks early in the season, and they still cut him because he was late all the time.

Dexter took over for him. By the end of his rookie year, Dexter was dressing better, and the press liked him. He had this big, raggedy Mercedes, a piece of junk. Every time we saw it, it was on the back of some tow truck. The seats of the Mercedes were so worn out, he put covers on them. It was like you were sitting on Slinkies.

When you rode with Dexter, he'd scare you by driving and talking and looking at you at the same time. He wanted to see your expressions.

Coy Bacon came up with some advice from time to time. Torgy used to tell me in practice to take the trap head on, which meant I would get crushed, and Coy said, "Do that all the time, boy, and you'll play just three years in the league."

Coy believed there was a way to take on the trap, but you'd do it with your shoulders. See, if you'd let them, coaches will run you into the ground in this league, like the Redskins ran Larry Brown into the ground in the seventies.

Well, the 1981 regular season was finally beginning, and Joe Theismann gave me another nickname—Manchild. I had two nicknames now and was ready to rumble. My first pro game was also Joe Gibbs's first game as a head coach, and it was against those snotty Dallas Cowboys at RFK Stadium. As a kid, the Cowboys had been my boys. My daddy loved Dallas, too. We lived in Houston, but we never went to Oilers games. We'd stay home and watch Dallas. Gregory was the only Redskins fan in the house, and now here I was playing for the Redskins against Tony Dorsett and Drew Pearson and Tom Landry and Ray—that guy on the play horse—and so on.

I actually didn't play much from scrimmage, other than a few snaps at left defensive end. I went in for the starter, Karl Lorch, and—wouldn't you know it—they ran a trap at me. I don't remember if I closed that trap or not.

But I was so much in awe of seeing the Cowboys play. I played well on special teams, and they triple-teamed me with Billy Joe DuPree, Anthony Dickerson, and with a cornerback who'd rub me downfield. I ran over Billy Joe DuPree, and, man, that just made my day.

As a kid, I had idolized DuPree.

We lost 26–10, and the game reminded me of Oklahoma vs. Oklahoma State. We were so close, just like the games against Oklahoma in college, and then they'd blow it wide open.

Over the years, I learned to hate Dallas more than sauerkraut. This one tackle they had—Kevin Gogan—called me a nigger on the football field, and I responded, "I screwed your momma."

He really said, "You fucking nigger," and I told him, "Your momma's a nigger."

When I came out of college, I idolized Tony Dorsett, but I lost some respect for him when he'd sidewind out of bounds all the time. I used to see Dorsett sashay out of bounds, and I'd say, "That's bull." I mean, I've had Dorsett come through the middle on me, and that homeboy ran right through my arms, he was so tough. So I couldn't understand him ducking out of bounds. I was an Earl Campbell fan, and that's who I was judging everybody on. There ain't too many Earls around.

On the other hand, probably the toughest tackle I ever faced in my career was a Cowboy—Pat Donovan. Maybe it's because I faced him just my first two years while I was young, but he'd finesse me and shut me down. He wasn't all that physical, but it seemed I'd be running in place against him.

But all the Redskins hated Dallas, literally. We heard you could piss off Randy White by telling him you screwed his wife. Tony Peters said that once, and Randy White started chasing Tony right on the field.

The next game of 1981 that I clearly recall is the fourth game, a 36–13 loss at Philadelphia. I recorded my first career sack that day, a blood curdler on Ron Jaworski. It was a great hit from the blind side. I nailed his ass, big league. The Redskins were high on me because I was getting off on special teams. Wayne Sevier said so:

We'd always put speed guys on the outside to cover punts, but what struck me about Dexter was how fast he could run for a big fella. The first day he was here, I said, "I'm Coach Sevier, and I've got plans for you." It was unheard of to have a release man that size, and the guy caused havoc. They'd double him with two DBs, and he'd run over one guy and be one on

one with the other guy until he'd just pound him. Then, he had the ability to
run the returner down.

That was the first thing he could hang his hat on, and then Coy Bacon
was let go, which is when Dexter became the starter. Then we backed him off
special teams, and he just took over on defense.

You know, to this day I still hear guys talk about Dexter on special
teams. And he only did it six games.

I finally started a game against San Francisco, which was our
fifth straight loss, and I racked up a sack against Joe Montana. That
name would come up again later.

It was finally doomed for Coy Bacon when he came in drunk one
day. He came into a meeting toasted.

Actually, it also had something to do with them taking him off
the goal-line defense unit and putting Matt Mendenhall there. Coy
would fuss. The man talked so fast. He never made sense. He'd be, "Ya
tink he can da betta ja' den me? Well, ga' dan, ga head and play um.
Ga' dan, let the muva play." That's how he talked.

So Gibbs just sent him home, told him not to bother coming
back. Coy Bacon was way out of line. He was late and drunk, too. You
can say all you want about my checkered past, but I wasn't late very
often.

Now, I will say Coy could rush the passer in his day. But when he
was with us, he couldn't rush to the store.

My boy had been Lamar Parish, who had long been an all-pro
cornerback. But Art Monk pulled me aside one day to say that Bobby
Beathard had said, "Don't hang around Lamar Parish."

Art Monk told me this, and I got the message. That year Lamar
went to buy drugs while I was with him one day. I hadn't messed with
the stuff back then.

I'd have a drink once in a while. I got drunk off wine my rookie
year and went riding with Mark May and Darryl Grant. That might
have been the time we went to McDonald's and I was talking trash. I
acted like a plumb fool. I couldn't handle liquor.

My daddy used to drink Cutty Sark and, I thought, Sprite. So I
used to experiment with Cutty Sark and Sprite myself. That rookie
season, we were playing the Miami Dolphins down in the Orange
Bowl, and I drank a boatload of the Cutty Sark and Sprite that Friday
night. I got drunk and was hurting that Saturday morning. I was
actually hurting for two whole days, even during the game that Sunday.

I was sick for two days. That was the game in which Lamar Parish and Dave Butz nearly fought on the field. It was the first time I'd almost seen a Civil War in a huddle. Lamar called Dave Butz a big fucking punk. He said he was fucking scared and didn't want to play. And it was true, the way Butz was playing.

Lamar yelled, "Butz, get pissed, you big-ass dude."

Lamar was a real shit talker. But when I heard that, I got fired up and started playing my ass off—with a hangover.

I was pissed at Butz, too. He was just walking around on the field. I mean, they nearly fought right there in the huddle. I was just thinking, Damn, why don't this big-ass dude do something? He's big as a house.

Later in my Redskins career, Joe Gibbs used to get mad at me for talking trash about Dave Butz. One time I said to the media, "Dave Butz, you've got to take a slingshot to his butt to get him going. I don't know if his elevator is going to the top floor." I also said, "You've got to get Butz woken up out there. You've got to shoot him in the butt with a BB gun."

Butz was so pissed when I said that, he said he was going to shoot me. With what? A BB gun? Mark Moseley was mad at me, too, because Butz was his buddy.

I can safely say there was a double standard on the Redskins. Curtis Jordan said something about me to reporters once, and Gibbs didn't get rip-roaring mad at him. But if I commented on Butz, Gibbs would be all over me.

In the meantime, Butz always tried to pull something. One time in 1983, we'd just flown back from a big Dallas game, and Butz was driving directly in front of me on the way home. Next thing I knew, he held a full can of Coca-Cola outside his window so the wind would blow it all over my windshield. That was Butz.

As my rookie season wore on, I grew nostalgic. I recalled the day I'd cried in the hallway at Yates, telling Coach Booker, "I've got to get to the NFL." Well, I knew all along I'd get there. That was my whole life. You know how you hear guys who say their whole life is football? I'm a victim of that. It's kind of sad to say that's all I had, but it's fact. Along the way, there could've been so many stumbling blocks, like injuries or flunking out of school. I'm so fortunate to have made it.

Well, we kicked enough butt to end the '81 season with an 8–8 record. I'd started nine games, recorded six sacks and—what mattered most—earned about $30,000 in incentives. That gave me enough cash to get Texaco out of my hair and sort of put me over the hump.

I'll never forget the last game of the season in Anaheim. We blew the Rams out, 30–7, and it was here I first saw the true screw-'em-at-all-cost attitude of management.

I'd seen Bobby Beathard on the sideline that day, and he said, "You had a great rookie season." We had had a handshake agreement in training camp that if I had a great rookie season, he'd renegotiate my contract. So I had gone to him on the sideline to talk about it, and you know what he did? He told me, "Oh, by the way, we're taking incentive clauses away from players."

Why did he say that? Hell, he figured that'd keep me from renegotiating because I had an incentive package in my original contract. I was a rookie, and he wanted to scare me and keep me away from renegotiating. So I just shut up.

But in January or February of the off-season, I called him back and said, "Bobby, remember we had an agreement we'd renegotiate?" No question, he knew I'd had a super rookie season. He'd said it, and Gibbs had said it.

Bobby told me, "Well, Dexter, as a matter of fact, we're taking Larry Kubin's incentive clauses away, and we're going to take your incentive clauses away."

They weren't going to do that. It was just a threat to scare me from asking for more dough. From that time on, I knew never to make an agreement with the white man, shaking hands. The best thing to do is to put it down in black and white.

And you know what? They tried to screw me out of the reporting bonus I was due when training camp opened the next season. I took my contract to a teammate, Perry Brooks, and showed him. It said, "Upon reporting in 1982, you receive $6,000." Perry said, "Uh huh, you better get on it. Don't let 'em screw you over."

It was then I realized they were trying to use me. I went to Bobby about it, and Bobby said, "How do you know you have a reporting bonus in there? Can you read it?"

AN IDLE THOUGHT

I learned from Coy Bacon in 1981 that veterans believe rookies should be seen and not heard.

I never forgot it, either.

I was in the training camp dining hall with Phoenix ten years later, in 1991, and I said to rookie Scott Evans from Oklahoma, "Go up and get me some more potatoes, rookie."

I believe he did.

C H A P T E R   15

Impersonating What?

T HE MONTHS FOLLOWING MY ROOKIE SEASON, I
had so little money that I memorized all my one-dollar-bill serial
numbers. I needed cash flow in the worst way, and Joe Gibbs and
Bobby Beathard had an idea: Send me to prison.

My $40,000 first-year salary didn't exactly have me living in satin
sheets, so Gibbs's and Beathard's solution was to find me a summer job
as a guard at the Fairfax County Detention Center. Hey, I'd had
nightmares about being behind bars, but never about being in front of
them. I had bills to pay, and I liked the idea of a job with authority and
with a badge. I'd finally be majoring in criminology.

It was thoughtful of Gibbs to be looking out for me. Coach Gibbs
even asked me to go to church with him that summer and to help him
with some underprivileged kids, and I agreed. If I'd gone to church
with him later on in my career, I might still be a Redskin. But I didn't
play the Bible-toter game later in my career with Gibbs—like half the
team did to get on his good side—but I did pack a Bible with him on
Sundays my rookie year. I even went to church with his family once.

The prison job he got me made me feel important. I wore a
sheriff's uniform, and I'd strut around jail like a hot shot, watching
monitors. Tammy said I'd come home cheerful, and she was glad I had
something to keep me out of Pall Mall.

I worked split shifts. If I had to work the overnight shift, my job
was to wake up the inmates in the morning and get a head count before
breakfast. I loved that part. I'd go in there sassy like my daddy used to
wake us up, banging my keys. Driiiiiiiiing, biiiiiiing. I'd pound on a
box and holler, "Up time! Up time! Up time!" Who wants to wake up
to that? I'd turn a slot in their cells and slide in their breakfasts as if I
was feeding bears at the zoo.

I'd jolt them from their sleep at about 6:45 A.M., and some of the inmates literally wanted to fight me. Most tough guys aren't used to my kind of alarm clock, and I treated 'em like the military. Hell, my daddy treated us like boot camp, too.

Those inmates knew I was a Washington Redskin, but they weren't impressed and would write me up to the sheriff. I would taunt them—talk trash—and I got in trouble once because I kicked a guy in his butt. I soon realized you can get in a heap of trouble with inmates; they can file a lawsuit on you in a heartbeat.

It also amazed me to see the inmates were predominantly white. The one unit I was really scared of was the C Unit. It was extra security, and I didn't like hanging around a bunch of murderers who'd maybe snuck in a hunting knife.

The only thing my prison bosses didn't do was give me a gun. I asked for one, and they said no. If they had, it would've been hilarious.

Nonetheless, the badge came in handy. One night I was late for work, and I was a little drunk and speeding like Mario Andretti. I might have been swerving a bit, because a cop pulled me over right by the jail.

I hopped out of my car and started fast-talking him. I'm sure he smelled the alcohol on me. I told him, "I'm late for work," and I flashed my badge. He let me go.

When the off-season ended, I figured the sheriffs would have me back again the next year. It was Tammy's idea to send them a kiss-ass letter saying, "It was wonderful working for you, but it's time to pick up and play ball again. But I'd love to be back next spring."

They never asked for my badge back.

My relationship with Tammy began to flounder. During my rookie season, we'd been like husband and wife, me rushing straight home from Redskin Park and her rushing home to cook me as much food as she could fit in the cupboard.

We had a dual checking account, and one time I accused her of writing too many checks. She got angry because all the checks she wrote were for my food or things we needed for the town house. She'd drive 80 mph to get home before I would, so she wouldn't have to listen to me bellyaching for my supper. And this is after I'd stop for chili dogs on my way back from Redskin Park.

I'm not certain how much Tammy liked Virginia. She and my sister had driven my raggedy Mercedes from Houston to D.C.—while I flew—and she said it was the longest ride she'd ever embarked on. She was worried the whole time because the locks on the Mercedes didn't work, and they'd check into motels at night wondering if their stuff would be stolen by morning. When they finally arrived in Virginia, two white guys called them niggers.

But I relied on Tammy. Although I carried *The Washington Post* to make myself seem worldly, I couldn't read it. Tammy would read articles to me, especially the ones about me. She'd tell me what every word meant.

From time to time, I'd try writing cards to her. I'd buy a card from a card shop and write "To Tammy, Form Dexter." I couldn't spell *from* right.

Tammy paid all the bills. She remembers me writing a check once and misspelling the word *hundred,* so she had no choice. I couldn't withdraw money on my own until ATMs came along. She would open all the mail. I'd come home and be pissed and ask, "Why'd you open my mail?" She wouldn't say anything. She'd just look at me and go, "Um huh." She later said she'd open the bills because it could've been the electric bill, and if she didn't rip it open, we would've been sitting in the dark before I'd take care of it.

In fact, that happened once later, when my momma and I were living together.

When my momma came to live with me at the start of my rookie year, she was not well. It was stressful having her. I knew she wasn't playing with a full deck. She'd wake up thinking she was in Houston or wake up not knowing my name. But I brought her to D.C. because she wouldn't have lasted long in Texas. It was a desperate situation to get her the hell out of there. It was either fly her to D.C. or she'd be roaming the streets with just her bra on.

She'd be trying to buy liquor at night or bootlegging or going to the bootlegger man's house at midnight to chug beer. My sister told the bootlegger man, "We've known you've been bootleggin' our whole lives, but if you turn our momma into a bootlegger, we're gonna call the police."

So he started refusing to sell her anything. Thank God, he'd realized my momma had gone from one extreme—a churchgoing woman—to the other—a boozer. Without his cooperation, she still could get her alcohol during the day, but not late at night.

My daddy had left her $40,000, plus his life insurance, but she must've spent all that money on alcohol. When she came to live with me, she had nothing left. From 1977 to 1981, she'd become empty-handed.

Momma didn't want a bed. She requested to sleep on a floor mat.

She'd just putter around the house in Reston, and she'd try cooking for Tammy and me, but she couldn't even boil water. Everything she did, she either burned or half-cooked.

I took her downtown once to D.C., and she was petrified. When she saw the bustle of the big city, she would not get out of the car. She was more content in Reston, which was more country. But even here she was kind of lost. She'd say she had nothing to live for.

She continued having her dream about the Schlitz malt liquor bull chasing her. What could I do? She said, "I don't want to be a burden," but her moods would swing like a saloon door. One day Tammy was in the kitchen, and my momma started howling, "You bitch! You bitch!" and grabbed Tammy by the hair.

I tell my drug counselors there were no alcoholics in my immediate family, but they question, "How about your momma?" Well, my momma was not an alcoholic until my daddy died. Did that drive me to use drugs? I don't know. I was seventeen when she began boozing, and I agree I had a lot of shame. I had shame because my momma had deteriorated from being a Christian woman to being a lush. But this all happened when I was seventeen. It's not as if it occurred when I was five and she was drinking whiskey instead of making me bologna sandwiches. I can't say if my momma was responsible for my eventual drug problem.

If only we'd known there was a tumor growing in her brain.

It was about that time—the spring after my rookie season—that I met Glinda Nelson, which is what eventually led me to drop Tammy like a hot potato:

Well, he did totally drop Tammy, and I felt real bad for her. I didn't like getting between them, but I loved Dexter. I fell in love so quick with Dexter, and he fell in love with me, too. Maybe we just needed each other. I think he was my security, and I was his.

When I met Dexter, I was married to Steve Sheppard, a member of the 1976 gold medal Olympic basketball team from the University of Maryland. I met Steve when he was playing for my hometown team, the Chicago Bulls. I hated basketball, but my girlfriend called one day and begged me to come to a game with her. She was dating Scott May [of the Bulls], and they were engaged. I pleaded, "Loraine, I really don't want to go."

"Oh, Glinda, just come on and go," she replied.

When we got there she said, "Well, the reason I wanted you here is that

Scott has a best friend, Steve Sheppard, who always says, 'Where are your pretty girl friends? Let me meet just one.'"

I already had a boyfriend, which is why I didn't want to go, but she wanted me to go so Steve would get off her back about meeting some of her friends. When the game ended, I was ready to get out of there, but Loraine was like, "No, just wait 'til Steve comes out so I can introduce him to you."

Well, he came out, and I was like, "Um huh."

I never thought I'd hook up with Steve. I didn't like him initially, but he was such a gentleman. I was dating a man who was fourteen years my senior and had just gotten out of a marriage, and here was someone young.

I was getting ready to leave the arena, and Steve conned me into agreeing that the four of us would go and have one drink. Steve didn't drink—he said he'd just order Perrier—and Loraine kept saying, "Come on, Glinda." So we got there and I ended up drinking something, and he started looking a little better to me. And then he danced real well, so he started looking even better. And I was like, "Oh God, this must be the alcohol."

At the end of the evening—Dexter did this, too, and won my heart— Steve gave me a kiss on the forehead when he said goodnight. Steve didn't kind of hook me, but I really found him as a really sweet guy.

I was in my last year of college, having just transferred to a school in Chicago from Arizona State, and Steve kept calling me. So he kept telling me, "Glinda, I just want to stop by and see you." I didn't really like him that much and he wasn't that cute, so I said, "Steve, I really can't. Because I'm studying for this final."

He said, "Glinda, I'll only stay for five minutes." But it was a forty-minute drive to the South Side. I said, "You're gonna drive forty minutes and stay for five?" He said yes. How could I tell someone no for five minutes! I said OK.

So he came over, and five minutes became dinner. We were engaged in two months and married in eight. He proposed to me in his mother's house over Christmas.

We were married in June, and it was the worst thing that could happen. Immediately, Chicago traded him to Detroit.

I hope Dexter's more prepared mentally for life after sports, because Steve started drinking when things went south. He became abusive. So he went to play in Rome, and I went with him. That was lovely, except for when he was around the house.

The abuse was real weird. I can't remember why we fought, but Steve was always on edge, in depression. If I said the sky was blue, he'd go off. He'd be ready to kick your ass.

When we got back from his season in Rome, we came to live at my parents' house. He'd been great in Italy, where they loved him. He was a king. But he was unhappy because he wanted to be in the NBA. He felt he was exiled.

His line was, "Let me go to Washington, D.C., by myself, find a place to live, and I'll send for you." I didn't really want to go with him, because I was afraid of him. In Rome I had even slept in my locked bathroom all night.

I told my parents I didn't want to go to D.C. with Steve, but my daddy said, "You need to go back. You're married. I'm tired of supporting you."

I took it as if my parents were deserting me as well, so I left. When I got to D.C., Steve wouldn't touch me. He wouldn't even talk to me. He moved me to Reston, Virginia, but he wouldn't show me around. He'd say, "Just get in the car and figure it out. Get lost. You'll find your way back."

I was like, "What did I do to you?" But it wasn't me, it was basketball. He told me, "Glinda, I don't love you, I love basketball. And my woman— basketball—has died, and I'm mourning her."

I got myself a job working for Xerox and supported Steve for a whole year. He didn't work, and he couldn't find an NBA team. I'd give him an allowance every week.

I'd say I was emotionally abused by him. We'd be lying in bed, and if his foot accidentally touched mine, he'd move his foot real quick. It was like I was a disease.

Why'd I stay? I felt sorry for him. See, I'm the wonderful caretaker. That's my job. I take care of people. My mother, my husband, whoever needs help. Great, huh? I'm always last. So that's what I need work on, because eventually it makes you resent the person you're helping, like "Why can't anybody help me?"

So it got to the point I didn't even like looking at Steve's face. Even the smell of him irked me. I said, "It's gone; there's nothing left."

Then Steve got an offer to play in Uruguay, and he was going to do it simply for the money. He said, "Glinda, maybe we'll do better if we go down there. Why don't you come with me?"

All of a sudden he wants me now. I told him no. No way he was going to get me in South America and then beat me. I was going nowhere with him. But he kept trying.

So I was coming home from work in the afternoon on a gorgeous, lovely day. I happened to be looking over to the side, and I saw this big black man in a Mercedes. I thought, Ohhhhhhh. I just love big black men.

He just looked so gorgeous, and from what I could tell, he was built. I'd heard there were athletes out there in Reston, but I wasn't into the Redskins and didn't know. There weren't many blacks in Reston, so I was thinking,

What is he doing here? Then he had Texas license plates, and I thought I bet he is a Redskin.

Well, we drove and drove. We both had stopped at a red light opposite Route 7. He was coming out of Clyde's, a bar, and then he was going to make a right turn on Route 7. I was making a left onto Route 7, and we saw each other as we turned. We played cat and mouse for twelve miles up Route 7 before we turned into Reston.

I'd look over at him, and he wouldn't look at me. He'd keep driving. I was like, *Why isn't this man looking at me? I know he thinks I'm cute. This was my ego.* He finally looked at me, tooted his horn, and smiled. When he tooted his horn, I thought he'd say something to me, but he sped off.

I thought, *Now he really thinks he's somebody! I couldn't believe he did that. I was thinking I'd lost something, but a red light caught him.*

So there he was, sitting at the red light feeling like an idiot, because here I came driving right up, like, *You goin' somewhere?* I didn't say anything, but I looked at him like, *Uh huh, you got stopped.*

He started laughing, because he couldn't even make a getaway. I'd seen an NFL sticker on the back of his car, so I asked him, "Do you know a guy named Reggie Haynes?" I had known Reggie at Arizona State, and I knew he played for the Redskins. He kept saying, "What?" He couldn't hear me. Finally he said, "I can't hear you. Pull over!"

We pulled over into this parking lot, and I was nervous. I really felt out of place because I was married. When I saw him unfolding out of his car, it turned me on. I said to myself, *Oh my God.* He just kept unfolding, and then he's taller and taller and bigger and bigger. I was like, *Whooa!* He walks up to me, and I was like palpitating.

This was in my days of smoking marijuana. I was so stressed with Steve, I had started to smoke about a joint a day. I'd heard that athletes like reefer, so I said, "Hmmmm, do you want to smoke a joint?"

You know what he did to make me feel even crazier? He said, "No, I'm a deputy sheriff." And he pulled out a badge.

He didn't crack a smile or anything. I was like, *Oh, my God, I'm about to go to jail.* I kept thinking, *Oh no, Glinda, no you didn't.*

I said, "Oh no, I didn't mean to . . ."

He said, "Oh, don't worry . . . You want to go have a drink or something?"

He'd seen me getting real scared and nervous, and then I saw him laughing. He said, "Just relax." I felt so stupid.

So I said, "OK, I'll get a drink." We went to Fritzbe's in Reston, right across from where Steve and I lived. We stayed there from three in the afternoon until nine at night.

He told me he was Dexter Manley, and he told me about Tammy, and I told him about Steve. It was like Dexter was an old friend. All he drank was orange juice. He wasn't drinking then.

I tried to hook him up with Steve. I called Steve to tell him, "Come across the street. We're at Fritzbe's, and I've got another athlete here." Steve had been working out every day waiting for that call from the NBA, and it was off-season for Dexter, so I thought maybe they could work out together. Dexter didn't mind. He was real cool. He probably didn't like it, but I was trying to be a righteous lady. I was like, I'm married. You're living with this girl Tammy. We can be friends.

I called Steve three times, and no answer. I was thinking, I'm the one with a job. Where the hell is Steve?

To this day, they've never met. Who knows what would've happened if Steve had been home! So then Dexter gave me the fatal good-night kiss on the forehead, and I was hooked. I felt bad, being a married woman. It was March 31, 1982.

I hadn't even heard of Dexter Manley. That really pissed him off. He kept saying, "You never heard of me?" He was really serious about it, and I said, "No." He said, "Shit, don't you watch the Redskins? Where you living, under a rock? I'm just one of the best players they have. I was a rookie last year."

I was like, Oh, a rookie. Because I knew how NFL rookies were. I had dated Ahmad Rashad for a few years, on the side.

Dexter said, "I'll give you a call sometime." I figured that was it. I went home, having dreams about him but knowing it would never come about. I was married, and he was living with this Tammy.

When I got to work the next day, a message was waiting for me: "Dexter Manley called. Call Redskin Park."

I kept it quiet, but then I went to Redskin Park. I could be flexible with my job. I was in the marketing department, so I'd say, "I've got to make some calls." After a while, Dexter would go out on calls with me. He'd sit in the car and wait for me. I mean, we were like that every day. I don't think it was healthy, but we were addicted to each other. There were some needs that both of us were missing, and the other one was filling.

Things got real bad. He had to go to Houston, and I drove him to the airport. In the meantime, we were seeing each other every day, one way or another, even if I was coming to Redskin Park to get a hug and a kiss. I didn't feel like an adulteress because I wasn't having any relations with my husband. I mean, none, physically. I'd already asked for a separation, but Steve didn't want to give it to me. But we weren't touching, we weren't having relations. It was all on paper only.

Dexter wrote down all his phone numbers, and I sat the paper next to my bed and didn't think anything of it. Steve found it one day and beat me over it.

The next day, I went to work all bruised. Steve had kicked me. I called Dexter and told him—I told people from work I was in a car crash—and Dexter said, "I'm gonna meet you. Meet me at the mall." When he saw me, you could see his eyes started to tear. He felt so sorry for me. He said, "God dang, I'll kick his . . ." He wanted to kill Steve, because how could somebody beat me? Dexter and I hadn't done anything sexually yet, so we became even closer. We became even more like allies.

It got to the point that whatever it took, we'd see each other. If it was Dexter running to get milk at 7-Eleven and us meeting there, so be it.

Tammy told Dexter, "I know something's up." When I'd call, he'd say, "I just have a friend named Glinda." Then I'd hear her in the background, "Oh, is that Glinda? You all must be doing something . . ."

I could tell she was starting to get jealous. When she'd answer the phone, she'd say, "Dexter, it's your girlfriend."

Dexter told me he was about to get engaged to Tammy. We were playing cat and mouse, after all this. So I messed with him and said, "What size diamond will you get her? You should at least get her a two-carat. Listen, I can help you shop for the ring." He was like, Gaaaaawd, what's wrong with her? I thought she liked me and now she's going to help me get engaged!

I figured that the last thing he wanted was somebody to clutch onto him. I'd be the total opposite, and that brought him closer to me.

We went on like this for a long time. Then one night we went shopping at the mall together. Dexter didn't have credit cards then, and I did. We both picked out some things, and he said, "Why don't you just put it all on your credit card, and I'll give you cash for my stuff?" I said fine.

He bought a couple pair of jeans and a silk shirt. We checked all the clothes before he took them home to make sure there were no receipts, no names, nothing Tammy could find.

Well, we didn't find one receipt. They must've stuffed it in his jeans pants pocket. It had my address on it because they wanted to put me on a mailing list.

Before that, Tammy never knew where I lived. That's what always saved me from her. She really felt something was going on, because she kept telling him, "I know you're seeing somebody. I don't know if it's Glinda or not, but it's someone who lives real close, like in Herndon or Reston." She knew it was somebody in the neighborhood, because she said, "You go out long, but not long enough to go downtown to D.C." She figured it all out. He said, "Damn, she's smart."

So, he got home that night from the mall—it was 2:00 A.M.—and fell asleep. In the wee hours of the morning, Tammy got up, went through his clothes, and came to my house.

Steve was leaving the next day for Uruguay. I wasn't going, but I was taking him to the airport. Guess what was on the door of my apartment when I walked outside? A letter from Tammy.

She wrote, "Hey, you yellow ass bitch, you can keep him for all I care. He ain't shit, he ain't gonna be shit to you, and here's his motherfucking clothes. I hope y'all rot in hell."

She had shredded all the clothes he'd bought. I was so embarrassed. I had all these men's clothes at the foot of my door, and everyone knew I was married. And this horrible letter stuck to my door for all the world to see.

By saying "yellow bitch," she was referring to my light skin color. Tammy was dark. Dexter would say brown-skinned, but I guess Houston darkens you as the years go on.

I couldn't see what Dexter saw in Tammy. She had a teenie waist, with a butt from here to that wall. I'd never seen a person built like that in my life, and I was like, Whoa! She was short and petite, kind of cute with long hair, but had a gold front tooth.

So I grabbed the letter. I didn't want him to see it, but he was so cool. He just walked down the steps and said, "Looks like his woman is pissed off at you."

I didn't know if I was going to get a backhand from him or what. I was scared. I had to drive him all the way to National Airport, and I didn't know if he'd stay that cool. That wasn't like him. He usually goes off. I kept thinking, Why is he so cool? He must be waiting. I didn't know what he was going to do, but he was cool. He didn't say a mean word the whole way there.

If anything, he was cracking jokes. He said, "Yeah, you better be careful. Now that she knows where you live, she might come and kick your ass."

What he said about her kicking my ass was his goodbye. He just walked out of the car and said, "See you later."

So, I drive home thinking, "Boy, this could be the goodbye of all goodbyes." And it was.

Tammy had gone right home from my apartment and hopped into bed. Dexter didn't know she'd been out. I thought it was pretty slick. She probably thought my husband would kick my butt for her.

When I returned from the airport, Dexter called. I said, "Dexter, I don't know if I should tell you this . . ." I knew how Dexter would get mad at Tammy.

"Tell me," he said.

I knew he could get hyper on things, and I was afraid he might hurt Tammy. So I thought, Should I tell him? "Well, I don't know if I should tell you . . . OK, Tammy . . ."

"What, what? Damnit, tell me." Then he said, "Wait a minute. Let me run to 7-Eleven, so I can really talk to you."

When he called me from the pay phone there he asked, "What'd she do? Did she do something to you?"

"Well, your clothes are shredded. Tammy was over here."

"What do you mean she was over here?"

"Wait a minute, when you woke up, was she in bed?"

"Yeah, asleep."

"Well," I said, "somewhere between the time we got home last night and the time you woke up this morning, Tammy got up, took the clothes, brought them over here, shredded them up, and put a big note on my door."

You know what he was mad about? His clothes. He was furious about his clothes being cut up, just like his daddy would have been.

I said, "Dexter, wait a minute. You've got to understand." I was trying to be on her side, because I didn't want him going off and doing something to somebody so little and ending up in jail.

But he kept saying, "Nah, nah. I'm fine, I'm fine. But she's going to pay for that. I'm going to kick her ass."

I kept repeating, "Dexter, don't kick her ass. Don't kick her ass."

I heard he went over there and did slap her around and put his foot through a window or something. I don't know what happened, but I know he put her on a plane that day.

So later that evening we celebrated. We were rid of everybody on the same day.

That was a sad way for Tammy to go. I felt bad for her because I know she loved him. I felt like they were married and I had destroyed their relationship, even though they weren't married. I knew Dexter was all she had, but then, I loved him.

Tammy had planned on leaving for quite some time. She wanted to go to school at Northern Virginia Community College, and I wanted her to work. That was a sour point between us. She figured that now that I was in the pros, she would finish her education. Well, I wanted a working woman.

Tammy was working at Woolworth's part time and going to school part time. When she was studying for finals, I wanted to bring my five-year-old son Derrick in, much to Tammy's dismay. She said she needed quiet to study, and I said, "I can bring my son when I want to." She wanted me to wait until later to bring Derrick in.

Tammy stayed by me in college. She loved me to death there. She was a good woman, but I was her meal ticket, too, to get out of the poor life. She tried to take care of me, and then I saw a pretty, educated woman—a working woman—in Glinda. I was young, so I said, I'm going with Glinda.

Sure I hurt Tammy. She probably thought I'd never leave her, but so many things happened. Even before that incident with my jeans, Tammy hurt my feelings by calling me dumb one day on a tennis court. "You're dumb," she said. "You can't even read or write." When she said I would end up back in the Third Ward some day, I realized she didn't love me. It was her way of lashing out.

Well, I said, "I don't need to hear this." She told me I needed to go back to school and learn to read and write. It was the first time she'd called me illiterate. She predicted that after football, I wouldn't get very far. When she cut my jeans all up like that, it was obviously the last straw for both of us.

I admit I hit her when I got home from 7-Eleven that day. She says I hit her in her ear and put a hole in her eardrum. I hope I didn't cause that. I owe a lot to Tammy.

I have friends who believe Tammy was the right woman for me, because she loved me for who I was. I can't speculate. I still believe I made it to the NFL because of her help in school. I don't know what else I can say about her, except I'm sorry.

Well, that next football season, I had a new woman but old worries, namely getting locked up.

Remember that sheriff's badge I kept? It sort of came in handy again.

My Mercedes was a piece of junk, and I told my agent, Joe Courrege, I wanted a new one. He said I didn't have enough money to buy a new one.

Hell, my Mercedes had snow tires on it. It didn't even *look* like a Mercedes. Besides, I wanted the car's title in my name. If I was going to pay money on it, I wanted it in my name; but Joe Courrege had co-signed on the car, and it was in his name. I think I paid $13,000 for that piece-of-shit car, and I had to put $6,000 in it the first week for repairs. So I stopped paying on it, and that caused problems. The bank started looking for me because I had gotten a bank loan to pay for the car.

Meantime, Joe Courrege was supposed to send me my new tags for the car. When he never sent them, he told me to change the date on the paper temporary tags so he'd have more time to get the permanent tags to me. That's what I did.

In November 1982 I was stopped on Reston Avenue by a cop. I wasn't speeding at all. He stopped me because I was a black kid in a Mercedes.

I wanted him to let me go, so I figured I'd subtly whip out my badge. I'd learned that all officers flash their badge when they pull out their driver's license. The other officer respects that badge and lets you go. I'd been pulled over three or four times before, and it'd always worked.

So I flashed it to this cop, and he asked, "What is that thing?"

"The same thing you have on," I answered.

I told him I was a sheriff's deputy at the Fairfax Detention Center, and he said, "You Manley? OK, go ahead."

He went back to the station, ran a check, and didn't find my name. Well, I hadn't resigned or anything, and I intended to work again at the center the next off-season. They'd gotten the letter Tammy sent, but I guess the police authorized my arrest. They railroaded me.

Next thing I knew, I got a call from the same cop, Officer Michael Mack, at Redskin Park.

He said I was no deputy and that there was a warrant out for my arrest. I was in the Redskin Park equipment room, and told him, "Go get your fucking warrant. I'll arrest your ass. Fuck you." I hung up on him.

The next morning I woke up with six or seven police cars and a SWAT team outside my house. I was arrested on charges of impersonating an officer and altering temporary tags. I could have gotten one to five years in jail and a $5,000 fine. I had to post $6,000 bail.

It turned out that Judge Frank Perry III imposed a six-month jail term on me and a $600 fine, but he suspended the sentence on the condition of my good behavior for a year. That meant I had to be a good boy. Can you imagine what would have happened if I'd been sent behind bars with the same guys I used to piss off as a deputy? They would've gang-banged me. Instead, my God-awful Mercedes was re-possessed—thank goodness. I also couldn't work at the detention center the next off-season.

But, hey, I got publicity for it. The story was on the news everywhere. People heard the "impersonating an officer" charge and believed I was out there dressing up like Sergeant Friday.

They thought, This guy's a character. He's some crazy guy. Now everybody had heard of Dexter Manley. It took something like that to get notoriety, but I liked it. I knew I was in trouble, but at the same time I felt like I was more popular.

Darryl Grant started spreading rumors about my "impersonating" stunt. He said I'd pulled someone over on the Dulles Airport toll road and ordered, "Slow down, I'm the sheriff around here," and that person got suspicious and called in my license plate to the police. Darryl also spread rumors that one of the inmates I had overseen at the detention center got out and stuck his finger in the back of my head while I was on a pay phone, as if it was a gun.

All I know is I considered 1982 the start of the real Dexter Manley era. That was when my teammates began calling me Sheriff.

By the way, I fired Courrege.

AN IDLE THOUGHT

One of my more famous quotes came while I attended a Washington, D.C., banquet with several politicians and powers that be.

Al Haig was there, and I started my speech by saying, "First of all, I want Al Haig to know *I'm in charge.*"

Tammy was responsible for that quote. We'd been sitting together watching TV when President Reagan was shot in 1980, and that's when Haig said *he* was in charge. I didn't realize it was a ridiculous statement until Tammy explained to me that the vice president was in charge, not Haig, the secretary of state.

Tammy may have alerted me about Haig, but I follow the news religiously. I mean, I *knew* who Oliver North was. Back when we were in the playoffs in 1986, Joe Gibbs was asked what he thought of Oliver North, and he said, "Who's Oliver North?"

I just can't believe Gibbs did not know who the hell Oliver North was. He must've been playing some game to prove he works harder than other coaches. I just cannot believe that Joe Gibbs—who is the second in command in the nation's capital behind the president—had not heard of Oliver North.

CHAPTER 16

MVP . . . Not!

EVEN TEAM OWNER JACK KENT COOKE KNEW who I was after I'd impersonated Andy Griffith.

Just kidding. Cooke knew all about me before that—in the training camp of 1982—when I asked him for $8,000, out of the clear blue. He just whipped out that heavy checkbook of his.

I guess because I was in my second season now, I was one of the boys. I was one of the dominating players on defense, so what was Cooke gonna say? No? He could have said no, but he admired me for what I did on the field and for what I'd say off of it. I believe Cooke was drawn to me. He wore an ascot around his neck, and I wore a bandanna around mine. We were almost twins.

I told him I needed a raise, since Beathard had reneged, and that I needed it *now* to buy a house. I'd told Beathard about my request, and he had relayed it to Cooke, who sent for me right away. We met on the Dickinson College practice field, and he forked over the eight grand right there. He told Jerry Gabries, the comptroller, to scribble out a check.

I may have been his boy then. But I guess my tongue grew sharper over the years, and our relationship soured like one of his marriages. What's he had? Two? Three? Four?

Anyway, the summer of 1982 had been complex. My momma remained with me after Tammy split, and—as Tammy expected—I forgot to pay the electric bill one time, and Momma was left in the pitch dark.

While I was in Carlisle for training camp, I forgot the light bill, and those electric company suckers switched off the electricity in a heartbeat. Glinda paid the overdue bill for me and made sure my momma hadn't found her way to the liquor store. Momma would always ask Glinda real softly, "May I have a drink of water?" That's how she was. She lived there, yet she was always asking Glinda permission for ice water.

Momma wasn't in good health, and when Glinda would come over to visit me, my momma would ask, "Can I come in and watch TV with you guys?" Real soft.

Glinda didn't even live with me, but my momma treated her like an empress:

Every day I'd come by and check on Dexter's mother, and a couple of times I spent the night. The time he didn't pay the electric bill, I came by with candles for dinner. She was perfectly OK.

She was just the sweetest lady, but I was shocked by their home. He had Tammy and his mother in this nice town house, but he'd only rented a dining room set and a bedroom set. All he actually owned was a stereo system, the only thing in his living room, and his mother slept on a mat.

One of the times I spent the night, I expected her to sleep in Dexter's bedroom with me, but she went to her own room. I said, "No, Miss Manley. Sleep in here."

She replied, "Oh, no," in that soft voice of hers.

Some people believe she was emotionally abused by her husband. He was a street fellow, and she was a church mouse. He dressed better than her, but she kept her mouth shut and could never speak out. I think she loved him so much, and he controlled her fully. Her brother Wilbur says she's been like that since she was a little girl. She wouldn't swat a fly.

But get a little alcohol in her, and there'd be a change. Dexter told me before he left for training camp, "Whatever you do, don't give her a beer."

"One beer won't hurt."

Dexter insisted, "One will."

One day she outfoxed me. She said, "Do you have a dollar? I've got some personal items to get at 7-Eleven." She didn't want me to go with her, so I gave her a dollar and let her walk over there.

Dexter called, meanwhile, and said, "You gave her money? Betcha she bought beer. You'll see another woman."

When she came in, I happened to say, "Miss Manley, tell me about Carl."

She said, "Shiiiiit, Carl?" She'd become somebody else. She was like a wino in the street. She looked evil when she was under the influence, like she'd fight you. The alcohol would bring out the suppressed Jewellean Manley.

By the end of the 1982 training camp, my momma was moving out of my town house. Her mother had taken ill in Louisiana, and someone in the family had to bring her hot towels and tea and nurse her. Since my momma was the co-dependent type, she volunteered.

Again, if only we had known there was a tumor growing in her brain.

Meantime, I was monogramming the football season "DM." In the first two games, I had four sacks, including two against this guy Doug Williams of Tampa Bay. We won the Tampa game, 21–13, in a driving rainstorm in Florida, and I kicked Doug's ass. Kicked it big time. Nobody could block me.

They didn't block me the next week either because we didn't play. The players' strike lasted fifty-seven days. I went back to Houston for a couple of days, but I basically stayed in D.C. because the team held informal weight-lifting workouts at a health club.

Torgy would call and ask, "Have you been running? Have you been working out?" With me, he knew the answer was yes.

I didn't have bills because I had moved in with Glinda after my momma moved out. Plus, I had the $8,000 Mr. Cooke handed me. That eight grand cushioned me, so I could sit in an easy chair.

When the strike ended, the Redskins kept eking out victories. Although we lost to Dallas, we believed we would come through in the end. We finished 8–1 in the regular season and did so with some unique suckers. Cornerback Jeris White, for one, would sit in the locker room speed-reading, and we kept relying on our kicker, Mark Moseley, to bail us out of games.

Moseley was a character. He had about ten mirrors in his locker and twenty bottles of cologne. Cooke used to call him a "broad." Moseley wore tight pants, jeans that stuck up his butt like he couldn't even breath.

He was hung up on himself. Blond hair, Jheri curls. I'm not saying he was a faggot. He just liked to admire himself in the mirror.

Our team had nicknames left and right. There were the Hogs, the Smurfs, and the Fun Bunch, but our defense went just by the word *defense*. We didn't need a nickname like the Hogs, who tried to make money for themselves, and I admire that. But I just didn't want any nickname for the defense.

I think Perry Brooks tried to come up with something, he and Tony McGee. Later, Charles Mann tried to come up with some baloney nickname—the Wrecking Crew—just as he tried coming up with National Defense in 1991. But I ain't into that kind of crap. I want to do my own thing. I want to be singled out and identified for me, myself, and I.

I thought the Smurfs and the Fun Bunch were super for the team. Don't get me wrong. It was a blast playing football in Washington.

We went into the playoffs with the home field advantage and opened against Billy Simms and the Detroit Lions. They penetrated our defense early, and we were lucky when they fumbled the ball away. Then on their next possession, our Jeris White intercepted a pass and hauled ass for a score. It was a waltz, 31–7.

On the field, Billy Simms told me he'd heard I'd been hanging out at a strip joint downtown. Right on the field, after the final gun while we were shaking hands, that's what we were rapping about. A sign of things to come, huh? Billy Simms and their wide receiver, Leonard Thompson, and I were talking about hookers and prostitutes. The Lions had come into town the day before, and I guess they ran out to a strip bar I'd frequented. I guess the girls must've told them, "Oh, Dexter Manley's been in here."

The next week, we took care of Minnesota, 21–7, and then I shot my mouth about Dallas, whom we'd be playing in the NFC championship at home.

That's when I first felt there was something special about the Redskins. The week before the Dallas game, the town was in chaos. They were even doing special events up on Capitol Hill, pushing guys in wheelchairs in connection with the title game. I think Rep. Walter Fauntroy had some kind of bet with a politician from Dallas. It was bedlam.

There's just something about a big football game. I love the sight of people tailgating outside as I walk into the stadium. They're barbecuing and throwing footballs around, and I see that on my way to the locker room, and I think, Hey, they're all coming to see me.

Everybody kept blowing their horns that week in D.C., like they had nothing else better to do. There were bumper stickers reading, Honk If You Hate the Cowboys, and you'd hear car horns from D.C. to Sterling, Virginia. I was sitting at home watching all this hoopla on the news, and I thought, This is right up my alley. See, I'd gotten it all going by shooting off my mouth like Muhammad Ali.

I'd said something about kicking Dallas's butts. But I'd also bruised my thigh against the Vikings and didn't practice much during the week before this Cowboys game. Joe Gibbs got to talking trash to

Above left: Me, Andre Hewitt, who taught me my ABCs, and my brother Reginald, my clone who took some of my tests for me (left to right). *Above right*: Me at about nine years of age. *Below*: My sister Cynthia and me posing on the front steps of our home in Houston. That house was fine, but it's a wreck now.

Above: My daddy thought he was the sharpest dresser in town. Here he is out on the town with my mother. *Left*: Momma posing in her Sunday best on the front porch of our home.

Right: Stephanye and I posed for our wedding photo. *Below*: Here I am feeding baby Derrick his bottle. Wasn't I a great daddy?

Left: Glinda took this photo of Mother and me. She was battling cancer about this time. *Below*: My sister Cynthia, who sacrificed so much to take care of our mother.

Above: My best friend Gerald Franklin, me, Cedric (I can't remember his last name—it's been a while), and Danny Johnson (left to right) ham it up on the sidelines at a high school game. *Right*: Al Dotson, Harold Bailey, me, and John Corker (left to right) chilling at Oklahoma State. They called me "Hollywood" there.

Name	MANLEY, DEXTER KEITH
Social Security Number	460-02-4682
Birth	February 2, 1959
Parent or Guardian	Jelleen Manley
Entered	August 29, 1977
Last School	Jack Yates High School Houston, Texas

GRADING SYSTEM

A Superior
B Good
C Adequate
D Minimum Passing
F Failure

I Incomplete
P Passing
W Withdrawn Passing
N Withdrawn Failing

DEGREES CONFERRED

ISSUED TO STUDENT.

233121 MANLEY DEXTER KEIT FA 1977

SPECIAL TOPICS	BUSAD	2010 03	A
ECON OF SOCIAL ISSUES	ECON	1113 03	D
INTER FOOTBALL	LEIS	1131 01	A
ARCHERY & RIFLERY	LEIS	1312 02	C
WEIGHT TRAINING	LEIS	1352 02	C
COACHING WRESTLING	PE	3822 02	A

233121 MANLEY DEXTER KEIT SP 1978

INTER FOOTBALL	ATHL	1131 01	A
FRESHMEN COMP	ENGL	1113 03	X
AMER HIST 1492 TO 1865	HIST	2483 03	F
INTRO TO SOC	SOC	1113 03	D
MAN AND SOCIETY	UNIV	2223 03	B

233121 MANLEY DEXTER SUM 1978 EXT

HPELS WORKSHOPS	HPELS	3010 02	C

CORRESPONDENCE August 25, 1978

Swimming Pool Management	HPELS	3010 2	D

THE FOLLOWING COURSES WERE EARNED AT SOUTHWESTERN COLLEGE, OKLAHOMA CITY, OKLAHOMA, SS 1978:

Denominational Survey	REL	---- 3	A
Total Semester Hours		3	

CORRESPONDENCE August 30, 1978

Metric System	MATH	4910 1	F

233121 MANLEY DEXTER KEIT FA 1978

EDUC & VOCATION ORIENT	A&S	1111 01	F
INTER FOOTBALL	ATHL	1131 01	A
BIOLOGICAL SCIENCES I	BISC	1114 04	F
INTRO TO REC & LEISURE	LEIS	2411 03	D
SOCIAL RECREATION	LEIS	2422 02	BX
INTRODUCTORY PSYCHOL	PSYCH	1113 03	D

233121 MANLEY DEXTER KEIT SP 1979

ECON OF SOCIAL ISSUES	ECON	1113 03	A
GENERAL GEOLOGY	GEOL	1014 04	D
CARE & PREV OF ATH INJ	HLTH	2533 03	C
INTRO TO THE HUMANIT	HUMAN	1013 03	F
BEGINNING GOLF	LEIS	1232 02	X
LEADERSHIP	MILSC	1211 01	A

233121 MANLEY DEXTER KEIT SP 1979 EXT

HPELS WORKSHOPS	HPELS	3010 01	B

CORRESPONDENCE August 17, 1979

Directed Study R.O.T.C.	UNIV	3110 3	B

233121 MANLEY DEXTER KEIT FA 1979

INTER FOOTBALL	ATHL	1131 01	A
INTRO TO ECON ANAL	ECON	2123 03	F
PHYSICAL GEOGRAPHY	GEOG	1114 04	W
AMER HIST 1492-1865	HIST	1483 03	D
BEG TENNIS & RACKETBAL	LEIS	1242 02	C
BOWLING	LEIS	1322 02	C

233121 MANLEY DEXTER KEIT SP 1980

INTER FOOTBALL	ATHL	1131 01	A
BASIC BUSINESS LAW	BUSL	3213 03	C
INTRO TO ECON ANAL	ECON	2123 03	D
LABOR PROBLEMS	ECON	3513 03	D
MARKETING	MKTG	3213 03	F
SOC OF AMER FAMILY	SOC	3723 03	BX

233121 MANLEY DEXTER K SP 1980 EXT

HPELS WORKSHOPS	HPELS	3010 01	C

233121 MANLEY DEXTER KEIT SUM 1980

ORGANIZATIONAL COMMUN	GENAD	3223 03	X
VOICE & SPEECH IMPROVE	SPATH	1713 03	D

THE FOLLOWING COURSE WAS EARNED AT OKLAHOMA CITY SOUTHWESTERN COLLEGE, OKLAHOMA CITY, OKLAHOMA, SUMMER 1980:

Church Bus Mgmt 11	GENAD	---- 3	A
Total Semester Hours		3	

233121 MANLEY DEXTER KEIT FA 1980

INTER FOOTBALL	ATHL	1131 01	A
LEGAL POLICY SYSTEMS	BUSAD	4513 03	B
GEOG OF MUSIC	GEOG	4223 03	X
MARKETING	MKTG	3213 03	C
PRIN OFFICE MANAGEMENT	OFFMG	4103 03	D
COACHING BASKETBALL	PE	4852 02	I

233121 MANLEY DEXTER KEIT SP 1981

MANAGEMENT	MGNT	3013 03	F
INTRO SOCIAL PSYCH	PSYCH	3743 03	F

Above: Check out my easy courses. This is my official college transcript. *Left*: A promotional photograph of me at Oklahoma State.

Above: In the Redskins locker room with defensive coordinator Richie Pettibon, Angelo Snipes, Charles Mann, me, and Steve Hamilton (left to right). Little Dexter thinks that game ball would look good in his room. (Nate Fine Photo) *Below*: Hey, folks, that's money on the ground! A sack was worth $2,000 in my incentive clause.

Above: My imitation of Joe Willie Namath at the Super Bowl in January 1983. I said I'd be MVP, too. *Below*: With Redskins teammates Virgil Say, Mark May, and Joe Theismann (left to right) on a team flight. I hated take-offs, and I'd sweat like a dog every trip. (Nate Fine Photo)

me, telling me I had to play now because I'd mouthed off and Todd Liebenstein would take my place if I didn't, and he didn't deserve to take a beating I'd instigated. It was Gibbs's way to get me to play hurt, but I told him, "Don't worry, I'll be there."

How had I mouthed off? I just said I was going to pancake Danny White, their quarterback. It was exciting, man. Nobody really thought we could whup the Cowboys in 1982. They were one of the most talented teams, while we were just eleven guys squeaking by. Art Monk was hurt, and we had Charlie Brown and Alvin Garrett, that little monkey, at wide receiver, and just me on defense. Matt Mendenhall was opposite me at the other end. Matt Mendenhall? Mark Murphy was in the secondary. Murphy was a good hitter, but he had big feet and was slow as a caterpillar.

I mean, who'd we have on defense? Rich Milot? I thought he always seemed bitter at life. Maybe he was insecure. In 1986 we played San Diego, and somebody, Gary Anderson, I think, threw a shuffle move on Milot and faked him to his knees. Seeing this happen, we were embarrassed for Milot.

Milot and I always had a running argument. We never saw things the same way. I'd be talking noise on the field, telling the other team, "Run the ball over here!" Milot was the linebacker on my side, but he wasn't making a single damn play! He'd order me to zip my lip, and I'd tell him to go straight to hell. Right on the field.

So, how were we gonna beat Dallas?

Well, I laid out Danny White, which was a start. The play we had called on defense was a "Tex." Both ends run a game. The tackles hit up inside and run outside, and the ends loop inside. The other end, Tony McGee, was in front of me, and I bumped him accidentally. It could've been Tony's free sack, but that's football. So I ran into Tony, and Danny White was there for me.

I shot that gap and cut Danny White's lights out. I hit his off switch.

Actually, it wasn't a big steamroll hit. Everyone thinks that was my biggest lick of all time, but I disagree. I preferred the Bert Jones KO my rookie year, and I decked Phil Simms big time my rookie season, too, injuring his shoulder so badly he needed surgery.

What I really liked about the Danny White sack was standing over him with my fist up in the air like National League umpire Doug Harvey. I was like, "He's out!"

That sucker was laid out on the ground, fingers all stiff, like he was about to have a seizure. I loved it, man. Every time I see that hit on a highlight reel, I think of those boys on the Miami Dolphins for some reason—A. J. Duhe and all them.

Why? Before we played the Dolphins in the Super Bowl the next week, A. J. Duhe and I both made a magazine cover, and my picture showed me standing over Danny White.

Late in the Cowboys game, I made one more huge play. We led by only a touchdown, 24–17, and we were so nervous we had ants in our pants. You just never knew if you'd put away the Cowboys. Although I knocked Danny White out of the game, they could still score in an irregular heartbeat. You had to kick them while they're down, which is what I attempted to do.

Not me or anyone else had heard of White's replacement, Gary Hogeboom, but he still had the nimble receivers—Drew Pearson, Butch Johnson, and so on. They still were matriculating the ball, to borrow a phrase from Hank Stram.

But Donovan came out to block me late in the game, and I side-stepped him somehow and had a clear path to the Hogeboom boy. I leaped and batted the ball, and Darryl Grant picked the wounded duck out of the air and scored. He made the cover of *Sports Illustrated,* thanks to me. It was the biggest play of the game, and we were Super Bowl bound, boy.

In postgame interviews, CBS had Grant and me on. Brent Musburger asked me about the clinching play, and I said, "I don't know that quarterback's name . . . Hoge . . . what?"

After the CBS interview, our quarterback, Joe Theismann, and I did a press conference in the cellar of RFK Stadium. It was the first time I was at a press conference with Joe, and I ran my mouth like a hyena. Theismann was trying to coach me, but I was just this young buck. I said, "I went for Danny White's jugular vein" and "Who is Gary Hogeboom?" It was the first time I'd done a press conference— and I was getting off on it—but Joe kept saying, "Be quiet. Watch what you say."

Joe's not one to be quiet himself.

But I didn't care. I didn't like the Cowboys, and I thought I was born to hold press conferences.

When we knelt down to pray after the game, Jimmy the Greek had his lard ass in the locker room. I almost forklifted him out of there. I was taking *everything* personal. The Greek had dogged us the whole week, saying Dallas would be victorious. I wanted to soccer-style kick him out of the locker room, but Joe Theismann said cool it.

I wanted to be like Joe in many ways. As a rookie, I'd seen he was more popular than one of "Charlie's Angels" and a good player. I liked what I saw—an arrogant and controversial guy—and I admired that. He was dressed to kill and a Republican. I wanted to imitate him.

During my rookie year, once Tammy and I were driving anonymously out of RFK Stadium, when we saw Joe flagged down at a red light by fans. I told Tammy, "That's what I want."

Hell, when it was all over, I was three times bigger than Theismann.

Joe always used to read *People* magazine before a game. We'd all be hyperventilating, and Joe'd be stretched out on the floor reading the gossip. He was looking for his own name in there.

Anyway, when we whupped Dallas and earned the right to go to the Super Bowl, Joe could only control me so much. I cut loose. The week before we played Miami, I guaranteed we'd win and predicted I'd be MVP.

There's no way Joe Gibbs would have tolerated such a thing before the Redskins' Super Bowl XXVI victory over Buffalo in January 1992. In 1991 Gibbs had a bunch of his religious robot clones who said all the right things, but in 1982 Gibbs was just out of the blocks as a head coach and had just a smidgen of control. I guess Joe Namath was on my mind the week before the 1982 Super Bowl.

I'd always been an admirer of Namath's. I was a show-stopping athlete, as he'd been, and I sincerely thought nobody could block me when I took the field. The week before the game, some reporter asked me what I envisioned doing on Super Sunday, and I said, "I envision myself making a couple tackles, a couple sacks, being MVP, and us winning." End of conversation.

Everybody was convinced we'd lose. They thought we'd shot our wad emotionally against Dallas. See, there was only one week between the NFC title game and the Super Bowl that year, and everyone suspected we'd be hung over. Little did they know, I *was* hung over.

We practiced at the Rams' facility, and it was just so gorgeous out in Los Angeles, where they held the Super Bowl. Darry Grant bought a case of Dom Perignon. Hell, I didn't even know what the hell Dom Perignon was. He drank it, and I might've had a sip. Knowing me, I probably got wasted off of it.

But I played as if I had a clearer head than the California sky. The Dolphins scored first to lead, 7–0, and they were marching again until I sacked David Woodley and punched the ball free. Big ole UPS courier Dave Butz took forever to recover the ball in front of the sidelines, setting up a Moseley field goal. I believe my hit turned around the ball-game.

I got very little credit for the play. NBC carried the Super Bowl, and Dick Enberg kept raving about Butz for recovering the loose ball. I videotaped the game, and they zeroed in on Dave Butz after the play. I was not even acknowledged. When I watched the game later on tape, I said, "What about me? This is bull!"

It was as if Butz had caused the fumble, too. My name wasn't called nor was my head shot shown to my momma on NBC. That was the biggest downer about that Super Bowl, though I guess Butz got the attention because he was a senior guy. Hell, he was so cotton-pickin' slow, the ball almost rolled out of bounds before he got his lard ass there.

It took us a while to get going that game. Fulton Walker returned a kickoff ninety-something yards for a touchdown, but, even so, Wood-ley hardly completed a pass in the second half. To be honest, the best defensive play was turned in by Theismann. One of his passes got batted, and Kim Bokamper was gonna swoop in, intercept, and score, but Theismann yanked the ball out of that boy's arms. John Riggins may have run forty-two yards for the winning touchdown and received MVP for his effort, but the largest play of the 27–17 victory, in my book, was Theismann's Night Train Lane impersonation.

About an hour after the game, Riggins and all them Hogs were boozing and drunk on their floor at the hotel. Our center, Jeff Bostic, started smart-mouthing me. He said, "You didn't have a chance for MVP. The Hogs brought you here."

I said, "If Riggins doesn't win it, who wins it? Me."

In fact, during the week of the game, Bostic and Butz were making smart-ass remarks about my MVP prediction. Why? Probably because they thought I thought I was better than them. Well, I was.

Listen, you find a football player who doesn't show arrogance, and something's wrong with him. I had a stellar game that day—a sack and caused a fumble. If Riggins hadn't broken that run, let me just say I was an MVP candidate. Theismann wasn't doing squat, other than playing his version of defense. Charlie Brown had one big catch in the end zone. But MVPs make a lot of plays, and I made them.

The next day, CBS wanted Joe Jacoby and me on their Mon-day "Good Morning Show," which aired at 7:00 A.M. eastern time, 4:00 A.M. Pacific. They chauffeured us before dawn to the CBS building in Orange County, put us on an elevator to the roof, and then hauled us in a helicopter to downtown Burbank for the show. I thought, This is it, man.

This was the first time I felt like, This is glamour. It was three or three-thirty in the morning, and it was so peaceful over the city. I mean, to fly in my first helicopter ride over Hollywood at three or four in the morning? That's why it was my favorite Super Bowl.

I was just pissed that Jacoby was with me.

When I returned from CBS, it was like five in the morning. I laid down for a couple hours, then got my luggage together. We all flew home to Ronald Reagan.

I mean—literally—President and Mrs. Reagan met our team plane at Dulles, along with Mayor Marion Barry and other dignitaries. The Reagans were standing out there, but I was oblivious, man. The first lady stuck her hand out toward me, and I didn't even acknowledge her. I just shook the president's hand and carried on. Glinda thought that was real rude of me, but I didn't do it on purpose.

But I was thinking like, Ah, the president is just jumping on the bandwagon. He and Mrs. Reagan would never come to a game at RFK.

By the way, when it was all over, Cooke handed me a W-2 form for the eight grand.

AN IDLE THOUGHT

John Riggins was the MVPee of that Super Bowl, all right.

That's because Riggins was famous for peeing in hotel lobbies around the NFL.

In San Diego, before a Monday night game in 1983, it's my understanding Riggins was peeing in the hotel lobby while Coach Gibbs was up there giving a speech.

At least when I peed, I peed in a cup under supervision of the NFL. Riggins peed in the nearest potted plant. He definitely showed up to play on Sundays, but he did a lot of drunken stammering in between.

We were getting ready to play the 49ers in 1984, I recall, when he came into a pregame meeting drunk and lewd. He stood up in the back of the room and interrupted Gibbs. "Coach Gibbs," he babbled, "Ahhhh, you're the best coach in the league."

John was holding his Jack Daniel's in his hand, and then he got up and left. On his way out, he told Gibbs to go ahead and fine him. "Sorry," he said, "but I'm going back to the bar."

During the episode, linebacker Larry Kubin must've said something derogatory to Riggins, because Riggins told him, "Ah, shut up before I flatten you." Kubin talked a lot of trash. He was a Penn State linebacker who always tried to hit Riggins in practice.

But one day during practice Riggins pancaked Kubin back. Kubin was on scout team, and Riggins ran over his ass during the Riggo drill. I guess that's why they had flak going on between them.

Anyway, I admired John because he stood up to authority. Of course, did standing up to authority make him a real man, or did it make him a fool? I personally thought he was a hell of a dude to do that.

The rumor also was that Stretch, one of the team employees, was feeding Riggins booze on the sidelines during games. That's only a rumor, mind you. I never saw it.

You'd have to say there was a double standard with Riggins. If I drank Sandra Day O'Connor under the table, you think I wouldn't have been ostracized? Gibbs let Riggins get away with that scene in San Francisco, too.

If it had been me, the Redskins would've called in the National Guard.

CHAPTER 17
I Needed Perry Mason

WHEN YOU WIN A SUPER BOWL, PEOPLE ASSUME you're up to your earlobes in cash. The 1982 off-season wasn't even warm yet when Courrege, my former agent with the awful taste in Mercedeses, sued me for money he said I owed him. A Dallas court had the Redskins garnish $21,000 of my playoff money to pacify Courrege, although he and I later settled.

Every Redskin made $72,000 for winning that Super Bowl. I cleared about $54,000 after taxes. It's a good thing I stored that cash away, because I was getting sued more than Al Davis.

Texaco was still hounding me, and during the 1982 season, I'd also haggled with my landlord. He wouldn't give my deposit back because of the broken window from my final fight with Tammy. And he sued me for about $950.

Then, my ex-wife, Stephanye, in her version of the Texas lottery, sued me for child support.

If my drug counselors believe all this affected me in the long run, they're frickin' right. I thought everyone was out for my money, and I grew more distrusting than I'd been in childhood. I needed an escape from all these legal messes. My counselors probably believe drugs could've been that escape.

I admit I'd grown reckless with my child support checks. Tammy used to suggest I mail Derrick and Stephanye $500 a month, but I said the hell with that. I'd just send him $100 here, $200 there. And when I'd see Derrick in person, I'd spend money on him.

When Stephanye took my ass to court, Glinda testified she'd sent Stephanye money for me. The lawyer said, "All you've got to do is show me the proof that you did, like canceled checks."

Glinda said somebody broke into the house and took them. She lied to protect me. Mainly, she lied because our lawyer told her to lie.

We lost the case, and the court ordered me to fork over $6,000 in back payments, plus $800 a month until Derrick becomes eighteen. I turned to Stephanye's attorney, Ronald Tucker, and threatened, "I'm going to whip your butt." I think he peed in his pants.

Well, truth is, the lawsuit strained things between Stephanye and me. We always spoke after that, but in soured tones. Stephanye had resentment toward me, and I had resentment toward her. Here I was, a pro football player, and I didn't need anyone telling me how to take care of my kid.

Of course, I wasn't keeping my child support responsibilities, so she was right. But coming from where I came from, you knew I'd be tight. I'd hold onto my money. I guess this is my way of justifying why I hardly sent diddly, even though I knew it wasn't right.

After we went to court, I was through with Dexter. I never pressured him to help with Derrick. There was a long time—before the court case—when he did nothing for me and my son, and I never said much. But what hurt me with Dexter—and only now have we talked about it—is his wife lying on the stand.

Like I told him, I'd never prevent him from seeing Derrick because Dexter was Derrick's father, but for a while Dexter wasn't really being a father to him. There were no checks sent, zero. We were living in Houston while Dexter was in D.C., and he'd tell Derrick to come to his games in Dallas. But as a whole, he was no father.

And I resented Glinda to some degree and still do. I just don't see how a woman can lie. I thought loyalties would be there between two women. There's no way a man could get me to lie, not when it comes to taking care of a child.

Why'd I sue him? Well, he offered a paltry $150 a month before the lawsuit, after the Super Bowl XVII in January 1983. I said to myself, well, OK, Stephanye, get real. This man has no loyalties.

Then, our relationship kind of ended. I mean, he'd drive up in our driveway and blow his horn for Derrick. But he never came inside.

After that trial, it took eight years before we could really speak again. Finally at Christmas 1990, he said, "Come on, Stephanye, let's go riding." We went to visit his mother. That was the first time I felt for him. He'd been banned from the NFL and was paying for his wrongdoings. That was when he admitted he'd been wrong not to pay child support, and I guess I needed to hear that.

I hadn't seen his mother in years, and to see him in the situation he was in—banned—and the pain he was in, it was time to throw away hard feelings. But in the eight years of silent treatment, I never prevented him from seeing Derrick or argued with him in front of Derrick. And sometimes he made that darn difficult to do.

He left me with a lot of negatives to deal with when it came to Derrick. His cocaine problem, for one. When Dexter was banned in 1989, he warned me ahead of time and I was able to prepare Derrick for the blow. But his first two episodes with drugs, I was not warned and didn't have time to tell Derrick. My child still hurts about that.

In 1990 Derrick went into a new environment, a new school that was mostly white—Hodges Bend Middle School. Nobody really knew who Derrick's dad was, and we liked it that way. Derrick never admitted who his father was. If they found out, no problem. But Derrick was never one to boast about it.

So what happened? Dexter came to visit Derrick's school. I resented that. I thought it was selfish. When Dexter came there like that, he brought his excess baggage for Derrick. Dexter came out and talked to Derrick's football coaches, but Derrick had been in school eight years and not once had Dexter participated.

I heard these other kids in Derrick's school saying, "Look, there's Dexter Manley! He can't even read, and he does drugs." If I was hearing this, imagine what Derrick was hearing. ABC "Prime Time" was doing a special on Dexter at the time, and Dexter used Derrick to help his image. I don't think he was thinking of how this could affect Derrick. Derrick has to deal with that stuff to this day.

Do you know how Derrick found out about Dexter's drug problem? From a teacher. I could see Derrick was upset when I picked him up from school that day. So I said, "What's wrong?"

"My teacher tells me Daddy's in rehab for drugs."

There was a big campaign back then, Say No to Drugs, so how can you let a stranger tell your son that? I went to that teacher and said, "How dare you?" The teacher said she thought Derrick knew. He should *have* known. Dexter should've prepared his family for something like that.

Don't get me wrong. Derrick's reaped benefits from being Dexter Manley's son. Who wouldn't want their daddy to be popular and be a football player? Derrick's also been to Europe twice to see my sister, who's stationed over there.

But I had to sit Derrick down and explain the drug thing. I said, "OK, Derrick, Dexter has a problem." He'd seen his grandmother—Dexter's momma—with an alcohol problem, but I was left to explain the cocaine, something I knew little about. All I could say was, "Your daddy loves you, *and he has a problem. People will try to make it look bad, but you've got to stick by your family and love him."*

Derrick tells me how mean his classmates are. They say, "Can your dad read? Does he need coke?" Dexter doesn't have to deal with that part of Derrick's parenting, but I've felt it's partly my fault because I never gave Dexter the responsibility of explaining it to Derrick. Of course, he didn't take the responsibility, either.

Derrick will not talk his father down. Derrick's different from Dexter. Whereas Dexter's quick tempered, I don't see that in Derrick. Derrick's easygoing. But Derrick's toes and hands are exactly like Dexter's. He looks like he'll be built like a football player.

Football? Boy, Dexter and I had an argument about that, because Dexter doesn't want Derrick playing. To me, Derrick needed a male role model around him, so I've had Derrick in football since he was eight. Growing up, Derrick's been around a lot of ladies, and he needed to be around males. I thought learning to be a part of a team would help. Dexter doesn't want him breaking any bones, but I said, "You're not here! He needs to be around male coaches."

Derrick could get hurt standing on the street corner. I understand the fear of injury, but I was team mother. I went to all the games. I've sat through the cold and rain for Derrick's football. So, I'm doing it. It wasn't easy on me, but I thought Derrick needed that.

Derrick seems to like basketball better. He didn't seem to like football this year and said he wasn't going to play. But I work until about 7:30 at night, and that would leave him with five hours on his own. That's not good for a young boy, so I made him play football. Now, if I told him he couldn't play, he'd have a fit.

Derrick has always told me he loved me. After my ban in 1989, I tried petitioning back into the NFL in June or July. I had a feeling they'd turn me down, but when I finally took the phone call from my attorney, Bob Woolf, Derrick stood by me.

When I hung up, Derrick said, "What'd they say? What'd they say?"

"They said no."

Derrick said, "I still love you, Dad, I still love you."

It's hard to believe I have a fifteen-year-old son. He's close to six feet and wears boats for shoes—size twelve. I wish he'd play tennis instead of football. Tennis is for rich folks. Me, I had motivation to play football: to get my butt out of the Third Ward. My momma and daddy couldn't give me much, and I was desperate. Without football, I'd probably be pushing a basket. Society told me I was dumb, but Derrick can read, write, and multiply. I'm proud of him for that. I wish I had that.

Daddy wants me to play tennis.
I think tennis is truly boring.

It bothers me that I'm missing Derrick's childhood years. My own daddy missed mine, but that doesn't make it right for me to miss Derrick's. If Derrick turns to drugs, I'll blame myself.

An Idle Thought

After all of our grumbling over child support, I guess Stephanye had a couple of ways to get back at me. She could turn my kid against me, which would have been cruel, or she could turn my kid against the Redskins, period.

She chose number two. Every year when the Redskins played at Dallas, I'd fly Derrick from Houston to watch me whup up on Danny White.

Problem was, Derrick got off the airplane one year wearing a Cowboys shirt, a Cowboys knit cap, and Cowboys knit gloves.

I raised hell. I told Derrick, "Take that stuff off around here!"

But Stephanye didn't feel guilty:

Hell no, I didn't feel guilty. I had to buy my son's clothes—Dexter wasn't paying at the time—and I'm a Cowboys fan. So why not buy what I want?

Derrick rooted for the Redskins, so who cared if he was dressed like Tony Dorsett. Shoot, if Dexter wanted it different, he could've bought Derrick Redskins clothes. Dexter made a big stink, and so did my mother. But, hey, Derrick had those Cowboys clothes long before that game.

Derrick liked the Redskins, but why should I buy a Redskins jacket while I'm living in Texas? Why should I make the effort when his daddy plays for Washington? All Dexter had to do is go to his own locker room and get a Redskins coat for Derrick.

You know how I always used to say I hated the Cowboys, and I always talked trash about the Cowboys in the media?

Stephanye, to this day, thinks I did it to get back at her for dressing my son up like Bob Lilly.

There may be some truth to that.

CHAPTER 18

Only Mohawks Allowed

FOLLOWING THE CHILD SUPPORT SHENANIGANS, Bobby Beathard and Jack Kent Cooke spoke rap music to my ears: "Let's renegotiate."

It was the summer after our 1982 season Super Bowl victory, and, listen, it was their idea. The newspapers said I was holding the team hostage, because my statement was, "They're paying me pennies, and I want dollars." But, hey, Cooke and Beathard brought renegotiation up first, and I merely said I deserved a contract like Randy White's in Dallas.

I guess that turned it into friction.

Cooke scheduled a meeting between him and me in the summer, but my new agent after Courrege—Jim Kiles—advised me not to attend. Cooke was going to have me chauffeured from Redskin Park to his farm in Middleburg, Virginia, driven by his son John Kent Cooke (whom I called "Johnny Cakes" because he hated that nickname), but I couldn't decide whether to show up or not.

I imagined Cooke was going to have me over to the estate, give me a grand tour of the croquet course, and bribe me into accepting a deal. The morning of the meeting, I finally headed over to Redskin Park an hour late. By that time, Johnny Cakes was bye-bye. Jaybird, our equipment manager, told me that because I'd been late the meeting was off.

Pretty soon, training camp started, and Richard Bennett and Bruce Allen conspired on that USFL scheme that worked to a T.

Bennett replaced Kiles as my agent in the middle of negotiations. Kiles had wanted me to sign for $525,000 over three years, or something like that, and he swore I'd be making out like a bandit. I said, hell no. Kiles was good friends with Beathard—I thought that was a conflict of interest—so I fired him. I enjoyed firing people. In the

147

newspapers, my explanation was it wasn't in my best interest to stay with Kiles. Kiles tried suing me for slander.

As I said, me and Al Davis, baby—either suing or getting sued.

Anyway, as the negotiations carried on, I wore the red Chicago Blitz cap to freak out the Redskins. I also wore a cap with the slogan that said, Money Talk, Bullshit Walk.

The Redskins went to great lengths to keep me from the USFL. During training camp, they even sent a black scout, Dicky Daniels, to talk me into staying in Washington forever. He caught me one day in Carlisle, sitting on a bench, and he said I shouldn't consider the Blitz's offer. I knew management sent Dicky to hook me. They figured I'd listen to a black man.

"You should stay in D.C., Dexter," he urged. "The old man will always take care of you." He said the Blitz offer of $1 million for three years was too much cash for me. "That's too much money for a young guy," he explained. "What would you do with all that money?"

I lost respect for Dicky Daniels right then. And get this: Dicky then took his ass to the USFL L.A. Express as their general manager for *more money.*

I mean, I'm a young black guy trying to get ahead, and here's another black guy whom I'd respected saying I shouldn't take the Blitz's offer? Dicky returned in 1985 from the L.A. Express to become the Redskins player personnel director, and now he's Beathard's assistant GM in San Diego. But I could never look him in the eye again.

To the contrary, I sort of liked Cooke. He was ruthless, but ruthless looked good on him. I'll have to say, though, that our relationship went downhill during that '83 training camp. He'd handed me that eight grand in '82, but he can sour on you quicker than milk left out overnight.

Earlier I've recounted how Cooke, Beathard, and I met in a Dickinson College office when Cooke tried luring me with a $100,000 bribe. But I stood on my own two feet and said no, and that's when Joe Gibbs came to me to say, "You're disrespecting the grandfather." So maybe that was the beginning of the end for Cooke and me. Beathard, by the way, thinks Cooke was good to me:

*M*r. *Cooke really cared about Dexter, and he did some things for Dexter that a lot of owners wouldn't have done. But Dexter always seemed to be suspicious. I never got the impression Dexter really trusted anybody.*

When we tried to do something for Dexter, he seemed to be always wondering, Why are you really doing this?

After all I'd been through in college—with cheating coaches and Social Security scams and no daddy around—it's supposed to be easy for me to trust?

To hell with them.

I unveiled a mohawk at training camp that year. Originally I was gonna shave my entire head just for the hell of it—not for attention— and offensive tackle George Starke said, "Put it in a mohawk, Dex."

I had the balls to take him up on it.

I swear I didn't do it *for* the attention—like my drug counselors believe—but once I realized cameras even followed me to the john to get shots of the mohawk, I kept it. Darryl Grant did the haircut for me, and Charles Mann reshaved my head and kept the mohawk neat.

Will that ruin Charles's squeaky clean image today? That he contributed to Dexter Manley's mohawk?

To be honest, I didn't really hit celebrity status until that mohawk in '83 and when I started calling myself "Mr. D." Mr. T, from the *Rocky* movie, had had a mohawk and had been popular, so somebody suggested I become Mr. D. It stuck like Superglue.

The Danny White sack hadn't made me huge. The "impersonating an officer" hadn't made me huge. The *mohawk* made me huge. Go figure.

That's when I felt special. No one wanted to talk about my Super Bowl prediction anymore; they wanted to talk about my mohawk. It was an accident that worked to my benefit.

I took a lot of crap from my teammates, though. John Riggins, who had worn an ugly ole mohawk when he was with the Jets, used to call me a skunk. He said I should paint a white line on top of my head and I'd look just like Ling-Ling in the National Zoo. Both Jeff Bostic and he said that. I took it as having racial overtones.

Joe Gibbs never said a word about the mohawk. The only coach who called me Mr. D was Wayne Sevier. He'd see me coming and shout, "Mr. D!"

I felt at the time that Mr. D was my way of expressing my individuality as well as my growing up. See, I felt I had to do something to set myself apart, and this was one way. For instance, after we won the Super Bowl in January 1983, Joe Bugel told some Texas newspaper that if it weren't for Riggins and Theismann, we wouldn't be world champs. Darryl Grant's dad read that and told Darryl, and Darryl told me. Well, that bugged me because I seemed to remember a huge fumble I caused in that Super Bowl.

And that same Super Bowl year, Moseley, Riggo, and Theismann were on a *Sporting News* cover, like it was those three who led us. True, they had great years, but being a black athlete, I just felt I and some others were being taken for granted.

Look, I have nothing against a guy like Moseley, I identified with Mark. I had sympathy for him. Here's a guy who's had some personal tragedy and has had a rough life. He got cut three times before the Redskins got him. But I just felt slighted when he and Theismann and Riggins were on that cover. I was in their shadow, and I had to break out. And to be honest with you, being Mr. D and also being arrested for impersonating an officer helped me get that identity.

So in 1983 I was a different guy, and I remember Theismann throwing a housewarming party that year. He was the king of the team. You know, the guy who had the biggest salary, biggest house, and so on. I was the only guy who didn't show up at his party. That day, Mr. D (that's me) had a limo waiting for him in front of Redskin Park. I was wearing a burgundy suit and ostrich skin boots, and I had a public appearance to go to. Theismann wanted to show off his house that night, but I wasn't gonna be there.

Well, he was pissed. The next day, he said, "Hey, big shot. You're Mr. D now, so you can't come to a party. I saw you in that big limo, big shot."

He was hurt because I didn't take the time to go, although everyone else went because he was Joe Theismann. How come I didn't go? It wasn't that I didn't like Joe, but I'd grown up on my own. I was my own guy, and I didn't run with the crowd. I didn't need to be there.

It wasn't meant to be a jab at Joe. Theismann was always cool to me. I remember doing the "Redskins Sidelines" TV show my rookie season, and I had no decent suit to wear. I was poor, and a guy gave me a raggy black coat to wear. After the show, I was walking to my car with Theismann and a female friend of mine, and Joe taught me that a lady should always walk inside, toward the sidewalk. My friend was walking outside of me at the time, and Joe corrected that. I appreciated that and have never forgotten it.

See, I looked up to Joe. He was a teacher to me. My rookie season at training camp, he gave me a ride from the dorms to the field, and he said, "Dexter, you have a million-dollar smile, and you're a handsome guy. If I represented you, I could make you millions." If Joe Theismann told me that now, it wouldn't faze me, but I was so impressionable back then. I was thrilled to hear it. It was an affirmation to me. But that was 1981. By the time of his party in 1983, I didn't have to be a yes man. I could be Mr. D.

I must've enjoyed that nickname. When I signed my renegotiated contract that summer, I signed it, "Mr. D. Manley."

It was all downhill from there. I started drinking like my momma.

I felt I had a very bad year in 1983. It was because I was out on the street corners of Georgetown every other day. I had eleven sacks—I was better than eleven sacks—and I even let UPS courier Dave Butz beat me out for the team lead with eleven and one-half. I didn't get even one sack in December. It was one of my worst years ever.

But it taught me a lesson. I wasn't in shape. My teammates on defense teased me about my motorcycle stance, saying the way I'd line up, I looked as if I was using a kickstand. My stance was bent over, and I was resting some plays. It was obvious something was wrong. While 1981 and 1982 had been Siskel and Ebert thumbs up, 1983 was a thumbs down.

I was out partying too much. I was a bachelor hanging out. I was going out every other night, loitering in the streets. It took away my endurance.

On the field, I kept tripping. I'd chase a quarterback and trip over the 35-yard line. I told a doctor, "I always fall down, Doc," and he examined me. He said I was in good health. So I asked him, "Then, what's wrong? Why do I chase a play and trip like Chevy Chase?" The doctor said if I was partying all the time, that would explain it.

I partied so much in 1983 that every field was a muddy field to me. Torgy kept saying, "You're falling a lot. Keep your feet."

When Dexter was Mr. D, he didn't like practice. I was the defensive tackle right next to him—Darryl Grant—and he'd try hard only in warmups. He'd hit the sled and run 100 yards. He liked lifting weights, but he didn't like the physical beating of practice.

All this started in 1983. Charles Mann was a rookie and started getting a lot of reps for him. Dexter had shoulder and knee problems for the first time, and Charles would take his spot at times.

Dexter'd get so hyped during games, though. He paid no attention in the huddle. He'd be playing up to the crowd, and I'd get the call in the huddle, and he'd say, "World!"—that's my nickname—"What's the defense?"

He'd be standing there asking us, "What's the call? What's the call?"

And the offense would be about to snap the ball. He'd ask me right during the cadence, and I didn't have time to respond. Some team broke a few long plays on us because of that. Once a stunt was called, and he didn't hear it, and I didn't have time to tell him what it was. Somebody broke a run about 15 yards.

But Dexter was there strictly to get the quarterback. Two sacks, and he'd call it a day. If he got two sacks on the first two plays of the game, he'd take the rest of the game off.

That's what they emphasized—sacks. You may be getting blown off the line 20 yards, but if you get sacks, that's notoriety. Dexter knew that.

Being right next to him, I was playing the run, because he'd be going upfield for the sack. It just meant more tackles for me. In that regard, it worked out well between us.

I agree I was so hungover from partying that I would take game days off. I remember a muddy game against Detroit, which we won at home, 38–17. I went up against Big Don Laster, who'd been on our team the previous season. I got off early, with two and one-half sacks and should've finished with five, but I didn't do squat in the second half.

That's the only year I took games off: 1983.

I can't say I loafed in an early game against the Raiders that year. The Raiders came into RFK Stadium with their bad dude image, and I wore black cleats especially for them. With all their skull-and-crossbone stuff, it was my vision to wear black. My thoughts were that they are an intimidating team, and it was a challenge to be on the same field with them, so I wanted to do black. I wanted to show I wouldn't back down from all their mess. I mean, there were articles about getting the women and children off the streets because the Raiders were coming to town, and it bugged me.

We won, 37–35, on a Joe Washington circus catch. Tony McGee had three sacks, and I had two. Hell, I would've had a lot more, but I slipped a few times, as usual that year.

That's also the year I started wearing suits to Redskin Park, carrying a briefcase and the *Wall Street Journal* or *The Washington Post.* I'm sure my drug counselors will agree with me when I say I was trying to cover up for all my partying and my illiteracy by dressing Wall Street. It was that Boy George makeup of mine.

But I was creating an image. Basically, I was marketing myself as a business man. Mr. T wore the gold; Mr. D wore the suits and had the briefcase.

The people at Redskin Park took it all wrong. To give you an idea, Joe Theismann's wife bought him the Presidential Rolex watch for Christmas 1983, and Joe gave me all the details about it.

Since we were headed to the playoffs with the best record and scoring more points than you can in Nintendo, I bought me a Rolex, too. But, see, my watch got notoriety. There wasn't any notoriety when Joe Theismann got one, but there was a ruckus when I showed up with mine.

It was like people were thinking, How is Dexter supposed to know about a Rolex watch? Where did he get this watch from? One of the Redskins' assistant coaches asked me, "Are you hanging around the right kind of people?"

It was as if they were saying, "Who did Dexter buy this watch from?" It was a big deal among the coaches to see my watch. They were wondering, Was it a hot watch? Did I buy it on the streets?

That's how I interpreted their comments. Because I was black, I wasn't supposed to know the finer things in life, and particularly about a Rolex.

They made me feel inferior—my drug counselors might want to mark this down—like I wasn't supposed to accumulate beautiful things. See, it was OK for Joe Theismann to prance around with that Rolex, but not Dexter.

Before a preseason game in Miami a few years later—I wasn't wearing the watch—Richie Petitbon, the defensive coordinator, asked me if I still owned it. I did, but I never wore it. I had it tucked away in a safe deposit box with my Super Bowl rings.

Richie kind of inquired, "Dex, I haven't seen you wearing that watch." He and Torgy wanted to know, "Where's the watch?" To me, they were wondering if I'd sold it.

So I checked the watch out of the safe deposit box and started flashing it again just to show their asses, "Yeah, I still have it." I was trying to say to them subtly, "I'm not one of the stereotype brothers, wearing watches and then driving to some street corner to sell it."

But this was just the state of my game in 1983. No one trusted me, so I trusted no one. When I started wearing suits to Redskin Park, coaches and front office people asked me, "Are you going to a funeral? Are you going to court?" Or it was, "You look like a preacher," or "Are you getting married?"

I thought people at Redskin Park hadn't experienced the world yet. They were lacking in their education about black men. What's wrong with a black man wearing suits?

Anyway, we had three Monday night games that season, and I remember incidents from each of them.

The first was our season opener against Dallas at RFK. This was the night Howard Cosell called our wide receiver Alvin Garrett a "little monkey."

It had racial connotations, naturally, but Jack Kent Cooke wrote up an accept-Cosell's-apology speech for Alvin. Why didn't he let Alvin respond for himself? In my mind, Garrett accepted Cosell's apology because the Redskins accepted it.

The one with monkey arms was really our other wide receiver, Charlie Brown. He had long suckers and big ole hands. I'll never understand what happened to that guy. We traded him in 1985 when he seemed to be in his prime. He had a Corvette that had "All Pro" written on it, and the next thing the Redskins dealt his keister to Atlanta. He was never the same.

The second Monday night game that year was a 48–47 loss to the Packers. Both teams kept racing up and down the field, and in the closing seconds Mr. Jeans-Up-His-Butt-Moseley missed the game-winning field goal. I couldn't understand why Moseley rushed the kick. We had five seconds left on the clock, which was plenty of time, and I believe there was a time out called before he shanked it. I shouldn't talk, because we gave up 48 points on defense, although I did have five hurries that game.

What I remember particularly about that night was the locker room scene before the game. I was keyed up and woofing. I ended up having all those hurries, but I really didn't bust a grape that night, even after all of that woofing and hollering in the locker room.

I mean, I was pacing and hyperventilating in the locker room. I usually do that every game—it's just my ritual—but that night I played an extra game in the gosh darn locker room. By the time I arrived on the field, I was sucking for air like a sixty-year-old. I didn't get my second wind until the second half. It was embarrassing chasing Lynn Dickey around and not being fast enough to fall on him. I think it was the Schlitz malt liquor in me.

Actually, my pregame was always the same. I'd rub hot balm on my body. It gets you hot and irritable, a good frame of mind for football. White guys generally aren't as fired up before a game as blacks are. It's a culture thing, I guess. White guys are more conservative, whereas me, I take a game as a challenge, as a war. White guys say, "It's just a game. Let's play."

Of course, there are some exceptions, like Pete Cronan, a white guy who was our special teams nut. Cronan was bananas, the all-time worst before a game. He'd tear up the locker room, as if you were trying to put a straitjacket on him.

There are quiet black guys, too. Art Monk's quiet; Charles Mann's passive; Darrell Green's passive. The whole damn 1991 season Super Bowl champion Redskin team was quiet, but Wilber Marshall was their exception. Wilber and I were like insane men on the field. There'd be so much noise and racket between us. I'd hear the defensive calls, but I'd forget them right away. I'd be preoccupied with talking trash with Wilber, or worrying about the referees, or taunting the other coaches.

At RFK Stadium I punched more chalkboards than Albert Einstein can count, and I hurled chairs like Nolan Ryan. One time I busted a chalkboard, and the coaches had to write around the big hole I put in it. I'd crash coffeepots when it was time to go on the field. You know who I feel like when I talk about this stuff? The Joker from the *Batman* movie. That's who I acted like.

Wide receiver Ricky Sanders loved it when I'd foam at the mouth like a Doberman. Maybe the Sudafed had something to do with it, but I'd been doing that crap since high school. All my teammates got fired up watching me go psycho. Today's Redskins are lacking that emotion. Doc Walker, my former teammate, has always talked about it:

Dexter'd be singing with his earphones on, and it was an awful sounding voice. He had his ritual, and it reminded me of a pro wrestler. I never took my eyes off him. It helped me relax. He'd pace, he'd rip things up. I think he broke glass in Dallas.

Joe Washington and I watched him in 1983. The thing was, the bigger show he put on before the game, the less he'd do in it. I remember that Monday night game he's talking about. He was huffing and puffing and pacing and blowing. Me and Joe and Tony McGee, we just said, "Well, wonder how he'll be out there on the field?"

Usually, on the trip home, we'd have the stats with us, and we'd take a peek at Dexter's totals. We were convinced he literally wore himself out before a game. It's a shame NFL Films didn't sit in one of his pregame deals.

Wayne Sevier, the special teams coach, used to have me hitting the ceiling before a game:

He'd have that headset on, singing. He probably thought he was singing along quietly, but he'd be screeching. We'd say, "What the hell?" It was like two cats fighting. You could hear it all over the locker room.

We had a special teams meeting eight minutes before we'd go out on the field, and Dexter would always sit in. Pete Cronan and he would just go off. I'd give a tirade, a real emotional appeal, and Dexter loved that. He never missed our meetings, even though he didn't play special teams.

Wayne's speeches got me riled. That's why I'd be sucking on the oxygen tank even before the opening kickoff. It's something I got from John Riggins. He and I used to come out of the tunnel and head like magnets to the oxygen. I'd take a whole glass of ice and pour it in the tank. That would get me good clean air. I'm always on the tank. That's my trademark.

The other thing I'd do, as I've said, is I couldn't stand still during the national anthem. I'd be too pumped up, like a Reebok shoe. All the other guys would be lined up single file, hand over chest, and I'd be behind them pacing back and forth, steam streaming out of my nose.

When I played for Phoenix in 1990, two of the Cardinal vets—Tootie Robbins and Lance Smith—told me they used to see me sweating and kicking dirt on the field, and they'd get petrified of me. They'd say, "What's he on now?"

Anyway, there was one more Monday night game in 1983, at San Diego, and I recall Riggins peeing in the hotel lobby again, Kathy Lee Crosby showing up at our hotel for some reason, and me almost ruining myself again with another pregame woof session.

I would keep playing first quarters in the locker room. I mean, let's say we had a 1:00 P.M. game. Well, I'd usually be suited up and behaving uncivilized by 11:30 A.M., breaking chairs and acting silly. I wonder if my drug counselors say this is addictive behavior.

Before I tired myself out before this San Diego Monday night game, our strength coach D-boy—Dan Riley is his real name—collared me and said, "You have to learn to settle down. Don't exert so much energy in the locker room, because you're exhausted by kickoff."

We won the game, 27–24. Mr. Jeans-Up-His-Butt *made* the winning field goal this time.

Oh, I'm just poking fun at Moseley when I mention his jeans. But I will tell about the time Moseley was inviting a bunch of players to a Thanksgiving dinner, and he was standing at the door of the trainer's room asking a lot of white guys to come: Bostic, Mark Murphy, Bubba Tyer. You know me, I say what's on my mind, so I asked Moseley,

"Mark, you didn't invite any brothers?" He replied, "The only [blacks] will be waiting on us." I'm sure he was joking.

Honestly, we used to hear a lot about mostly white Redskin parties. We'd hear about Fourth of July parties at Russ Grimm's house, with the Hogs drinking up a storm and the Boss Hog, Joe Bugel, jumping off Russ's diving board after having a few beers himself.

I'd seen Kathy Lee when we checked in at the San Diego hotel, and I wondered, What is she doing here? Next thing I knew, I saw her and Joe Theismann having breakfast in the morning. I'm not sure if Joe was still married or not.

That night Howard Cosell told me that if I wanted to get rich, I should be controversial.

Hell, that was easy.

The 1983 season came down to a ballbuster, a late regular season game in Dallas. If we won, we'd just about clinch the NFC East and the home-field advantage through the playoffs. I'd also be able to shut up Cowboy fan Stephanye.

All season long, Riggins had worn army fatigues on road trips, so the rest of the team—attempting to be Mountain Men for the Cowboys—got on the airplane to Dallas in camouflage, too.

But I was my own man. I wore my Mr. D suit and tie.

Hell, Joe Theismann wasn't going to wear that camouflage crap, either. But 80 percent of the team wore those army fatigues down there.

Gibbs did not like it. If we'd have gone down there and gotten our butt kicked, how would that have looked?

We ended up stomping them, though, 31–10. As you can imagine, we were on our path to the Super Bowl.

But the Super Bowl in Tampa against the Raiders was disgusting. First, we didn't even stay at a Marriott. We stayed at a lousy Holiday Inn. The Raiders stayed at a Hilton, which was three times better than a Holiday Inn.

The week before the Super Bowl, I didn't make any Muhammad Ali predictions. I just said their star running back, Marcus Allen, was a "broad." I said he "wore a skirt."

Hell, Marcus Allen ended up gaining 200 yards on us.

I said Marcus was a "broad" and that "he probably won't even show up." I said he was one guy I didn't have respect for because he tried to avoid contact. So that mother came out and got 200 yards and beat us, 38–9. He had a 79-yard run—Charles Mann had replaced me for that particular play. Since then Marcus has said my comments fired up the Raiders.

Gibbs scolded me for talking like that. Joe Gibbs thought he was my daddy. He had a fit.

It's not that Gibbs gets angry or anything. He'll just make a comment with his teeth clenched. You all see this born-again, humble guy on TV, but you should see him with his upper teeth showing.

The guy Gibbs should've been pissed at was Theismann, who gave the game away when he threw an interception for a touchdown with twelve seconds left in the first half. It was that infamous "Rocket Screen" play to Joe Washington, and Joe put the ball in Jack Squirek's lap. I believe that play alone may have driven me to drugs. Mark that down, counselors.

I played out of my mind that day, screaming for Tom Flores—the Raiders' coach—to run the ball at me. But Darryl Grant got angry and started yelling, "Shut up! You ain't making no god-dang plays, so don't tell 'em to run the ball over here. If you're gonna tell 'em to run it here, make a frickin' tackle."

We got in each other's face, and Rich Milot had to get in between us. Darryl and I almost fought on the field.

Grant actually got a sack in the fourth quarter. I caused two holding penalties on Bruce Davis. I kept telling the Raiders to run it at me, and they did. Despite what World said, they were not accumulating yards on my side. I played the best of anyone on defense. It may have been my best game all year. And as soon as they gave me a breather and put Charles Mann in for me, Marcus Allen went on that 79-yard run.

I don't know why we were so flat, but the Raiders had a curfew and we didn't. And you know how some guys on our team liked to booze, not just me. Plus, we'd won the Super Bowl the year before, and maybe our hinies got soft. We'd also routed the Rams, 51–7, in a divisional playoff game, and we believed we were unbeatable. All I know is the next morning after the Super Bowl, I was depressed and the wind was howling through that Holiday Inn. It was like a ghost town in Tampa.

I didn't catch the plane home with the rest of the team. I said, "Forget it, man." They were up early in the morning to go, and I just couldn't hack catching that flight. I split the next day.

It had been a lousy year for me. I realized I'd have to cut back on my street life and train as I did in high school when I'd run those train tracks like Kip Keino.

So I added workaholic to my alcoholic, right after the '83 season.

AN IDLE THOUGHT

Joe Theismann, working for ESPN, broadcasted my last NFL game.

My team, Tampa Bay, was hosting Minnesota in a Sunday night national TV game in 1991, and Joe bumped into me at practice the Friday before. I already knew I'd had a positive drug test and would be retiring soon. But, hell, I had to put on my Boy George makeup and give Joe some crap.

We hugged, and I said, "Joe, the last time you were here in Tampa, you threw the Super Bowl. You blew the game, Joe. How much did you get paid? How much, Joe?"

Man, I caught him so off guard.

Joe said, "I helped you win one Super Bowl. What else do you want?"

Do I know how to work a guy who has a big ego or what?

I said, "Ah, Joe, you threw that ball to that sucker right before halftime. Why, Joe? Why?"

Joe replied, "I couldn't do it all by myself," and he kind of stomped off. I think he was actually pissed.

C H A P T E R   19

Cancer Sucks

IT'S ONE THING TO LOSE A SUPER BOWL, IT'S another to hear your momma has a brain tumor the size of a superball.

It was February 1984, not long after our loss to the Raiders, when I admitted my momma to the Houston Methodist Hospital. One good thing was I knew she couldn't get booze there.

After her surgery, my sister, Cynthia, took Momma in and waited on her hand and foot. Unfortunately, that was also the downfall of my sister. It drove her to use crack.

Cynthia devoted her life to nursing Momma, and I told her, "Hey, you've got to love Momma enough to let her go. Fight for your own life. What you need to do is go get a job. Because you have a daughter, Qwindella, and a life."

I sent her $700 to help her out, and next thing she was on drugs. My sister never had done drugs, so the thing with Momma had to be the impetus for her to use.

Cynthia had been acquiring a lot of money—Social Security checks and cash from me—and had idle time. She couldn't leave Momma alone, so she turned to you know what:

My momma had a tumor in the third ventricle of the brain. She couldn't remember people's names; she just knew she was sick. When she was in Louisiana, she had diabetes, but she didn't want anyone to care for her. She'd say, "I just want to die. And when I die, bury me next to Carl."

After surgery, doctors suggested sending her to a nursing home. I couldn't allow it. The doctor said her illness meant constant supervision and she'd get that in a nursing home, but I refused. She would have to be in my care.

It was far from easy. I lost nineteen pounds in one week. The doctors were actually called to check on me. I slept about four hours a day. Momma had to be turned constantly in her bed, about once every hour or half an hour. She was like an infant. She couldn't talk or move. She'd gained weight from the diabetes and was over about 200 pounds. I'd try to roll her over and fail. If she soiled the bed, I couldn't lift her out of it, and I constantly had to get new linens. The hospital lent me a lift machine, and they eventually donated it.

I couldn't leave the house. My whole life changed. I had no social life, and I was only about twenty-seven years old. But she had been there for us when we were young, so . . .

With her diabetes, she'd have mood swings and give everybody fits. She was a very proud lady, and if the nurse wanted to check her bandages, Momma didn't want anyone looking. "My daughter's going to do it," she'd say. The nurse took so much abuse from my mother she quit.

The therapists would try working with her, too, but Momma'd say, "I'm too tired." I'd tell her, "Momma, the therapists are here," and she'd pull the covers over her head.

Eventually she got to the point where she could scribble again. It was like when you're in first grade, first learning how to write. Her speech got a lot better, too, and she finally was able to walk, so she got out of her wheelchair.

When she'd been in her wheelchair, my apartment doorways were too small for her to pass through, and I had to move into a house. Thankfully, Dexter helped.

Then the cancer recurred. She was in and out of that hospital for the rest of her life.

For years, I didn't get a break and I developed a problem. I'm trying to take care of it.

I bought Cynthia a Honda Civic in 1986, and she sold it for drugs. Glinda gave Cynthia her lady's Super Bowl ring in 1987, and Cynthia pawned that for drugs.

You don't think that Glinda and I were upset when she sold that ring? I do understand the strain of having to nurse Momma, and I still love my sister, but at the same time, I get mad at her for getting on drugs. I had the loot to use drugs, but she didn't have the money.

Her getting hooked means she'll use her last dime to buy drugs. For drugs, she'll let the utilities people turn off the lights and the water in her house.

AN IDLE THOUGHT

I wish today my momma could hear the way my seven-year-old son, Dexter, prays.

The morning before one of my 1991 games against Green Bay, I asked Little Dexter over the phone to pray I would get two sacks.

"If you don't want to pray for two sacks, you don't have to," I said. "No, I want to," Little Dexter replied.

"OK."

"Close your eyes, Daddy."

"OK."

"Dear Lord . . . Dear Lord . . . Dear Lord . . . Daddy, you're supposed to repeat Dear Lord after me."

"No, you just go ahead," I urged.

"Dear Lord . . . Please let Daddy have a great game and win . . . and get him three sacks or two sacks . . . and no cuts on his face and no hurts . . . and let him get up strong and tackle those people . . . and have fun . . . and a great win . . . in Jesus' name . . . Amen."

CHAPTER 20

Michael Jackson, Prince, and Me

In 1984 I FIGURED IT WAS TIME TO GIVE GLINDA a ring for wedding purposes. Of course, she says she had to bribe it out of me:

Dexter's mother was sick at the time, and Dexter had to fly to Houston to see what was up. They still hadn't done the brain surgery.

It was after the Super Bowl loss to the Raiders. Dexter was working out every day, but he was still partying. He didn't even come home one night, and I went to work pissed off. I was afraid he was doing one of two things: cheating on me or getting wasted.

Well, he must've called me twenty times that day at my office, but I wasn't taking his calls. I told my secretary, "Tell him I'm out in the field."

My secretary said, "Oh, Glinda, he sounds pathetic. You've got to take his call." She bought his act.

He kept calling. She kept saying, "Please take it," and I kept saying, "No."

Finally, he told my secretary, "Tell her I'm going to Houston, and I need someone to take me to the airport."

I said, "No!" again. But I thought about it and felt I'd hate myself if I didn't see him before he left. So I went home to get him but entered the house mean, saying, "If you're going to Houston, you might as well take all your clothes and stay."

I'm thinking it's goodbye and good riddance for our relationship, and then I see his long arm holding a velvet box. He said later it was the only way to get back in my good graces. Of course, everything I ever got from Dexter was after something made him feel guilty. That was his first gift, the engagement ring.

I fell in love with him again. Of course, he lied to me about where he'd been, but I chose to believe it.

We were going through some shaky times up until then. He was staying out all night, and my first inclination was he was screwing women. I was more angry at that than the possibility of drugs. Because if he was messing around with cocaine—he says he was drinking—it was at a time when they weren't sure cocaine was addictive. He could still play, so I was more worried about him being out with other women. When he first started staying out all night, I threatened that he had to move out, because he was living in my apartment.

One such time, when it was raining, I threw his clothes over the balcony. Why his clothes? He throws conniption fits if you mess with his clothes. He was so furious he kicked out the front door, which was metal. Then he ordered, "You get down there and pick up every last one of my clothes." And I did.

I was scared. I was no fool. I had to. I had never seen him like that. And then I thought, Damn, he went off on Tammy because of the clothes.

I told him, "You love your clothes more than anything else." He's still pretty much like that. He loves his things.

Anyway, we'd been living together two and one-half years before we finally tied the knot. It was January, after the Raiders Super Bowl—I already had the engagement ring—and I asked when were we getting married. He kept repeating, "I'm going to marry you. I'm going to marry you. Don't worry about it."

Then I issued an ultimatum: "OK, Dexter, look. I've been with you for two and a half years. I'll give you a year to marry me. If you're not married to me in a one year, we'll have to break up."

I knew Dexter was dependent on me. I figured, He isn't going to let me go, but he's really scared of marriage.

So he said, "OK, I've got a year? Until the end of the year? OK. December 31!"

We agreed on a Hawaiian wedding on December 31, 1984, provided there was no playoff game that day.

Not long after, my father came to visit us in Virginia, and we went up to New York on a May afternoon. I was eating everything in sight that day. Every corner we passed, I had to have a hot dog or a pretzel. My daddy asked Dexter, "Does she eat like this all the time?"

Later that week I got tested because I got to thinking I might be pregnant. I was right. The baby was due in February 1985. I told Dexter, "I'm not going to be too pretty a bride at a December 31 wedding. I'm going to be humongous. I'll be eight months pregnant."

Dexter said, "Oh no, It'll be fine. It'll be fine." That boy did not want to move the wedding date up. "Everyone knows I love you and I'm not marrying you for the baby."

In July, on the eve of training camp, I told him I wasn't waiting until New Year's Eve. "Dexter," I said, "I'm getting married before I start showing."

He finally said, "Pick a date."

I said, "OK, when you get out of training camp. September 1."

We looked at the 1984 Redskins schedule, and he said, "Oh, that's the day before our season opener against Miami. OK, we'll do it then."

So we got married. After the reception, everybody came to our house for an after-party, so we couldn't consummate it. Dexter had to go to the team hotel that night because of the game the next day, so he said, "Shhhh, come on upstairs real quick."

Everybody else was downstairs or roaming through the house, and we locked the door for a quickie.

Dexter said, "Now, we're married."

Yeah, I spent my wedding night at the team hotel with the boys, and then I spent the next day with a crick in my neck as Dan Marino's passes blurred by me. The Dolphins tore us up, 35–17.

I still was too inconsistent in 1984, although I improved to thirteen and one-half sacks. I had three sacks against Detroit one game, but there were six other games where I had none.

Coming into the season, I buried Mr. D once and for all. I got rid of the nickname. I felt keeping it would remind me too much of my bad year in '83.

Of course, I still wore my suits and carried the *Wall Street Journal*. And I was still grandiose. My best quote of the season was, "The three most famous people in the country are Michael Jackson, Prince, and me."

I wore Blues Brothers glasses during noncontact drills. I thought it would add comic relief, and it did, especially when I immediately tripped over a dummy bag.

After two straight Super Bowl appearances, we started the season, 0–2. In the second game, a Monday nighter at San Francisco, we were trailing, 37–31, real late in the contest, and we needed to get the ball back for our offense. We held on third down, meaning we'd get one last shot for Joe Theismann. But the dumb referee called a 15-yard penalty on *me* for kicking a 49er running back. The 49ers then ran out the clock:

We stop Montana, and Dexter kicks Wendell Tyler in the head! We force fourth down, and Dexter gets a personal foul! Dexter told me, "Darryl, I didn't do anything." Shoot, the coaches went nuts. I said, "Wow, Dexter, that was dumb." I guess he was frustrated he hadn't gotten a sack.

The coaches did not get angry at me, no matter what Darryl Grant says. Besides, I thought it was Roger Craig I kicked, not Wendell Tyler.

Earlier in that game, I got into it with one of the 49ers tackles, beefy Bubba Paris. My childhood buddy, Gerald Franklin, had just finished playing for the Oakland Invaders of the USFL and was at the game that night, and he loves this story so much. Bubba had been holding and chopping me, and cutting my legs out is one thing I don't appreciate. I'm a speed guy, and my legs are my money.

So I started cursing, and Bubba said, "Why are you using all this profanity? Do you believe in God, Dexter?"

I answered, "Don't bring God into this ass-whupping."

Anyway, I think I would've had a much better season if I hadn't been cheap-shotted by Steve Wright of the Indianapolis Colts in the sixth game of the year and had my ankle injured. He now plays for the Raiders, and I saw him get a slew of holding calls in last year's playoff game against Kansas City. It serves him right.

Wright had been the right tackle that day against Charles Mann, and Chris Hinton had been the left tackle against me. On one play, though, I stuffed Hinton in the hole, and Grant fell on his leg and injured him. So Hinton had to leave the game, and Wright moved over to Hinton's side to block me. Charles Mann had been kicking Wright's ass the whole day, so I said to Wright, "I'll kick your ass, too."

Well, they ran a dash play—with the quarterback sprinting out— and Wright peeled back and then dove on my ankles. I learned right then: Don't talk to offensive tackles.

I was crawling to the sideline, screaming to my replacement Perry Brooks, "Get him, Perry! Get him, Perry!" I kept hollering, "You sorry cheapshotting SOB!"

The season ended with us collapsing to another SOB, Mike Ditka, in the playoffs. The Bears beat us at RFK, 23–19, and I couldn't see how. Ditka isn't very imaginative. It's usually run the ball right, run the ball left, run the ball up the middle, run the ball to no daylight whatsoever.

Personally, I've always questioned *his* IQ.

An Idle Thought

I'm not sure if Perry Brooks retaliated on Steve Wright or not, but you hope your teammates will come to your defense in a situation like that. I learned over the years that some of my Redskin teammates were punks.

We were playing in Seattle in 1983, and Doc Walker—a black guy who was a charter member of the Hogs—found himself in a scuffle. Not one of the other Hogs came to help. You'd think they'd at least leap in there or point a finger, but they just trudged back to the huddle. That homeboy was down there fighting by himself.

Now, let somebody fight one of the white Hogs? Everybody's in on it. Even the blacks. But I'll never forget that day in Seattle. It's like, Wait a minute. Why would nobody go to Rick Walker's aid? This was supposed to be a team. But I understand. I clearly understand.

Maybe offensive players are more subdued. It seems like defensive players have a different mentality when it comes to fights. I got into a tussle with Daryle Smith of the Dallas Cowboys in 1988, and Neal Olkewicz—a white guy—came charging in there for me. On the other hand, after Olky dropped somebody for me, Danny White sneaked in there and stoned Olky from the blind side.

Hey, the Cowboys offensive players stuck up for each other.

CHAPTER 21

Things Didn't
Go Better with Coke

I THOUGHT IT WAS NEAT THAT JOHN RIGGINS did Ford truck commercials.

Maybe that's why in 1985 I took my Ford truck out for a serious test drive.

On Wednesday night, October 30, with our record 4–4, I went out on a street corner and raised hell. Remember how my daddy wanted me up by 8:00 A.M.? That night, my head hadn't even hit the pillow by 8 A.M.

What slipped my mind was practice.

I showed two hours late to Redskin Park with a glass of vodka in my palm. The team had broken out of a meeting and was dressing for practice when I pulled my truck through a side gate and parked next to the weight room. I stumbled through the locker room door to take a leak. Our defensive coordinator, Richie Petitbon, was taking a leak, too, and he would not talk to me or even eye me. He seemed so petrified of me, I'm amazed he could even pee.

I crashed all the combs, shavers, and shaving cream off the counter. I raked 'em off with my forearm. I don't know what I was mumbling, but I was buzzed and slamming things around. One of our linebackers, Mel Kaufman, was also scared to say a word to me. He and my other teammates saw this look in my eyes, and, basically, it was real sad. This is not funny at all. This is sad.

Then I bolted for my truck, with Dave Butz—the UPS courier—and Mark Moseley—Mr. Jeans-Up-His-Butt—trying to catch me from behind. I beat them in the 40-yard dash to my Bronco and locked the door because they would've held me down and taken my keys. They didn't want me driving.

168

Butz kept hollering for our trainer, Bubba Tyer. He was going, "Bubba! Bubba! Dexter's gone crazy."

Butz and Moseley were pounding on the window, and I was going, "Hee, hee, hee." I revved the truck up, did a doughnut, and shot out of the gate to make a left turn onto Redskin Drive.

Hell if I saw an eighteen-wheeler tractor-trailer headed my way.

It was *zoooooom! booooom!* We crashed right in front of Redskin Park. The front end of my truck was crushed in like a soda pop can. If that sucker had rammed me a little further in front, I'd have been with Reginald.

Butz and Moseley saw the whole thing, and Bubba and all of them came sprinting as if I were dead. Joe Gibbs came running out, too, as I recall. I still had my glass in my hand, and they convinced me to come in to Bubba's back training room.

I put on my Boy George makeup. I conned them. I was lying down on the training table telling Gibbs the Redskins didn't like black ballplayers and they treated us all wrong. I said, "Nobody cares about me. Nobody loves me."

I brought my momma into it, saying, "Momma's sick, and I'm depressed and nobody loves me here." It was true, she *was* sick, but I admit I used her. It was just another way to manipulate the Redskins. I had to cover my ass.

I started pumping them full of this poor-me stuff, and Gibbs grew sympathetic. Whether he bit for the whole story, I don't know, but he said, "Dexter, just go and get some sleep. We'll get you a room at the Dulles Marriott."

Doc Walker found me a new shirt. I splashed water on my face and cleaned up. By that time, the police had showed up, and I passed a field sobriety test. How? It was a black police officer. Everyone thought the Redskins fixed it up real good with the police.

Bobby Mitchell, from our front office, then brought me to the Marriott:

Before I took Dexter to the Marriott, I had a talk with the police. The main thing I tried to do was make sure they didn't arrest him. They tested him for alcohol, and he was up there pretty good. They allowed me to get him away from there.

Dexter has a tendency to come down hard on himself and on everybody else when things don't go well. At that particular time, the thing to do was save him from himself.

I got him to the Marriott, and he was skittish. He was immediately concerned what might happen to him and concerned about his truck. It shook him up, and he was worried what people would think later. That was pretty much Dex. He'd come to me and go, "What'd they say? What'd they think?"

Anyway, I was under the impression it was alcohol, and the police were under the same impression.

I had just started to experiment with cocaine and the night of October 30, I'd done just a little. It was more alcohol in me than anything else.

One of my teammates, Vernon Dean, later said he checked my truck for drugs. If I'd had any in there, he would have cleared it out for me. But I didn't have any drug paraphernalia in there.

Our special teams coach, Wayne Sevier, thinks some of my teammates may have helped me make it look like an alcohol-only episode. I certainly wasn't going to admit to management I'd been using coke:

I was looking out a window when it happened. From what I understand, Dexter poured alcohol on himself to make it seem he'd only been drinking. I don't know if he did it or if other players did it, but he reeked of alcohol.

He'd wanted it seen as an alcohol problem. I'm not making excuses for us coaches, but unless a player's play falls off, no one suspects drugs.

I doubt the organization was suspicious of my drug use in 1985. I never got the feeling I was being watched. Never. Maybe that's because I was silly. People are *always* watching, but when you're on drugs, you don't have any perception of what people are doing. You're not in reality.

The first time I saw coke was in 1981—my rookie year—when we played the Rams in Anaheim. One of our veteran players on the Redskins had a home in Los Angeles, and we went to visit his place the day before the game. I tagged along, with Darryl Grant, and about four or five Redskins snorted right there. Darryl and I hopped in our cars and left. The veteran player didn't know we saw their stash, because they had shut the door. But Darryl and I got out of there.

The first time I really heard about drugs was from one of my teammates, Perry Brooks. Perry told me about coke, how it made sex great, and I said, "Hmmmm." I was impressionable. My drug counselors want to say my upbringing drove me to cocaine, but it's not like I was depressed or disturbed about something when Perry told me about it. I was happy as a clam when he told me about coke. I don't believe I was driven to it by a gruesome childhood.

The only thing I can say is maybe I had some lingering low self-esteem and maybe I was bored in the off-season. Maybe that's why I tried it. What else was I to do in the off-season? What was my hobby? Nothing. I couldn't read or write. So some guy told me about drugs, and I tried drugs because I wanted to. And I got hooked. That's the real deal.

So if counselors want to dissect me like a frog, I guess the low self-esteem is the factor. You can argue that people with high self-esteem do drugs—doctors, mayors, lawyers—but deep down they probably feel like trash inside like I do.

When I first tried coke, I tried it out of curiosity. I was with this girl, Diane, in Tysons Corner, Virginia. and I asked her about coke, and she smuggled me fifty dollars' worth.

All I could think of was this singer from back home in Houston, Johnny Taylor. I was sitting there with Diane, wearing slacks and no shirt and chopping up the coke, and I was reminded of Johnny Taylor. Johnny sang and used drugs and would try to steal my girlfriend in high school. He was a handsome man, and everyone admired him. I used to look up to him.

So when I used cocaine for the first time, I thought I was doing big-time Hollywood crap by using coke. I thought, "I can afford to buy coke! I've made it!"

I was drinking Asti Spumonte and sniffing coke. I knew *this* was the answer. Sex. Coke. And being the famous Dexter Manley, too? That was euphoric. My low self-esteem temporarily flew the hell out the window.

The first time you take that hit of coke, you cop an overwhelming feeling. But the second and third times, it's never the same. You keep chasing that first feeling, but it got to the point I'd do coke, and then I'd want leftovers by eating the boogers out of my nose. I don't mean to be crude, but I'm explaining the addiction.

The second time I did coke was probably three or four days later, but then I ceased. I stopped because I never envisioned myself on drugs, and I didn't appreciate what I saw in the mirror afterward. I don't know if I was addicted right away, but I know I wasn't willing to stop for good. I crawled back to it the way a heart patient wants a cigarette after open-heart surgery.

The only thing I really didn't like about coke was it made your hair hurt. Has your hair ever hurt before?

As Redskins trainer—I'm Bubba Tyer—I wasn't sure Dexter had a drug problem. At the time Dexter came up, we were just being educated on drugs. We had a player that a couple of times a year would get in a depression or whatever, and I never knew what was wrong. I always felt he had the flu because the symptoms were like having the flu. It turned out it was probably something else. When one of our great players told me about it two years after the guy left, I said, "He did what? Drugs?" I couldn't believe it. So through the seventies and eighties, we were all being educated.

You don't know those things are going on. You might suspect something, but it's hard as heck for a trainer or a coach to have a suspicion and then confront the player. If your suspicion's wrong, you may lose that guy forever. So to this day, I don't know what Dexter was up to.

The day he crashed his truck, there was no way we could tell [drugs]. I remember him coming in and Bobby Mitchell and I had him in the doctor's office. We were afraid the police were going to arrest him and take him off, and I think we were trying to calm him and settle him down. Dexter was nervous about the accident, but I couldn't really say he was intoxicated one way or the other.

I remember somebody talking about Dexter, that he had a bottle of vodka or something. I miss Dexter sometimes. He was fun to have around here. But the drug problem, when it kept popping up, I knew he wouldn't be able to survive it.

Following the crash, I wondered if my teammates knew I was coked out. They shouldn't have, because I never hung with them.

Sometimes I'd visit the house of Mark May, an offensive lineman. Mark gave a party every year, and I'd go to his house with nosebleeds. He'd lay me down in his bed and put ice under my nose. It was because I'd done coke, but he never knew.

I didn't befriend them, and they didn't befriend me. First, I thought my teammates would reject me. Second, I was doing drugs, so we didn't have much in common. I was more secretive while the other guys wanted to pound beers and sit around with the guys. That wasn't me.

So, they didn't have a clue what was going on. The closest person to me on the team, Darryl Grant, wasn't even sure:

Dexter always told me he was drinking, but as a rookie Dex couldn't hold more than one drink. Two drinks back then, and he couldn't stand up. But I didn't press the cocaine issue. I was like, "OK, what happened?" And he'd say, "I drank too much." That was that.

In 1985, there was hysteria surrounding me all the time. If it wasn't the truck crash, it was Chicago Bears players crashing into my knees.

Before our game at Soldier Field, I'd been quoted in the Chicago *Sun-Times* as saying, "We'll have to knock Walter Payton out of the game. We're going to have to do that."

Well, I don't know if that SOB Ditka ordered this or not, but tight end Emery Morehead chopped at my knees the entire day.

That crap can end a career. The Bears do it a lot even today, but you don't see them doing it to white boys. Seems like they're always doing it to brothers. They put their tight end or a receiver in motion, and he comes back and chops you. That day in Chicago, I was surgery waiting to happen.

Gibbs came out in the media after the 45–10 loss and complained about Morehead, but he also told me to shut my mouth. He said maybe they'd chopped me because of what I said about Payton. It was a chorus I'd hear from Gibbs my entire Redskins career. "Clam it, Manley."

My truck crash came about a month after the Bears game. The accident happened on a Thursday, but I played my ass off the following Sunday in Atlanta. I think I had two of my fifteen 1985 sacks that day. In fact, through 1985, I had more career sacks than any other active NFC player, even more than Lawrence Taylor.

There were some positive things happening in 1985, and I'm not talking about positive drug tests. In February Glinda and I had our first child, Dexter Manley II.

I gave him Roman numerals after his name because that sounded classier than Dexter Manley, Jr. I wanted to be classy because deep inside I felt unclassy. My drug counselors will want to read this. I figured if I couldn't be classy, maybe my kid could.

Then, the day of our Monday night season opener in Dallas, Glinda called me as I was leaving for Texas Stadium. I got her message from the front desk operator, and told the operator to tell Glinda I'd call her back from the locker room.

When I called her, she told me she was pregnant again.

Since I was in Dallas, we decided to name our second baby after the Cowboys, boy or girl. When our little girl was born, she was called Dalis Joy Manley. I know we spelled Dallas wrong, but it was on purpose. Again, Dalis looked classier than Dallas.

All I can say is it's a good thing we weren't playing in Green Bay that night or my daughter would be Green Bay Manley, or Lombardi Manley.

An Idle Thought

I guess it's not fair to say a teammate *never* came to my aid.

Glinda was pregnant—this is way back before Little Dexter and Dalis were born—and we agreed she'd get an abortion. The problem was I didn't get to the bank the night before her procedure and I had no cash on me. I didn't know how to write checks very well, and I had no ATM. Glinda needed her money that day.

The abortion was going to be in the morning, and by the time the banks opened, I'd have to be at practice. I mean, I was up a creek.

But another defensive end, Tony McGee, bailed me out. We met at McDonald's at 8:00 A.M., before we reported for 9:00 A.M. meetings, and he whipped out his wallet.

Glinda had the abortion, and I swear I paid him back the next day.

CHAPTER 22

A–B–O–U–T

I T WASN'T ONLY JOE THEISMANN'S LIFE THAT changed when he broke his leg. It may have been the most significant day of my life when Lawrence Taylor sacked Joe on a flea flicker and mangled Joe's leg in the process. L.T. put his hands over his own helmet earholes and frantically signaled for our trainer.

In the matter of a second, Theismann's career was over, and I began thinking about second grade.

I'd seen the play happen. Usually, I didn't pay much attention to our offense, but I tried to watch against the New York Giants. I wanted to see if L.T. would go off.

I was standing on the 35- or 40-yard line, and I knew it was an awful injury to Theismann by the way L.T. leaped up. I didn't know who was injured until everybody said, "It's Joe . . . It's Joe."

Reality hit me. I learned that your career can be over in a heartbeat. We didn't know the severity of the injury at first, but when the reports came in about the compound fracture, I thought, "This guy's through. Joe'll never play again."

I got so I couldn't watch the replay. It hurt me inside to watch it, but it also made me wonder, What if that was me? How could I find a job? I can't even read the directions on a bottle of cough syrup.

If only I had learned to read in second grade at Douglas Elementary, it wouldn't have battered me that way. But as Theismann was gurnied off and Jay Schroeder promptly hit Art Monk for 40 yards, I began realizing I had to go back to school.

Gee, I'm glad I could help Dexter by breaking my leg.
I always felt Dexter had a reading problem. He'd carry that Wall
Street Journal *around, but I don't know who Dexter was kidding. You'd*

175

figure it made him feel better about himself, but so what? When I was recruited out of high school, I didn't think I was very bright either. I signed a grant-in-aid to North Carolina State—though I ended up at Notre Dame— and people'd say, "Why did you sign at N.C. State?" Well, I wanted to sound smart, and I knew N.C. State was one of three schools that had a nuclear reactor. So I'd tell people I signed there because I wanted to study nuclear engineering. I wanted everyone to think I was bright, and I hid behind that.

Same thing with Dexter, and, at some point—maybe my leg was the impetus—he needed to face reality.

Three months after Joe's accident, something else motivated me to get on back to school.

It was in January 1986, and I had discreetly entered drug and alcohol rehab at the Hazelden Foundation in Center City, Minnesota. Not a single Redskin teammate, Redskin coach, or Redskin anything knew about it. They still wouldn't know about it today if I weren't writing of it in this book.

See, I checked into Hazelden to save my marriage, and I went in under an assumed name.

One of our first assignments was to complete a diary, to write down whatever was bothering us. I couldn't even spell the word *about*. Literally. I could not picture the word. That also was a real catalyst for me to go get a real education.

As I sat heartbroken over my stupid, empty diary, Redd Foxx's nephew, who was in treatment with me, scolded me. He said, "Dex, you can work on it."

I was boo-hooing and crying, I felt so sorry for myself. I was really on the pity-pot. I started reflecting back to when I was a kid. All the things I wasn't able to accomplish in school came back to me. The low self-esteem things I'd tried to banish from my mind chillingly returned. I thought, "How did I make it this far?" I felt worthless.

Here I was, twenty-seven years old, and I couldn't read, couldn't write, couldn't spell *about*.

Why? I probably was doing drugs at the time, and you know I wasn't practicing my writing.

But I'll never forget Redd Foxx's nephew. He saw the distress written all over my face and the nothing written on my paper, and he let me know I could go back to school, that there was a place somewhere, where I could get help.

I told Glinda about me not being able to spell *about* and she consoled me:

I figured he had a problem. Dexter was a celebrity guest at the Apple Blossom parade in Winchester, Virginia, once, and they were planning an autograph session. I had anxiety about the autographs on the way over because I knew how much writing it would entail.

He asked me to spell names for him the entire day. Some girl said, "Can you sign it 'To Ann'?" and he whispered to me, "Shhhh. How do you spell Ann?" I answered him out the side of my mouth, "A–N–N." That's when I assumed he had a serious reading problem. I thought it was more than him just being slow, but I never knew for sure until that day.

I mean, he could fool you. When we first started living together, he'd call me on the phone and say, "Glinda, get the newspaper. I heard there's an article on me. Read it to me." He'd act as if he needed me to read it to him because he didn't have a paper. But as I'd read, I could hear the rustling of a newspaper over the phone. He was actually fingering the words on his newspaper while I read.

I never knew he couldn't read a menu. He fooled me by ordering what other people ordered. Sometime's he'd just order what he liked to eat, and because he was Dexter Manley, the restaurant would fix him whatever he desired.

But he'd act as if he was reading the menu. He'd glance at it real fast and announce, "I know what I want! I don't need this menu."

Glinda's mother saw an ad in the newspaper for the Lab School of Washington. It specialized in adult reading classes and in learning disabilities for kids, and it was conveniently in Washington.

So I enrolled at age twenty-eight. The Lab School was a small brick place, but there always seemed to be 100 eyes on me. People would see me there and think, What the hell is *he* doing here?

When I took an evaluation test in early 1986, I tested at a second-grade reading level. That was about right, considering second grade was the last grade I flunked before entering special ed at Douglas Elementary.

Immediately, they included me in evening adult reading class. Of course, everyone knew I was a Redskin. Hell, I was the best quote on the team, so I was on the local news about every night.

One guy in my first class asked, "How can you play football if you can't read or write? How do you study the plays?"

I wanted to say, "I'm not as bad as you are," because my feelings were hurt by his comment. I felt ashamed, but my teachers told me I was ahead of most students in there. I mean, there were guys in there who were trying to spell the word *cat*. I was a *little bit* better than that.

So I just answered the guy, "Well, I just study my plays a lot."

But, still, during the first days at the Lab School, I hid and put up a wall.

I received one-on-one tutoring, but—from my former experiences—I didn't trust the teachers farther than I could throw them. Going one-on-one with them was helpful, though, because I noticed I was back to my cheating ways in the class settings.

For instance, while I was in a phonics class, I would look at another person's paper rather than try to learn it myself.

I thought, Why do I want to think about sounding out words? When I became frustrated, I automatically looked at someone else's paper. I wanted to learn, but I didn't want the humiliation that went with it.

My defense mechanism was to act up. It went back to my childhood. I don't think one of the Lab School teachers, Sara Hines, liked me one bit:

*T*he first time I saw Dexter was at night school and, yes, he was a cutup. In a group, he'd be silly, and he'd have the other students all silly. They'd be too focused on him. Here was this football player . . .

As I recall, when he first came to night school, he had three different teachers, but it didn't work. I don't know if people kept asking him for his autograph, but I sensed he was embarrassed and didn't want people knowing he was learning disabled. He was in a class with two twenty-one-year-olds, and they thought he was so cool. I couldn't handle it. Eventually, I became his private tutor. He couldn't make it to class for a while, so we also tried having a tutor go to his house.

He wanted us to hide it from the media, so I never told anyone. He'd say, "Don't you tell a soul."

He'd come in the side door because he didn't want kids asking for his autograph, and at first he pretended as if he could read. He'd say, "I can read this, but I don't feel like it. I'm tired. Let me read it on my own, not out loud."

He had to ease his way. You just don't learn it overnight. I started with him in 1986, and it took a good while.

I would rush in the back door of that school, or I'd hide. I didn't want to be seen because the kids would insist, "Why are you here?"

I'd lie, which I was skillful at. I'd say, "I'm here because I have to do a speech, and I'm here to talk to a teacher."

A couple of times, kids knocked on the door of my tutor. They slipped paper under the door for autographs. Even other teachers knocked and wanted autographs.

Sara had no choice but to tape manila paper over her door window so no one could see in.

My drug counselors probably figure this, but you think the fear of going back to school led me to drugs a little bit? Because I was facing up to a childhood ordeal, I needed an escape? Hell if I know.

It was stressful, though. I did not want it known that I was learning to read. I didn't know how people would react. I wanted no publicity.

I didn't tell a single Redskin teammate, not Grant, not Gibbs. I went on Tuesdays during the season—that was our day off—and Tuesdays and Thursdays during the off-season.

See, I was still dealing with shame. I didn't want a soul to know I was pushing thirty and coming to a brick schoolhouse with twelve-year-olds.

An Idle Thought

I'll tell you why I didn't want a soul to know I couldn't spell.

Back in college, I walked off the practice field once and had a Houston Oilers scout ask me if I'd take an intelligence test.

I naturally begged off, but since it was an NFL scout, I tried to be polite.

I said, "Uh, let me take a shower first."

This hick scout, a white man dressed in an all-white suit, said, "Don't worry about it, son. It's not difficult. Earl Campbell can't even read the darn test."

Now, here was Earl Campbell, busting his ass for the scout's team, and he's talking badly about him to another black athlete? Earl busts his ass and someone in his own organization belittles him? After all Earl Campbell had done for the Oilers?

Even if that hick scout believed Earl couldn't read, he certainly shouldn't have told me. It just made my secret safer with me.

CHAPTER 23

Hazed at Hazelden

WHILE I WAS ADDRESSING MY READING PROBLEM, I sure as hell wasn't addressing what I was putting up my nose. Although I checked into Hazelden in January 1986, I treated the program and counselors as seriously as a Redskin minicamp—I paid no attention.

It's my loss. I could've gotten off the boat in 1986, and I probably would be making a million bucks right now. But I sleepwalked through the rehab program.

I stayed thirty days and was in total denial. I was in such denial that if they'd told me the Redskins wore burgundy and gold, I would've denied *that*.

All I wanted was to keep Glinda from packing up my son, our silverware, and our TV and moving out.

Dexter was staying out all night on cocaine—this was a month after the 1985 season—and he'd always come in remorseful. I'd say, "Dexter, be strong. If you want to stop, just stop."

See I figured he could just stop because I had just stopped myself. On his birthday that year we had been using cocaine together at about 2:00 A.M. I'd taken a hit, and when I walked into the bathroom and looked in the mirror, it didn't look like me. It wasn't the girl my parents had raised. I decided not to take another hit, and I flushed his stash down the toilet.

He was mad at me for flushing it, but I was seeing the addictive side of him, and it scared me. I was able to quit that night. I had voices talking to me. One voice would say, "It's his birthday, just finish the cocaine." Then this other voice would say, "Why let Satan trick you into using cocaine?" So I flushed the coke. I had to prove to the devil that God was king.

I could've overdosed that night by trying to keep up with him. Dexter was the type who couldn't sit there and use if you didn't. He'd say, "Come on, do it with me."

But I just flat-out quit that night. I quit cigarettes, too. Later I still had an urge to use coke at work, and I'd think, Let me find this drug dealer's phone number, but it wouldn't last. You know how I quit? I literally would fuss at the devil out loud. I'd treat the devil—or this voice in my head—as a real person. I'd scream out loud in my car, "I will not use any more drugs. Get away!" It worked for me.

So I didn't realize cocaine addiction was like a disease. I thought Dexter could quit, too, if he wanted to badly enough.

He continued to stay out all night, and I began to hate him. I was pregnant with Dalis and was getting plumper, and I'd think, Oh God, he's going out because I'm not this cute little size eight he married." I was like, How dare you want to go out with another woman who looks better than me at this point? Here I am carrying your baby, and you're going out on me?

So I hated him. I'd say, "Why can't you just stop the drugs and so on? What is your problem? Are you deaf? Stop!"

He didn't stop, so I left him. He hadn't come home one night, and I left the next morning before he did get home. It was Christmas time 1985. I had Little Dexter, who was ten months old, with me.

Dexter was out screwing around, so I left for my folks' house in Chicago. I didn't tell him where I was, and I told my parents to say I wasn't there.

Then my mother said, "He sounds so pathetic on the phone. He needs to know where you are. We can't lie to him." So she told him.

It'd been a whole week since we'd talked. I said, "Dexter, we're not coming home unless you get help."

That's when he went into Hazelden under an assumed name. I was so happy he checked in. Now I'd know where his butt was every night, and our marriage would be saved.

But the first day, he called and said, "I'm coming home. This is not for me. These guys are addicts and alcoholics and homeless. They are nuts!" He kept thinking he was better than everyone. Then after a couple weeks, he adjusted.

I wasn't adjusting. I was conning. I was bored off my rear end, so I started calling my teammate Darryl Grant every day.

Except Darryl didn't know where the hell I was calling from.

I'd call him and tell him I was in Hainesville, Louisiana, visiting my grandmother or in New Orleans or anywhere else in the country. I felt like the Riddler:

*D*exter'd call me and say, "I'm in California!"

Or I'd say, "Where are you?" And he'd answer, "Oh, I'm at my grandmother's house in Louisiana."

But that was fishy. Like, yeah, your grandmother lives in an auditorum! You could hear an echo in the background when he'd call, and then he'd say, "Darryl, I gotta go. Someone wants to use the phone," as if his grandma would be pressing him to use the phone. I heard him shout at somebody, "OK, OK, I'll be off in a minute." Something didn't sound right.

So I kept saying to myself, He's not at his grandmother's. He was on a dang pay phone.

After about three weeks at Hazelden, it was time for the family portion of treatment. Glinda had to come up and be with me.

They gave her a questionnaire to fill out right away, and one question was, "What do you think of your significant other? Is he in here because of a lack of willpower or because it's a disease?"

She wrote, "Lack of willpower," and she tagged on, "Stupidity."

I did not want to be there. My son was going to have his first birthday while I was up there. Because of drugs, I had to miss my son's first birthday.

But the counselors said, "If not now, never." I hated Dexter while I was up there. I missed my baby, and I cried. The counselors asked me how I felt one morning, and I said, "I hate being here. It's my son's birthday, and I hate my husband."

When we left a week later, we left together. But the thirty days up there had done Dexter no good. He kept saying the people in the program were nuts. I'd learned about drugs while I was up there, and I told him, "Just because they're poorer than you or they'll end up on the streets or skid row doesn't mean that you can't get to that point someday."

But Dexter wasn't low enough yet. He hadn't lost anything. The only reason he went was to hold onto me. To buy time.

I thought I could stop cocaine with the snap of a finger. I didn't know I was out of control. One word I did learn in the program was *unmanageability*, and I guess I knew I was unmanageable.

But this other word they kept bringing up—*powerlessness*—I didn't get that word. I said to myself, I ain't got powerlessness. How can you be powerless over places, things, and situations?

That's when Redd Foxx's nephew said, "You'll be back." He predicted a lot of things about me. None of them were flattering.

I returned home from Hazelden. In just a couple of months I was on the edge again. Or shall I say on the ledge?

It was April 12, 1986, and I passed out in Garfinckels department store on M Street in Georgetown. I can't remember the details, I was so wasted. Glinda remembers:

He started going out all night again, and it was scary. I figured he'd kill himself. You hear about other athletes running their cars into something, and after his truck crash I figured it was inevitable for him.

I couldn't sleep at night. Every time I'd be about to doze off, I'd think the phone would ring and it'd be the coroner's office or the cops telling me they'd picked him up.

Well, one night in April, the phone rang, all right. But it was Dexter. "Glinda, come get me."

"Where are you?"

"I don't know . . . Just come get me . . . Come get me, Glinda."

A security guard got on the phone. He was a black guy, and he told me Dexter was at Garfinckels. He said, "Miss Manley, come on down. I've got him with me, but come on down."

I said, "Is he OK?"

The guy said, "Yes, he's fine. I've gotten him away from everybody. Nobody knows he's back here. But come on down."

So I drive down there with my babies, a one-year-old and an infant. I ran inside holding both of them and asked, "Where is he? Where is he?" Somebody pointed, "Go back there." I went back there, and the guard said, "Oh, you just missed him. I had to call the ambulance because he passed out."

I was sure he was dying. The guard told me to go to Georgetown Hospital.

Dexter was in the emergency room. His eyes were rolling in the back of his head, and he didn't recognize me. I almost started crying, and I guess this is how I knew I really loved him. I wanted to punch him for being out all night, but he looked as if he was dying. They had all these tubes in him, and someone took the babies from me. I kept saying, "Dexter, it's me . . . it's me."

Well, the hospital covered it up, except for one doctor who refused to cover it up. They kept him in there for six hours, trying to get him together.

They took all this blood for tests, and I said, "You've got to take blood?" I was trying to protect his career. I kept thinking, Oh shit, they'll see the level of cocaine in him. There goes our life!

They said, "Ma'am, we have to take blood to see what's in him, so we know how to treat him." And my babies were screaming.

Soon, I was paged to see this doctor, and he said, "Miss Manley . . . um . . . you know what we found in your husband's urine and blood . . ."

"Yes, ."

"Well, it's kind of a lot," he said. "Quite a lot. I hope from this he seeks some help. We'll keep the records confidential, but I just want you to know this is pretty serious."

I said, "Well, thank you," and that was that.

Dexter stayed hospitalized most of the night—until he was lucid enough to come home. At the house he was his typical remorseful self. He felt bad but also was like, Phew, got out of that one.

We worked up a scheme—a real killer scheme—to fool the media. I talked to my father-in-law about it the day after I'd blacked out. I knew it was going to hit the papers, and we tried dreaming up something I could've passed out from. He said, "Aren't you allergic to seafood?" Bingo.

So I had the newspapers believing I blacked out because of an allergic reaction to seafood. I said I'd been passing out from seafood since grammar school, which was true.

The media asked the logical question: If I was allergic to seafood, why had I eaten it? My answer was, "'Cause I like it."

I thought I had the Redskins wrapped around my fingers, too. For a couple of days after my collapse, I was working out at six in the morning at Redskin Park. That was my way of showing them I was as healthy as a bull. They'd see me lifting weights at the crack of dawn, and they had to be thinking, He ain't doing drugs. How can this guy be doing drugs if he's here at six in the morning? That was the picture I painted.

But soon Joe Gibbs called me in for a meeting. My cover was finally blown to smithereens. Gibbs and Bobby Beathard told me they knew I had done drugs.

Before, they had never had an inkling, but somebody from the hospital must have told the team internist, Doc Knowlan. I know that's what happened, because I visited the hospital after the incident to make sure those records were not released to anyone, not even to the Redskins. I was told Doc Knowlan had been milling around down at the hospital. So somebody must've told him, and he spilled the lima beans to the Redskins.

And—damn—that was right when I was negotiating my contract. Any leverage I had was shot to hell.

Gibbs and Beathard told me that day they were not going to cut me just because of the cocaine. They said everything would be copacetic, and I just needed to get my act together.

They hooked me up with some square drug doctor, a Doc Flynn at Georgetown Hospital, and I was to see him on Saturdays or Tuesdays. He would counsel me and also drug test me on his own.

The Redskins were overseeing my recovery. The league had not one iota to do with it. It was not even considered a first strike against me under the NFL drug policy, from what I understand. Hell, how would the league be involved? They had no record of it.

My teammates still had no clue, not even Grant:

I was hearing everything after the fact. The day after this so-called seafood incident, he left a message on my answering machine, "World, call me. I need your help."

I wasn't home, and he didn't leave a number where he was. The next day, he got me at home and said, "Why didn't you call me back? I needed help to find my truck."

This was the truck he'd driven to Georgetown that night. He couldn't remember where he'd parked it.

I asked him what happened, and he said, "I was drinking . . . I ate seafood, and I had a couple drinks." He swore to me, "I just had too much to drink." It sounded strange, but I didn't press it.

He was most pissed that the paramedics tore up his $200 shirt trying to revive him.

The Redskins must have trusted me worth a nickel; they drafted a defensive end with their top pick in the 1986 draft: Markus Koch. They wanted Markus Koch to unseat me so they could eliminate me. I was a cocaine risk now.

But Markus Koch couldn't play dead. Even if I wasn't concentrating on playing the run, I penetrated the backfield. Markus Koch couldn't penetrate the backfield. They were not going to get rid of me until Markus Koch proved he could bust a grape. I believe they held onto me all those years because not one single person they lined up at right defensive end could carry my jock.

Let me tell you, Bobby Beathard always used to accuse guys of being on drugs or on steroids, but Bobby would put up with it, if necessary. He has to. If you want to win, you're always going to have a certain amount of good players on the juice.

Of course, the Redskins figured their Doc Flynn would keep me under control, but I'd bring Little Dexter to distract him. I figured Doc Flynn would see me with this cute little boy and think I couldn't have a major problem. But after I'd see Doc Flynn every Tuesday, I'd leave to do drugs. By the time the next Tuesday rolled around and I had to take a leak for him, the coke would be out of my system.

I particularly remember June 1986, a couple of months after the Redskins had drafted Markus Koch. I sat Indian style in the Key Bridge Marriott doing lines of cocaine. Then I turned on the TV, and the anchorperson had a news flash: Len Bias was dead.

Len Bias, a twenty-one-year-old basketball stud, died of a heart attack. A couple of days later, they said he died of cocaine ingestion.

And you know what? It didn't scare me an inch.

See, rumors flew that he'd died of free-basing cocaine. I said to myself, I don't free-base. I'm not going to die. It was just denial that it could ever happen to me. I'd never heard of anyone who'd died from snorting coke—I thought you could just croak from free-basing—so I carried on. It scared the whole country, but hell if it frightened me. The only thing I did was continue to see Doc Flynn.

I still had to negotiate a contract for the 1986 season, and this time wearing a Chicago Blitz cap wouldn't cut it.

Talks dragged from February until our last preseason game in August. As you can imagine, it was a strain to keep my mouth shut.

First, I tried bringing the USFL into it again. My quote was, "Maybe I'll be signing with the Memphis Showboats . . . Or it'll just be me and Donald Trump. We can go one-on-one. Better yet, I can go work in the Trump Tower. Maybe he'll let me run the elevator. I think he'd pay me $400,000 a year to run the elevator, don't you?"

Then, I went live on WAVA-FM one morning—I was there because the station was talking to me about a full-time job, and I called Jack Kent Cooke a miser.

I was only trying to be funny. I called Mr. Cooke a couple of days later, and he said, in his Katharine Hepburn cadence, "Don't you call me behind everyone's back noooooow . . . You said it. We have a tape heeeeeere. And I'm upset. I don't want to hear that apology noooooow."

Mo Siegel, a writer who's tight with Mr. Cooke, told me Cooke really loved it. I was telling everyone I was misquoted, and Mr. Cooke said he had this tape.

Man, he didn't have no tape.

Meantime, I was off coke during the holdout. I needed the contract, and I chilled the whole holdout. I'd sit at home, work out, train . . . I did what I had to do.

There was no movement on the contract whatsoever. They made the same offer in September they made in February. It was a four-year deal worth $360,000 in 1986, $385,000 in 1987, $405,000 in 1988, and $480,000 in 1989, and it never really altered from day one. So I got pissed at my attorney, Richard Bennett.

I mean, Bobby Beathard wasn't budging:

Dexter changed agents a lot when an agent wasn't successful renegotiating, and Dexter wanted to renegotiate every year.

He'd start by joking around about it. Like, "Hey, I need more money. This other guy's getting this." It was a certain way he'd approach you. I guess he figured, I'm serious, but I'm not gonna let Beathard know I'm serious. But after a while, you knew, Oh no, this is just the start of this. And, boy, could he turn unhappy just like that. The money thing could really make him unhappy. Money didn't make him play any better, but it kind of ruled him. The Rulon Jones contract became a big issue with him, and it took me a long time to get all the figures on it. That contract was paid out over so many years—with all the deferrals—that the contract we offered Dexter was equal to the Rulon Jones deal. But then you had to get into the discussion of present value, and that was something Dexter either didn't understand or didn't want to understand.

Because of the drugs, the Redskins never intended to increase their offer. They decided they'd just pump the contract full of incentive clauses. They knew about the drugs now, so they said, "Oh oh, we can't trust him. It's got to be full of incentives."

So I told them I wanted cash for every quarterback hurry. Richard Bennett didn't know what a "hurry" was. He said, "They're not going to put that in there."

Listen, a hurry is important. It's when you get close enough to the quarterback that you can smell his breath, but he gets rid of the ball anyway. A lot of times the result is an interception.

Well, I met with Beathard and Gibbs on a Sunday, without Richard Bennett. We were in Beathard's office, and I said, "Hey, I'll take the deal, but there's one more thing I've got to have."

"What's that?" Bobby asked.

"I've got to have my hurry clause. Let's say I get two grand for every hurry."

Bobby replied, "A hurry? Oh, no problem, Dexter, whatever you want." Then he added, "Just don't tell Mr. Cooke."

So I signed, but I was still a little confused and angry. I kept remembering what Redd Foxx's nephew had told me at Hazelden, that the drugs were going to get worse. He was right.

The Redskins had found out about the cocaine, and they held it over my head like an anvil. Them knowing about my cocaine cost me about one hundred grand a year.

It turned out to be the last contract I ever signed with those boys.

An Idle Thought

Agents are hired to be fired. I had four representatives in my pro career, and I axed three of them:

1. Joe Courrege (1981–82). His downfall was that he couldn't find me a decent Mercedes.

2. Jim Kiles (1983). Besides him being too tight with Beathard, he also tried selling me a real estate deal in Florida. He only represented me a month, and he'd already gotten out of hand.

3. Richard Bennett (1983–86). His maneuver to bribe the Redskins with a Chicago Blitz offer was brilliant, but his 1986 negotiating was nothing special. I had to sign the same deal in August that I'd been offered in February, and then Richard was pissed I wouldn't pay him what he wanted.

People may think that's irresponsible of me, but I'm not gonna get screwed over and pay Richard Bennett for doing nothing. So I paid him $5,000. He said I owed him $25,000 and I said, "What are you basing that on? What did you get in the way of an improvement?"

In 1983 he asked for $10,000, and I gave it to him. But in 1986 he didn't deserve a dime.

4. Bob Woolf (1987–). I remember talking about Woolf with

Bennett, long before I ever met Woolf. Bennett and I were still partners, and we were eating at the Maison Blanc. Richard asked me if anything ever happened to him, whom would I ask to represent me. I said Bob Woolf.

Woolf, you see, was big time.

Bennett told me not to go with Bob Woolf, to choose Howard Slusher, who cared about his players and would fight for them like Richard would. Well, I don't know if Woolf has ever fought for me, but I know I freaked ole Bob out right from the start.

About a month after I signed with Woolf, he found out about my drug problem. That's how I welcomed Bob Woolf to Manleyville.

C H A P T E R   24

Joy of Sacks

I'M A BORN PASS RUSHER. I MEAN, OUT OF
9,000 sperms, I finished first place in the race to get my momma
pregnant.

Nobody can convince me quarterback sacks aren't bigger than a
touchdown. If sacks ain't the end-all, how come we printed up T-shirts
in Washington that read, Another sack, Jack [Kent Cooke]!

If sacks ain't the end-all, how come Johnny Cakes—Cooke's
son—and I had a bet about 'em? The bet was if I got a certain number
of sacks, I could park in Johnny Cake's parking space, about ten yards
from the front door of Redskin Park. He and I started the bet because I
used to park in his space all the time anyway. It was like my Cougar
days in college.

So Johnny Cakes said, "Three sacks, and you get the parking
space." Or he'd say "two sacks." He even posted a sign that said,
Manley's Parking, though I never did win the bet. We only did it for a
few games, and the offensive tackles must've been chop-blocking me.

Then Cooke started including Charles Mann in the bets. He'd
say, "You have to get more sacks than Charles." I could see Charles was
becoming the Redskins' boy.

If sacks ain't the end-all, then how come Bobby Beathard used to
offer me dinner every time I recorded three in a game? It just shows you
defensive end is the most glamorous position in the NFL:

*Well, I'd offer Dexter dinner for sacks because of how he was
motivated. Dexter might've fallen into the category of player whom you could
give a million dollars a year, but if you told him you'd give him fifty dollars
after the game or buy him dinner if he got a sack, that'd get him going more.
They think that's what they are getting for the sack. They don't look at the*

million dollars as having anything to do with playing well. They figure that's just what they deserve. They want you to give them something for what they're supposed to do: get sacks.

Dexter was a challenge, a real challenge.

In the 1980s, NFL sacks became huge. My personality would change when I'd cop one. I'd get a little more arrogant or wouldn't listen as well to coaches and teammates.

I may have played a bad overall game, but if I had two sacks, that was the bottom line. I think I had two sacks against St. Louis in 1985, but I failed to stop some runs by Ottis Anderson. Gibbs told me, "Dexter, you didn't play well." But I had two sacks, so I could live with myself.

If Dexter didn't get a sack, he'd mope. He'd tell me, "Grant, I need a sack." Against St. Louis, Neil Lomax was running around in the pocket, and Dexter's butt had been blocked to the ground. But Lomax didn't see where Dex was lying on the turf, and Dexter tripped Lomax's ankles. Then Dex leaped up waving to the crowd as if he'd worked his butt off for the sack.

In the 1989 Monday night opener against the Giants, I'd driven my guy back, and my guy tripped Phil Simms to the ground. Well, Dexter dove from five feet away to touch Simms and get a piece of the sack. Then Dexter jumped up, arms raised, and not a single person acknowledged me.

Dexter would claim sacks. If a quarterback went down, and Dexter was nearby, he'd claim it. Just by leaping up and raising his arms.

But if he didn't get a sack, he'd seem suicidal. We could've won by thirty points, but it was as if his world had ended.

It's not impossible to get notoriety playing the run. It depends on who's running. It's no big deal kicking Ottis Anderson's behind, but I wanted to lasso an Eric Dickerson or a Bo Jackson. If I could knock a Bo out, then that would give me a name.

But any sack gives you a name . . . and money. I used to dream about third and long in the fourth quarter. It's what I lived for.

That's why I'd incited the RFK Stadium crowd. If I couldn't hear myself think, how could the offensive players hear? And if the opposing tackle flinched, I'll beat him off the snap nine times out of ten. And that's a sack, Jack.

I wasn't being a hot dog. I was simply utilizing the masses. I mean, on second and third down, I'd be into it. And I'd go on Frank Herzog's show—Frank was our play-by-play announcer—and I'd say, "What I need from you fans is to be on your feet on second and third down."

Grant complains about the time I dove on Phil Simms and stole his sack. Hell, that's money laying on the ground. My incentive clause called for $2,000 a sack up to ten sacks, $3,000 per sack up to seventeen sacks, and $4,500 a sack after seventeen sacks.

The reason I'd jump up and claim sacks was for the benefit of the stat man. In the pile of bodies, how's he supposed to know who got the sack? I'm making his job easier, man.

Listen, sacks were a huge thing at Redskin Park. Sacks and hurries. We'd be watching films with Torgy, and I'd be yelling, "Torgy! Torgy! Is that a hurry?" Grant and I would argue about what was a hurry and what wasn't:

Dexter was a trip in meetings. He'd sit in the front row and laugh at every one of Joe Gibbs's jokes. He'd Ed McMahon him.

During film, he sat right by the lights and would go to sleep with his head twitching back, with that bandanna around his neck and his mouth wide open. I'd say something to him like, "Isn't that right, Dex?" And he'd spring up answering, "Yep."

I'd whisper, "Dex!" And he'd shoot up, "Yep, Darryl, right. That was a nice play."

Watching film, you knew Dexter played football with his image in mind. Some fast running back would break a run, and Dexter'd be sprinting right alongside him to prove he was JUST AS fast. We knew he was doing it, so we'd say, "Look how fast Dexter is." But Torgy'd be screaming, "Darnit, Dexter, make the play! Don't run with him!" I specifically remember Dexter doing that once with Eric Dickerson.

When Dexter'd fall asleep during film, Torgy would take a light beam and shine it in Dexter's eyes. And Dexter was silly enough to sit by the light switch, which meant he'd have to be awake at the end of the session to flip the lights on.

That's true, I used to have to operate the lights. When I'd fall asleep, Torgy'd say, "I'll throw this damn eraser at you!" If it wasn't Torgy shining the light in my eyes, it was Dave Butz. Butz would shine it at me more than Torgy.

Meetings were cool. I'd make rookies get the hell out of their chairs. At minicamp, a room would be packed when I'd walk in, and I'd say, "Hey, one of you rookies has *got* to get up."

As for Gibbs's meetings, I'd always sit up front. I've always been a front row man. I try never to sit in the back, because you might miss something. It's a carry-over from my school days. Sitting up front was buttering up the teacher, and I guess maybe I was buttering up Gibbs. I'd be up there nodding my head at everything he said, and I'd die at his jokes. Gibbs had a dry sense of humor, actually. Grant says I'd "Ed McMahon him." That's a good one.

Gibbs definitely tried to amuse us, and his famous one was the Eskimo joke he'd tell every year before a cold weather game. He'd start out explaining how when he used to coach in St. Louis under Don Coryell, Coryell gave the old Eskimos-and-the-Alaskan-pipeline speech before a blistering cold game. He told the team that when the Alaskan pipeline was being constructed, the white men had a horrendous time bearing the cold. They could work on the pipeline for only an hour before having to race in for a hot coffee break. Frustrated, the person building the pipeline decided to hire Eskimos to do the work. They were able to stay out all day in the cold.

Scientists who heard about this were curious and checked the Eskimos' blood to see what the difference was, but it was the same as the white men's.

The moral of the story? Coryell told his Cardinals that playing football in cold weather was simply mind over matter, just as it had been on the Alaskan pipeline. At that moment, Cardinals tackle Dan Dierdorf stood up and said, "Coach Coryell, what if I line up across from a guy Sunday, and he's an Eskimo?"

Well, Gibbs told Dierdorf's line *every* year. After he'd told it one year, as I sat in the front row, I asked, "Coach Gibbs? What about us brothers? Where are the brothers in this joke?"

That cracked up the whole room.

Hell, I recorded more sacks in 1986 than any other season, and this was after the off-season that included the incident at Garfinckels, the contract dispute, calling Mr. Cooke a "miser," and skipping training camp.

I reached every incentive clause imaginable. I had eighteen sacks, which accounted for $46,500 in incentive money, and I had thirty-one hurries, which accounted for $62,000. Also included in my incentive package was cash for batted passes and recovered fumbles. I was making out like Gordon Gekko.

I also held the NFL record for most sacks since 1982: sixty-five.

And I got held a lot by linemen. I should've had an incentive package for holding penalties.

This also was the season I said I'd "ring Joe Montana's clock" in a Monday night game. Montana had just returned from back surgery, and our whole team was pissed I said that, especially Gibbs.

Gibbs is paranoid that you'll fire up the opponents. As we walked to practice, all the media kept asking him about my quote. When he strolled by me, Gibbs said, "Ring his clock, huh?"

That night, the 49ers crack-back blocked my ass, sort of the way the Bears had done in 1985. It was vicious. I was sore for two weeks after that game. Their tight end, Russ Francis, is a big ole boy, and he crack-backed me all night.

On the sidelines, Torgy told me, "Next time you see Francis, go attack him." The next time I grabbed Francis's neck.

He growled, "You fucking dumb nigger."

I shot back, "Fuck your momma, you fucking white boy." I tried to hit him right in the jugular vein. This is what happens when you shoot your mouth off about Joe Montana.

But I still whammed Montana that night. I rammed him near the sidelines, right in his disc, and the man somehow climbed up. That damn Ronnie Lott talked so much crap from the sidelines when I hit Montana. Ronnie Lott was always talking crap.

Well, pretty soon the whole league was chop-blocking me; they certainly couldn't block me straight up. At Green Bay that year, the Packers chop-blocked me all day, and I nearly fought their coach, Forrest Gregg. Hell, even my own teammates hammered me that weekend in Green Bay.

We got to our hotel the Saturday before the game. I was tearing the league up with sacks and attracting all kinds of media. So that Saturday, Clint Didier, Donnie Warren, and Jeff Bostic—just a bunch of white guys sitting in a room together—pulled a hoax on me.

Bostic called my room and said he was a reporter doing a front-page story on me for Sunday's paper. He asked if I would come to do an interview in Room 210, and I said, "You bet."

Hell, I didn't know it was Jeff Bostic. I mean, I'd never talked to Bostic on the phone. He faked me out.

I knocked on 210, and Bostic, Warren, and Didier opened the door laughing. I said, "Oh, I must have the wrong room. I was looking for the press room. Is there another 210?"

So, I walked around for twenty minutes looking for another 210. I'm like some airhead looking for this room. Bostic and those guys didn't tell me it was them until months later. They said, "Remember that call in Green Bay for an interview?"

I cracked up. Hell, it was funny. I didn't have to retaliate or anything. Matter of fact, they routinely messed with me. In preseason Murphy or Milot or somebody like that would open their preseason checks—which I thought were $500 for all veterans—and they'd say loud enough for me to hear, "What, only $800 this week?" I truly thought I was getting screwed over, but eventually I caught on. But that was typical of them.

However, I generally didn't take too much crap from anybody. For instance, someone once let the air out of my truck tires, and I went straight to Bostic, to Rich Milot, and so on. I tell you, I knocked on some doors. Bostic swore it wasn't him. I can tell you, though, nothing ever happened again.

That was our first full season with Jay Schroeder as quarterback, after he replaced hop-a-long Joe Theismann. Immediately after Jay had some success, the Redskins ruined his head by granting him a $1 million contract. Jay had a decent arm, but his footwork was like a duck's, and he completed a very low percentage of his passes. He started making this bull excuse about how he was simply a low-percentage passer and a big-play quarterback. Hell, that was a cop-out.

Before Theismann got totaled by L. T., Schroeder had been the scout team quarterback. I used to piss Jay off in practice. I'd harass him like Clarence Thomas and smack him. The quarterback coach, Jerry Rhome, told me not hit Jay's hands or anything, but Coach Wanser was still in the back of my head.

I used to plaster Theismann in practice, too:

Dexter was cute. He'd run into me just enough to knock me down, and then he'd pick me up with that big smile of his and say, "I'm sorry." It was like he got caught with his hand in the cookie jar, took one bite, and put the cookie back.

As the 1986 season headed into its final month, I was getting off. As of December 7, heading into our second Giants game the fourteenth week, I had seventeen and one-half sacks. The national media were pounding on my door.

Until then, I had not been using coke that year. But the rave reviews made me feel *larger than life* again. Just so my drug counselors know, that's when I'm dangerously close to using cocaine—when my head is so big it can't even fit into a taxicab. At those times, everyone's telling me I'm Superman, but deep inside I don't feel worthy of the glory and need an escape. Drugs become so tempting then.

I was still seeing that Doc Flynn on Tuesdays, but he was absolutely useless. I had a relapse because I wanted to relapse.

In the final three games of the regular season I had only one-half sack and finished with eighteen. Publicly, the Redskins said the reason for my slump was an injury to pass rushing defensive tackle Steve Hamilton, which enabled teams to double- and triple-team me.

To hell with that. It was probably the coke. I used to think cocaine was performance-enhancing. At first, I was all hyper and speedy, and I thought, Oh, this is the answer. This stuff is too good to be true.

But I think it wore me down. Lawrence Taylor beat me out for the lead with twenty sacks. I still made first team All-Pro and my first ever Pro Bowl. I should've made the Pro Bowl the year before in 1985, when frickin' Dan Hampton made it over me with five fewer sacks and thirty-one fewer tackles. But players probably didn't vote for me because they were jealous or didn't like my fat mouth.

But in 1986 they had no choice but to write "Manley"!

So here I was in the Pro Bowl, and here we were headed to the playoffs, and here I was feeling grandiose. That takes us up to Christmas Day, a Christmas that "snowed," if you catch my drift.

AN IDLE THOUGHT

One of my greatest defensive plays wasn't a sack. It was a spit.

In a 1988 game at RFK Stadium against New Orleans, the Saints were driving late to pad their seven-point lead. They were in field-goal range when I started wrestling with guard Jim Dombrowski and spit all over his face mask.

What I did was bait Dombrowski into punching me. The ref saw his punch—not me drooling all over him—and penalized the Saints 15 big yards. It pushed their kicker, Morton Andersen, out of his field-goal range, and we came back to win by three.

Afterward, reporters wanted to know what the hell happened.

Darryl Grant told me to say I sneezed on Dombrowski, so that's what I said. I said, "Hey, I sneezed. What's the big deal?"

Little did the reporters know, I couldn't have sneezed that day if I'd wanted to. I'd taken my Sudafed.

By the way, at the Saints' next home game, a banner was unfurled at the Superdome reading: Dombrowski—Spit Happens!

CHAPTER 25

White Christmas

'TWAS THE NIGHT OF CHRISTMAS AND ALL through the house . . . Hell, I wasn't even *in* the house.

This was three days before our 1986 Wild-Card playoff game against the Los Angeles Rams, and I'd stayed out all night—Christmas night—with a batch of cocaine.

What slipped my mind was practice the next day.

I was asleep somewhere—who knows where—when the Redskins practiced on December 26, the Friday before the game.

When a guy mysteriously misses a practice, you *know* he has problems. You see it in sports all the time. He misses a game or a practice, and then he comes up with some lie like he had a flat tire. It's bull. When my name started surfacing like that, it was humiliating.

I was just out snorting with some girl Christmas night. It's not as if I was doing coke the whole season, but I left practice Christmas Day absolutely knowing I was going to snort coke. It's an urgent feeling I always get before I use.

I didn't show again at Redskin Park until late Friday, *after* practice. I had had my personal PR guy, Roy Robertson, call Beathard and tell him to meet me at the Dulles Marriott. That's where I was hungover. But Beathard instructed me to venture to Redskin Park, which is where he eventually found me leaning unstably against a Redskin Park wall, crying. He just eyed me.

My career flashed before my eyes. I knew I had let my teammates down. Missing a practice? That's big. I felt like a horrible person—irresponsible.

Bobby said, "Our coaches are in a staff meeting now, and they'll decide what they're going to do." I was kicking the wall.

Gibbs and our equipment man, Jaybird, eventually ushered me through the equipment room. Gibbs told me, "You're ruining your career." He never mentioned drugs. He just said, "You're throwing away your career. If you aren't careful, you're going to wind up in the gutter." He was a good coach and a prophet.

He told me to return the next day, the Saturday before the game. In the morning I met with Richie Petitbon, our defensive coordinator, and then with Gibbs. Gibbs and I talked privately. He wanted me to come meet with him every Friday for a Bible study.

He genuinely tried to help me. We were leaving for the Dulles Marriott, which is where we stayed the night before home games, and he requested I bring a Bible so we could talk.

When I was in his office that day, he pulled out his Bible, and I cried. That's what I did. We met a couple times after that, but I wasn't a big Bible-toter. So we never stuck to our plan of meeting Fridays.

I don't believe the team came close to suspending me from that Rams game. Gibbs met with Russ Grimm and Art Monk, who represented my teammates, and asked if they thought I should be allowed to play. Apparently, they said they thought what I'd done was unforgivable, but they didn't tell Gibbs not to suit me up. That was fair. Gibbs got the rest of the team involved, yet made the final decision himself. Getting the team involved was good politics. If I was coach, I'd have done the same thing.

He fined me $1,000, and I immediately began a coverup. First, I said my absence was contract-related. Second, I changed my story and said I'd had just too much eggnog.

I wondered what my teammate Grant thought this time:

*W*e *were geeked up for this playoff game, and then Dexter didn't show. We all thought he wanted more money. I was thinking, We want to go to the Super Bowl, so he could've waited.*

We were just out at practice waiting for him . . . waiting.

I tried bluffing the team and the coaches into thinking it was totally alcohol. The morning of the Rams game, I consented to an interview with Bill McAtee of NBC. He asked why I'd missed practice, and I replied, "I had too many drinks and fell asleep and didn't wake up until later."

He asked me about the rumor of drugs, so I went off on him. I said, "Look here, man, do you have a cup? Hey, I'll piss for you. I'll take a leak for you right now, buddy. I'll take a leak right here."

He said he was extremely sorry.

I had them all conned. Then I went out and had a decent game to boot. That strengthened my case. I had no sacks, but I had some tackles and put pressure on their rookie quarterback, Jim Everett.

This is also the game in which Darryl Grant said I ran alongside Eric Dickerson as if I was racing him instead of making the tackle. Why did I do it? I'd attribute that to a residue of the drugs.

Having defeated the Rams, 19–7—my cousin Eric fumbled, which helped beyond belief—we took on the defending Super Bowl champion Bears in Chicago. All I can tell you about that game is that I clotheslined their quarterback, Doug Flutie, big time. I jumped off-sides, then carried through with the play and cleaned him out. I didn't mean for him to fly 10 yards backward. It's just he's as light as paper.

I got flagged 15 yards for the hit, but it was an intimidation hit. We played the Bears in the playoffs the next year. Jim McMahon was their quarterback, not Flutie, and when he was asked why the Redskins beat them in 1986 with Flutie, he said, "We were too short last year." After we beat McMahon again in 1987, my quote was, "Maybe, they were too tall this year."

Anyway, we whupped the Bears and Flutie, 27–13. Art Monk had a big game. Unfortunately, we didn't bust a grape the next week in the NFC Championship game against New York, a 17–0 loss. I didn't record a sack in the playoffs, for obvious reasons.

A week later, Glinda and I went Hawaiian. We finally got to see what all this Pro Bowl fuss was about:

The way Christmas had gone, I needed that Hawaii trip badly. I could tell Dexter was antsy Christmas Day. It was as if he had some things to do. So I had my brother Greg hang with him and keep an eye on him. Greg said out loud, "We're gonna go out, Glinda." I figured Dexter was safe with Greg.

At about 11:30 Christmas night, I heard Greg coming through the garage and sighed with relief. But Greg was alone. I asked, "Where's Dexter?"

I'd figured as long as Greg was with him, Dexter wouldn't use drugs or pick up women. Now I was scared.

"Oh, he just dropped me off," Greg answered.

"Dropped you off? Why?"

"He said he was just going up the street to get gas."

"Greg, why didn't you go with him?"

"Well, he didn't make no big to-do. He just pulled to the side and said he was getting gas. Just right up the street."

"Greg, he ain't coming home."

Greg was like, "Oh, Glinda, he wouldn't do that, would he? Christmas night, with me here? He wouldn't do that, would he?"

I repeated, "Greg, he ain't coming home."

Sure enough, he didn't. I was like Tammy in those days. I had a feeling it was some woman living close by in Herndon or Reston. I said, "It's somebody near." Turns out, that whole day he missed practice he'd been hanging with this girl who lived one block up from us.

I hated him for what he was doing to us and to himself. And this was during the holidays, which are supposed to be happy times. I hated him all the way through New Year's Eve.

So we finally go to the Pro Bowl, and Dexter says, "Glinda, we never had a honeymoon because our wedding was the day before a game and then we never had a honeymoon because we had the kids. So let's make the Pro Bowl our honeymoon."

I really looked forward to Hawaii. He'd been screwing up, but I felt like, This trip is it. This is going to be the time we're gonna get together.

The first day we were there, he called Eric Dickerson, then said, "Oh, Glinda, you don't mind tonight if I just go out with the fellas?"

I talked to Eric on the phone and said, "You all going out?"

"Yeah, a bunch of us," Eric replied. "About eight of them. We're just going to go to this club."

I trusted Eric because I knew he didn't get high. So Dexter left, and at 2:00 A.M. there still was no sign of him. I knew the next day was photo day, but Dexter never made it. He did coke. He admitted to me, later, that he was with two women, two stewardesses from Europe whom he met at the club. He fetched cocaine and went to their hotel room.

Finally, at about 6:00 A.M., I called Eric to see where Dexter was. When Eric answered, I could tell he hadn't been out all night because he'd been asleep. "Eric," I asked, "where's Dexter?"

"Oh, shit, don't tell me he didn't come back."

"Eric, what happened?" I persisted.

"Well, I left," he said, "but he said he was going to come on, and I really thought he had gone on home."

"No, Eric, he didn't show up."

"Oh, Glinda, I'm sorry. I don't know where he is, but he'll be there." Eric felt really bad, I could tell.

Well, I never heard from Dexter, and it was now our second day in

Hawaii. I ran into Joe Gibbs, who was the NFC head coach, and Joe's wife, Pat, and all these people I knew. They kept saying, "Where's Dexter?"

I wouldn't stay in my room because I knew the phone calls would start flying in, so I lay on the beach all day. I wanted to dodge the players and the coaches and the phone calls. Finally, I got to the room and took my messages. I didn't know what to say if I ran into Coach Gibbs again, so I ignored his messages. What could I say other than, "I don't know"?

Dexter finally sneaked in the room at about three that afternoon. I came up from swimming, and Dexter was lying there sleeping it off. I started yelling. "Dexter, I don't believe it. You swore to me you were really going to try to get off these drugs, and you said this was our honeymoon! Not only do I know you did drugs, but you must've been with some women. Otherwise, you would have called."

"I was never with no woman," he insisted. "You're crazy. Why do you always think it's some woman?"

"Well, if it's not," I replied, "why couldn't you call?"

That whole week was hell week. I couldn't stand him, because I knew he'd been screwing around.

The Pro Bowl was a stupendous disappointment. I was so thrilled, originally. At first, I just knew I was on my way to making the Pro Bowl an annual thing.

But when we got there, I immediately went out with Eric, LeRoy Irvin, Jerry Gray, and Mike Quick. Glinda told me, "Don't go out," but I told her I was gonna be out with the boys.

We were at this club, and this guy approached me and some girls about drugs. The other players had no clue what I was up to, and I missed the team practice the next morning. I didn't get home until 11:00 A.M. I met Mike Singletary and asked him, "Were they looking for me at practice?" And he said he didn't know. You know Singletary, he speaks in such perfect English.

Then I bumped into Eric Dickerson. Eric said, "Man, they're looking for you. Emmitt Thomas [a Redskins assistant] was looking for you. Coach Gibbs was looking."

Torgy phoned me that night to make sure I would be there the next day. When I arrived, I had my con all planned out. I told Gibbs, "Coach, I missed the bus and caught a cab, but I went to the wrong place. I went to the University of Hawaii instead of Aloha Stadium."

He probably didn't buy it for one minute. But, as I say, when you're on drugs, you're a liar. You're covering your ass. At least, you think you are.

It was just a bummer of a Pro Bowl. The worst part is that because I missed the photo day, I'm not even in the team picture. There is no proof I was in that game. That bothers me to this day.

If there was a best part, it was the game. I had two sacks and about five hurries. Hey, it was the Dexter Manley and Reggie White Show that day.

From what I understand, the NFL wanted to give me a drug test. That's what our trainer, Bubba Tyer, said. Somehow or another the Redskins blocked them from testing me. Listen, Joe Gibbs is smart. He didn't want to lose me.

I would have volunteered at the Pro Bowl to take the test. I would have bluffed them, just as I did after I missed the Rams practice.

After I missed the Rams practice, I told Coach Gibbs, "Hey, test me, I'm not on anything." I kept repeating, "Coach, I'm willing to take that test." It was me manipulating them. I kept saying, "Test me, test me."

Gibbs finally said, "OK, we'll think about it." Hell, they never tested me. I knew Gibbs wasn't going to. See, the league wasn't involved in testing me back then, and the Redskins didn't want to know.

Which was smart.

After the Pro Bowl game, Glinda and I went to the other side of the island for the Superstars competition—my longtime dream—but I didn't believe Glinda was enjoying herself:

The first night on the other end of the island, Dexter came clean with everything. We were in bed and he said, "Glinda, I have something to tell you."

"What's wrong?" I asked.

He said, "I just want to come clean, because I'm tired of living lies."

Because I was hurting, I was still being evil to him. And then he told me all. He ruined the Superstars week for me, too, because he admitted to all his playing around. He told me the name of the girl in Reston he spent Christmas night with and where she lived and worked.

On the outside, I acted calm. I said, "Oh, Dexter, well, I feel really good about this. I'm glad you told me."

I played it real cool. I got as much information about her as I could. In case it happened again, I'd know where to find her butt.

I asked, "What does she look like? What kind of car does she drive? Where does she live? Oh really? She does?" Before I let him know it hurt, I made sure I knew where she worked and lived.

Then I went off. "Golly, Dexter, how come you tell me about her, but you've never told me about any of the others? You know, I had to find out about them on my own. This relationship with this girl must be pretty serious if you want to tell me. It's almost like you want me to be your policeman and watch you now . . . now that you've told me."

He kept saying, "Oh, Glinda, do you really think I'll see her now, now that I've told you everything about her? Do you really think I'd be so stupid?"

All I know is this made me even more scared. I said to myself, This must be a relationship he has going.

Then he told me it had been going on for months. I was like, Wow, this isn't fair! He also said, "She's told me she's seen you a couple of times in the grocery store and outside with the kids."

That really hurt! "This bitch knows what I look like, knows where I live, has seen my kids, and I don't know who she is? How dare her! How dare you!" I yelled.

So I was even more depressed at the Superstars competition, because he'd also told me about those two stewardesses at the Pro Bowl. I felt terribly rejected. Hawaii was total hell for me. I couldn't wait to leave.

When we got back to Reston, he kept telling me, "Glinda, I'm so sorry. I'll never see her again. I promise you."

Well, it was Little Dexter's birthday—February 4—the day we got home. Lester Townsend, who was Dexter's close friend, came by with his wife, Odessa. We sang "Happy Birthday," and Odessa had made a birthday cake for Big Dexter, too, because his birthday was February 2.

Where did Big Dexter go that night? Here I was trying to start to forgive him, and he didn't come home. I went to my Bible.

By about 5:00 A.M. I was full of rage. More than anything, I wanted to see them together and look at him and give him a look that said, You dog! How could you do this to me after what you just did? You swore to me . . . I wanted him to know I knew and that I thought he was scum.

Well, the kids were in my bed and my parents, who were visiting, were sleeping in the basement. I decided not to wait any longer. I threw on some jeans, but in case she was cute, I threw on a little makeup so she could see he didn't have a dog for a wife. All these things went through my head, because I didn't know what she looked like except for what he said. Then I put on my tennis shoes in case I had to run.

Dexter had taken my BMW that afternoon, so I drove his truck over to her apartment. It had a parking garage underneath, but I didn't know where

206 • EDUCATING DEXTER

to go. I was in the dark at five in the morning, and as I looked to the side to pull out, I saw eyes staring up at me.

It was the woman. She knew I must be Dexter's wife, because I was in Dexter's truck. She had guilt all over her face, and she looked like she meant to say, "Oh, shit." The thing that made me mad and probably made me kick her butt was the fact that she got out of her car.

She should've driven off.

She should have known she was wrong. She should have known I must be a crazy woman to be out at five in the morning looking for my husband. I pulled that truck right next to her car, and she got out of her car and was locking the door when I said, "Are you Debbie?"

When she said yes, I just took her and flung her. I broke her nose. She had to have two surgeries, and her nose is still messed up.

The thing that made me beat her up was that she never fought back. She never tried to protect herself.

She kept going, "Huh, Huh, Huh," like she was having an orgasm or something, and it made me even madder.

I could only think, This must be what she sounds like when she's with him. I never hit her, but I banged her into cars and pillars. And once she was down, I kicked her ribs.

The police were at my doorstep an hour later. She had called the cops and was pressing charges. I heard the doorbell ring and saw police cars. My parents told me to go upstairs with the babies and they would keep the cops away from me.

I wouldn't come downstairs, but the police wouldn't leave. Finally, I told Dad to send them up. Here I was, looking like a poor little housewife with my two little babies. I was real quiet, saying, "Yes, officer?"

"Listen, Miss Manley, I know this is very humiliating for you, and I know what's happened. She did tell me she has been with your husband tonight, and I can imagine what you're going through. I feel really bad having to come here, but I'm not going to make you feel worse than you already do. I'm not going to make you come down to the station . . ."

He was supposed to take me down and charge me, but he told me to come to the station later that day, and he'd serve me the papers.

Dexter didn't even know this had happened. He didn't call home until three in the afternoon. "I guess you talked to your girlfriend, huh?" I asked.

"What're you talking about?" He was defensive.

"Dexter," I said, "where are you?"

He answered, "Uh, around the corner at a restaurant. Come meet me.

Come meet me for a drink. Come on, Glinda. I feel so bad. Because I love you so much."

"You don't even know what's happened, do you?" I persisted.

"No, what?"

"You haven't talked to Debbie?"

He said no.

So I told him I'd kicked her booty, and, "The worst thing is, Dexter, she had the audacity to press charges. I'm the wife, and she knows she's wrong, and she presses charges on me!"

Later she called Dexter at our house and I said, "Listen, Debbie, I really don't want you calling here. I don't want him calling you." And Dexter was like, "Be quiet. Don't make her mad. She's already going to press charges."

"Don't make her mad?" I was incredulous. It was as if he was protecting her more than he was protecting me. He had it so screwed up.

Anyway, Debbie ended up getting $9,000 in damages. She went in asking for 50 grand.

Each time I'd come home from using drugs or my other vices, I'd cry. I'd see Glinda feeding Little Dexter in his high chair, and I'd find that so beautiful. Maybe—and this is for my drug counselors—it'd flash me back to some pain from my own childhood. It was like my whole day was messed up, and I couldn't sleep. I'd think, Look at what I'm doing! I wouldn't know what to do with myself. Then the next morning I'd wake up and still feel like crap, yet I'd go downstairs and see Glinda feeding Little Dexter in his high chair. And I'd cry again.

I was headed nowhere fast. By March 1987, Glinda had caught on to all of my drug tricks.

One was the way I dressed before I'd use drugs. I didn't know I got dressed in a certain way, but I guess I'd picked up the trait from my daddy. When I was a little boy, I used to watch him lay out his fancy clothes. He'd be talking and singing in the house, and then he'd try to dance. You knew he was going out.

Dexter had a ritual when he got dressed to go out. It was like a ceremony. I used to call it his "get-high clothes." He even put makeup on.

I saw him once with the makeup—I guess it was to help cover the scar—and I said, "Dexter, will you please promise me you'll never let your son see you put that makeup on? He's not going to understand, and he's going to think something's wrong with you."

He first started the makeup for TV. He'd see himself later on videotape, and he'd notice how his face looked smoother. So, at first he only did the makeup for interviews. But I noticed he'd also do it before he went out.

He also was into smelling good, and new underwear. I'd say, "Oh, new underwear?" It used to be, "Dexter, why don't we give this underwear a break and throw it away?" He would not get new underwear. He'd let it rot. So I always knew when he wasn't screwing around, because if any woman saw that underwear . . . no way!

But then he started buying his own little underwear, real sexy stuff. When he pulled out his new underwear and the new socks, it was get-high night, and that also meant screwing-around night. Although he'd swear to me nothing would happen, he'd fib so well, I would almost believe him. Then I'd be on pins and needles until he came home. A lot of times he'd come home while I was having breakfast and feeding the kids.

He'd try to sleep, but I kept him awake. I'd say, "Oh, no. You're not sleeping. You should have slept last night." I'd throw things and carry on so he couldn't sleep.

Then I couldn't talk to him for days. I could not look at his face. I used to tell my mother this, and she would respond, "Glinda, you still love him."

And I'd say, "No, Mom."

She disagreed. "No, as much as you hate him, you still love him. And if you looked in his eyes, I think you'd know."

One time I even tried doing what she said. I looked in his eyes, and it was true. I couldn't look at him. He looked so rejected and dejected and remorseful.

He never walked in cocky after doing drugs, or evil. He'd be like a little boy, as if he never did wrong. I used to jump on that feeling and treat him real mean. I said horrible things.

By the time things got back to normal, he'd be ready for another relapse. Every ten to fourteen days, this would happen. I became like an addict, because I'd start itching at the same time he'd be itching. I was on his same cycle, even though I wasn't using.

That's what they say happens. When you love an addict you become a co-addict. I'd be fine, and then I'd be waiting for the bomb. Him, too. He was waiting to do it again. His body would start to go through a craving, and mine through nervous anxiety.

I'd even mention it to him. "Well, it's almost about that time, Dexter."

He'd say, "Oh no, it's different this time."

I'd say, "Uh uh." And then he'd start dressing in his get-high clothes, and I'd say, "You're about to use."

"No!" he'd say.

Maybe 80 percent of the time he told me no, he really meant it in his heart. But he would use. He couldn't stop.

I felt there was nothing I could do. Where could I go with my two little babies? I wasn't working anymore, and my self-esteem was low because I had gained weight. And the more he disliked the way I looked, the more it kept me eating.

So I came up with a new tactic—when I was close to God—and it drove him crazy. He'd come in from drugging feeling remorseful, and I'd say, "Dexter, I'm going to pray for you." Then, I would hug him, and he would cry, and I would pray. I would be so good to him, I would even give him love.

This made him even more remorseful. He kept saying, "Glinda, how can you love me when I just did what I did?"

At that time I was really close to God, and God gave me an unusual love. I did love him, and I felt sorry for him. I said, "It's not a human love, Dexter. It's not. You're absolutely right. What you did I do not like, but God has given me this love to give to you."

That lasted a year, but he never got better. And after a while, I said, "I don't have no more love." It just got so tiring. I called my mother and said, "Mom, I just can't do it anymore."

She answered, "Baby, I understand."

"Mom, do you think I've given up on God?" I asked.

"No, I don't think that. You're just tired and you're human, and you just don't have nothing left in you," she replied.

And that's about when I turned Dexter in to Coach Joe Gibbs.

Joe Gibbs's wife, Pat, had a women's group, sort of a Bible study. I called Pat one night—this was after the 1986 season and after the Pro Bowl—and I said, "I need to talk to you. Can I come and see you?"

She said, "Sure, come on."

To me, it was a life or death situation. I felt my husband might die. I was afraid he was going to kill himself with this drug.

I had to go to Pat. Was I supposed to let my husband die? Let him run his truck into a gas station and blow himself up or OD in a hotel room? I took a chance on my husband never playing football again, but I wanted him alive.

I prayed, and I asked Pat Gibbs to pray. I said, "I'm telling you something that could cost my husband's career, but I love my husband and want him alive. But you have to promise you won't tell Joe."

She said yes.

I told her Dexter was doing drugs and that I feared for my marriage because he was messing with all these women. And you know what she said? "But, Glinda, haven't you always known that?"

She knew it, and I didn't! That was an awakening. I wasn't telling her anything she didn't already know. I wondered how many other people knew.

"Glinda," she said, "that's been going on a while, hasn't it?"

I felt really mad. "Pat," I said, "I'm asking you as a confidante. I don't want you mentioning any of this to Joe. Will you promise me that?"

She agreed not to say a word unless I told her she could.

After I told her everything about Dexter's drugs, I asked, "Now, Pat, tell me. What do you think your husband would do if he knew? Do you think we should tell Joe? I don't want to be the reason for Dexter to be out of a career, but I also don't want my husband to die."

"Glinda," she said, "I'll be honest with you. Joe is a good man. I think he'll understand. The bottom line is we've assumed drugs for a year. We figured he had a problem. But he never told my husband, and that's what Joe's been trying to do—to get Dexter to admit it."

Then she said, "Why don't I have Joe call you?"

So Joe Gibbs and I started talking on almost a daily basis. Joe would say, "Glinda, Dexter was just in here, but he wouldn't tell me anything." Joe and I kept tabs on Dexter over the phone.

Pat would call first and ask if Dexter was with me. If he wasn't, she'd say, "OK, here's Joe."

Joe was a very good man. He really did look out for Dexter. He really tried to help.

I also could tell he had a heart and that he gained more respect for me because I was a wife who could put her husband's career on the line for his health. That also let me know I must really love Dexter.

Originally, I'd heard Joe didn't like me because he thought I was this fast-talking Chicago woman who was going to take Dexter for a ride. Maybe he thought I was the one who was making him go crazy!

Joe kept saying, "I'll never tell Dexter I've talked to you. That's not going to help your marriage. We'll try to get him to admit it, and then we'll get him help."

I said, "I just want my husband."

Joe and I were in cahoots. If Dexter went out, I'd call Coach Gibbs and say, "Dexter was out all night using." And I'd tell him the area where Dexter

went. That way, Gibbs could call him in and say, "Dexter, I have information that you were out all night using."

We figured maybe Dexter would say, "OK, you're right. You caught me."

But Dexter would deny it. Joe would report, "Glinda, I don't know
what to do. I mean, he just won't admit to it. He's still lying." I told Coach
Gibbs, "He's not trying to lie. He's on drugs, and that's part of his disease.
He lies."

I could tell it really bothered Coach Gibbs that Dexter could look into
his eyes and lie.

On March 10, 1987, it finally came to a head. Dexter came home after
another coke binge. I had not seen him look like this since the night of the
Georgetown incident.

When he came in the house that afternoon, he would look at me and
slip in and out of consciousness. His eyes were rolling up in his head, like the
Georgetown thing, and it was scary.

The first thing I thought was, Somebody must be protecting this man.
He should be dead trying to drive home in a state like this. I don't know how
he made it home.

He went down into the basement, and I heard him moaning, "Glinda,
I don't feel good . . . I don't feel good." And he lay down on the floor. He
started rolling around on the floor, and when I turned him over, his eyes were
still rolling.

I cried, "Oh Dexter, I've gotta call 911. Tell me you're OK, because I
do not want to have to call the ambulance." I knew the story would get out if
I called the ambulance this time.

He kept saying, "Yeah, I'm fine." But as soon as he'd say it, out he'd
go again. My mother was there, so I ran upstairs. "Mom, I think I'm gonna
call. What should I do?"

"Glinda, if you call, it'll get out in the papers, and his career's going to
be over."

So I went back downstairs, and he looked worse. I knew I couldn't live
with myself if he died because I was worried about it getting in the newspapers. I really thought he was dying. So I called 911.

The rescue squad arrived, and went to the basement—about six of
them. I think, deep down, they didn't want to bring him in. One of them
even said, "You know, ma'am, if you bring him in, the world's going to
know." There were trying to protect him.

They started to walk away, and then Dexter's eyes opened back up and
it scared me again. And I said, "No. Just take him."

They asked, "Ma'am, are you sure?"

"Yes, take him."

When they left, I frantically called Coach Gibbs at home. He wasn't there, and Pat said, "Glinda, he's in a meeting at Redskin Park, but he'd told me to get him from whatever he's doing if you call." That's why I still respect Joe so much. He was in an important meeting, and he stole away from the meeting to talk to me on the phone. He really cared about Dexter.

When he returned my call, I told him, "Joe, we've got him now. He's in the hospital. It's public now. You can just say someone called you and told you it was cocaine. It doesn't have to come out that I've been talking to you. Can you please help him?"

Joe sent Dr. Flynn to the hospital. When Dexter finally got lucid and saw Flynn, he knew Gibbs knew. Dr. Flynn told him, "We all know at Redskin Park, and we're going to get you help, Dexter. You're going to be OK."

It didn't bother me that Glinda went to Joe and Pat Gibbs. I've never been mad because I know the unhealthy situation I was in. I thought it was gutsy for a wife to do that, knowing we could lose it all. She showed courage not to care about the material things. I'm just glad I have a woman like that who's willing to turn me in and sacrifice herself, too, to get me well.

She didn't want me doing drugs, but she couldn't stop me. So she had to tell. I really hadn't answered to anybody since my daddy died, except the Redskins. Glinda, she knew that. She had no other choice.

I knew something was fishy, though. Gibbs would call me on the phone and say, "I want to talk to you." I'd see him, and he'd say, "Dexter, I know you're back on drugs. I know that you'll stay sober for a while, but when you get down, or get angry at us, or whatever, you go do drugs."

Then he suggested, "Go to Hazelden. Sneak into treatment. Nobody'll know. It's the off-season. Do it before something bad happens."

He would compare me to Lawrence Taylor. He'd build me up and then say, "Don't let something happen to you in the streets."

I couldn't understand how Gibbs knew I was doing drugs and where I was doing drugs. I figured, He don't have any proof. But it was as if somebody was following me. I would tell myself, "Ah, he don't know. He's never seen me. I've never been caught, so how does he know?"

Well, three days after I left one of my meetings with Gibbs, I did a

Haiti shipment's worth of coke, and I came home sick and throwing up. That's when it all hit the fan.

Yet, even as the news blurbs got out about my collapse, we still told the media it was alcohol only. Alcohol didn't carry the stigma of cocaine.

Even Doc Flynn and the Redskins went along with my alcohol story. It was one hell of a cover-up.

I left detox and had no choice but to fly off to my winter home—Hazelden—for my second go-round with drug counselors.

An Idle Thought

One game, I lost my cocaine spoon in the RFK Stadium locker room.

It was a miniature spoon I used to shovel the coke up my nostril, and I had it with me before the game. But I couldn't locate it later. Hell if I didn't get on my hands and knees and search for it right in front of Gibbs. If someone had asked me what the heck I was doing, I would've said, "Oh, searching for contact lenses."

I didn't wear contacts.

I mean, what if some Redskin equipment guy had found the coke spoon? Think he would've stood up and said, "Whose is this?"

CHAPTER 26

Dexter Does Dalis

CONSIDERING MY DAUGHTER DALIS HAS NEVER walked without a cast, brace, or high-tech cage on her leg, I've wondered if I'm to blame. She was born with a rare leg condition, and I question whether cocaine had anything to do with it. At the time my baby was conceived, I was probably laced with the crap.

Dalis came into this world with a leg curved in the shape of a harp. When the doctors first saw her crooked leg, they weren't alarmed. Babies' bones can easily straighten out. Still, they took X-rays to double-check.

The X-rays were conclusive. They showed the white of the other bones, but where her tibia bone should have been was clear. In other words, she was born minus a tibia bone.

The morning after delivery, an orthopedist woke Glinda to tell her that little Dalis had fibrous dysplaysia, and that it was the worst case they had ever seen; it affected the entire limb—knee to ankle—and it could affect Dalis's growth plate. They knew of twelve cases of the condition in the world and assured her it was nobody's fault, that it was a genetic birth defect. But I still pointed a finger at myself, thinking, The coke, the coke, the coke.

When the doctor wanted to amputate, Glinda asked, "This disease, does this hurt her? Is it cancerous? Will it spread?"

Their answer was no.

"Then why cut off the leg?" she asked. "She won't walk anyway."

They just answered, "From what we've seen, nothing will change."

Me being my usual self, I said, "Who's talking about cutting off my daughter's leg? I'll kick that person's ass."

Dalis was put in a leg cast that went all the way up to her thigh. Since she would wiggle out of it, the doctors nicknamed her Houdini.

Another day, when we took Dalis to the hospital for a new cast, our regular doctor was in surgery and unavailable. Suddenly, this Indian or Pakistani—I don't know which—walks in, doesn't announce himself as a doctor, and picks up a circular saw that had ugly teeth on it. Dalis screamed. We were worried and protective. You know how parents are.

"Wait! Hold it! Who are you?" I demanded.

The doctor looked at me and said he was Doc So-and-so.

I asked, "What are you doing?"

"Cutting a cast off."

"Doesn't that hurt?"

"No," he answered. He was talking matter of fact and sounded pissed off I'd stopped him.

"How long have you been a doctor?" I inquired.

He didn't answer.

I repeated, "How many years have you been a doctor?"

He finally looked up, said twenty years or something, and gave me a glance like, What the hell is he asking me?

He turned the switch back on, but as he was doing so, he snidely said, "Oh, I've never cut a cast off before in my life."

He may have meant it facetiously, but I was ready to ring his clock. I grasped him by the collar and flung him out of the room. I shouted, "Well, you ain't cuttin' this one off then."

"Come on, Glinda," I said, "we're out of here."

Ever since then, little Dalis can't tolerate noises that remind her of the saw. When I was playing for the Phoenix Cardinals in preseason of 1991, they shot off fireworks over Sun Devil Stadium during lineup introductions and also when the Cardinals scored—if we could score. Dalis heard one firework and started screaming—and she's got some serious lungs—"Let's go! Let's go!"

Glinda had no choice but to leave the game and take her back to the hotel. As soon as they made it to the car, Dalis gave Glinda a high five and said, "We're safe now."

Soon after Dalis's birth, Glinda and I were facing the prospect of having Dalis in a wheelchair forever, in a cast forever, or with no leg forever:

When Dalis was three months old, my mother called and said, "Do you know Rev. Fred Price is coming to D.C.?"

It was mid-August—during Dexter's 1986 holdout—and I said, "Mom, I didn't know Fred Price did healings."

"Well, he does," she said.

I'd watched him before, and I had a lot of respect for him. I knew he wouldn't heal her but that God would. I said, "OK, I'll go. What do I have to lose?"

It was the same day Dalis was to get a new cast at Children's Hospital, but we decided to go to the faith healing first.

Once we were there, the Reverend Price said, "All people here for healing, please come down." Hundreds moved forward, and we followed meekly. Dexter had agreed to be part of it. He was a trouper.

I'd never seen a faith healing done in person. I always thought it was hocus pocus, charlatan stuff, but I learned healing comes from faith. I didn't care if Fred Price had any power. All I had to worry about was my faith, my salvation.

Fred Price had everyone close their eyes. Then he explained, "This is not an emotional thing. You don't have to scream. I don't want anyone watching what's happening to the other people up here, so just please close your eyes and listen to my words. Soak it in. I have no power, yet I can be a channel. You must only be receptive."

He continued, "When this power comes through, it'll be like a bolt of lightning through our hands." But he said if we resist him and don't have faith, it will wear him out.

I peeked, anyway, I saw people passing out. Very gently, he'd touch them, and their knees would buckle. After a minute, they'd come to. He'd say something real quick, and they'd be passed out before he'd finish. He'd just touch them on the forehead.

When he got to me, he said, "Ma'am, open your eyes."

I was carrying little Dalis, and he asked, "Do you want to heal your child?"

"Yes."

He said, "I want to know what's wrong."

I told him about the possibility of amputation, and he responded, "No! Na uh," like he was angry. "No one mess with her!" He put one hand on her forehead and another on her leg, and he gave the most powerful prayer. He said, "Satan, I rebuke you. You will not claim any parts of this child."

He said a prayer, and through his hands all God's power went into Dalis. But he also touched my head for a second. I'm not weird, but it was like electricity in my body. It looked like white light in my mind. I was losing my equilibrium, but I couldn't fall, because I had the baby. The ushers helped me step over people who were all laid out, and Dexter urged, "Come on, let's go."

But I couldn't go. My legs were like spaghetti noodles. Reverend Price had said that when you go through this experience you'll be tired the rest of the day, and he was right. I thought, Imagine what's happening inside Dalis, imagine what's happening inside her body. I had to sit ten to fifteen minutes before we could leave.

When I came to, Fred Price said to me, "Miss Manley, you are just the mother of this child. But it does not work except through faith. She's too young to understand, but through your faith, your daughter can be healed. Satan will work on you, will tell you what happened here today is a joke. And every time Satan tells you your daughter is not healing, you say, 'Thank you, Jesus, for healing her.' Let it be a chant. Scream it. Shout it. Don't whisper. But don't do it around people, because they'll think you're crazy. At those times, say it softly to yourself. You may not believe it today or tomorrow, but you'll have reprogrammed your computer. You'll believe it 100 percent eventually."

Fred Price also said, "Be prepared for Satan. It'll happen today. When you walk out that door, Satan will tell you she isn't healed."

He gave me a little booklet to read, and we left for Children's Hospital.

I didn't know what to make of this holy-rolly stuff, but Dalis was to get a new cast that day. Immediately, the doctors touched her leg and started talking among themselves. They called a specialist in, and Glinda asked, "What's the problem?"

They replied, "Miss Manley, touch her leg." It was hot.

Glinda said, "Why is that happening?"

The doctor explained, "It's so hot because there must be a tumor in there. We must do a biopsy."

Glinda looked the doctors dead in the faces and said, "No. She's been healed. We've just had her healed by Reverend Fred Price."

"That's nice, Miss Manley, but we have to do this X-ray," they insisted. Little Dalis's head wasn't hot, just her leg.

On the X-ray they were expecting to see a huge tumor, but you know what? They saw white matter coming into the tibia where it used to be clear. This was bone matter. Glinda shouted, "I told you, I told you. She's healing."

I mean, just two weeks before at our last appointment, there'd been no bone.

The doctor said, "Wait, Miss Manley. This doesn't mean it's good. This just means she doesn't have fibrous dysplaysia, because you don't get bone growing in with fibrous dysplaysia."

I was telling these doctors, "Told you so, told you so," but now they began telling me she had something worse than fibrous dysplaysia. And I thought of what Reverend Price had said, that Satan will try his hardest to deter my faith. So I was prepared for whatever they said.

Well, the doctor goes, "We believe Dalis has neurofibromatosis—NF." That's what the Elephant Man had. I was like, "Oh, my God."

I said, "With tumors?"

They said the tumors probably wouldn't start until she hit puberty, and they said it was possible she could go blind.

I was so thankful Fred Price had said, "Satan will work you harder than ever," because that's what Satan was doing.

Dexter was dumbfounded. It hurt him. Even today if we talk about it, he almost cries. When we would put a cast on her or take one off her, he couldn't even be in the room. He'd be ready to beat somebody up if they hurt her. He wondered if his use of drugs did this to her. It really bothered him.

I told Dexter, "I'm not going to read these pamphlets on NF because then I'll believe the doctors."

Then I said, "I'll totally believe that God's healing her."

We agreed to let them do a biopsy, although I just believed it would prove the doctors wrong. It was a week before they did the biopsy, probably the longest of my life. I'd rock her at night praying, "Lord, please let my faith grow more and more. I'm a baby Christian, and I need help. I need a sign." The bone in her leg an hour after she'd seen the Reverend Price had been a sign, but I needed more.

When the doctors took her in for the biopsy, they were all grim. They had no doubt it was NF. My doctor—Dr. Malawar—never smiled, and he came out of that X-ray room cheesing it. "Miss Manley," he said, "the bottom line is she does not have NF. We did every test imaginable. What she has is fibrous dysplaysia, but it's the only kind in the world where it's actually healing itself. Never before has this happened."

I thought Dexter would become a Christian right there. I thought that through these tribulations he'd understand God, that maybe that's why God gave me Dalis, to help the salvation of Dexter.

No, I didn't turn into a born-again. All I knew was from that point on, there was bone coming in. By the time Dalis was nine months old, you could no longer see the break. Her weaker leg was two and one-half inches shorter than the other and was a little crooked at the ankle, but she was strong enough where we could take off her cast.

She began walking at nine months, and she hasn't really missed much of a beat since. They don't have a name for it; it's just the rarest form of fibrous dysplaysia known to man.

The doctors still considered amputation a frickin' option because there was a small hairline fracture that kept breaking from the stress of her walking on it. We then were referred to a doctor in Baltimore, a supposed genius.

This Doc Paley in Baltimore was so sure of himself. I like cocky Pro Bowl doctors like that. Other doctors had said, "We *may* be able to help her," but Doc Paley said he could undeniably heal the bone and lengthen it at the same time.

Glinda said, "What?"

He replied, "Miss Manley, it could've been done when she was one year old. But thank God you're here now and they never amputated."

"Sign me up!" Glinda announced.

Dalis's weaker leg was two and one-half inches shorter than the other at this time, and in two months, this Doc Paley had it fully lengthened.

He put a high-tech cage on her leg, connected by screws and pins. It's called an Illizarov after the Russian doctor who designed it; Doc Paley studied under him for five years. The device was on little Dalis from February 1990 until October 1990, but then they saw she was slightly knock-kneed; so they put it back on.

Her brother, Little Dexter the evangelist wanna-be, prays for her. He'll hold his hand up and go, "Dear Lord, I know you can do it. You can heal. You're the almighty powerful king. In the name of Jesus, please heal her."

Well, Dalis is five years old, and all she has to do is wear a brace for protection at school so there's no shock or trauma to the leg. She'll be able to go to gym class with a brace on. Listen, that's Doc Paley's baby, too. He's not gonna let anything happen to her. By puberty she can discard the brace.

That will be a gigantically happy day. I have cried over and over about Dalis. I've said, "Why her?" I was called dumb and was neglected by my daddy; and I thought I was ugly, and I've been on drugs. And now I'd done this to my kid? It was just another whack to my self-esteem.

Poor Dalis wakes up at night nowadays and says, "I hate myself, I hate myself." I can't stand it that she's getting a complex, too.

Some moms and dads are afraid for their kids to hit puberty.

We can't wait.

An Idle Thought

If Glinda had left me, I'd have never received custody of the kids.

I mean, one time I'd taken Little Dexter with me to Denver for the John Elway Celebrity Golf Tournament, and—my luck—it turned out he was nearly kidnapped.

When I asked Glinda if I could bring Little Dexter to Denver, she had said, "Are you sure? Dexter, you know they'll have all kinds of functions you'll want to go to, and you won't be able to if you have Little Dexter with you."

I explained, that was why it'd be great Little Dexter was coming. He'd keep me off drugs.

Well, Little Dexter—being sort of a momma's boy back then—called Glinda the second day we were there and asked, "Mommy, will you tell Daddy not to leave me in the hotel room when I go to sleep?"

Glinda answered, "Little Dexter, he's not going to leave you."

Little Dexter repeated, "No Mommy, no Mommy. Just tell him. Just tell him not to do that, OK?"

Glinda made Little Dexter hand me the phone. She said, "Dexter, say it out loud so your son can hear. Tell him you're not going to leave him once he goes to sleep." So I told him I wasn't gonna leave.

Then Glinda tore into me. She said, "Now Dexter, you just promised this child you will not leave him. Don't you dare leave him, even to go get ice, unless you take him with you. You promise? If you leave him, he'll never believe you again. He's going to count on your word."

Well, addictions own you. I left that night.

There was a dinner party in the lobby of our hotel; and a few hours into it, I was standing there minding my own business when I saw Little Dexter in his pajamas, holding his baby doll. He was with a maid, who was walking him toward the kitchen.

Who knew what she was gonna do to him in there?

I stole him from her. The next morning, I called Glinda as if nothing had happened, but that Little Dexter has a big mouth. He spilled the beans to Glinda.

Little Dexter told her, "Mommy, Daddy left me last night. I didn't know where he was, and it was all dark in the room. I ran out of the room, and I couldn't get back in because the door locked on me. I just started walking, and I didn't know where my daddy was."

Glinda says that since then Little Dexter has this fear of abandonment. I can't believe an incident such as that would influence a kid like

Little Dexter, but—to this day—whenever he sees an Embassy Suites Hotel, he says, "That's the hotel daddy left me in."

It only goes to show that you are a product of your childhood. Maybe I'm starting to believe that now. I admit that little boy of mine has a lot of fear in him. Whenever he sees another big man or musclebound man, he tugs on that man's shirt and asks, "Are you stronger than my daddy?"

Other than me, Little Dexter's favorite football player in Charles Mann. He once asked Charles, "Are you stronger than my daddy?" Charles said, "Noooo. No one's stronger than your daddy."

Even at home, Little Dexter, asks me, "Daddy, are you strong?"

One time, I said, "Daddy ain't strong anymore."

Little Dexter got scared. I freaked him out. He said, "Daddy, yes you are. You know you're the strongest guy. You may not be strong in football, but you're the strongest on this block, right?"

I'm his protection. It's like if I'm strong, he can go ahead and sleep at nights. And when I tell him I'm not strong, he'll start panicking. He'll want to talk about it all night.

Glinda and I both notice he will check all the locks on the house every night. He'll double-lock and triple-lock. If I'm not home, he'll tell Glinda, "Just in case, Mommy, I've got my rifle upstairs and a big stick. So if someone comes up these stairs . . ."

Glinda tells him, "But Dexter, that's a toy rifle."

He'll say, "I know it's a toy rifle, but if the crook doesn't have a gun and they see me pointing it at them, they may think it's real and run away."

I took Little Dexter to Astroworld in Houston about two years ago, and he was afraid of every ride. I said, "Dexter, I'll get on the ride with you," and he replied, "No, something will happen to both of us, Daddy."

I decided I'd have to go on a rollercoaster myself. I hoped he'd want to hop on, but when I sat down on the seat, he shouted, "Hold it! Hold it!"

The rollercoaster man was about to start the ride and told Little Dexter to back off.

"Wait!" Little Dexter screamed, "I've got to talk to my daddy!"

He came up to me and said, "Daddy, are you going to be safe? Promise me. Promise me you'll be safe. You know you always get into trouble, Daddy."

"I'll be fine," I told him.

Then he said, "Daddy? Do you love me, Daddy?"

When the ride was over—and it did toss me around some—Little Dexter said, "Listen, Daddy, that ride is dangerous. They should close it down."

We found a slower ride—for three-year-olds, and he was five. Little Dexter agreed to ride it, so I went to get popcorn. But then I heard a ruckus and saw security guards rushing from everywhere. I said, "Must be Little Dexter."

I was right. The ride had started spinning, and he'd jumped up and said, "Stop this machine! Stop this machine!"

That is one frightened kid, and I hope to hell it's not *my* fault.

CHAPTER 27
Define Dysfunctional

WHEN GLINDA AND JOE GIBBS LED ME BY A leash to Hazelden in March 1987, I had to check in under an *unassumed* name—Dexter Manley. This time the whole world knew I was in rehab. I couldn't call Darryl Grant, and say, "Yo, Darryl, I'm in Tahiti."

The night of my collapse in our basement, word leaked out I'd been rushed to the hospital. Glinda had to appear on TV to dispel all the drug rumors. She put on a hell of a show.

I had to fib. Totally. God, that was hard. I don't like cameras too much in the first place, and then to sit up there and lie about it.

Rick Walker—Dexter's old teammate who worked at the NBC station in town—did the interview. Everyone wanted to interview me, but I said only one person: Rick.

He had the camera crew with him, and I told him, "Listen, don't ask me certain things." I felt I could do that with him. I went on, "If you ask me something I don't want, I'm not going to do it."

He said he was going to ask me two or three questions, and I insisted on knowing what they were. Then I stated, "Well, don't ask me anything else. That's all you'll get."

On TV I said it was alcohol only. I hated myself for lying.

Why'd I do it? To protect him. That's what co-dependents do! I had to protect him. He was my livelihood. But I didn't realize that by lying I was enabling him to do more damage to himself.

I just figured I was protecting the family. Dexter wouldn't go on the air, and all the reporters and Rick kept saying, "Something's got to be said. If it's not Dexter, Glinda's got to do it." So I did. But as soon as I finished it deep down I hated Dexter.

If I was going to benefit at all from the drug treatment, the people at Hazelden had to convince me I was an addict. And also show me *why* I was an addict.

They said I came from a dysfunctional home, but I didn't buy it. These drug counselors tell you 95 percent of the people in America come from dysfunctional homes. So I had to look at myself and say, "Well, my momma and daddy didn't fight. We took family trips. We had entertainment. I was always a happy kid."

I could understand them saying we were dysfunctional if I came from a home with one parent, struggling. Of course we were poor, but both of my parents worked. We had money.

At Hazelden they told me I was addicted from childhood. They said I had an addictive personality. They also said it's hereditary. They say if your parents are alcoholics or addicts, you are. Well, my daddy and momma drank and played cards over at the Irvin's house, but it was nothing out of the ordinary. I mean, hell, yeah, I remember my daddy coming home drunk two or three times. One day, he came home drunk and pulled out all our clothes from our dresser and took a shit in our drawer. But there was no violence, as I recall.

Another time, Daddy came home drunk, went in the bathroom, and peed in the dirty clothes hamper.

To everybody else it sounds vicious that he took a dump in our bedroom drawer. But what did we do? We laughed. To my knowledge, he wasn't an alcoholic.

My two uncles on my momma's side were alcholics. They drank; so it was in my family. But not in my immediate family.

My daddy may have come after me once with a baseball bat, but he wasn't drunk when he did it. That was his way of disciplining. Hell, he ran me out of the house, but he wasn't drunk when he did it. Now, if he came home beating on us, that would have been a problem. Or beating on Momma. Or not paying his bills. Or not getting to work. But no, those things didn't happen. Daddy was a literate man. I'd see him up at night paying bills.

I could accept myself being an alcoholic or addict if I could say, yes, my daddy was. Then I could see a link, but I didn't see a link.

As for Momma, we all know she started drinking after Daddy died. Was she an alcoholic before then? In my opinion, no.

Consequently, it was hard for me when I first went to Hazelden—and also the second time there—to accept the idea that my family's past made me an addict.

Yes, it's true everyone in my family had been through crap, but does that make it hereditary? I don't know. To me, that's part of life. People drink. Some can handle it; some can't. And I don't know too many people who can't handle it.

In my case, I drank and did drugs because somebody said, "Hey drink this." So, I drank it. Or somebody said, "Hey, try this drug." So, I tried it. Am I weak? When Perry Brooks told me about cocaine, I wanted to try it. That's how I started.

Maybe it's just my metabolism. I don't think it ever took much for me to get drunk. Matter of fact, my old buddy Gerald Franklin thinks when I take just one sip, I get violent:

N*o, man, Dexter didn't drink growing up. He didn't smoke joints or cigarettes. But I do remember one night in high school when Dexter and his brother Reginald drank Thunderbird, and then Dexter cut off all his hair. He was a skinhead like Isaac Hayes.*

Then we all went over to a party. Some girl came up with this dog, and it kept barking. Dexter—boy, he was drunk, and 'cause he never drank, the alcohol really affected him greatly—picked up the dog and slammed it.

I think that dog died instantly. We were drinking spiked punch, and I guess Dexter was stooged. He was about seventeen at the time.

So then some guy came out of the house talking crazy, and Dexter picked him up and tossed him in the thorn bushes.

But, like I said, Dexter didn't drink often.

So that was the struggle I had with the people of Hazelden: I felt deep down I wasn't an alcoholic and addict. They did, and I lied to get the hell out of there.

One of their deals was to put me in the middle of a circle, in what they called the "hot chair." When you're in the hot seat, you tell your story. You tell what led you into treatment, and your peers evaluate you. Afterward, your peers decide if what you're saying is a bunch of bull or real.

I told them what I thought of myself—but I didn't exactly blurt out that I was addicted—and a couple of people said, "Hey, get frickin' real."

Most of the time there, I was visiting with two doctors. Both of the docs said I was slick as a fox. They said I had street sense but wondered if I was serious about the program or not. Hell, no, I wasn't.

They said I was in there for bullshit reasons, just to get my wife back and to stay in the NFL. They hit the nail on the head.

They also asked all of us patients to write a letter to whomever you were most mad at—the person didn't have to be alive, and you didn't mail it—and I contemplated writing mine to my daddy because he never told me he loved me.

But I never wrote the letter. Hell, I couldn't write. But the people who were functional did write letters to their ghosts. It's all part of learning how to grieve losses, deal with anger. You write a letter to whomever you're pissed at, and then you bury it or burn it up. When you bury it, you supposedly bury your anger.

To be honest, I didn't verbalize any anger to anyone. Why? There's no one I've been angry at in my life. No one! Who would it be? Not my daddy. I miss it that he never told me he loved me, but I'm not angry with him. If he had beaten me up, then I'd have a right to be angry and to wear chips. But I ain't angry at nobody.

If anything, I would've written a letter to Daddy apologizing for not telling him I was married. I wish I could clear that up. I've *been* angry at my dad, but not since he's been dead.

I was trapped in Hazelden for about a month in 1987. Redd Foxx's nephew wasn't there to rag on me this time, but my doctors probably figured the same thing he did in 1986: Dexter'll be back.

I have to admit I listened a little more during the second trip in. I returned home with a book of sayings called *Touchstones*. It was a very wise book, and I like to consider myself a wise man; so I carried it in my Louis Vuitton bag. I'd keep it available in the toilet, too. I liked carrying books around. I imagine it made me feel better about myself, but I also imagine it was a little bit of my con.

I also returned with motivational cassette tapes I'd play in my truck. I liked those suckers. One I've often played, even to this day, is "You've Got to Be Hungry" by Les Brown, the motivator. I can't say the tapes worked. The trick, I guess, is to have a Walkman with you just as you're about to do coke and slip in the cassette before you snort. Unfortunately, I never packed a Walkman.

Hazelden always stressed the importance of Alcoholics Anonymous meetings as a form of aftercare. When I left Hazelden the first time—in 1986—I began going to a group therapy every Wednesday night in D.C., though I don't think it was AA. A minister there had a drinking problem, and we got into a discussion. I was young and didn't know squat about addiction. I told him what I thought he wanted to hear; I said, "All I need to do is go to church, and God will cure everything."

"That's not so," he said.

Someone suggested I go to AA, too. But I'd never been to an AA meeting, and I didn't know the content. My fear was—I guess because I was a Redskin—that people would recognize me and tell my secrets. I was embarrassed to go. I mean, you hear stories about a bunch of old drunks.

I went to my first AA meeting in a church basement and hid behind a wall. As soon as that meeting was over, I dashed out of there. They had asked me to talk, and I said I was there for someone else to learn about AA.

Even to this day, if I go to a meeting, I'm almost like the first guy out of there. I get so uncomfortable when it comes to talking to people afterward because I feel so much like a phony.

I just don't enjoy sticking around after the meeting and shooting the breeze with a bunch of people I don't know. I guess the AA theory is that recovery takes place before a meeting and after, when you make associations with people, but it's still as if I want to do it my way. I need to get out of my head and think I'm a normal guy and socialize with everybody.

I just feel I have to watch what I say in there to protect my anonymity. I can't open up because everyone knows who I am. They say you can let your shirt out, but you can't. They begged me for autographs in those AA meetings. Jim Vance of WRC-TV in Washington says, "Don't give autographs at AA meetings. You're in there for a reason like everyone else."

So, unconsciously, I wanted out of AA meetings. I felt they'd tell their friends whatever I'd said in there.

Once a woman spouted to me, "Oh, one of the anchor people in Washington, G———, comes to our meeting." Why would she say that to me? So is he supposedly an alcoholic? I don't know, but she wasn't very cool to open her big mouth. She's just a human being, and humans talk.

It might make their day, but it doesn't let me open up. I'd rather speak one-on-one to a psychologist. Being in a group doesn't make a well-known guy like G——— or me want to be their friend. It's a mixed signal when I go to meetings and everybody goes out of their way to speak to me. It's a mixed signal because I'm in there feeling like I'm worth two cents.

For me, it's Alcoholics Un-anonymous.

But back in 1986, I forced myself to go to AA meetings. And I'd sit there and say, "Hi, I'm Dexter and I'm an alcoholic and addict."

Eventually, someone said I'd feel better if I had a "sponsor," someone to call, to listen, and to give me advice, who would not get pissed off if I called them at five in the morning.

A sponsor can't stop me from doing drugs, because first I've got to want to stop. But he or she can be a sounding board for whatever is on my mind. Obviously I needed a sponsor, and I found myself a doozy in 1986. Pham Chopra.

I met Pham through this guy named Chuck Brewster, who has since died. Chuck went to the Christian Fellowship Church that I attended, and he somehow knew about my problem. Chuck said he had the perfect sponsor for me.

Pham was from India. Although he was from a very wealthy family, he'd come over with just $200 in his pocket. He went to the University of Michigan, earned a master's degree and became an engineer.

He came from a family of doctors. Everyone in his family was a doctor, except him. I don't know if that has anything to do with him becoming an alcoholic or not:

Sixteen years ago, I went through something similar to Dexter. Not drugs, but alcohol primarily.

Dexter's wife would go to church, and one of the guys there—Chuck—looked up to me and knew I worked with tough guys. You know, hard-asses.

He told me about Dexer Manley, and I said, "Dexter who?"

Chuck said, "You don't know Dexter?"

I went to Michigan; I loved Bo Schembechler. But I didn't care much for pro football. If I watched, I'd watch the Dallas Cowboys.

When Dexter and I first met, there was a lot of pain and fear inside of him. He reached out. He said, "I need help."

My approach to these things had all the elements of a kick-ass approach. I knew Dexter shook hands with a hard grip, so when Dexter put out his hand to me, I knew I needed leverage. You've got to slam your index finger in, and I got him on that one. He said, "Ouch." I do remember telling him, "If you want me to work with you, you've got to call me every day, so you hear my voice at least twice a day.

I had reconstructed my own life. I was once diagnosed as an acute alcoholic with little chance of recovery. I could tell it like it is to Dexter.

By the time I'd finished my second Hazelden stint in 1987, I was mentioning Pham publicly. I just loved Pham's sayings. He'd say, "The same man will never swim in the same river twice." What he meant was the river and the man will eventually change.

Intellectual people think that crap is a bunch of bull, but I loved his expressions. He'd always say "cultivate your garden," things like that. I wasn't used to intellectual talk. It made me feel like an intellect for the first time to be able to quote Pham.

Pham was definitely my man. He used to help me get out of things I didn't want to do or help me prepare for interviews by letting me borrow some of his wise sayings. The Redskins, though, still had me going to see Doc Flynn, too. I guess Bobby Beathard could see I didn't like Doc Flynn:

That's because Flynn had picked up all Dexter's tricks, and Dexter wanted people around whom he could control, like that guy Pham.

I imagine the Redskins and the public didn't know what to make of Pham.

See, Pham walked around wearing a turban. I thought it was kind of strange myself. I figured it was probably some sort of cult thing, but here I was being seen all the time with a guy in a turban. It was like he was some guru, and people would say, "Oh, Dexter's hanging around with a voodoo person to try to break his addiction."

It contributed to my extravagant aura around D.C. heading into the 1987 season.

AN IDLE THOUGHT

As you can tell by now, Joe Gibbs has a control fetish.

I mean, before the 1987 season started, he made a big scene and ordered me to drop my radio show.

I was going to do morning broadcasts on DC-101, which featured this knucklehead DJ called Greaseman. Hell, I was all for doing these shows. They were paying me 200 grand.

But Gibbs called me into his office before the season and told me to tear up my DC-101 contract. He said, "How can you work for that kind of station?"

See, a few years earlier, Greaseman had made what you might say is a racist comment. On the first anniversary of the Martin Luther King birthday holiday, he had said, "Hey, I drove to work today and there was no traffic. Shoot four more, and we can take the whole week off."

Well, not too many people knew what Greaseman said until *The*

Washington Post wrote an article a couple of days later. Then all the local TV stations picked up on it, and it became quite a hullabaloo.

That's what Gibbs was talking about when I signed up with DC-101. Gibbs said I'd be "turning my back on black people" if I worked there, because Martin Luther King was a "great man."

Hell, you're damn right I think Martin Luther King's a great man. But does that mean I give up $200,000 for an isolated incident? And an old one at that?

I asked myself how I could be turning myself on black people? I'm supposed to walk away from 200 grand?

Gibbs was trying to manipulate me. He didn't give a hoot about what the Greaseman said. He probably was laughing when he heard it.

Gibbs was just trying to control. He was trying to con me into walking away. What was his motive? Maybe he didn't want me getting too popular, or maybe Gibbs thought with that extra money I wouldn't be as motivated to play.

Maybe he thought I was too talkative and might give away strategy on the radio. He probably never had respect for me, thinking I'd talk about the game plan or rip somebody on the opposing team. Or maybe he heard I was getting more than he was getting for his show on WTOP, and he was pissed.

I mean, he's the head coach. Maybe he thinks he should be getting the big bucks. It's like what he used to tell guys when their contracts were up. He'd say, "Well, look how much money you make as a football player. You make more money than I make."

Well, if I make more money than you, it's because I've paid the price to be a football player. I *deserve* to get more than you.

When I held out in 1986, Gibbs said, "Well, Dex, you'll make more money than I do. And you're a *football* player."

Hell, that's the life I chose! I'm supposed to. He was the coach, and he deserves to make exactly what he makes. Just because I play doesn't mean I shouldn't make more than him.

Well, after Gibbs asked me to leave DC-101, I walked out of his office and went straight into John Kent Cooke's office. Beathard was in there, and I said, "Bobby, Coach Gibbs wants me to quit the Greaseman show. What do you think?"

Beathard said, "The hell with that."

Beathard also said, "Do it. I like DC-101. I like the Greaseman. I think it's a good thing, Dexter."

Beathard also said, "Oh, the hell with Joe Gibbs. But don't tell him I said that."

Above: At an Easter Egg signing on the White House grounds. I'm still mad I never got to the Oval Office. *Right*: Mr. D wants you!

My wife Glinda didn't know what she was getting herself
into. Here we are on our wedding day (*left*), in a family
photo (*above*), and during a day on the town in Paris
(*below*). Isn't she fine!

Above left: My pride and joy. Little Dexter and sister Dalis hugging in the breakfast room. *Above right*: Derrick, who's getting to be a regular adult, and I. Where does the time go?
Below: Dalis, Glinda, Derrick, and Little Dexter (left to right).

Left: Dalis and Little Dexter dressed up for Halloween. *Above*: I always wanted to be Santa Claus, but I was in too good of shape. *Below*: Autographing for fans following a practice session. I used to sign some, "Say no to drugs?" (Nate Fine Photo)

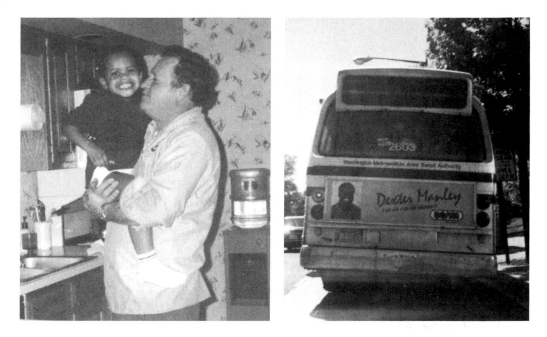

Above left: My best friend Lester Townsend holding Dalis. Lester worried about me even more than Glinda did. *Above right*: Joe Gibbs ordered me not to do this radio show, but the hell with that. The Redskins used to tape it for Gibbs every morning to see if I'd been outrageous. *Below*: Pham Chopra was my mystery guru.

Above: Secretary of Defense Casper Weinberger meets the secretary of *the* defense, Dexter Manley. *Below*: It was an honor to meet President George Bush, though I noticed a hole in his pants.

Today is the day that I have prayed would never come. After an emotional meeting with my friend and attorney, Bob Woolf, he has agreed with my decision to call you here and break the news to you myself.

For the past year, since Commissioner Tagliabue gave me the opportunity to resume my career in the NFL, plus the year undergoing successful drug therapy treatment, I have been tested for drugs three times per week and have attended (AA) meetings regularly several times per week without any problem.

Nobody knows better than I do how difficult it is to try day by day, week by week to draw upon one's deepest reserves and strength, to dig in and fight this insidious disease that has plagued me and so many others.

For two years, I have worked long and hard to restore my self esteem and self dignity. As a recovering addict, it is essential and critical that I be honest with myself, my family, my teammates, the fans, everyone depending on me not to be dependent on drugs.

I recently have had a setback and the fact that it has happened, even if only once, shows me that I am in trouble and that I must renew my battle with this disease.

Therefore, it is with a heavy heart that I have come here today to announce my immediate retirement from the NFL.

It is the end of an era for me, and I would like to express my deep appreciation to the NFL and to the Tampa Bay Buccaneers. I will miss all my teammates who have stood by me throughout the years, and most especially the fans who have been supportive of me.

The struggle on the field is over, while the struggle off the field continues. From now on the only clock I'm going to clean is my own.

The battle in football is a game, the battle for my life is not. I may have lost a battle, but I will win the war.

Thank you.

Right: I cried like Jim Bakker when I read my retirement announcement on December 12, 1991. Below: This is one of my final sacks. They made me famous.

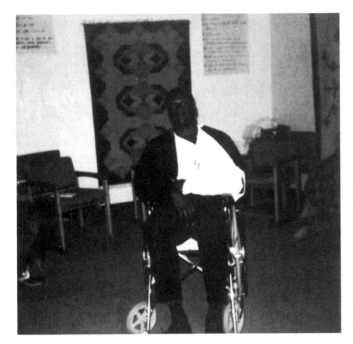

Left: In rehab at Sierra Tucson, they tried to show me what cocaine can do. I was required to live in a wheelchair and only have the use of my right side. *Below*: I hope Little Dexter always remembers this. He and I sprint down the field together after I signed with the Ottawa Roughriders. Look at his stride. [Photo courtesy of Wayne Cuddington]

Beathard also said, "Oh, Joe Gibbs is a religious guy. You've got to understand his thinking. But the hell with that. Do it."

Well, that boosted me up. I also asked Charley Casserly, who was the assistant general manager. And I asked a couple of other white scouts what they thought, and they all said, "No way, you've got to do that."

And you know what? Gibbs came walking out of his office, and I said, "Coach, I can't do what you asked me to."

Gibbs gnashed his teeth and said, "You're gonna regret this!" Just like that.

CHAPTER 28

Redskingate

I SHOWED UP FOR THE 1987 TRAINING CAMP with an uncharacteristic edict: no interviews.

Obviously, it's hard for me to shut my mouth, but at least I could talk on my morning DC-101 radio show with Greaseman, the show Gibbs hated.

The year 1987 brought the NFL strike and the replacement games, and I was a focal point throughout. I loved it. I kept threatening to cross the picket line and play on the scab team. Hell, I never meant a word of it. I was just stirring things up to get on TV.

Neal Olkewicz, our player rep, went 'round and 'round with me the entire strike:

We had a players-only meeting before the strike, and Dexter was screaming, "I'll stay out as long as it takes!" Then, the next day he says on the radio, "Hey, I'm going in."

After a while, I kind of hoped he'd go in. He was being such a pain in the ass.

One time, we were deciding as a team whether to go in, but he was saying the opposite on the radio. He and I had a big blowup about it. He said, "I wish you guys kept me informed!" and I said, "I have forty-five players to keep informed, and I can't wet-nurse you, Dexter." It got to the point where we hoped he went in, but you know Gibbs wouldn't have let him.

Gibbs kept a few guys out: Dexter, Jay Schroeder, George Rogers. Gibbs made it clear that sticking together had been our strength in 1982, and he wanted us to do it again. Gibbs had as much to do with keeping our team—and Dexter—from crossing the line as I did.

232

I'd never recommend another strike. I was the first to tell Gene Upshaw that year, "I'm not gonna do this unless everyone is serious about it." I saw what happened the first day. Our player reps said, "Everyone be here at 7:00 A.M. to stop the bus taking replacement players into Redskin Park." Only two guys showed up on time.

I was never going to cross, man. I just didn't like it that we weren't following our game plan. As for Joe Gibbs, I remember him saying publicly that he would not comment on the strike, yet he was running the show behind the scenes.

One day we all decided to cross as a group, but Gibbs told us not to. We made a decision at the Ramada to go in and practice, and nothing would hold us back. But then Gibbs held us back. Gibbs had a bunch of those boys wrapped around his fingers.

Gibbs was calling the shots, and Jay Schroeder was telling management everything the players were doing. Schroeder was our leak. He was like Bubba Tyer, our trainer. Hell, from the locker room, Bubba was strictly a pipeline to John Kent Cooke and Joe Gibbs's offices. Bubba and Schroeder, the two of them were offshore drilling pipelines.

I admit I had the herd mentality in the end and followed whatever the rest of the team decided to do, but here's why: I knew in the long run I had to play with these guys.

I sounded as if I was uncontrollable for Olky, but part of it was just to get on TV. I wasn't ever going to cross the line, but everything I said was such big news and it turned me on. I just couldn't believe what big news it was. I was toying with the media. One day, I'd say, "I'm with the group, " and the next day I'd say, "I'm going in. I need the cash."

Hell, I walked the picket line only once. I went that first day, but nobody else was on time; so I said screw it.

I guess I must've really pissed some guys off, because quarterback Doug Williams ripped me on TV. Doug was asked if I crossed the picket line, would it influence other guys to cross. He said no. But he said if Art Monk crossed, that would influence guys.

Well, Glinda called Doug on the phone and sassed him:

I thought Doug got too personal there. The Redskins portray themselves as family, so he could say that to the boys when they're sitting around, but it wasn't appropriate to say it on TV. I lost a lot of respect for Doug, my blood curdled, and I said, "I'm gonna call him."

Dexter said, "Go ahead."

Dexter knew he couldn't stop me anyway. So I called Rick Walker's restaurant, where Doug had done the interview live on TV, and asked, "Is Doug there?"

Dexter was already playing on a racist team, and the white guys loved to hear Doug say that about another black man. To me, it didn't look like the Redskins were sticking together as a family.

When Doug got on the phone, he said, "Glinda, you don't understand."

I said, "I heard you. You said no one would care if Dexter crossed. It was basically you guys don't give a shit about Dexter. Bottom line, Doug, I think you're jealous of Dexter and of all the publicity he gets, and it's small of you to talk about another black man like that."

Doug got off the phone and told the whole world I cursed him. Well, I didn't curse at him, but he made everyone around Redskin Park think I was crazy. At that time the team was segregated, and I thought it was poor judgment for one black man to say that about another.

By the time the strike mercifully ended, a knee injury I'd suffered in training camp was about healed up. I still hadn't had a full sack since the fourteenth week of 1986, and the media were implying I was through. I went along with them. I kept telling them, "I'm washed up. Print it."

This was about the time I began stopping at 7-Eleven for my breakfast of champions before ballgames—my Sudafed. I'd stick them in my duffle bag and have them lying there for everyone to see in the locker room.

That Buffalo game—that's the one when I took ten Sudafeds—I got my two sacks and started howling at the Buffalo fans, "Do I look washed up? Do I look washed up?"

As the season wore on, I also slipped back into my cocaine regimen. Doc Flynn was still testing me, but I kept my calendar and knew exactly how many days in between urinalyses.

The league office had no idea I was being tested. It was under the Redskins' jurisdiction, and the team sure as hell wasn't turning me in.

I'd also wondered if someone like Bobby Beathard could tell I'd be trashed at practice:

Oh, yeah. He acted so different. He'd act so skittish, and then he kind of lost his stinger and didn't want to hit people. There were a lot of changes, and [drugs] is what we suspected. He was wild sometimes and superhyper and sweating profusely. All sorts of things.

You know that big Buffalo game I had? Well, I was supposed to see Doc Flynn the Wednesday before that game, but I had to skip my appointment with him because, homeboy, I was still wasted on cocaine that Wednesday. I'd stayed out on the street corner Tuesday night and had come in Wednesday morning a zombie. I ain't just saying this. Joe Theismann says he used to come to practice drunk, but I never saw him drunk. But *I'm* telling you the truth. I came to Redskin Park plenty of times under the influence of drugs and alcohol. No question.

I used to think one guy always noticed something—Joe Bugel. He was our offensive line coach at the time and always wanted to look people in the eye, like, Are your eyes dilated? Are they red?

I'd get real paranoid around Redskin Park. I'd sit in those meetings and sweat. I'd pray to God that I wouldn't sweat so much. I mean, I went through hell just to cover it up.

Actually, I didn't cover it up; I hid from everyone. When you're on drugs, it causes you to withdraw. It makes you unsociable, and you isolate yourself.

When I'd come to Redskin Park under those drugs, there was just one guy I'd talk with. I'd say, "Are my eyes red? How do they look?" I'm talking about my buddy "World," Darryl Grant.

World would say, "Dex, what're you doing? You look all right. You look all right." In that high-pitched voice of his.

One time, Vernon Dean, one of our ex-cornerbacks, made a call to our quarterback, Doug Williams, the day of a game and told Doug, "Please watch Dexter. I know personally he's been out doing drugs."

When I walked by Doug that day in the locker room, he was talking to Emmitt Thomas, and I got paranoid. That's what coke'll do to you. I thought, Oh oh, somebody knows something. Coke makes you worry. You peek out of peep holes and look out of the hotel door to see if any footprints are walking by. You hear footsteps.

Anyway, Doug told Darryl Grant about it, and Darryl came up to me before kickoff and looked in my eyes. He said, "You all right?"

I got a sack that day, do you believe it? I won't say which game it was, but I actually fell asleep on the bench in the fourth quarter. Going up against the offensive tackle that Sunday, I kept thinking, Boy, he's a good one today. Of course, I was playing half asleep. Ordinarily, if I'm awake, I'm gonna crush any tackle in the league.

Later in the season, we beat Dallas, 24–20, and I was supposed to collect an award at the D.C. Touchdown Club the next day. Unfortunately, I had to get my feet to touch down first because I'd been out partying. It was my normal routine. I did my drugs in a hotel. I'd take the hotel mirror off the wall and do the lines of coke on the mirror. Boy, I could trash some hotel rooms.

I was so messed up by the time I arrived at the Touchdown Club, they hauled me into a little office there. I called my best friend, Lester Townsend, and Lester dragged me by the arm and drove me home.

Lester was a white guy, and he was the most loyal friend I've ever had. I didn't even need to call Lester that night at the Touchdown Club; he was going to meet me there anyway. Wherever I was, he'd be there. Lester worried even more about me than Glinda did. Glinda used to tell me, "Dexter, you're going to kill Lester, 'cause he's a worry wart." He'd worry about me to the point he'd get ulcers and headaches. He'd call Glinda in the evening to ask, "Did Dexter make it home?" He wouldn't sleep at night 'til he knew I was home from partying.

I simply needed to go out at night. I could not sit still if I tried. The only way I could stay in the house was if I'd get two sacks or if I had a big game.

See, I was more liable to go out if I had *no* sacks and a *bad* game! I'd be so depressed that I had to go out and get adulation. If I had a bad game, I'd go to Redskin Park on a Monday and wouldn't hear people say, "Hey, great game." So, in my mind, I had to go out in the public and get fans to tell me I was great. I needed the excitement.

I know I shouldn't rely on other people to make me happy or sad. Happiness should come from within. But I'm sure that's the same with everybody. I'm sure after Desert Storm, George Bush didn't want to sit in the Oval Office. He wanted to go wherever presidents go so everyone would come up, pat him on the back, and say, "Good war, George."

Now, if I had a two-sack game, I'd come straight home from Redskin Park and wouldn't go out. Then I want to be private. After a big game, I'd want to be the star that *no one* ever sees, like Michael Jackson. Then, sometime during the week I'd show up, somewhere, unannounced, and everybody would say, "*Wow,*" and pat me on the back and buy me drinks or dinner. And then I wouldn't go back to that spot again. Was I larger than life or what?

Sometimes, I try to be a good parent and husband by staying in the house. But if I stay in the house two or three days, it just gets me bored. I've got to go. I've got to be seen. Glinda says that when I go out, I turn my wrist a certain way so people see my Rolex watch. She might be right. Going out is like a cycle for me. My counselors probably think this is part of my addiction.

The 1987 season ended with Doug Williams beating out Jay Schroeder at quarterback and me slipping out of the house again to do coke around Christmastime.

It was actually on December 27, the Sunday after our final regular season game in Minnesota. We had defeated the Vikings in the Metrodome, and New Year's was coming. We had a bye week before our first playoff game against Chicago, so I did coke. I might've even started snorting the night we got back from Minnesota.

Tuesday morning—the twenty-ninth—Doc Flynn called me to take a urine test. I had figured I wouldn't have to take a test that week because we had a week off, but Doc called me for one anyway. I had to ditch him for five or six days so the crap could leak out of my system. I wasn't home when he called, and I didn't call him right back because his message to me said he was going to a party that night. I figured I'd call him back later while he was at the party. His son answered, and I told him I was going out of town to the sobriety anniversary party of my sponsor, Pham. Pham was helping me cover up.

I was lying. I wasn't going anywhere. I had to stay away from Redskin Park, too, because Gibbs and Beathard and Flynn were all working together. Flynn kept calling me during the week, but I ducked him.

Since then I've wondered if someone tipped off Flynn that I had done drugs after the Vikings game. I did my cocaine at the Sheraton Hotel-Tysons Corner, and I remember thinking someone was following or watching me. I never spotted the sucker, but I felt like someone might have snitched to the Redskins.

I stayed out of sight until Monday, January 4, when we had to report back for practice. I had to take my drug test Tuesday, seven days after I'd done my coke.

Since it had been that long, I thought my system would be cleaned out. Usually the drugs were out of my system in five days. I'd calculate it to a·T, although some tests are more sophisticated and can detect drugs for up to nine or ten days. Robert Shelton, a friend and counselor of mine at a Virginia rehab clinic, told me all about these tests. Sometimes he would even test me as a favor to see if I was cleaned out before I had to go take a Redskins' drug test.

Do you see all the craziness here? I was like a woman and her period. I'd ask myself, When did I do drugs? and I would count the days. I'd calculate my cycle, like a woman who didn't want to become pregnant would do.

I thought I would pass that test; seven days would have been more than enough. Normally, I left Redskin Park right after practice, but this day I went into the front office area. I was standing by the film rooms talking to a secretary when I saw Doc Flynn sneak up the steps and run into Joe Gibbs's office. I wondered what the hell Flynn was doing.

I drove home paranoid.

I kept wondering, Why was Flynn there? When I got home, I told Glinda, and she was mad because now she knew I'd messed up. I called Flynn at about 7:30. "Doc Flynn," I said, "I saw you over at Redskin Park today. Why were you there?"

"You flunked that test I gave you."

"Oh, so you told Joe Gibbs?"

"Well, yes. They're making a decision on what to do with you."

About eleven or twelve o'clock, Joe Gibbs called me at home. He would have called me sooner, but he had to film his weekly TV show with George Michael.

Gibbs said I was suspended, that I would not be able to play in the Bears playoff game Sunday. He also said Mr. Cooke would try to get the thing resolved so I *could* play in the playoff game.

I don't *know* if the league was involved or not, but it sounded like Mr. Cooke was handling the matter. I really don't think the league was aware. Again I went into rage. I said to Gibbs, "Well, I ain't dirty. I haven't done drugs." I was real defensive, talking about how I was clean.

I couldn't understand how after seven days, the test had come back dirty. I figured maybe they'd used another stronger, more elaborate test on me.

Well, Gibbs finally said, "Be here tomorrow morning at eight, and I'll need you to take another drug test. If you flunk this test, we can't help you."

In the back of my mind, I knew Gibbs had said Mr. Cooke was trying to get it resolved or get involved. So I wasn't too panicky, yet.

The next morning, Friday, January 8, it was snowing heavily. It was the kind of snow people can't get to work in, but I took my butt over there at 8:00 A.M. and leaked for them. Bubba Tyer issued the test, and by this time I'd been about eleven days since I'd done coke. I watched one of the assistant equipment guys—Ed Allen, I think— take my urine over to Georgetown Hospital for evaluation.

Evidently, it must've been clean, because I didn't hear from them. Whatever Mr. Cooke aimed to do, he must've done. I went ahead and prepared to play.

Naturally, I was scared, and for a lot of reasons. First, I thought maybe the Redskins knew I was doing drugs again. I was nervous, too, for my image. In 1986 I had done coke, and here it was surfacing again. The Redskins were my employers, and I wondered, Will they put up with me?

But as far as playing in the game, I didn't think they'd pull me out. Not if they wanted to win.

This was the game where Bears coach Mike Ditka had said during the week, "Dexter Manley has the IQ of a grapefruit." I was paranoid over the drug test, and now I hear this from Ditka? A former Oklahoma State trainer was working for the Bears at the time, and I figured this trainer had told Ditka I was dumb. I couldn't figure out how Ditka knew I couldn't read or write. Surely he didn't know and was just mouthing off, but I really believed he knew me. I said to myself, How does he know my secret?

To be honest, that statement from Ditka got our entire team fired up to play even more. At least, I heard our guard, R.C. Thielemann, say that to the media after we won, 21–17:

That did psyche us up. It was a team thing. It's like someone picking on a private in the war. We were a unit. Dexter was not ostracized on our team. We knew he was a little different, but when someone questions someone's intelligence, that isn't cool.

I flew all over the field that day, boning Ditka every time I made a tackle. What I mean by bone is I'd point a stiff arm at him every time I made a tackle. I'd scream, "Run it here! Run it here!" And I was making the hits, too.

The Monday after that game, I was still adamant that I hadn't done drugs. I told Gibbs, "See how well I played? I wasn't on drugs. Man, I'm telling you, I wasn't on drugs. Look here, I had a great game, so how can you accuse me?"

Gibbs said, "Well, maybe they made a mistake."

We were sitting in Bubba's office. We shut the door, and I said, "I want the hell out of here 'cause y'all are accusing me of drugs and all that crap. Trade me."

Gibbs started apologizing. He said, "We'll talk about it in the off-season."

I was just using my great game as leverage, as my con. If I'd had a horrible game, oh boy.

Gibbs asked, "How could this confusion come about?"

"Well, there was something wrong with that test," I suggested.

"You sure did play a great game," he conceded.

And I predicted, "I'll do it again against the Vikings in the NFC championship."

But, you know, those people were right, and I was the one who was sick.

Jack Kent Cooke was in the locker room after we beat the Bears, and I could see that he was pissed at me. Everyone was happy because we had won, but I could feel Cooke's bad vibes. He wouldn't talk to me. I was getting dressed, and he didn't come near. It's not that I cared—I really didn't—but when an owner comes over and congratulates you, it helps your morale. But he didn't. He knew what the hell was going on.

There's no question in my mind that Cooke withheld my positive test before the Bears game. My relationship with him had begun deteriorating after I missed that Rams practice in 1986, but it was definitely never the same after this Bears incident.

Naturally, I didn't do coke the week after the Bears game, heading into the NFC championship at home against the Vikings. Against Minnesota, I had another great game, with one and a half sacks. Our defense came up with a crucial game-ending goal-line stand, although Darrin Nelson choked and dropped the potential game-winning catch on fourth down. You should've seen Gibbs kneeling down like a kid, praying before that fourth-down play.

We escaped, 17–10, and replays show me sprinting to the sidelines and getting in the middle of Gibbs's and Beathard's private celebration. Gibbs and Beathard were hugging on the sideline, and I wanted to be in there with 'em.

I didn't want to hug just anybody. I felt like I was third in command and should be in there with them. I want to hug the big boys because that's where the cameras are. What can I say? I wanted to hug the Big Cheeses.

After we won, Home Team Sports printed up T-shirts—I guess,

in honor of me—that read, "Grapefruit—The Breakfast of NFC Champions."

Thanks to ole Mike Ditka, I also received grapefruit spoons and a case of grapefruits from a company in Florida. And a restaurant in D.C., Joe and Mo's, had a "Dexter Manley Special" that featured pancakes, bacon, and *grapefruit* juice.

It wasn't grapefruit I ingested the night we won the NFC championship; it was cocaine. I was back at it, not that I'm proud about it. We had some days off before leaving for Super Bowl XXII in San Diego, and I felt that gave me a cushion to use drugs, sauna, and flush them out of my system before the next test.

We had to report to Redskin Park for some quickie meetings and practices right after we beat the Vikings, but everyone was in such a hullabaloo over going to the Super Bowl, nobody tested me. I'd been out partying all of Sunday night, and I came in the next week and saw John Madden and Pat Summerall of CBS. I was hiding from them and everyone else. My eyes were red, and I was paranoid that people would know. I've been told people don't necessarily know when someone's on drugs, but I *can* tell. I can instantly see coke in someone's eyes.

Well, I made it out of there without being issued a Dixie cup. Drugs will also make you a smart ass, man. When we held our final practice before leaving for San Diego, Col. Oliver North showed up as a guest of Coach Gibbs. I paid no attention to him.

North gave a speech to the entire team, and I just wasn't impressed with that crap. When you're on drugs, who wants to see an Oliver North? Like, who cares? While he spoke to the team, I was the only one who stayed in the locker room, ripping tape from my ankles.

I brought my wife, Derrick, Dalis, Dexter, my mother-in-law, Pham, and my drug pusher to San Diego. Actually, I didn't *bring* my drug dealer, but he showed up. His name is Freddie, and I'll explain more about him later.

Once in San Diego, I soon was walking around with $10,000 or more in cash. Naturally, I'd taken some personal money with me—about $1,000—but the rest of the money came from scalping tickets. Sometimes, I had $12,000 to $15,000 on me.

Freddie, my drug dealer, actually came to all three Super Bowls. Glinda says everyone had to know Freddie was a dealer by the way he dressed, but it wasn't obvious to me. He wasn't dressed in gawdy jewelry or crap like that. He wore conservative clothes, sometimes a warmup suit. Nothing too slick or sleazy.

I promised myself I would do no drugs in San Diego, not that I didn't want to. The first night I was tempted, but I wanted to be clear-headed and play a phenomenal Super Bowl. The last time I had done coke was the night we beat the Vikings—January 17—and I wasn't so sure I could pass those urine tests anymore.

The Redskins finally got around to testing me on our third day in San Diego. I had to pee in a cup in Bubba and Doc Knowlan's hotel room on Tuesday, January 26.

It turned up positive.

I still played in the Super Bowl.

That frickin' coke had stayed in my system nine days! With this new technology, it was getting out of hand.

Here's the deal: The Redskins didn't test me the first week after the Vikings' NFC title game, but they did in San Diego. The question then is, How long did it take for the test results in San Diego to return? Did they know before kickoff that I'd had a positive test and still let me play? It's *possible* the results didn't come in until after the Super Bowl game, but I believe they did know before the game. After all, they took my urine to a lab in California and should have gotten the results back in as little as four hours and certainly in no more than two days. Shoot, I took the test five days before the game. They *had* to have known and had to have covered it up.

How do I know? Well, I got a letter from the commissioner's office early that next off-season, saying I had flunked a test at the Super Bowl. The thing was, the league wasn't involved with my drug testing during the Super Bowl.

So the Redskins probably knew I was dirty and waited to tell the league. They *had* to have gotten the results back before kickoff. The league's tests take about a week to come back, but that's because they double-check the urine if it returns positive. The Redskins didn't need to double-check.

I was a little uptight that week. The drug test was an irritation, but so were the zillion idiotic questions about Denver's quarterback, John Elway. Not to mention another question I got asked: "If you were a tree, what kind of tree would you be?"

What really got me was the Elway crap. It was like he was God or somebody. John Elway is only as good as his offensive line, and I knew I could beat their asses.

I got so sick of the Elway questions, I made a scene one day at my group interview session. I came in there requesting that all questions be submitted to me in writing and that I would review them overnight and only then would I respond. I was surrounded by so many writers, and I was sweating bullets, and, for some reason, I shouted at all of them, "I want your questions in *writing!*"

I then bolted from the interview session. Coach Gibbs had to pull me aside, saying, "You've got to go back out there because it's league policy. I don't want you to get fined." So I tried to be civil.

What people don't know is that later in the week I also went off on Al Michaels, Frank Gifford, and Dan Dierdorf of ABC television.

In preparation for their Super Bowl broadcast, they called in Darryl Grant, Charles Mann, and me for an interview, and I started screaming at the top of my lungs. I scared the crap out of them. I was all fired up for the game, and I was hollering in their interview room, telling them what I was going to do to Elway. I told them I was gonna kick somebody's ass. Part of it was that I was a hell of an actor, and part of it was I was sick and tired of Elway.

I took it out on Elway on the field in our 42–10 victory. I had a phenomenal game, with one and one-half sacks. Phenomenal!

After we won, it was as if the Bears incident had vanished into thin air. *Nothing* came of it. When I had sat in Bubba's office earlier and pleaded with Gibbs to trade me, it was all a con to get him on my side. He had said we'd discuss it in the off-season, but I had no plans whatsoever of meeting with him. I was a Redskin and wanted nothing else.

I tell you, there's nothing like a Super Bowl parade. I've experienced that three times, and in 1987 I smoked a foot-long cigar on our way to the White House. I felt like the "Boss," Bruce Springsteen.

But when we arrived, I immediately felt slighted. They took four people to visit President Reagan in the Oval Office: Gibbs, Beathard, Doug Williams, and Dave Butz. Not me. I wanted to feel important, and I felt it should've been me instead of big ole UPS courier Butz. What the hell had Dave Butz done? I guess it was a seniority deal, but I was peeved.

So I had to concoct something to say at the White House podium to get attention.

The ceremony was in the Rose Garden, and it was staged for President Reagan to throw a pass to Ricky Sanders. Before all that, he walked down the line and shook everybody's hand. When he got to me, I said, "You should renegotiate for four more years."

Reagan thought that was just fantastic. Then, when he gave his speech to the team, he said, "Happy birthday, Dexter." It really was my birthday—February 2—and I thought that was neat. I couldn't believe the Redskins had told him that.

I wanted to march right up to the microphone and say out loud what I'd told President Reagan about renegotiating. Rennie Simmons, our tight end coach, had heard my conversation with the president, and he said, "Go to the podium and say that, Dexter." That was my green light.

I moved toward the microphone, and Joe Bugel said, "Where are *you* going?" Bobby Beathard was like ga-ga. I said, "Look here, I have something to say."

I pounced on that mike, and I pronounced, "The president needs to renegotiate for four more years!" The entire audience started cheering, and they showed it on "World News Tonight." You just knew all the Republicans loved it.

I wished my daddy could've seen that.

When I got off the podium, it seemed everyone wanted a piece of me. I agreed to go on George Michael's sportscast at five o'clock. By the time I got home from the parade, his limo was already waiting for me. I did his show, and then I kept Michael's limo out all night, coking it up in there. Michael never sent me a limo again; the bill cost NBC $800. I kept it the entire night.

Two days later, the phone rang, and it was the White House. Those Republicans must've taken to what I said on the podium, because they were having a birthday party for the president and wanted me to come to the White House again to present him with a jersey.

When they called, I still was in a daze from my drugging in George Michael's limo and I didn't take their call. I asked Pham if I should go, and we decided I should say no. I didn't exactly look the part.

I told the White House I was leaving that day on vacation, and Glinda and I actually did hop to Cancun for a spell. Unfortunately, I returned to D.C. to hear a double dose of bad news.

Put it this way: I wasn't around for the Redskins Super Bowl ring ceremony the next August.

AN IDLE THOUGHT

Most of the Redskin players were hip, except for big ole Dave Butz.

One time I was on the toilet before a game at RFK Stadium, and Butz tip-toed up to my bathroom stall and peeped down on me.

Hell, Butz thought I was snorting coke in there.

CHAPTER 29

Benedict Arnolded

I RETURNED FROM MY CANCUN VACATION IN March 1988 and fingered through my mail. There was a letter from the National Football League.

As I read it—the Lab School had made some progress with my phonics—the telephone rang. It was my buddy Lester Townsend, who was talking so fast he sounded Japanese.

"YaheardboutWilberMarshallWilberMarshall?" he rattled off.

When Lester finally cooled, he asked, "Did you read the paper?"

I found a football headline on the front page of the *Washington Post*: "Redskins Sign Marshall for $6 Million."

So, in one hand I had a letter from this guy Pete Rozelle telling me I'd failed a drug test at the Super Bowl—I'm wondering how the hell *he* knew about it—and in the other hand I have an article telling me that some joker who's never played a down for the Redskins is gonna make seventy times more than me.

I have to say, I was sucking on raw eggs.

The letter from Rozelle was staggering. He mentioned the positive test from the Super Bowl and requested a meeting. The Redskins must've Benedict Arnolded me.

The Redskins had always kept my drugs top-secret, but now the league was saying, The drug issue's in our hands because teams are cheating and sweeping positive tests under the rug and letting people play while dirty. We're going to clean it up.

I figured it was the beginning of my end, unless I could make it stop snowing, if you know what I mean. From then on, I was under the league's Gestapo jurisdiction. I'd never been to jail yet, but in a way I was being punished under the judiciary system of the National Football League.

Before Pete Rozelle's letter arrived, the Redskins had looked the other way. Hell, yeah, Jack Kent Cooke covered my drugs up for me. Probably for his own gain. You think the Redskins were going to turn me in? Gibbs probably was just threatening me when he said before the Bears playoff game I might be suspended. The league was never in control then.

The Redskins were in control, and their only decision was to send me to Doc Flynn. They were the ones having me tested. When I'd show positive, were they gonna suspend me right on the spot? Hogwash. Didn't they want to win the Super Bowl? I'm one of their best players on defense, so they're gonna take me out? N–O! They knew what was going on. They just never took action.

But they sure as hell let it out *after* the Super Bowl. They knew they were gonna go after Wilber Marshall, and they sure as hell knew I'd freak out and want to renegotiate and hold out when they did. By turning me in to the NFL they had me by the balls. Now, I'd have to be a yes man.

'Course, I had put myself in this dang situation. If I'd never used drugs. . .

I went to see Rozelle in April of 1988. I sneaked in the league office on Park Avenue, and nobody knew. Rozelle set guidelines for me, including periodic testing by a league doctor, Doc Goldstein. It was sayonara to Doc Flynn.

I guess the league considered my positive Super Bowl test as the *first* strike against me. The league policy was like baseball's: Three strikes and you're out. So I had two to go.

Little did the NFL know I'd already had many strikes with the Redskins. Do you think the Redskins would tune the league in to the truck incident, the Rams incident, and the Bears incident? And lose their best pass rusher? Hell, no.

Naturally, in the spring and summer of 1988, I was in a desperate search for self-esteem. It was then that I began living like His Majesty. I bought the Rolls-Royce and rented limos whenever possible. In June 1988 I booked a limo to drive me two blocks to the Tyson–Spinks fight in Atlantic City. I could have walked to ringside from my hotel in fifty-three seconds.

I also rented bodyguards. See, I gauge the power of a man or woman by whether I can count their bodyguards on one hand. If anything, bodyguards are a façade, but the public doesn't know that. They see you with bodyguards and picture you as King Tut.

That's what I wanted for me. I heard Joe Montana had people

working for him at the Pro Bowl. He rode all around the island in a limo. If I'd had my way, I'd have hired a twenty-four-hour, year-round limo driver, but Jack Kent Cooke wasn't paying me enough.

Still, that spring and summer I'd go to *any* event. Anything in any town, any social function. I needed the lift. And I'd hire two body-guards to keep the hounds off me.

It didn't matter I could squash anyone who bothered me. It just looked good to have bodyguards and a limo. I'd find them anywhere. I'd look for young, big guys and say, "Hey, you want to work? OK. Go put on a frickin' suit and tie. Let's go."

College boys want to do that kind of work. All kinds of people in life want to be go-fers. Hell, I'd be a go-fer for Michael Jackon or some other big wheel. But it's got to be a *big* wheel. If I go-fer for Michael Jackson, man, I'm gonna be seen.

Of course, there were many times that spring and summer of 1988 when I *didn't* want to be seen.

One time was May 17. I had just finished conducting a radio interview with Los Angeles Dodgers manager Tommy Lasorda for DC-101. It was a radiant day, and I was cruising in my Mercedes like a big shot. I was heading down the D.C. beltway when I remembered I was supposed to be at a photo session at a warehouse near Redskin park at 5:00 P.M. Mr. Cooke had flown in photographers to do a charity calendar—he was copying the '85 Bears—and Cooke had picked me as one of the players to pose.

I'd agreed to do it, but that day on the beltway I did a 180-degree switch. I started thinking bitterly about them signing Wilber Marshall for beaucoup bucks, and I wondered why they'd pay Wilber Marshall that much cash when he hadn't done crap for the Redskins, and we'd just won a Super Bowl.

I got cocky and said to myself, The Redskins screwed me. I ain't showing up.

Instead, I went out and got obliterated. Obviously, I didn't show up for the five o'clock photo shoot. John Kent Cooke—the son, not the "grandfather"—called my house while I was out snorting to ask, "Where's Dexter?"

Glinda had no clue herself, and Johnny Cakes told her to make sure I showed at 3:00 P.M. Thursday to complete the photo shoot. Johnny Cakes, who loves flaunting the authority his daddy grants him, said to Glinda, "I want him *there!*"

Hell, I didn't show up at three o'clock Thursday either. I was just coming in from Wednesday. I was in the basement—sick as a dog—

trying to sleep it off. I wanted the stuff out of my system so I could sleep, but I couldn't sleep because the drugs wouldn't let me.

On a typical day after cocaine, I'm like this:

I CREEP IN. I'M SAYING, "GOLLY, IS GLINDA UP THERE?" I'M LOOKING AROUND. I'M SAYING, "WHY DID I DO THAT? WHY?" I'M RUBBING MY HEAD AND NECK. I'M PEEPING UPSTAIRS. I HAVE THIS VISION—ME SLEEPING IN AN ALLEY AND MY KIDS LIVING IN SOME HOUSE IN CHICAGO WITHOUT ME.

THEN I SNAP OUT OF IT 'CAUSE I'VE ACCIDENTALLY SET THE HOUSE ALARM ON. SO I SNEAK DOWN IN THE BASEMENT AND PEEK TO SEE IF GLINDA'S COMING. I HEAR MY KIDS GETTING DRESSED, THEN I HOP IN THE BED IN THE BASEMENT. THEN I HOP OUT OF BED AND SAY, "WHY? WHY?" I'M HOPPING IN AND OUT OF BED LIKE A SCHIZO.

I PICK UP THE SPORTS PAGE TO SEE IF MY NAME'S IN THERE. I PEEK UPSTAIRS AGAIN. I HEAR GLINDA COMING, SO I HOP IN THE BED. I HEAR HER FUSSING. UGGGGHHH!

When I was so fried on coke that day I missed the photo shoot, I called Pham to rescue me, and he came over. He would drop everything to help.

Pham and I heard the doorbell, and he went to the door. Standing outside were two Redskins employees: John Konoza from the PR office and Paul Denfeld from the marketing department. They were begging to see me, obviously having been sent by Johnny Cakes, and Pham guarded the door with his life.

Pham said, "You cannot come in his house. There has been a family dispute. He does not want to talk to you."

They insisted, "Just let us *see* Dexter."

Pham was covering up like Oliver North. He was my sponsor, although he was also enabling me to do drugs, which is sort of backward. But those two guys had no right to barge in my house just because I worked for the Redskins. Of course, I wasn't in any condition to stop them from prying inside—I couldn't even see straight—but Pham put up a steel wall for me.

Konoza and Denfeld went back and told Cooke I was in the house, but some guy with a turban wouldn't let them in. So Johnny Cakes telephoned Warren Welsh, the NFL's security advisor, who called Doc Goldstein. Goldstein—the new Doc Flynn—called me at 10:05 P.M.

I answered the telephone real sleepy. Doc Goldstein said, "Dexter, I need to see you at 8:00 A.M. in my office. I said, "OK, OK." Hell, he was gonna make me take a leak.

But Pham and I were scheming. Pham told the poster people I'd do the photo shoot at 6:00 A.M. Friday. I then booked a 7:00 A.M. flight to Houston.

The next morning, I showed up for my photo shoot. I charmed the socks off the photographers, and they flat-out loved me and didn't mind I'd given them the runaround. Then I was off to Dulles Airport for my flight to Houston. I was supposed to fly to Texas that weekend anyway for a roast of my college coach, Jimmy Johnson, who'd just won the NCAA national championship with Miami. I left a day early— Friday—to escape Doc Goldstein's Dixie cup.

In Houston I called Doc Goldstein from the airport and played like I'd been half asleep the night before when he'd called. I said, "Now, what was it that you wanted?"

He said, "Where are you, Dexter?"

I said, "Oh, I had to fly to Houston to do Jimmy Johnson's roast. He just won the national championship, and he used to coach me in college."

The roast was actually in Port Arthur, Texas, but I planned to stay an extra week or two in Houston and let the coke seep out of my system.

See what I was doing? I was hopping on airplanes to escape drug tests. And, boy, the NFL was looking for me in Houston. I was afraid they were gonna slip me a Dixie cup. If they'd nabbed me, I could have been suspended. I was playing tag with the NFL.

The Houston police almost did the NFL's job for them. As I was leaving the airport, I was pulled over for speeding with five grams of coke in my top pocket. About three police cars pulled me over; I assume they had seen me in my rental Lincoln Continental, weaving in and out of traffic like I do, and assumed foul play. The police were obnoxious. They kept calling me "boy."

They said, "Boy, get up. Walk that line, boy. Boy, blow on my face, boy."

I blew in their face lightly.

One cop said, "Boy, I said blow on my face, boy."

So I did it again.

He said, "Boy, have you been drinking or something, boy?"

I walked the line for them and was praying to heaven they wouldn't search my coat.

Then I remembered my briefcase. Before I left, Glinda had told me to put the Super Bowl program in my briefcase to take to my momma in Houston. I figured maybe I could impress the cops.

One of them said, "Boy, where's your driver's license, boy?"

"Sir, it's in my briefcase."

"Open that briefcase, boy."

So I unlatched the case. With five grams of coke still in my pocket, I could see myself out of football and back in the Third Ward.

I whipped out the program and said, "Officer, I've had a few drinks. See, I just won the Super Bowl."

He asked, "Whatya talking about, boy?"

I told him I was a Washington Redskin. "Look here. That's me on this magazine cover."

"Are you Dexter Manley?" he asked.

"Yes sir."

"Get the fuck out of here."

I told myself right then I'd never ride with coke again, but that didn't last. Twice since then, I've been sirened over with coke in my boots or in my sleeve. Each time the cop saw I was Dexter Manley and said, "OK, slow down, Manley."

On this Houston trip I managed to escape Doc Goldstein, but when I returned home, the league still had their dogs sniffing for me. I realized how complicated it was going to be with the league now having jurisdiction. When the Redskins had jurisdiction, it was like taking candy from a baby.

I had Robert Shelton, my drug expert friend from Virginia, give me urine tests prior to my actual league tests. That way, I'd know if I was clean or not going in.

My drug counselors must be nodding their heads. See my state of denial? See my con game? I'm not proud of it.

Well, I kept fiddling with drugs, and finally I must've miscalculated my drug calendar because I failed a urine test right after the Tyson–Spinks fight in early July. I passed one in June, but in July the urine didn't lie.

I was hoping the league would miss it. Training camp opened for veterans on a Monday, and I stopped by Redskin Park the previous Friday to lift weights and pack my gear for Carlisle.

I was driving home on the Dulles Airport access road, and as I neared the Reston exit, I spied a Federal Express truck. I said to myself, "That sucker's coming to my house." At the time I didn't know I'd flunked the drug test, but I felt it. I got home and sweated a month's worth in ten minutes and, sure enough, the doorbell rang. It was a letter from Pete Rozelle ordering me to meet him in New York.

I could've kicked myself in the ass five hundred times. When I looked in the mirror, I knew I'd caused this. I couldn't point the finger and say, "Well, it's the Redskins, they don't like me," or "It's the Pete Rozelles, they're after me." No! I'd caused my own problems.

The Washington Post printed I'd tested positive for a "minor substance." Whoever leaked that to them helped my butt. Is coke a minor substance? Hell no. But it threw the media and the public off. I sort of saved face.

I was hoping that Rozelle would go easy on me, so I went up to New York wearing an immaculate gray suit. Hell if I was going to look like an addict. Prior to the meeting, I sat in Bob Woolf's New York apartment waffling on whether I should wear my gold Rolex. It was a big ole Rolex, and I didn't want to wear it.

"You think I should wear this Rolex?" I asked Bob.

"Why not?" he answered.

I was trying to paint an image. I wanted to be all conservative. I didn't want Rozelle thinking, "Here's this gaudy Rolex. Manley's probably running with women on the streets and doing drugs." So I thought I should tone it down.

My memory flashed back to college, to the day I was sentenced in court at Oklahoma State. That day I had worn a loud, white handkerchief in my coat pocket, and Jimmy Johnson and Larry Holton—the defensive backs coach—told me, "Don't wear that."

They wanted me plain as can be.

So that was my mindset going to Rozelle's, but Bob Woolf said, "Wear the Rolex." Hell, the whole time I was in Rozelle's office, I held my hands under the table so nobody could see it.

That was one nervewracking day. Woolf and I were walking down the street to the NFL office on Park Avenue when I suddenly saw a boatload of minicams and reporters. My natural instinct was to run; the Houston Third Ward in me came out. I actually turned around and walked the other way.

"Where are you going?" Bob asked. "Come back here."

Man, I was really going to run, even though I was wearing a $1,500 suit and carrying my Louis Vuitton bag. I was dressed sharp. I didn't want those NFL stiff collars thinking I did drugs like a junkie; I went down there like a CEO. I wanted that Wall Street image. Was I under an illusion or what?

Well, Warren Welsh of the league office was waiting for Bob and me at a side door so we could avoid the media. We were escorted to Rozelle's office, and that sucker was pissed. He pounded his fist on the table and yelled, "If you want to do drugs, then wait until your career is over! Why are you ruining your career?"

Paul Tagliabue was there, but hell if I knew who he was at the time. He was just a lawyer taking notes. I think Woolf requested that they stop taking notes. We left the room for a recess, and then Rozelle and all his stiff collar men came back with a bunch of newspaper clippings. He had article after article from *The Washington Post* and other papers in which I'd been quoted as saying I was clean and wouldn't mess up. Rozelle threw those suckers on the table, and said, "You said this then. What's different now?" Bob Woolf and I were floored. Rozelle talked to me like a mad father. He scolded my butt.

Crap, all those high-power NFL guys were there with their guns loaded, their white collars pointing at me. Bob Woolf and I went in with our flag and said, "We surrender."

Saying this was my "second" strike, Rozelle suspended me thirty days from the start of training camp. You should have seen how Bob Woolf maneuvered. When the league released news of my ban, Bob played with the language so it said I had violated the league's "guidelines." Woolf came up with that word: *guidelines.* This way, cocaine or drugs were never mentioned.

The league wanted to use harsher words. They wanted to say I was barred from training camp, but instead Randy Vataha, Bob's assistant, suggested they use the words *excused from training camp.* That sounded smoother. The league could tell Bob Woolf was slick, but they went along with it.

The league also wanted us to slip out a side door to avoid all media whatsoever, but Bob said, "No, we'll go out this way, through the front door." The league wanted zero publicity, but with me there were always hordes of reporters. It was Bob who wanted the publicity. Who wouldn't? It was national, and Bob was a natural. He'd turn his head to the right, to the left, all for the cameras. Hell, I liked it, too. Who wants to plop in a cab and feel miserable?

I was exiled from the team for a month. I missed the Super Bowl ring ceremony. I think they mailed the ring to me from Tiffany.

But I stayed in stellar shape. I trained at George Mason with my personal track coach, Bob Brown, and I ran hills or pulled a harnass attached to my back. I was a stud, and TV crews came out to film me.

I was the first Redskin to run hills, and now—starting in 1992—I hear Art Monk has convinced the team to build a manmade hill at their new Redskin Park. Hell, I started it. Wherever I go on the road, I look for steep embankments to train on.

There is no doubt I was one of the most workaholic Redskins. Dan Riley, the Washington strength coach, can attest to that:

Dexter never, ever, had to be motivated. If anything, there were times he was so obsessed that he actually overtrained.

One year he was doing his radio show at 7:30 A.M., so he'd be in the parking lot of Redskin Park at 5:40, Monday, Wednesday, and Friday. He never missed a workout. Never late.

He'd warm up with 315 pounds on the bench. That's enough to rip somebody's chest off, but he'd warm up with it! I'd say, "Dexter, you've got to warm up," and he'd go, "Oh, no, this is good, this is good." He'd just strap that weight on and start rolling. He'd warm up with weights most people train with. It was 6:00 A.M., and there was no easing into it. He just pushed a button and he was going. A good man.

Maybe I'm too sensitive, but during my thirty days suspension, not one teammate called me. Not one.

There was no effort. I understand they were in Carlisle for training camp, but they broke camp before my suspension was up, and still nobody came over to say, "Hey."

But I was a loner, so what could I expect? They probably felt uncomfortable calling me. Even Grant didn't call. The only person who called was Bobby Beathard to say I was suspended.

I can't say why my teammates ignored me. I used to think it was my fault and that players didn't like me, didn't like my bragging, and didn't want to be around me. I felt they thought I showed too much confidence, or they thought I was ignorant, or they thought I was foolish.

I thought my teammates didn't want to be around me, so I accepted that role and acted as if I was a cut above everybody else. I know I wasn't, but it was a way to put up walls and stay isolated. I'm comfortable when it's just Dexter.

But I also grow uncomfortable around myself. I get lonely and fearful. Most of all, lonely. When I have friends and teammates around, I'm like a kid. I feel accepted. Just for being Dexter.

In other words, I wanted Redskins players to like me, but when they acted as if they did not, I'd act braggadocious and get into myself. Drug counselors, does that make any sense?

My personality, I guess, can turn people off. My attitude and flamboyance, my arrogance and stupidity baffle them. And I'm think-ing, Well, I'm not one of the kind of guys they like. I think I'm a likeable guy, but at the same time people probably consider me an asshole.

I'm Bobby Beathard, and I'm telling you I really wanted to like Dexter. He can be so nice and so much fun to be around, and he still even remembers my kids' names and my wife's name.

I think Dexter needed people who believed in him and wanted to be his friends. Though you wanted to be his friend, it was difficult. There were times when you thought you were getting along with Dexter, and then he'd do something that would destroy his credibility. He was his own worst enemy.

I mean, we'd be getting ready for the playoffs, and he'd disappear for a couple of days. Or you'd get along, and then all of a sudden he wanted a new contract. It was always something . . .

He wasn't a real popular guy with the players. There were times when people didn't like him, and at times I would stick up for him. Toward the end, though, I don't think anybody could stick up for him. We got to thinking it would be better for the Redskins if Dexter weren't around, because it got to the point where he was going to hurt the team, and no one guy is bigger than the team. It built up gradually, but the best thing for Dexter was to go somewhere else.

Did I come close to trading him? No. Very few players understand what's involved in trades. Most players feel they're better than they really are and that any number of teams out there want them. But when you go to trade a pretty good player, it's, "What wrong with him?" It's a buyers beware market, and you know there might be something wrong, so you're a little leery. Everybody knew about Dexter's problems. Not necessarily the drugs, but that he had disappeared here and wasn't here, and they would ask, "What kind of problem is he?" So he would have been difficult to trade.

But toward the end in Washington, I just held my breath. I didn't know what was next. It got to where we couldn't count on the guy. We knew something was going to happen, but we didn't know when.

Washington's a small town. You can't hide there, and that's particularly true for a Redskin. Even special teams guys would sign autographs at the malls, so can you imagine how it was for a popular player like Dexter? Things about him kept coming back to us from all sorts of sources. People would tell us where he was hanging out and who he was with. We knew it would be just a matter of time.

There wasn't a heck of a lot we could do with the rumors about him.

We had several confrontations with him, and I guess all of his promises to change were well-meant. But after a while, we knew it was just talk. But we were naive and weren't certain what he was doing, so we bought his story a little. We thought it was drugs, but I guess when you're around a guy who's doing it, he'll say anything to hide the problem. There were a lot of great times with Dexter, but at the end he just became a real distraction.

After his 1988 suspension, I tried to be his friend. If any little thing would help him get back his confidence and let him know he was wanted, then it was worth doing. I had strong feelings for Dexter—good and bad— but more often than not I'd come back to feeling that I wanted to help him.

Dexter was hard to do things for, because he didn't trust anyone. I couldn't talk about the drugs with him—he would deny it. Consequently, some people didn't want him because they felt he let us down one more time, so to hell with him.

For me, I always felt there was hope.

After my thirty-day suspension, not very many Redskins— players or coaches—approached me on a personal level to talk. On defense, only coach Emmitt Thomas, a black guy, did. On offense, Joe Bugel and Dan Henning said something, and Bobby Beathard did, too, but not another soul.

The Redskins called themselves a family, but I thought that talk was bullshit after the Super Bowl XXII in January 1988.

That "family" bull sounds cool when you're winning, but I never bought it. I sensed it was strictly PR.

After that Super Bowl victory, they tried to make it seem like family when Cooke promised to renegotiate MVP Doug Williams's contract, but as soon as Doug hurt his back, it became a business.

The team didn't want to pay Doug because he hurt his back in the off-season on a treadmill, but how about all the blows on his back before then? Doug caught a whupping in Houston during one Sunday night game in 1988. All that contributed to Doug's injury. I'm not a doctor, so maybe I'm speaking out of turn, but when they sit down and say they don't want to pay a guy after he's gone out there and fought blood, sweat, and tears? That's how you treat family? That's bull. You don't lie to your family members (Of course, I did, sadly).

The Redskins aren't as pure as everyone believes. They used to give us slush fund money, and we'd get gifts from the community or a quick $50 in cash if we got a sack. I'm not saying that's a lot, but it's play money. If a running back gained 100 yards, the offensive line would get cash. If a special teams guy made a tackle inside the 20, he'd come in Wednesday with his hand out. If you recovered a fumble or forced one, you had itchy palms. If we stopped 'em 3.8 yards per rush on defense, the group would get $100, and we'd put it together for a party at the end of the season.

We even got money for KO's, knocking people out. It was the Big Hit Award. Is that like the bounty Buddy Ryan once put out?

As far as my 1988 football season, it was nothing to sneeze at, if you catch my drift.

That was the year of my sneeze/spit incident against Jim Dombrowski of the Saints which, as I said before, moved Morton Andersen out of field goal range and gave us the 27–24 victory. Afterward, not one person in the Redskins front office said, "Don't spit (or sneeze) anymore." Hell, they were just glad we won.

On the other hand, the Grinch, Pete Rozelle, sent me a letter saying he didn't appreciate the incident and I'd better watch it. The league already took my urine, and now they wanted to take away my saliva?

In 1988, I got four of my nine sacks that season in one game, at home against the Giants. That's the game where I read the Mike Tyson article prior to kickoff, tore it up at halftime, and assaulted Phil Simms in the second half.

The season basically went down the tubes when we lost a Monday night game in San Francisco, 37–21. John Taylor went 90-something yards on a punt return, and we were toasted.

While I was out there, I went to Alcatraz and envisioned myself in prison and how I could break out of there. Speaking of which, there was no escape from drug tests in 1988, because I had Doc Goldstein on my tail during the regular season. Once we finished the season in Cincinnati, I used again. I was like clockwork. It's sad.

Originally, I was supposed to go to the Super Bowl in Miami to watch the Bengals play the 49ers, but I made a third trip to Hazelden instead—to escape an NFL drug test.

I'd partied on a Saturday night after the season ended, and I'd taken the Rolls-Royce with me. Eric Herring, my old friend from Yates High, was visiting from Houston and came with me, but he wouldn't join me in the hotel room to snort coke. I was in the Capitol Hilton, on K Street in D.C., and Eric sat in the lounge for seven hours.

I took the elevator downstairs and said, "Eric, come up and get the keys to the Rolls. You can try and find your way back to my place in Virginia."

Once he arrived, Glinda conned him. Eric told Glinda he was not involved at all and that I'd gotten coke and had gone in this hotel room. Glinda said, "Oh, Lord, Eric, you must tell me where he is. He could be dead having seizures."

Eric spilled the beans, and pretty soon I heard Glinda knocking on my hotel door, with Little Dexter and Dalis along. She had Eric's key, so I chained the door real quick and called the security guard. "Sir," I said, "this is Dexter Manley, and you need to get my wife and kids off this floor."

The security guard ushered Glinda off. This was January 14, 1989, and I was full of coke and had to escape my upcoming drug test. I didn't know when Mr. Fred Ford, who was now issuing me my urine tests, would call me.

I decided to hide at Hazelden. I wasn't gonna be able to sneak into Hazelden under an assumed name anymore, so I told *The Washington Post* I was going there for a renewal program. What I didn't tell them was I'd been coked up. Nobody knew I was coked up, not even the Redskins. I simply told them I was voluntarily going in to continue learning about treatment. It sounded good. I made it seem as if I hadn't had a relapse, that I was voluntarily taking care of Dexter.

It was my con game. Hazelden would be a place for me to camp out. I had two strikes against me, and if I got one more, I would be banned forever from football. I said to myself, Bingo, if I'm in Hazelden doing my renewal, the NFL can't make me take a test there.

I hid there for a week instead of going to the Super Bowl.

I even did my DC-101 report from a Hazelden pay phone. I mean, the show must go on.

An Idle Thought

I am the Redskins' all-time leading sacker, but you'd never know it by the way Joe Gibbs talked.

Hell if I *ever* heard any praise from Gibbs. By the end of my career in Washington, Gibbs was playing up the left defensive end, Charles Mann, over me.

I guess I understand. I did coke, and Charles did Diet Coke.

I'll never forget our Monday night season opener in 1989 at home against the Giants. I had a great game, and in our Wednesday meeting after we lost, Gibbs said, "Charles is the only one who played well Monday night. He tried to win it by himself."

They'd been trying to negotiate a new deal with Charles, and that was their way of kissing up to him to get Charles to sign it. I was an older veteran, so I didn't fall for it.

After the meeting, Charles said to me, "What's Gibbs talking about?"

I said, "Charles, you know the deal. They're trying to get you to sign."

But they were never interested in playing me up. Following my first-ever touchdown against Minnesota in 1986, Gibbs went on his George Michael show and said about my run, "Manley has good speed. He's a 4.6, 4.7 guy in the 40-yard dash."

I almost fainted. At minicamp that year, I ran a 4.55 40-yard dash. Like I said, Gibbs was never interested in blowing me up.

When I had that four-sack game against the Giants, Gibbs never said in the meeting, "Manley tried to win the game by himself." But if Charles had four sacks? Whoooooooa! Charles is his guy, Charles is a Bible guy. Of course, Charles is also a lot more humble than I am. I'm not a humble guy. I'm Sweet Potato Pie.

CHAPTER 30

IQ Higher Than a Grapefruit

I USED TO ENVISION MYSELF AS AN EIGHTY-YEAR-old man with a humped back and wire-rim glasses, not knowing how to read or write.

It's this same vision that kept me heading out to the Lab School, where I was surrounded by kids younger than Derrick, kids who needed Clearasil and Ban deodorant. This is where I learned what sound a *J* makes.

It's "Juh."

When Derrick was a little kid, I couldn't even read to him. That's another reason I needed to stick with the Lab School: for the benefit of my kids. There were so many reasons to be literate. What about medicine bottles? I might need to know, if I'm by my lonesome, how many pills to give my sick child. If I can't read the label, I may give little Dalis too much medicine, or not enough.

Before I went to the Lab School, the extent of my book reading was Dr. Seuss. Dr. Seuss wasn't difficult to read; it's your basic first- or second-grade masterpiece. That's what I *could* read to my kids. *Cat in the Hat* is something I particularly recall reading.

Contrary to what my daddy believed, my problem was not being falling out dumb. My tutor, Sara Hines, figured out after some private examination that I had a *learning disability*. This was a huge break-through for me. From my first days in elementary school, I considered myself an idiot, and who knows what kind of damage that caused inside.

There's such a stigma, being black and being an athlete, and then hearing all the old traditional crap about dumb, black jocks. I truly thought I was a dumb, black jock.

When I went to the Lab School, I learned it was no black thing or white thing. It was a human thing. The Lab School taught me that there are white people with learning disabilities, too. I didn't know that. I thought there were more blacks, and I stigmatized myself.

If I'd stayed in special ed in junior high, where I should've been instead of in the mainstream, maybe someone would've diagnosed my learning disability.

As it was, Sara Hines didn't diagnose it until I was about twenty-nine years old:

When I met Dexter the first time, he was nervous, and he was big. I'm not even five feet tall, so it was an alarming moment for both of us.

He was fine after about a month. He had learned to fake read, and I wanted to teach the fundamentals. He was skeptical. He'd say, "You're not teaching me right. You don't know what you're doing." He had to learn to trust.

He would look at the first three letters of a word and guess. He'd memorized certain words, but he couldn't read a word by sounding it out. He didn't know what sound a C makes, for instance.

Let's take the word conservation. *Dexter would glance at the first three letters of the word—*con—*check the context it was used in, and he would guess.*

He'd see conservation *and guess, "Convention?"*

He'd often guess with words he'd memorized. He memorized re-member, *for instance, and when he'd see the word* repeat, *which had an* re *beginning, he'd guess "remember." Or when he saw the word* reverse, *he'd guess "remember."* Remember *might be one of his words.*

I made him go back to basics. At first, he didn't like going back to the beginning. I showed him words that looked alike and sounded alike, such as bat *and* cat. *He had never mastered phonics before, and didn't read phonetically. He read by linguistic patterns and seeing word parts, but he only knew word beginnings and not word endings. It was probably overwhelming for him to do more than word beginnings.*

See, his strength was visual memory, or visual analysis. But Dexter doesn't remember what he hears. His auditory memory is weak. He's always had a vocabulary, but he couldn't remember how words sounded, so that's why he'd mispronounce words. Now that he knows what words look like and sound like, he can pronounce better. Before, when he couldn't read or remember what was said, his fund of information was limited.

For instance, when he stayed at a Residence Inn hotel, he'd call it the

Renaissance Inn. That's his memory. He meant to say residence, but there used to be a Ramada Renaissance near Redskin Park, so he'd say renaissance instead of residence. That's his auditory memory problem.

We worked twice a week, and it was fine after some initial stubbornness. I knew what the problem was fairly quickly, but it was difficult finding what would work. The traditional methods of teaching someone to read didn't work with him, because of his disability, so we worked on it together by trial and error.

Our breakthrough was really his learning how to piece words together. He didn't know a lot of word endings and word parts, for instance, tion. He never looked at that when he read a word. So, we worked on that.

His motivation was great. I'd say he was almost angry about learning to read. He was almost desperate. I liked working with him.

Had he had help earlier in his life; he'd been in special ed. But in college, his tutors merely helped him get by. He needed remedial help. I'm not surprised he made it through. He was good at hiding it. I mean, he even fooled Glinda.

At first we fought. He would be difficult, saying things like, "You're not teaching me nothin'."

I'd say, "Dexter, sit down and get to work."

He thought I didn't know what I was doing, and just answered, "I think I can teach you how to read, but if you don't want to do it, I can't."

After that he was more cooperative.

I was never intimidated by him. I didn't think of him as anyone but a student. I was never scared because he was sweet. I didn't think of him as a Redskin.

After the 1988 season, Sara and I would read the newspaper together. I'd bring the *Wall Street Journal* in, or *The Washington Post* business section. I liked business because I'd started working at Commonwealth United Mortgage Company as sort of a PR guy.

At this stage of my life, I was trying to become cultured. My drug counselors can probably figure out why. I wanted to cover up the emptiness inside by putting on a sophisticated face. Again, it was a con.

I started taking tennis lessons, for instance. Tennis is more white collar. I joined a tennis club, and I met a guy named Chris Applegate in the shower room. Chris ran the mortgage company, and we ended up talking business. He thought my name could attract customers, so we dreamed up a job for me. I had a business card and a desk and a salary, and I was supposed to keep my ears open for potential deals.

Companies would meet with Chris and me, and they'd end up wanting me to sign autographs the whole time.

That off-season, after I returned from Hazelden, Glinda and I visited Paris and the south of France. But on the flight over, Glinda and I met an older couple, and I had an interesting chat with the woman. She was a teacher, and I told her about my reading lessons. She said it was brave of me to go back to school. I liked her reaction, and I began thinking about coming out of the closet.

Later that spring, I flew to Florida for the cable station I hosted a show for, "Home Team Sports." By fate I sat next to some woman from *USA Today* on the plane. I told her what I was doing at the Lab School and that I'd been an illiterate through high school and college.

She put one little blurb in *USA Today*, and the rest was history. In the three years I'd been at the Lab School, I'd never breathed a word of my reading problem to anyone. Suddenly I was getting interview requests from every Tom, Dick, and Sam. So was Sara.

One phone call came from Sen. Paul Simon's office. He called me twice. I never took the calls because I didn't know the magnitude of what I was doing, but Senator Simon and his staff kept pushing for me to appear at their senate subcommittee hearing on illiteracy. They wanted me to give a testimonial on national TV.

I think Sara was against it:

*D*exter said he wouldn't go unless I went. I personally didn't want him to. I didn't know if it'd be good for him. I thought it'd be better if his reading was not in focus so much, but I left it up to him.

Some guy wrote a speech for Dexter to read at the hearing, but I told Dexter not to read it, to just improvise from his heart. This agent guy said the committee wanted him to read, but Dexter gets so nervous reading in front of people. I thought he should just talk. He decided to read.

Well, he did get nervous right there on national TV and lost his place and cried. When Senator Simon told him to forget about reading his speech and said, "You're doing fine," Dexter spoke from the heart and was brilliant.

If you have a learning disability, any anxiety makes it worse. He'd never read in front of anybody before. He practiced the speech with that man, but not with me.

When he cried, there I was on camera sitting next to him. I knew I didn't want to be on TV, and I felt uncomfortable. I sat there frozen when he broke down, because I didn't know what to do and I knew the TV cameras were there. I always worry about people exploiting Dexter, but Famous

Amos—*who also has a learning disability and was there that day testifying—
came up to help Dexter relax.*

*Dexter was very upset that he had to look at himself on TV, crying. He
ended up making an eloquent speech to the subcommittee, but all they
showed on TV was him crying. I believe he found that humiliating. At least,
that's what he told me. I think he should've stayed out of the media because it
was confusing. He was getting adulation for something he'd always tried to
hide.*

Overnight, after that illiteracy hearing, I became a role
model. That was a first for me. I'd always had this bad-guy image—the
drug guy, the loud-talking guy—and now little kids and illiterate adults
were writing me letters—misspelling my name—saying I was brave.

I became a good guy overnight. I don't know why. Maybe because
of my courage, people probably saw the human side.

Athletes are put on a pedestal, but just like politicians and
entertainers, we are ordinary people. That day, millions of people
identified with me as an ordinary person.

But I was in such disarray that day. I was so disappointed. I
wanted to show those people I could read, but I wasn't adept at keeping
eye contact with the panel and keeping my eye on my speech. See, I
wanted to act professional and read it like an anchorman, with eye
contact.

Hell, I didn't even write the speech. A guy named Brown wrote
it. He was trying to do some PR for me, and I'd never met him before
that hearing. Thomas ("Hollywood") Henderson, who was my confidante, had told me about him. It was a brotherhood thing. Thomas
said, "Give him a chance. He wants to help you out." So I said OK. I
figured if he could find me some business and extra endorsements, fine.
This Brown guy was talking about getting me a Campbell Soup ad or
something.

I told Brown on the phone what was going on with the senate
hearing, and he wanted to get involved. So he put together a speech,
though Sara didn't want me to read it. I practiced with him the
morning of the hearing, and I had it down pat. But when I tried to
make eye contact, I lost my place and panicked.

I thought I'd made a fool out of myself. I was trying to be
somebody I really wasn't. That's the way I felt sitting at the hearing. I
didn't mind giving my message, I just felt better talking it.

When Senator Simon said, "You're doing fine, just tell us your
story," it went great. It was just too formal before. I think they wanted

to get to hear my real side, anyway. They wanted to have their hearts moved. And that's what I was able to do once I stopped reading it and just told my story.

So, that day, I felt shame. But I also knew I'd made great strides from where I'd come from in 1985 and 1986.

All the hoopla started the next day: mail and phone calls to my home. But I was nowhere to be found.

Guess where I was? Here I had done something good, and I went and did something bad.

The same day of the hearing, I went and did cocaine.

As I left the senate building, I made up my mind to get blitzed. Everybody was talking about how great my talk was, and I was like, "Man, I feel so positive." Right then, I decided to do drugs because deep inside I didn't believe I deserved the adulation. I guess I wanted an escape.

That testimony could've really changed my life. It was something I could've taken and run with. People gave me so many ideas on what I could do as an illiteracy role model. People said, "Hey, this is your niche, this is something you should adopt. This is something you can touch a lot of people with."

I thought about all of that, but my thing was still to train and get ready for the upcoming 1989 season.

Then there was my drug use. I was so confused. Should I stay sober? Do drugs? Be an illiteracy spokesman? How would I accept the adulation? How do I accept all the things people are telling me? For the first time, I felt wanted.

I mean, Joe Gibbs never asked me to go anywhere! Before that, Joe Gibbs never asked me to visit his boys' ranch for underprivileged kids at all. But here came Coach Gibbs now asking me to visit the ranch. It's as if he wanted to jump on the bandwagon. That's the way I looked at it. Joe Gibbs never came to me before and asked me to do anything in the community. Not since my rookie year anyway. I felt like, "Wow."

But then the Redskins said I was doing *too* much. They said there was too much Dexter Manley out there. They told me, "That's enough."

John Kent Cooke—Johnny Cakes—called me in his office. I knew instantly when he called me in that he was attempting to control me. He was real smooth, but he was manipulating me. I looked him right in the eye and knew what he was about. I didn't fall for it.

Johnny Cakes said, "You helped my son. I have a son with a

problem like that. This reading thing is great. But now you need to concentrate on football. That's enough talk about reading."

Here I was, someone who always had a great work ethic. I'd always shown up for training camp on time—most of the time—and they never had a problem with me coming in out of shape. So why would an owner be telling me I needed to concentrate on football when it's June and football doesn't begin until July? Does he think I'm a rookie?

I just played along. I acknowledged him, but it just went in one ear and out the other.

Maybe I was getting too big and making them look bad. I could never figure it out. Why would I put football in the background? What kind of money was I gonna make off illiteracy? I'm sure it was about control.

What irked me most was that Cooke was trying to take something away from me that was becoming special to me. I went through a lot of struggle and pain with reading as a kid, and all of a sudden I had adulation with it. And he's gonna tell me, "That's enough"?

He told me no more personal appearances, but I didn't stop. I did what I had to do. Johnny Cakes's daddy got him a good education; my daddy wasn't able to get me a good education. I wasn't diagnosed early and sent off to some private school to get my problem taken care of. So it was unfair for him to tell me, "Hey, that's enough." That eats me up to this day.

On the other hand, I never considered my testimony would cause a backlash at Yates High School. Everyone there, including my old assistant coach who was now the head football coach, Maurice McGowan, said I was lying about being illiterate:

I read all that business about Dexter being illiterate, and I didn't believe it. Everyone came running to me—I'm Luther Booker, and I was his head coach—and I said no. I've had a lot of discussions with his former coaches and teammates, and all these boys have known each other since elementary school. We'd ask those boys, "Could Dexter read?" And they'd say, "Sure, he could read."

They think it's a gimmick thing, something he could cash in on. They said, "He must be running his mouth."

My opinion is you can make a Ph.D. look like a fool if you ask him about football. What I'm saying is, I could give a group of people a test and let me grade the test, and I can make that person illiterate. And I can give that same test to a junior high student and make him come out a genius.

It's all up to whoever's giving the test.

What is reading? I've got a grandson in kindergarten, and he can read. But give him a test, and he can't recall a word. Now, is he illiterate? The way I see it, this Lab School said, "We can get some publicity off Dexter. Great."

How about those people at Oklahoma State? He had to fill out their applications and pass their tests. How did he stay there four years? How did he do it? How did they do it? I can't see how he can fill out the necessary forms. As an illiterate?

You can't stay in college that long and let people do the work for you. If he had the ability to do that, then he's a very unusual case and a genius in his own right.

His hearing in the senate definitely didn't make our school look good, but it made Oklahoma State look worse. Everybody gets mad at Yates High School, but what about his junior high and elementary school? People learn to read in elementary school. Why did the elementary school pass him on?

You should've heard McGowan:

When this all came out, I was the head coach at Yates—I'm Maurice McGowan—and we thought about it real hard. We knew Dexter wasn't the smartest in the world. Not even close. We knew he was passing by his chinny-chin-chin.

But he always had his newspapers. Kids like to look at the city statistics in the paper, and he'd look at them like the rest of 'em.

We didn't tell teachers to pass him. Of course, when Dexter came through high school, it was a different time. Nowadays, there are standardized tests and high school exit exams. Back then, all you had to do your senior year was take a test, and you didn't have to pass it. Nowadays, if you don't have a 70 or above at the six-week grading period, you have to sit out six weeks. If he went to high school now, Dexter would've been one of those. He didn't pass every six weeks.

Listen, we didn't cheat for Dexter. But we did try to get a kid eligible. A lot of these kids, all they have going is athletics. If you kick 'em out of athletics, they're out on the street or maybe robbing your house.

But no! We didn't give kids test answers. We had no way of knowing about tests. That is the furthest thing from the truth.

You've got to know about Yates. It was founded by the Reverend Jack Yates as the third black school in Houston. During the 1940s, all these teachers and doctors lived in the Third Ward, and this was an influential place. The kids who went to Yates had money, so people called it Sugar Hill. Everyone hated Yates. They had everything there. One year, Yates brought its homecoming queen to the stadium in a helicopter. That was the type of money they had.

Yates has had only one losing football season in its entire history, and that was in the 1940s. It has so many famous alumni: Debbie Allen, Phylicia Rashad, Elvis Patterson, and so on.

But over the years these rich Sugar Hill people moved out of the Third Ward. What were we left with? The Third Ward is an area that's gone down. But in the 1950s these were homes that looked new, and the people living in them had jobs.

So what I'm saying is now that we're down, people are kicking us. People have always been jealous of Yates, and now they're making up all kinds of tales . . . saying we helped Dexter cheat.

We all said, "OK, Dexter's lying again." I even called him up and said, "What're you doin'?"

As far as passing him to play, no! The kids who knew him are saying, "Dexter's lying, Dexter's lying." A lot of Dexter's old teammates are upset with him. He's come out before and said he had no friends in Houston, and he's pissed them off. He came over to Yates a few years ago, and one of his old friends was in the weight room. Dexter hollered over at him, and the guy just looked at him.

You tell Dexter I still think he's very stingy. He went out and made money, but never has he sent anything back. I asked him to buy us some weights, but he never gives anything back. All we get is, "We didn't teach him to read." If we failed you, Dexter, you failed us.

And let's say we did pass him through—and I don't think we did—but that's some way to repay us for helping him reach the pros. Saying, "They didn't teach me nothing," puts a black mark on us.

I understand he's upset he had to spend his money and pay a private tutor to teach him how to read. But how'd he get that money? Playing football. Where'd he be right now if the teachers had failed him? Dead. Knowing Dexter, he'd be dead. A lot of his old partners are dead. Or you can't see 'em on the streets as skinny as they are.

To hell with McGowan. McGowan's one of those guys who told me I'd never make it. He is an ignorant man.

I went back to Yates a couple years back to film a spot on ABC

"Prime Time," and they asked McGowan, "Aren't you proud of Dexter?" He answered, "Yeah, we're proud of his *football* accomplishments." That's all he said.

He's ignorant. Listen, he's just mad at me because all he cares about is parents sending their kids to Yates. He doesn't want bad publicity that'll make kids go elsewhere.

He says my old teammate was mad at me in the weight room? That's Danny Jackson. I'm supposed to care if Danny Jackson, who's been in jail three times, is pissed because I put down Yates? Like I care if these guys don't speak to me?

I won't forget what McGowan said to me. He put Gerald Franklin and me down. He told us we'd never amount to anything. He never in his wildest dreams thought I'd make it. He said I'd get kicked out of college for rape or for peeking in a girls' bathroom. I never listened to him, because I'm strong-willed. I knew in my heart of hearts what I could do.

He is right about Yates never getting good publicity. There always are fights there. I don't want my son, Derrick, or my nieces going to Yates. It's prestigious for sports, but not a good school. It ain't nothing but a place to house kids for a day. That's how it was when I went there. That's why I never learned to read.

McGowan's denying I have a learning disability because I'm a reflection on Yates. You think parents want to sent their kids to Yates when they hear that? He's worried about that. And if he doesn't win, he knows he'll get replaced.

He's right, too, that I may have been dead without football. No question. But a lot of kids at Yates today are just like me. I did them good by getting it out in the open.

When I left Yates, you know how I'd read? I'd see a paragraph, recognize about four words in the paragraph, and then guess at the paragraph's meaning.

But these people think I'm lying. Bobby Beathard, too:

I was surprised to hear he was illiterate. People remember going into Redskin Park, and Dexter would be in there reading all the papers and all the sports pages. A lot of people suspect it was played up a heck of a lot bigger than it was to get sympathy . . . I don't know.

If it's true that he learned to read, that's great. Because it's pretty tough to get by if you can't read.

See how good of an actor I am to attract all these cynics? I didn't *want* people to know I couldn't read. That's why I'd fake reading the newspaper, moving my lips. I'd really just be searching for my name. And then I'd call Glinda to ask her to read the article to me.

Listen, Sara Hines knows my learning disability is true:

*H*e *wasn't faking it. No way. He wanted sympathy? No. He was in our school for three years before it ever came out. And he didn't get sympathy and attention from me.*

He couldn't read. Trust me. But his whole life had been faking it and getting Glinda to read the menu to him or getting his girlfriend to do his homework. In high school there's no way Dexter could've ever passed a test that entailed reading. Unless he copied or cheated. And he's told me that's what he did.

That senate hearing was no con. After the 1988 season, my only cons were my hideout trip to Hazelden and my enrollment in a Japanese class.

That's right, I told the world that, in addition to my reading classes, I'd enrolled in a Japanese course. On my flight back from Paris, I was sitting by a Japanese girl, and we talked the whole way. She got me thinking Japanese was a good language to learn. I mean, I was interested in business, and the Japanese were taking over the business world.

It was a way to cultivate myself. I thought it'd be very impressive. When I was in Paris, I was so amazed at how those Frenchmen spoke English. It was like our language was international; and it was like Americans are so arrogant, we demand they learn our language. So I figured maybe I should be less arrogant and learn another language.

I also figured it would get me publicity—Manley learning Japanese. Kinichi Wa. It was just another fad.

My family in Texas saw through my Japanese phase though. I went to visit my Aunt Monneola and Aunt Joycee in Sealy, and they held this exchange:

Monneola: I guess he really couldn't read.

Joycee: Yeah, but why is a man who can't read English gonna try and read Japanese?

Monneola: Uh huh. He ought to get his English down first.

AN IDLE THOUGHT

My first practice of 1989, I caught serious crap from my teammates.

Darryl Grant said, "Yo, Dex. If you couldn't read, how did you get home at night? How did you read the street signs or the highway exit signs?"

It was a fair question. To be honest, I'd have problems getting places. Once I'd been somewhere, I'd have to remember how I got there because, no, I couldn't read street signs.

Now that I can read, I've noticed I try paying attention to street signs. In the old days, Glinda used to write out directions for me. All I had to do was match the name of the street on her sheet of paper with the one on the street sign. As long as they matched, I didn't have to read signs. But Glinda used to say she didn't know how I got around so well in D.C.

People ask me how I read menus. Well, I'd just order simple crap. My rookie season, I went to a restaurant with teammates Doc Walker and Jeris White, and I just ordered what they ordered. I figured I'd have their kind of tastes.

I'd experiment with different foods that way. I figured I'd just try them. I didn't know how to read the menu, but I didn't want a soul to know.

Do you know I just learned how to read *fettucine?* I've seen the word so many times, but I never knew what the hell it was. The first time I tasted it, I ate it at Sal's restaurant in Virginia. I used to point to the word and say to Sal, "What is this like?" And he'd say it tastes good.

Over the years, I've learned to cope. But I had a lot of anxiety. The thing that scared me most was, what happens when I no longer have people around me?

CHAPTER 31

My Beloved Drug Dealer

I'M LUCKY I'VE NEVER BEEN BUSTED BY SOME hotshot cop.

The NFL has put my ass in a sling, but it would've been a lot worse if it was the D.C. police department nabbing me in a sting. Like Mayor Barry.

There were times when I'd buy drugs from a total stranger. For all I knew, he could've been the police chief working undercover. The worst time was in downtown D.C. when I met this stranger and said to him, "I know these girls who want to buy some drugs. Do you know where?"

To cover my ass, I said somebody else wanted to buy, but how foolish could I have been? I was asking just anybody. It could've been a cop.

This total stranger gave me his phone number. I would never give a drug guy *my* number. I called him a couple of days later, and I guess I was fortunate he was a true, blue dealer.

Originally, I bought drugs from a guy named Terry, who only used his first name. I don't think I knew his last name. Anyway, I think I first met Terry through my ex-teammate Lamar Parish when I'd go over to Lamar's house.

I wasn't doing drugs, but Lamar was an all-pro whom I looked up to. He had it goin' on. Women would walk around dressed only in robes in his house, and then this guy Terry would show up. I was a rookie when I met Terry.

I saw Terry somewhere else years later, and I began going over to his house every Friday night. He had so much coke laying around, including a can full of the stuff downstairs. It was like a Pennzoil can, only you'd unscrew the top. When he was upstairs, I'd scoop some of the coke out like coffee and drop it in a plastic bag I'd bring. It was Christmas morning.

Freddie worked for Terry. I've seen Terry count $300,000 in one sitting, but his big connection was out of New York. Freddie was one of Terry's partners, but he was like a carrier. If Terry called Freddie over, he'd be right there.

I believed Terry and Freddie were legit. One time, Terry showed me a check he'd received—presumably for a coke purchase—from a Washington, D.C., media personality. When he showed me that check, I figured, Hey, if this other guy's coming here, it must be cool.

Terry didn't horse around when it came to business. He wouldn't give me crap for free. Unless I stole it from the Pennzoil can, Terry charged me. Freddie? Freddie gave me drugs free.

In fact, Freddie gave me drugs free for a long time. He was a nice guy. He never seemed to me to be an evil-spirited guy. I didn't spend a lot of time around him—I'd just pick up the stuff and split—but he seemed pleasant.

All drug dealers tell you you're getting a good deal. I probably wasn't. But if I spent $300 for coke, I'd want Freddie to give me an extra $100 worth. He'd do it all the time. Sometimes, he couldn't because it'd already be sealed up, but he'd try.

When I checked into Hazelden in January of 1986, Freddie didn't think I had a drug problem. He'd say, "Hey, you don't have a problem. Just don't let it get out of hand." He warned me not to free-base. That's one thing he stressed. He said the drug would be a lot more addictive if I free-based and that it would be a very, very hard thing to quit doing.

Later on, maybe he could see I was getting hooked. Sometimes, if I bought coke from him earlier in the day and came back later for more, he'd say, "Cut it out. I'm not gonna sell to you." I'm not saying he encouraged me to stop, but the girl he was living with would tell him not to sell to me.

Glinda, she didn't like Freddie. She used to say, "Watch out for Freddie" . . .

That Freddie is scum of the earth. He looks like a drug dealer. He's forty years old, maybe fifty now, with no teeth in his mouth, and unattractive.

He always wears sweat suits and tennis shoes, and he looks like a dope dealer. I told Dexter, "If people see you with him, they will know what's up."

Dexter said he didn't see Freddie that way. Dexter said, "Ahhh, people don't know."

That's not true. They do know.

*   *   *

Well, I do remember my Aunt Billie and Uncle Wilbur coming to the Super Bowl in January 1988 and asking, "Is Freddie a drug dealer?" To me, he just didn't look the part.

So I still associated with him.

AN IDLE THOUGHT

In Washington, D.C., lore, I'm linked with Mayor Marion Barry. I'd like to fake you out and say we snorted coke together—the mayor and a Redskin out on the town—but it never happened.

We were, and still are, friends. I originally met him at some function in the city, and I later had him as a guest on my radio show.

We grew closer after he got arrested for cocaine and after I got banned from the Redskins in 1989. I wired him a telegram, saying to hang in there. It was a fellowship thing.

But, Lordy, I did not party with him. I did not want to party with some of the women he was running around with. Some of those girls didn't look very good to me.

The one thing I remember about Mayor Barry, though, is the day we bumped into each other outside the district building downtown. It was spring of 1990, and I was at a red light on Pennsylvania Avenue. The mayor happened to walk in front of my car with his secretary, and I hopped out of the car and embraced him.

Suddenly, everyone on the street was honking horns and putting up power signs. It was just righteous. I couldn't believe the ruckus. But in the back of my mind—and this is just my own paranoia—I figured people were thinking, "Uh oh, there's the mayor and Dexter Manley making a drug transaction in front of the district building."

CHAPTER 32

Hell to the Redskins

By 1989 THE REDSKINS COACHES DIDN'T TRUST me as far as they could see. And a lot of those old boys wore glasses.

They test us in the 40-yard dash on the last day of minicamp, but in 1989 I didn't run because of a sore leg. So while everyone else was getting timed, I hopped over to my bank right quick for a withdrawal. I was bored, it was a Saturday, and the banks were closing at noon.

Well, Gibbs, who trusted me worth a penny, couldn't find me. So his alarm went off.

He went to the offensive line coach Joe Bugel and said, "I think we lost Dexter."

He thought I'd bolted to do drugs. When I returned with my wallet full, one of the Redskins PR guys said, "Coach Gibbs wants to talk to you."

Coach said, "Dexter, you made me scared. I thought you'd left for good."

And you know who then took time to talk to me for thirty minutes? Not Gibbs, but Bugel. Bugel and I stood on the football field so long the Astroturf must've grown half an inch. He gave me advice. He said people never thought I'd make it this far and not to mess it up now. He talked to me like a father, and I'd never had a coach try that before. Joe Gibbs never did. He and I would talk if I shot my mouth off before a Dallas game, or if he was pushing the Bible on me, or if he wanted me in Hazelden. But he never really talked about philosophy and life.

Bugel's chat meant a lot to me, and little did I know that he and I would hook up again in another time and place. But it was also scary. I'd let my guard down in front of a coach, and that was never supposed to happen.

274

It was also obvious the entire Redskins coaching staff felt I was on the brink of another big fall to drugs.

There were too many hints in 1989 that they were losing faith in me. Gibbs called me aside for a meeting early in the season to say I needed to fly around on the field more and play the run. It sounded to me as if they weren't pleased.

Gibbs said, "Dexter, you don't talk anymore." What he meant was in training camp I used to run my mouth at our offensive coaches. I'd say, "Run the frickin' ball over here, Don Breaux!" Or "Run the ball over here, Bugel!" Gibbs made the comparison of how I *used* to be. He said, "You used to say, 'Run the ball at me.'" He said I didn't practice the way I used to practice. See, earlier in my career I was a phenomenal practice player. But now I'd gotten to the point where I was saving it for the game. I got wiser. Gibbs didn't like that, though.

Once the season began, the coaches screwed with me. Richie Petitbon took me out on second-down-and-long passing situations, which was the move of an imbecile. Here I was, the best pass rusher in football, and they're taking me out on passing downs! They said they wanted to get linebacker Ravin Caldwell in for our 3–4 package on second downs, and I was the one replaced.

Gibbs and I almost had it out. I almost asked to be traded. I felt the Redskins were cutting my plays down because they knew I was up for a new contract at the end of the year. If I'm half-ass, I'm still a better pass rusher than Ravin Caldwell. But, see, if I'd had big numbers, the community would've backed me up in a contract dispute. So that's why they took me out on second and long. Gibbs says my contract situation didn't enter into playing time situations, but I really think it was all about control.

Those Redskins coaches have a stellar reputation, but coaches are only as good as their players. They only put the X's and O's up there. Who couldn't have coached the Lakers when they were in their prime? Coaches don't make tackles. The one thing coaches do is make adjustments during a game, and the Redskins coaches are very adept at that. Otherwise, it's the players busting their ass and getting it down.

Speaking of adjustments, there was a game on October 15, 1989, that Redskins coaches seemed to hold against me. Up at Giant Stadium, I had two sacks in the first half against Jumbo Elliott. Man, I was coming to put 'em away. But the Giants made some adjustments, and I wasn't able to come through anymore, and we lost by three points. But the Redskins thought I coasted in the second half.

Well, in late October 1989 we were about to play the Raiders in

Los Angeles. I was fired up because Leonard Goldberg, the Hollywood producer, wanted to make a TV movie about my life. Everybody tells me Danny Glover would have been the perfect actor to portray me. Goldberg, who also made *Sleeping with the Enemy,* was about to move from Julia Roberts to me. He was inspired about my story of illiteracy, and I believed he was one smart man.

On Saturday, October 28, the day before the Raiders game, my attorney, Bob Woolf, and I spoke specifically to Goldberg about *The Dexter Manley Story.* I was on the top of Mount Everest. When Bob and I left Goldberg's place, we got to talking about Paul Tagliabue, who had just replaced my old buddy Rozelle.

"Well, we got a new commissioner," Bob said.

"Who?" I asked.

"Paul Tagliabue," Bob answered. "Don't you remember he was always in those meetings with Rozelle? Taking notes?"

"I don't remember him," I answered "and I don't want to know him. Thank God we don't have to meet with him. Everything's going great."

Well, two days later . . .

Here's what happened. We lost to the Raiders—we got shellacked, 37–24—I was feeling almost too much glory. I felt grandiose. I felt like, well, look at me, I'm well. I'm doing things. I'll have a movie. I don't have a problem anymore. The idea that there were conversations about a movie . . . I got selfish again. I figured I'd be making money: I'd be larger than life.

Deep down inside, I didn't believe I deserved the accolades. My drug counselors believe that's why I needed cocaine as an escape.

I used to be afraid of cocaine, but with the movie deal the fear had left me. I had no fear of getting caught. I'd stopped going to AA meetings a few weeks before the Los Angeles trip, and my complacency had set in. Maybe I'd go to some meetings, but not regularly.

The urge was back, the carelessness. We returned from Los Angeles, and the team had a workout the Monday after the game. I asked Emmitt Thomas, our black secondary coach and my confidante, whether I had a good game. I regard Emmitt as a man of integrity. He always told me the truth. I wanted to hear from a coach's point of view how I played against the Raiders, so I went to him.

He said, "We thought you played well. You didn't lose us that game."

Right then, right on the practice field, I said to myself, "Man, I'm gonna do drugs." I cut out of there quick.

I mean, when Emmitt said I played a good game, the only thing flashing in my mind was cocaine.

I said to myself, I'm playing good, I've got a radio show, a TV show . . . Man, nothing's wrong with me. Everyone snorts a little cocaine now and then. I'm not an everyday user. I'll just do drugs.

You know what else? It was Halloween time. As I said earlier, that's my go-crazy time. My 1985 truck crash was on Halloween. I wish I'd just gone trick or treating with my kids.

Instead, I called Freddie. I was still getting tested two or three times a week. I don't know what I was thinking.

I even had to do my regular TV spot on the Fox Station in D.C., Channel 5, that night. Originally I told Freddie to meet me downtown, but I changed my mind and got a room at the Holiday Inn near the TV station in upper northwest D.C. That way, I wouldn't risk driving across town to do the show under the influence, weaving all over the road and getting pulled over by some cop. I preferred to be closer to Channel 5.

So before I touched drugs, I decided to get into a hotel first. That way I felt safe. Freddie met me there.

I actually thought I'd show up, cheery-eyed, for the TV show. Instead, I was dazed in my hotel room watching the sports anchor, Steve Buckhantz, tell the viewing audience I was nowhere to be found. The camera then focused on the empty chair I was supposed to be sitting in.

I didn't think that was nice. See, I worked at Channel 5. He didn't have to mention I was missing, although I guess he had an obligation. He's a journalist or a newsman, so he just did his job. But it didn't help me to show this empty chair. He could've just said, "Dexter isn't here."

So here I am coming up with bull to justify my wrongdoing. I was *wrong*. I *should* have been there. I had an obligation and didn't live up to it. I was just coked up at the time. Patrice Jordan from Channel 5 called me, and Freddie was answering my portable car phone. He was my answering service. My heart is palpitating just envisioning it now.

So the whole city knew I'd stood up Channel 5. Then I missed the filming of "The Dexter Manley Show" on "Home Team Sports" the next morning. I missed my reading lesson with Sara as well. I missed a meeting at the mortgage company, too.

I eventually called the mortgage company, and they told me a zillion people were on the lookout for me. My buddy Lester Townsend took me over to Dale Morris's house—Dale was formerly with the

Redskins in marketing and is a friend. Dale drove me around as it poured rain. From there, I went to the Regency Health Club to sit in the sauna and sweat. I had to drench the coke out of me. I knew that eventually I would have to take a pee for the NFL. One more strike against me, and it would be three: I'd be banned for life. Pham came over and we sat there at the Regency Club, talking. I eventually took my butt home.

At practice the next day I showed up as if nothing had ever occurred. That was my exterior. Inside, I was dying. I grabbed Charles Mann and we shut the door to Bubba's office and talked about my relapse. Charles said, "Are you all right? Are you gonna pass the test?"

Charles, who is quite a religious guy, then said it was a shame I didn't have a support group on the team. He said that on the Redskins team, he had a number of guys he had to answer to—other religious guys, guys like Art Monk and Monte Coleman. That was their religious group. But I was like an outsider. Who was I gonna answer to? I had no one to answer to . . . except Glinda. Those other guys had support through their religious group. They recycled the Scriptures. If they didn't get it, they'd talk about it. I had no one to go to. If I did, maybe I could've called them before I used drugs.

At a time like that, you need someone to answer to. That's when you need an older brother or a daddy—somebody—around. Charles had that. I could see the cohesion among those guys who packed the Bible.

I was jealous of them because I was doing drugs and they had a good, clean life. They were doing the right thing, the positive thing, and they always had someone to answer to.

Art Monk would give a guy feedback. He'd tell Art something, and Art would say, "That ain't right, man" or "Get your act together." I wanted that so badly, but I didn't know how to reach out. I stayed so secretive and isolated because I did so much wrong. I did drugs, so I closed up.

The one guy I could answer to was Grant, but we weren't *that* tight. When I'd come to practice with hangovers, I'd be halfway going to sleep on the field, and I'd say to Grant, "I haven't been home, man. I don't think I'm gonna make it, Grant. I'm sleepy."

Darryl would say, "Goddamn, man. Why don't you chill? Why do you keep screwing up?" Darryl talks with hands, like a rapper. And plenty of times he'd say on the field, "Take your ass home, Dexter. Get some sleep. Take care of your wife. Get your ass home."

Those initial days after my Raider game relapse, I'd stand away from everybody on the field. I'd isolate myself. I knew I was on my way out, baby.

Wayne Sevier, the special teams coach, noticed something was up with me, and had a talk with me at my locker about staying straight. I had already relapsed with the drugs at the time, so I was lying to him, telling him, "I'm all right, Wayne. I hear you, Wayne." The chat with Wayne was so confusing:

As an assistant coach, I noticed some things and thought some-one should say something. I saw some actions in Dexter that made me wonder what was going on. It was just one person to another person. I told him I was worried about him and was noticing changes in him from earlier years. I saw a little dropoff in practice. I noticed whereas he once was a fierce hitter, he wasn't approaching it with the same tenacity.

I wasn't accusing him of anything, nor did I want him to say, "Yes, I'm on something" or "No." I just wanted to talk.

The two weeks following my relapse were agony for me as I waited like an expectant mother for my test results. No one else knew, so I was business as usual, even making a trip to the White House to see George Bush. He was honoring adults for their work with learning disabilities, and I was invited, as was the governor of West Virginia and the CBS president.

President Bush was real tall. Personally, I felt Ronald Reagan was more handsome and attractive, more sharp. Since Bush is from Texas, he's probably got a little hillbilly in him. I even saw a hole in his pants—on the pocket seam. I don't mean to be rude, though. He might not invite me to the White House again.

The thing was, the cocaine was still in my system when I visited the White House on Monday. On Thursday—three days later—I learned I'd failed my test. So, here I was at the White House, feeling like a Rolls-Royce on the outside but like a garbage truck inside.

To make matters worse, Freddie was starting to shadow me. He began waiting for me outside Channel 5 on nights I'd do my show. He came by once, and I hopped in his car, and I was like, "Hey, man, stop bugging me." He'd say, "Let's go and have a good time" or "Hey, I've got some. What do you want to do?" Either that, or he wanted me to get tickets for him to a game. He'd just want tickets and wouldn't even offer coke. He was a big Redskins fan.

It was the first time he'd ever propositioned me about buying coke. You know how kids say they get offered the stuff? When I did it, no one offered. I just knew where to go get it. But now Freddie was coming to me.

I played in a game against the Cowboys on November 5—Dallas's only win that year—and still my positive test hadn't come back from the lab. See, they check it twice to make certain. Our next game was November 12 at Philadelphia, and that's when I started getting vibes that I was outta there.

On the Saturday before the Eagles game, the Redskins kicked my buddy Lester out of Redskin Park, which startled me. Lester used to wash cars over there and was generally welcome among the players, but the Redskins never liked him hanging around. Why? Probably because Lester was white and doing hard labor, and that probably was an embarrassment to them. Still, I never thought they'd mess with Lester. He was my friend, and I was big time there. If they tried running Lester off, I was gonna get involved.

On Saturday we were getting ready to go to Philly, and Lester came over to Redskin Park to get doughnuts as if he were a player. They never had said anything about it because he was my friend.

Well, Lester came to me that day and said, "Shhh. Dexter. Come over here." He took me outside by the football field and said, "Man, Bubba Tyer [the trainer] said something disturbing to me. I went in to get a doughnut, and Bubba said, 'Get your ass out of here. Because neither of y'all will be around here next week anyway.'"

And that same Saturday, I had an argument with the new general manager, Charley Casserly, and Joe Gibbs. Casserly called me upstairs in his office regarding a quote I'd had in *The Washington Post* about how the offense needs to be more productive. Charley was pissed, although Gibbs didn't say much. Charley said, "You're not having an all-pro season, so you don't have a right to talk that way."

I retorted, "Look here, man. I can say what I want to say, and I'm not putting down my teammates. I'm not criticizing them at all. I said if the offense put more points on the board, we could do better. Hell, we just lost, 10–3, to Dallas."

He said I wasn't having a good year. Our record at the time was 4–5. Ain't nobody on that team was having a great season.

Then he added, "I'll deal with you in the off-season." So I got up and walked right out of there. Gibbs didn't say much, probably because he knew what was going to happen with the drug test and Charley didn't. Things weren't exactly looking up.

When I got to Philadelphia that night, I kept thinking about what Lester said. The thing was, Bubba never said a word to me. But Bubba would've known. If a test comes back positive, they retest it; so I'm sure Bubba knew what the first test result was before the Eagles game.

In fact, Glinda and Little Dexter had driven up for that Sunday's game, and we got to the stadium at the crack of dawn. In the old days, Bubba used to always come kissing on Glinda, but at Veterans Stadium that day, there was none of that. Bubba just walked right on by Glinda.

I *knew* something was up at the team hotel Sunday morning. Coach Gibbs walked right by me on his way to the pregame breakfast without even looking at me. Larry Peccatiello, a defensive coach, was the only one laughing and smiling a little bit. I could tell by their attitude toward me that something was amiss.

I was paranoid, I agree, but I still sensed it.

I just sat on that bench before the game thinking about what Bubba had said to Lester. It was early still, and the Eagles' cheerleaders were practicing. Little Dexter had come on the field with me and was running around playing. As I watched him, I thought, I can't do this drug crap anymore. I saw all the joy in my kid, and I said to myself, You've got to stop the drugs. Little Dexter may want to run on the field again. I felt as if I was playing Russian roulette.

Do you frickin' believe I sacked Randall Cunningham three times that day? I knew it was maybe my last game ever, and I sacked that joker three times, including once when we were trying to preserve our 10–3 lead. Joe Gibbs hugged me when we won and gave me a high five. After the game he tried denying to the media that he'd done any such thing. He said, "I don't do that with my players."

After my three sacks, which had me well in front of Charles Mann for the team lead, I found Casserly in the locker room and said, "Look here. I don't need to make any tackles. I make sacks. And don't you forget it." Then I stalked off.

Being on drugs normally will hinder your performance. I felt my speed was still there, but drugs give you illusions. Maybe I was wrong about my speed. Maybe I was losing it. And, for sure, drugs take away your endurance. So how did I catch Randall three times? Put it this way: I was still the fastest thing the Redskins had in their stable. If I did slow down, I was still the fastest on defense besides Darrell Green and A.J. Johnson. Hell, I still ran a 4.58 40-yard dash

I had such a phenomenal game, I nearly did drugs again that Sunday night. I thought, I played studly. I'm not out of the league. I can use drugs. Sad, huh? While Glinda and Little Dexter were on I-95, driving back from Philly, I was off the team airplane, free until they got home. I sat at the Sheraton-Tyson's Corner for two hours, sweating and contemplating, Should I use? Do I want to? I'd just had a big relapse, and I was recalling its hell. And here I was having the same thoughts after the Eagles game! I couldn't decide whether to phone Pham. First, I wasn't going to call Pham, but then I knew I'd have to get to Redskin Park Monday; and if I used coke, it'd be the same crap all over again— me incapacitated in a hotel. So I dialed Pham, and he talked me out of it. That's the first time I saw how AA works. I went to his house at 10:00 P.M., and he just talked my ass out of it.

Pham made me remember the last time I'd relapsed, the night of the Eagles game. I was in his car, literally begging and crying saying, "Oh, God, just please help me." Pham made me see what I really looked like: pathetic.

My final day at Redskin Park, my stomping ground for nine years, was the following Thursday—November 17, 1989. It was around two o'clock, and I still hadn't heard official word of my positive test. I knew I'd been a bad boy and knew they'd catch it, but I tried to block it out. The optimist in me was saying, Maybe they missed it. My denial was so strong.

I was at my locker stall when I spied Doc Knowlan walking my way. Immediately, there was fear, anger, and no saliva in my mouth. He said, "Dexter, I've got to talk to you."

Everyone has a thermometer in their body, and mine instantly felt a rush. I started sweating. Doc Knowlan said, "Dexter, we've got a problem."

My defense mechanism sprang up. "What?"

"The league says you had a bad test," he answered.

I had so much denial. I desperately wanted to cover my ass because I was afraid I'd lost everything I'd worked for. "That test is wrong, 'cause it took so long to come back," I said. I insisted the NFL had made a mistake.

Was it all over? After all the cheating in high school and the running the train tracks? If so, I knew I'd be a liability for my family. At that moment I was no longer an asset.

I went into a fit. The Redskins had an FBI meeting scheduled that day—a league rep briefs them on the rules against gambling and so forth—and I was panicky, running up the back steps of Redskin Park. Gibbs was coming up the steps, too, and I said, "Coach, I need to talk to you."

"OK," he answered, "but let's wait until after this meeting."

Hell, I couldn't wait. I left. It was a long time before I spoke with Gibbs again.

This was after practice, and I said to hell with that FBI meeting. I met instead with Johnny Cakes in his office, and he said I had to meet the next morning with Commissioner Tagliabue.

But I had to go on my Channel 5 TV show that Thursday night and talk about our next game against the Denver Broncos. I had to go on that show and lie. I sat in the office of one of the anchormen—James Addams—and said, "James, it was nice knowing you, man." I wanted to tell him the whole truth, but I couldn't. I didn't know whom I could confide in anymore. I was so sick, knowing I had to go on TV and not being sure I could hold myself together. I had to be an actor, a phony, though I'd always been one anyway.

I even told the audience which Denver player would be blocking me.

As I left the station, glad I'd been able to cover up, I was greeted outside by a *Washington Post* reporter, Tom Friend, my co-author. When Tom asked me about the positive drug test, I knew it was over. Someone at Redskin Park must've leaked it. Confidentiality? Man, there was no such word. Before I saw that reporter, I was hoping Tagliabue was going to say the next morning, "We made a mistake, Dexter. Go back and play." But when I saw *The Washington Post*, it was a repeat of 1988.

I slammed my fist on my truck and cried.

I was with Sal, that friend of mine who owned the Italian restaurant and served the good fettucine. As we were about to leave Channel 5 with me in tears, I saw someone evil in a parked car across the street: Freddie.

Freddie was sitting there with two other guys. I ignored him, but it was as if Freddie was laughing, as if he was the devil.

I don't know if Freddie felt remorse for selling me the coke. I'd have to guess that he didn't. We weren't friends or anything. We were just drug associates. And really, it's not his fault. He didn't call me the night I did coke; I called him. If he had called me and set me up, and I had gotten busted, it would be different. I went to him under my own power. So point the finger at me.

I had my meeting with Tagliabue, and there was conjecture about me suing the league over its drug-testing procedure. I was being advised by Doc Goldstein, who used to supervise my NFL drug tests but was now in private practice, about the ins and outs of drug tests. That might've scared Tagliabue. I don't know.

I lied to the commissioner, that's for sure. Hell, if I'm about to get banned from football for life, my back is against the wall. Just the nature of drugs makes you a liar. So I went in there fibbing, hoping to save my butt. I was in his office crying for sympathy, and so was my wife. We both denied that I did drugs. Glinda didn't know; I was trying to protect her. I figured maybe I could convince the commissioner that I didn't do drugs, that there was a bad test reading. To be honest, I thought he'd let me off. Was I sick or what?

I threatened to take Tagliabue to court. Glinda and I and Bob Woolf were in a conference room with Tagliabue, but then Tagliabue and Woolf convened in another room for a few minutes. I don't know what they were hashing out in there, but I'm sure everything was done in good faith. Here were Glinda and I in this conference room—all alone—and I was like, Darn, this is my career in the balance. Why do they have to talk in private?"

They returned stroking each other. Tagliabue said, "Oh, you have a wonderful attorney," and Woolf said, "We're lucky to have a commissioner such as this."

Then Woolf told me privately, "If you stay clean Dexter, we'll have the leeway to get you back in football in less than a year." See, the league rules were if you had three strikes, you were subject to permanent ban. But you were also allowed to petition for reinstatement after a year of staying clean. Apparently Woolf struck a deal with Tagliabue that if I didn't sue the league, I'd have a shot at getting reinstated in *less* than a year.

So when the NFL exiled me, the language in the press release was ambiguous. It said I could be reinstated the next season. It never said I'd definitely have to wait a full year.

See how I kept getting new chances? All my life—my entire life—everyone looked out for me. My drug counselors say people enabled me. Maybe that was a detriment.

Anyway, when it banned me, the league used the language that contained a loophole. It didn't say I was banned a full year. It said: banned until next season. Next season could've been July 1990, during training camp.

To make a further good impression on the commissioner, Woolf orchestrated a press conference where—for the first time publicly—I admitted to using drugs. I'd always said alcohol, but this time I said drugs.

It was a con to pacify Tagliabue. I had nothing to lose and, hell, Woolf pulled out all the stops. He's a PR man. He held the press conference at the ritzy J.W. Marriott in downtown D.C., and I felt like a celebrity. I admitted I used drugs and then left early to let Woolf answer all the questions. Hell, I didn't even write my speech. I went back up to my suite. I felt like Cher or somebody; I still had that celebrity mentality. It was like, Don't sit around at the press conference. Look like you're important and leave, like you've got somewhere to go.

Where I almost went, that night, was to go use drugs *again*.

I mean, I'd already screwed up and was banned. I still had money. I figured, I'm going to sneak and get me $200 or $300 worth of coke. Who was going to know anymore? Nobody.

Pham talked me out of it again. I was seeing firsthand that this AA crap worked. All you had to do was call someone before you went out to use. What a concept.

Woolf put me in touch with John Lucas, the former NBA player who ran a drug clinic in my hometown of Houston. It was decided I'd leave for a *fourth* visit to rehab, and it would be with John in Houston.

When the ban became official, Lester came in my house bawling. He cried worse than I was crying.

TV minicam crews were outside my house waiting for my comment. I found it amusing. It showed me I was still famous. Glinda, though, hated it:

We locked ourselves in the house while Little Dexter and Dalis were outside playing with the cameramen. It was wild. I left a note on the door, "Don't bother ringing, because we aren't talking," and Gayle Gardner of NBC rang the doorbell anyway. I was mad. I was like, Can't you read?

That bothered me, but, deep down, it excited Dexter. I'm the only one who hated it. He thought all these people standing outside was funny. He said, "Yeah, Glinda. I must really be somebody." See, again, he took the worst and turned it around, thinking this was great publicity.

He felt he must really be important for all this press to come out like that. It just reassured him who he was. I'm the one who felt I needed to hide. He didn't. I rolled up the windows and locked them. And he would open them right back up.

He'd say, "Damn, Glinda, you see this? I love it. I must really be somebody."

I was like, you stupid sonofagun.

I took all of the humiliation he should've had. I was scared to go in and out of the house. I didn't even want people seeing my face, because I was shamed. But I took on his shame. He didn't seem like he had any shame.

* * *

The worst part of leaving for treatment was saying goodbye to my kids. Little Dexter, who was about four years old, had seen on the news that his daddy was out of football. When I was *in* football, he used to say, "Daddy, I don't want you to play football. You'll get hurt."

But when I got kicked out, he said, "Daddy, why can't you play football anymore? Were you bad? I want to run on the football field again."

I started crying. He kept talking about running on the field, and that hurt me the most, to have to witness my kids go through pain.

When I left for Houston, expecting to be gone through Christmas and New Year's, I told Little Dexter one thing: "Son, I'm going to Daddy School."

An Idle Thought

If you asked me if I had a preference between Pete Rozelle and Paul Tagliabue, my answer is yes.

I'd have rather seen Tagliabue any day.

Rozelle tried to be a hard-ass. If he'd been the commissioner when I relapsed in 1989, he would've moaned and groaned and said something like, "How many more times are we going to have to go through this, Dexter!"

But Tagliabue, he's a lawyer. He uses discretion. He picks and chooses what he wants to say, while Rozelle wouldn't give a crap and would just rip you.

CHAPTER 33

"Repeat After Me: You Are Not a Pro Football Player"

BOB WOOLF DESCRIBED JOHN LUCAS AS "THE voice of God." At first, I described him as just another homeboy.

The first time I talked to Lucas on the phone, just after my visit with Tagliabue, I told him, "I don't have no drug problem, man."

Then both he and Bob Woolf called me on a three-way hookup. I hardly thought I needed to go back to rehab again. Hell, I'd already been once, twice, three times to Hazelden. Plus, I'd been clean for *three weeks* after my positive test. To me, *three weeks* was like I'd licked the thing. Crazy, huh?

I'd started going to AA meetings again, and I'd been to a psychologist; and I thought checking into another rehab center would be just a waste of money and time. As far as I was concerned, all I had to do was stay sober until July, when Bob Woolf would have me in somebody's training camp. I'd always had the easy way out before, so why not now?

But Thomas ("Hollywood") Henderson, who once was so stoked on drugs he hid in the Astrodome parking lot, told me to get my ass in treatment.

I had met Thomas in January 1987 on my way out to the Pro Bowl. Glinda and I had stopped in Los Angeles to attend the Giants–Broncos Super Bowl game and we were out on the town one night with Doc Walker and his wife. We went into a hotel to use the john, and that's when we ran into Thomas Henderson.

He had been an idol of mine, one of the fastest linebackers who ever played and also a garbage talker. Speed and a big mouth were my assets, too.

That night, I recognized him and he recognized me. He'd just gotten out of prison, and I'd just missed that practice before the Rams playoff game, so we were two of a kind. He said, "You sound just like me, man. Your behavior is my behavior. Are you doing coke?"

This was in '87 when *nobody* knew my secret life. I replied, "No, just alcohol, Thomas." He offered his phone number, and I took it. I never called him. Eventually, after I'd been to Hazelden, Glinda suggested I phone him. So I did:

I'm sure Dexter had a fascination with me because I was a mirror of him. We both grew up in dysfunctional homes, and I'm sure his identification with me came through the way football was played in the neighborhood. Play ball, and talk shit. It was from the 'hood.

I ran into Dexter the first time at a Howard Johnson's hotel in Los Angeles. I had picked up a friend at the airport for the Super Bowl, and I was dropping the friend off at the hotel, and here's Dexter Manley in the longest limo you'd ever seen. He was darker than charcoal and wearing a white silk suit.

I'm thinking, A limo at a Howard Johnson's?

He got out of the car like he was it. I said. "Dexter, I'm Thomas Henderson." He wasn't like "Wow!" I caught him looking like, I'm it, and you ain't.

I told him, "Watch where you're going, man." He was loaded. You know, it's funny, I was sitting in jail once, reading an article about a player—it may have been Dexter—who said, "I don't want to end up being a Hollywood Henderson."

When I read that in jail, I thought, Yes, you do. Because I was clean and staying that way.

So I befriended Dexter that night. I told him he could stay sober if I did. When he finally called me, I told him, "I just want you to be clean and sober, and everything you tell me will be in the strictest confidence." Over the next few years, he learned to trust me.

After my relapse in 1989, Thomas asked me to check into a rehab center he was associated with: Sierra Tucson in Arizona. I was talking to Thomas and to Pham and to Bob Woolf and to Lucas and even to Clarence Kay of the Denver Broncos, who'd been in town to play the Redskins. Clarence had had his own problems, and he said it would do me absolutely no good sitting around at home. He said the league would smile upon me going into rehab.

I was all for conning the league into thinking I was healed, so Glinda and I both leaned toward me checking into Sierra Tucson. But I ended up choosing Lucas's "New Spirit" program at Houston International Hospital. At least I'd be around family and near my favorite barbecue restaurant: Lott's Barbecue.

Lucas and George Gervin, another former NBA player, met me at the Houston airport. They kept looking at my Louis Vuitton bags and Rolex watches, and John said, "Ain't nothing wrong with you, man."

I guess they were expecting a guy on drugs to be sucked in and looking destitute. But I looked like my daddy—sharp.

I checked in on November 26, 1989, and stayed a whole two months in Houston. It was night and day different from Hazelden. Hazelden always reminded me of Harvard. When I was in Hazelden, I used to daydream I was in Harvard Business School. But Lucas's place was the inner city.

There were pluses to both places. Houston was more controlled and strict. The pay phones weren't as accessible, so I couldn't call Grant and trick him. At Hazelden, if you needed a breath of fresh air, you could walk outside and not feel closed in. That was one of my concerns about going to Houston, but Pham thought I should go there and do like twenty-eight days of jail time.

I didn't like it there at all. I had to stay cramped on this one detox floor for twenty-four hours; you weren't allowed to leave. I woke up the first morning, hit the elevator button to go downstairs, and the button was locked. I was pissed. I thought, This ain't treatment. Hell, this is crap. Who wants to be locked up?

I wondered if I'd made the right decision coming there. I wanted to take a walk, get some serenity, and reflect, not sit up on the fourth floor of a building twenty-four hours straight.

I thought that first day would never end. They said it was strictly for observation, and what they must've observed was one antsy brother.

I couldn't wait until morning, and when morning came, I called Pham and told him I was getting the heck out of there.

What kept me there? I don't know. I think one of the reasons was my momma and sister were in Houston, as well as Derrick. I couldn't have visitors for the first four or five days, but it was nice that they were a car ride away.

It got better. I was allowed to go to AA meetings, and one day I had Stephanye and Derrick meet me at the 610 Club, which was a

Cocaine Anonymous meeting. I asked them to "Please bring me some Lott's Barbecue." The treatment center had a driver with me who was supposed to make sure I wasn't up to no good. I couldn't leave his sight, but at least I could sit there with Derrick and Stephanye and eat barbecue.

I eventually accepted being at the rehab center, but I did not want to open up. I'd open with John Lucas, but not with anyone else in the group. To me, it wasn't the kind of place you could open up in; there were too many people checking in and out. It wasn't a place that committed people for thirty to forty days where you build cohesiveness with a group of other people.

You might see a guy one day and not the next day. There was too much turnover, and I felt there was no confidentiality. You might spill your guts to these people, and they could be on the street the next day talking about you. All that paranoia was still inside me. I was still full of my crap.

One good thing about John was that he was a former athlete who understood all the temptations of pro sports. When I first heard of John Lucas, he was playing with the Washington Bullets, and he'd myste-riously missed a game. He came out and said he'd had a flat tire.

Ha! I'll never forget his TV interview. He was walking down the street with ABC's Tim Brant, and John was just plain lying about this flat tire. That was my first recollection of John Lucas.

But he was good for me because he'd been there. You can't con another con.

A little later during my stay, John told me another black athlete was coming in for treatment, Chris Washburn, another basketball player. Washburn joined Roy Tarpley and me in there, and John felt we athletes could build a nest of friendship throughout the NFL and NBA. It didn't quite work out that way with Chris. Washburn ended up stealing a $450 belt from me, and Lucas gave me the money for it because everyone knew Washburn had ripped it off. I later saw Washburn wearing it. Later, Washburn went to jail, but not for lifting my belt.

Washburn was my roommate, and one day I walked in to find that homeboy on the floor having seizures. He'd been gone for three days. He looked frickin' pathetic, and that made me so grateful I was clean.

Although my treatment was in Houston, I didn't exactly have a parade of friends visiting. Eric Herring was mad at me because I didn't call him when I checked in. Hell, I was the one who got busted; he should've called me.

Gerald, my oldest buddy, came to see me. But he begged me for twenty dollars.

It was a real eye-opener. Eventually, I was allowed to leave, though they wanted me to stick around town as an outpatient. During the day, I would drive through the Third Ward. It was an opportunity to see the condition of my people and reflect on how far I had come in my life. Lordy, I saw that place, and I said I do not want to live there again.

Of course, I was no different from those people. I was on drugs; they were on drugs. And in a way I felt I'd let them down. I was a hero to them, and now I was on drugs. I was no different from the addicts standing on the corner.

Maybe I was finally waking up to my disease. In treatment, they'd always ask me who I was, and I'd answer, "I'm Dexter, and I'm a husband, a father, and a professional football player."

My counselor would insist, "You ain't no football player. You're kicked out."

They'd say, "Repeat after me. You are no football player."

But I'd reply, "I'm Dexter, and I'm unemployed."

They were trying to break down my way of thinking. Did they? Hell, no. They thought I was arrogant, that I was always performing, on stage the entire two months. They thought I never let my real self come out and that I was saying I was an addict to pacify them, the same way I'd done at Hazelden—three times.

They were right.

They couldn't have broken me down no matter what. They wanted me to think of myself as an average guy, not as some football star. They'd say, "You're just another addict and recovering person. You're nothing special. *You are not special.*"

That crap sounded good, but I *knew* I was special. How can somebody say I wasn't special when I was a pro football player? I was a pro athlete, and people liked me for what I did on the field. So let's not disregard that, like they wanted me to do. To hell with them, I thought.

A typical day in treatment? I'd wake at 7:45 A.M., and there'd be a group meditation that I'd always skip. Because I was an athlete, I was on a slightly different program; so I'd get up and jog.

I'd come back, and we'd undergo group work, sitting around watching a tape or lecture.

We'd do recreational therapy, too. We'd work with our minds or make things, and we'd even go to Chuck E. Cheese's for lunch. They didn't do that to break us down to our childhood state; they took us to Chuck E. Cheese's 'cause it was cheap.

Or maybe we'd go bowling. I don't know what the purpose of that was. I'd be reluctant to do it, and I'd give counselors a hard time. I had the biggest mouth. Or I'd pretend I was running off and escaping.

After lunch, we'd return to the building, and thing I liked most was psychotherapy. You'd relive what brought you there. That was good because it was like you were performing and acting it out. I did a skit about me. I had one guy in my group portray Tagliabue, and I told him to act like a calculating lawyer.

There was a guy who kept having relapse after relapse. So our woman therapist picked up a towel and threw it to him. Then she picked four or five of us to play tug of war against the guy, with this towel.

She was making an analogy to drugs. The tug of war symbolized the fight, the struggle to stay clean. This one guy would try to tear the towel away from the four of us, and she said that's how much energy it takes to beat drugs. When you're on drugs, you have to war against them; and when he tried to rip that towel away, he couldn't. He couldn't move.

She was saying to all of us, "This is how it'll be when you walk back out there on the street." She said, "If you want your life, that's what you've got to do—fight." I could identify with that because it's easy to say, "Oh, well, it's too difficult a fight. I'll just do drugs."

I only got the drug urge once during the two-month period. Some girl started talking all sexy to me, and that made me think about drugs. With me, it was always women and drugs together, but it was just a fleeting urge. It crossed my mind, and that was it.

Well, Christmas became New Year's, and New Year's became spring. I was spending most of my time in Houston. It's a good thing I was in Houston, too, because Momma was dying.

It's sad, because in the mid-eighties I'd sort of neglected her. Our relationship kind of split up after she had that brain surgery. She wasn't 100 percent any more, and I was screwing up with the coke.

See, when you use drugs, you don't respect people. You don't keep your responsibilities, you don't show up for TV shows, you're not a good daddy, you're not a good husband, you're not a good son. When you're under the influence of drugs, drugs take priority.

One time I had to get my momma to the hospital for her surgery, but I was late. This was life and death, and I was late. I was doing drugs, that's why.

She made it to surgery without me, but what I had done hurt me. It also showed me the power drugs had over me. I *wanted* to be there for my mom. I *wanted* to show concern. I *wanted* to be a respectable son. But I showed up late, after the surgery, and I thought to myself, This drug stuff is beginning to be a bummer.

In Momma's final months, in the spring of 1989, I thank God I started to spend quality time with her. I bathed her once. I got joy out of that. I was helping my momma. In the end, my sister was on drugs, and she'd leave Momma, who was incapacitated, sleeping in her own shit. She would stay with soiled underwear for two or three days.

The housing authority had to break into the house and get Momma out of there. They put her in the hospital. Someone told me about what was going on with Cynthia, so I called the housing authority to get Momma out.

I guess looking after Momma just wore Cynthia out.

My momma died on May 4. It was a relief. She was just so sick. She didn't deserve cancer. She had put her body through so much with that drinking, and then she had that brain surgery and breast cancer. No one deserves to suffer like that. She'd come to visit sometimes, but Glinda and I both knew it wasn't my real momma:

The kids would be playing around Dexter's mother, and she'd sit in her room and never move. I came in one time, and it was pitch dark. I figured she was asleep, but she was just sitting in the darkness. She hadn't moved for five hours.

The kids were about two and three at the time, and they'd be yelling and making noise, and she'd never say a word. But then, out of the blue she'd suddenly say, "Goddamn, shut up!" They'd run up to me and say, "Grandma cursed and raised her arm to hit us!"

I was taking care of her, and I was tired because I had two little ones. Dexter wasn't coming home at night because of you know what, and so I was afraid what she might do to the kids. One time, her feet were cold, and I said, "I'll put some socks on you." She resented that and kicked me and looked at me with a killing look. She snatched the socks from me.

She wasn't the same woman she had been. I believe she resented the fact she couldn't do for herself anymore. There was no in-between with her. Either she had anger, or she was nice.

When she left, I didn't want to take her to the airport because I was afraid she might cause a scene. But I wanted to give her something. Since she liked this one raincoat of mine, I gave it to her. She said, "Oh, this is beautiful. " On the way to the airport, with the kids in the back screaming, I *was terrified that she would explode. When we get there, a man came up with a wheelchair for her, and I thought Thank God, a man. He can protect me if . . .*

We loaded her on the Dulles Airport tram to her terminal, and suddenly her eyes changed. She started looking at me evil. See, she'd go in and out. I asked her, "Do you want to keep on holding your raincoat?" and she must've thought I was taking it back because she snapped, "Yes, I would!"

When she died, she was the prettiest person I'd ever seen in a casket. At the funeral, I said, "Dexter, look how pretty she looks." She looked twenty years younger in the face. I said, "It must've been from all that pain she was carrying around. It made her face mean." But not in that casket. Dexter said, "Glinda, you're right. She had been carrying pain."

By June Bob Woolf was ready to apply for my reinstatement into the NFL. That deal he'd supposedly struck with Tagliabue must've been bull, because Tagliabue turned me down. I had to wait until my full year was up, November 1990.

Still, I left treatment for good, believing I was ready for football. The thinking was that I'd hit such a rock bottom, I'd be prepared to stay clean forever.

But had I really hit a rock bottom? I still had my house. I still had cash flow. I still was renting cars. I still had my Rolls. Hitting rock bottom is being stuck in a ditch with no money and having your house boarded up. That's a bottom.

I still had everything . . . Well, almost. Glinda asked me for a separation.

AN IDLE THOUGHT

They could suspend me or tar and feather me, but I was gonna live on in NFL infamy.

Just as Wilt Chamberlain is responsible for the widening of the three-second lane in basketball, I believe I was responsible for the NFL's "noise penalty."

It was some communist rule they passed after I kept calling for crowd noise at RFK Stadium. I mean, I used to play Simon Says with the fans at RFK. I'd wave at them to get up and go wild, and they would. I'd raise my palms facing the sky, and they'd go off.

So the league passed a rule where you couldn't prompt the fans to certain decibel levels. I didn't give a crap. During a game against the

Saints at RFK—the same game I spit on Dombrowski—the ref warned me not to incite the crowd. I said, "Hey, no problem." Instead of standing up and waving for the fans to yell, I got in a three-point stance and did it. I'd move my hand in a circular motion while I leaned into my stance, or I'd move my head in a circular motion. When the ref called me on it, I told him I was doing neck rolls.

Still, the ref tossed a flag on me at the end of the first half. Hell, he threw the flag *at* me, and it hit me.

Richie Petitbon, our defensive coordinator, was so pissed he benched me for the start of the second half. He told me, "Markus Koch is starting instead of you."

I had no choice but to stay on the bench, but next thing you know, Richie was ordering me back in the game. That fool Markus was getting his ass kicked.

CHAPTER 34

The Good Witch Glinda

GLINDA WASN'T THRILLED I SPENT MOST OF THE spring and summer of 1990 in Houston. I wanted the NFL to see I was involved with treatment there, but she wanted my ass home to help with the kids. I told her, "I'm not coming. I'm gonna stay in Houston."

So she announced, "Let's get a separation."

I said, "OK, you're gonna have to go to the attorney." And then I told her, "I don't think it's a good idea to separate." But she had to think it over for herself:

People ask me all the time why I stay with Dexter Manley. Sometimes I don't suppose I know.

People say I'm like a rock on the outside, but I'm going crazy inside. He literally drove me to drink and to have an affair. What kept me going? First of all, my friends. I'm a member of a club with five other women: Effi Barry, the former wife of Mayor Barry; Carol Fenley, who was Mitch Snyder's close friend before he committed suicide in her bedroom; Dorothy Ford, who's the wife of a congressman from Tennessee; Mary Wilson, the ex-Supreme; and Linda Green, a D.C. socialite. Linda's the hub. She and her husband know everything about D.C.

We call ourselves the F.O.C. Club, which stands for Friends of Charity. We meet for dinner, get together at each other's houses, and put on benefits and fund-raisers, real positive things. But sometimes I call it the "Fucked Over Club" because we've all had shit hit the fan.

I've particularly been equated over the years with Effi because her husband, the mayor, had his drug and women-chasing problems, too. I know Effi fairly well, and we've talked about it. I'll say, "Girl, I've been praying for you," and she'll say, "Honey, I've been praying for you, too." We've both gone through it, though hers is on a grander scale. I keep telling her I don't know how she sat through those court things, watching and hearing it all on national TV. I told Dexter, "Dexter, I've been pretty much humiliated by you through all the years of our marriage, but I don't think I could sit there and watch on TV these women talk about what you did with them and then—with everyone else in the world—hear you saying in some video, "Baby, give me some.'"

I said to him, "I don't know how that Effi did it. I think I'd have to be on Valium."

So Effi's someone I could turn to. And, well, my mom was a big factor in my keeping my sanity.

I grew up in southeast Chicago with a mom and a dad and two brothers in a middle-class neighborhood. The boys are really much older. See, I was a surprise. My mom was finished with kids, and the doctors found me when she was going in to have a hysterectomy because of a real bad cyst. That's how they found out she was pregnant.

Well, I grew up fine, with a mother who probably did too much for me. In fact, I was her life. I think my dad was jealous of me.

She was living through me. I used to hear her say, "When I was a little girl, I used to wish I could play the piano," and the next thing you knew I was in piano class. Or the same thing with ballet. So I thought I was living my mother's life, and I resented it. And then I remembered how unhappy she was with my dad because in his earlier years he used to drink. When he'd come in in the wee hours, he used to be abusive to her, yelling and stuff.

So I learned very young how to live in an uptight house. As soon as I'd hear my dad's key turning, I would get nervous and start thinking, OK, what am I gonna do if he hits her? So, I'd go to my neighbor's house, and that was further humiliation for me. I'd lie on their doorstep until two or three in the morning, which was humiliating.

I think that's when I learned how to leave a crazy home and walk outside and say everything's fine. So, that's how I learned how to deal so well with my first husband Steve's mess and with Dexter's mess.

When Dexter got banned, it really hurt me that none of the other Redskins' wives called me. Not one. I was never real close with them because I didn't really want them in on what was happening with us. I couldn't get too close because I figured they might be able to see what was going on.

But at football games or if I ran into them, I really liked them. If I'd see a couple girlfriends, I'd hug them. I felt that close to them, but that was as close as I could get.

And then when that happened to Dexter, it hurt me that they showed no interest in me. See, Redskins' wives are very close. First of all, they're Christians, and I felt if they were Christians, they should've come to my aid, whether I was close to them or not. Just as a sisterly thing.

Dexter couldn't soothe me after his relapse. I didn't want to listen to him. At that point, I was at my worst, and I started drinking.

I had a friend, and she and I would drink champagne. And I felt like, Oh, it's nothing. But all of a sudden, I noticed I was thinking about going over to her house every other day. And why? To drink champagne.

So I would go to escape, and sometimes that wouldn't be enough. I thought I was going crazy, because I'd have insomnia. I started resenting Dexter because he would sound so healthy on the phone from Houston, talking that therapy stuff. And here I was, not getting any help and being a single parent, for all practical purposes. I was taking all the abuse when I hadn't done anything wrong. So I started hating him.

I started thinking about getting away from it all, I was so sick of everything. A couple of years earlier I had been so close to God and had been so sure that God was going to deliver me from these problems. But it just kept getting worse and worse.

I can't say I didn't love God anymore, but I did stray away. I'd sit in church stone-faced, feeling like a hypocrite because I kept thinking of drinking, or getting high, or maybe having an affair.

One night I felt like I was going crazy. I was screaming at the kids too much, and I felt I was close to abusing my children. They were having a tough time, too. Their daddy was gone, and they could tell their mommy wasn't happy, and I think that made them even more hyper. I knew something was going to happen, and I was worried for my kids.

So I called Thomas Henderson. It was 2:00 A.M. when I called him in California. He wasn't home, but I left a message. I said, "Thomas, call me. I'm ready to go to Sierra Tucson now."

See, Thomas used to call Dexter trying to convince him to go into treatment. Thomas would be like, Man, Dexter, you're going back because you are not for real. You haven't lost anything yet. Thomas knew Dexter's bullshit, and you couldn't bullshit the bullshitter.

But sometimes Thomas would ask me, "How are you making it?" I'd say, "Oh, I'm fine."

He'd say, "Yeah, that's fine. You sound totally co-dependent. You're using the F.I.N.E. word." He said the f in fine stood for fucked up, and the n for neurotic. The i was for insecure and e for emotional. I started laughing, and he explained, "Glinda, you need help, too. So, when are you going in for treatment?"

"Treatment? Treatment for what?" I'd ask.

"You're just as sick as he is. You know how I know? Because if you weren't sick, you would've left him two years ago."

Finally I agreed with him. So I called him. It was a cry for help. Thank

God Thomas called me back. He gave me the number at Sierra Tucson and told me to call them immediately. I did call that night and agreed to go in for thirty days on January 1.

At first they wouldn't let me call home, which upset me. When I finally was able to call, Meko, our baby sitter, told me, "Oh, we're fine. Everything's fine. We're getting ready to go to the movies."

I was real concerned about Little Dexter, who had peed in his bed every night of his life, and she said, "Oh, he's fine, too. He doesn't pee in his bed anymore." In fact, he didn't do it again the whole winter I was gone, which was a sign to me that I was doing the children a favor by getting help for myself.

What I learned at Sierra Tucson was self-awareness. Things that are happening to you now are from your childhood. Admitting this doesn't mean we should put blame on our parents; it helps us understand and know we're not crazy. I, for one, thought I was crazy.

What they taught me was that I was setting myself up for my problems. Both of my marriages pretty much required me to take care of my husbands. What I've learned is that, from the way I was brought up, I didn't have a loving, touching father to tell me I was OK, to give me self-esteem, which kind of screwed me up for other relationships. Consequently, I'm attracted to sick people. I'd probably been a sick, co-dependent person since very early on.

And as a co-dependent, I protected Dexter. I even went on TV and lied for him, for instance. And I hated that.

So I had an affair. It was very, very brief, but I did. I felt like I needed somebody and that Dexter never appreciated me and took me for granted, and was never there, physically or emotionally, for me. I needed someone at that time who was strong, who was decent, and who wasn't into drugs. That was another reason I went to Tucson. I was like, Uh oh, I'm changing, and I didn't like what was happening to me.

In Tucson they told me that I was blaming Dexter for my affair. "Glinda, even though he's screwing all the women and he did drugs, you had a choice." They said, "You did not have to go out there and be with another man."

When Dexter came to visit me from Houston, we went for a walk, and he said, "Glinda, I want you to be honest with me." I think he kind of felt I'd had an affair, because I'd started not liking him. So he asked, "Glinda, are you seeing someone? Or have you seen someone?"

He kept asking me, and I kept saying, "No, why do you ask?" I felt totally guilt-ridden. At Sierra Tucson they explained there was no reason to tell him. You don't tell people things to hurt them, they said, and this was going to hurt him.

But Dexter conned me. He said, "You're not being real. I'm being truthful. I'm coming out and telling you that I've been doing it."

When he said, "Well, I've been doing it in Houston," he hurt me so much.

"Gawl, Dexter," I asked. "Aren't you in treatment?"

"Yeah, but I get out," he answered. "See, I'm telling you this for a reason. I'm not trying to hurt you. I'm showing that I really want to be honest with you and want our marriage to work. This is why I flew here. But I think it has to start on honesty. So you've got to be honest with me, and if you've had an affair, I promise I won't get upset. I'll understand. If you tell me the truth, I'll just think you are just as honest as I am."

So I told him.

But he went off. "You did what?" He went, Well, who was it? Where does he work? Duh, duh, duh.

"I'm not telling you anything," I replied. "It's irrelevant. It wasn't even longstanding, and it's over. We were basically friends, and it just happened. It was one time."

He told me to forget it. The marriage was over. Here, after he had conned me into telling him, he said the marriage was over.

"Well, you know, Dexter, you're full of crap," I said. "I've been with you through two paternity suits, and I don't know how many screw-arounds. I even had to go to court because I beat up one of your girlfriends. How dare you!"

He insisted that he was leaving. That night, I talked to our counselors and said, "This was supposed to be a week of healing, and now it's gone haywire." At first they were mad at me and asked me why I told him.

When I explained how he'd conned me, they said, "Oh, he suckered you again. You fell for it."

"Yep," I agreed.

"See, it shows how easy it is to go back into the co-dependent mode we're trying to get you out of."

The week turned out decent. Dexter threatened to leave, but my counselors were all on my side and backed me up. He got to express his feelings, but he couldn't harass me. Basically, my support group said, "Glinda, if that's what he's done to you and he says he wants to leave, let him go. You don't need him anyway. You are not an object; you are a human being." They also explained to me, "He objectifies you."

They eventually told him, "You objectify your wife. You look at her as an object for sex, for pleasure, for taking care of your family, and that's it. But you don't see her as a person who has feelings and hurts and does all these other things."

They also diagnosed him with a sex addiction. They told him one addiction can lead to another and that he would have to deal with all of his addictions, like him always wanting to go to strip bars.

He thought they meant he was a pervert, walking around with his thing hanging out. He didn't take it right, like when someone calls him an addict, he pictures someone with needles hanging out of his arm. He has problems with labels.

The main thing was that his cocaine went together with women. His addictions were women and drugs. The counselors asked him, "Dexter, have you ever been with a prostitute?"

He said yes.

He said something leads him up the street to strip bars, that he doesn't get turned on, but he does it anyway, that he feels bad when he leaves. "I feel disgusting when I leave those places," he admits, "like one of those fat beer-belly men." That's an addiction!

Thursday was Reconciliation Day. After we'd said all the things we hated about each other, on Thursday we were to say all the things we loved about each other. On that last day you find out how much people care, how much they love you.

For the first time, I stood up to Dexter in front of everybody. They kept saying I was carrying his shame and I needed it to be his. It belonged to him, and I should dump the garbage back on him.

He saw a new person in me and told me, "Glinda, it's going to be hard, but I do know I still love you. And I don't want to leave you. It's just hard for me to envision you being with someone else."

I said, "Well, Dexter, it's just as hard for me. Why do you think a woman can deal with it better than a man?"

So we learned a lot. A lot.

Dexter and I have always said we're going to have a second wedding on our tenth-year anniversary: 1994. I wonder what the odds are of us making it.

Glinda has gone through hell with me, but it would have been a lot worse if some of my old girlfriends hadn't had abortions for me. Who knows how many kids I'd have running around? I would've been playing football for almost nothing.

On the other hand, if Glinda and I had never had our two beautiful kids, we wouldn't be together now. She'd have left me long ago. It was a shock when Glinda told me about her so-called affair. I never thought she would do that, and when she told me she had, I was just hurt.

Yes, I'd cheated on her. And that's the only thing that made me understand.

AN IDLE THOUGHT

Glinda wants to change Little Dexter's name:

I worry about Little Dexter trying to fill his daddy's shoes, especially having the same name. If I had it to do over again, I would never name him Dexter Manley II. I felt bad when Big Dexter went down on drugs. I asked myself, What's going to happen to Little Dexter? I seriously thought about changing his name. I could just see him sitting in a classroom one day and everybody thinking he's a normal little boy until they say, "Dexter Manley?" He'll go, "Here!" And then those kids might say, "Oh, your daddy was the one who got bumped out of the NFL. Is he still a drug addict?"

I don't want him going through life like that, going out looking for a job someday and having someone ask, "Are you related to that Dexter Manley?"

People often ask Little Dexter what his name is, and he answers, "Dexter." Then they say, "You wouldn't by chance be related to . . ." When Little Dexter says he's Dexter Manley's son, people sort of gasp. But they've never said anything mean—yet.

C H A P T E R   35

Joe Gibbs,
the Plastic Man

CONSIDERING BOB HAD CRIED WOOLF, I HAD TO sit out of football for a full calendar year: November 18, 1989, to November 18, 1990.

When I was in Houston rehab for two months, football didn't enter my mind. Lott's Barbecue did. But when I'd go back to Washington, I couldn't help but see Redskin commercials, Redskin stores, even kids wearing No. 72 jerseys, which was my number. The emptiness would overwhelm me; I wanted to sack again.

In the spring of 1990, the NFL's director of security, Warren Welsh, called me for a meeting. We sat down at the Marriott Suites near Dulles Airport and chatted for an encouraging two and one-half hours. I realized then the league would eventually let me back if I stayed off the sauce. But it also hit me I would never again be a Washington Redskin.

That was the day Warren Welsh said to me, "Dexter, do you think you can handle not coming back with the Redskins?"

I could tell that Welsh had inside information from the Redskins. He probably knew they didn't want my butt back, and I told him, "I don't have a problem with that."

I lied. The Redskins had been my life, and I'd once told Glinda, "When I die, I want you to sprinkle my ashes over RFK Stadium." I meant that wholeheartedly.

Still, when Welch and I parted, I was in an upbeat mood because I knew I'd suit up again one day. In the interim, not very many of my old Redskin teammates were calling me. During my entire year off, I talked to one guy, Art Monk. Darrell Green also called, and so did

Torgy, Wayne Sevier, and Bobby Mitchell but I wasn't home for them. Art was the only guy I spoke to—in April.

I'd model my kids after Art Monk if I could. He is real, and a lot of other Redskins weren't. They'd act like holy-rolly Bible toters just to get on Joe Gibbs's good side, and Gibbs fell for it. For a lot of guys, religion was a way to get their feet in the door, and later a way to hold on. These guys had just as much con in them as I. They saw that Gibbs was tight with the Bible, and they said, "Well, I'll be a Christian now."

I wonder if Gibbs would take me back today if I went over to him with my Bible. Do you think if I was a born-again, he'd give me a tryout?

A lot of those boys were acting. I could've acted too if I had wanted.

But not Art Monk. Let me tell you, there aren't many Redskins I would've taken advice from. I'm a lot smarter than people think; I'm street smart. Maybe I'm not smart academic-wise, but I have a real interest in politics. I think I had a broader vision than most of my Redskin teammates. But Art Monk? Art Monk is the type who *can* give me advice.

Darrell Green can, too, I suppose. But I missed Darrell's call:

Yes, I called, but I missed him. I spoke to his wife, after leaving a couple of messages. And probably a lot of people other than me left messages.

But let me make a point. My sister-in-law's dad passed away recently, and they came over to my house to get their kids because we were keeping them while she was at the hospital. And it was like I felt funny seeing her, like I really don't want to see her. There was nothing I could say to her.

But I could look at her and tell she wanted a hug, and eventually we hugged. Now, I'd say it doesn't make the same sense in Dexter's case, but that's the way it was. You felt for Dexter, but you felt uncomfortable being with him, calling him. You felt funny seeing him. It was the same thing.

Well, minicamp turned into training camp, and training camp turned into midseason, and every leak I took for the league was clean as a whistle. I was about to be reinstated, and still no phone call from Joe Gibbs. Not one.

Tagliabue ordered me up to the NFL offices in New York for an appraisal. He was angry that some paperwork from John Lucas's treatment center was missing, but I presented myself like a CEO again. Just like the last time I'd been at the NFL office, the TV cameras were camped outside for me. Bob Woolf and I held a press conference out on

Park Avenue at about 4:30 P.M., and every car honked, every New Yorker yelled something, things like "Dexter, go get 'em!" or "Go Giants!"

There was so much commotion. It was like some nigger had been shot on the street, and everybody was standing around trying to get a glimpse of the body. Usually, people do that when there's an accident, and that's exactly how people were stopping to look at me.

Bob and I then stepped aside to do a one-on-one interview with Gayle Gardner of NBC. Right then, Tampa Bay owner Hugh Culverhouse was leaving the league office. We finished with Gayle, and Bob and I walked down the street with Culverhouse. I'd never met the man, but I remembered how Doug Williams had criticized him. I figured I'd judge for myself. He had some expensive-looking shades on, but his suit looked like . . . orange. He also had rubber shoes on so he could walk comfortably. One of Bob's clients was the Tampa quarterback, Vinny Testaverde, and Culverhouse told Bob that Coach Ray Perkins was benching Testaverde and that Bob might want to phone Vinny. But I was thinking, I hope this guy Culverhouse gets me. Please rescue me! And lo and behold, it was Dexter who later stepped to the altar with Culverhouse, but that's getting ahead of myself.

Anyway, on Thursday, November 15, 1990, the telephone rang at my house, and I finally heard the familiar voice of Joe Gibbs. It was the first time we had spoken since I'd nearly wrung his neck on the back steps at Redskin Park before that FBI meeting.

I said, "Hello, Coach, how ya doin'?"

He said, "Hi, Dexter. I know you're hanging in there. I just know you're hanging in there." It was as if nothing had ever happened.

Boy, I was happy to hear his voice. I was a big admirer of Joe Gibbs. That may sound like a contradiction, but what I'm trying to say is Gibbs represented my daddy to me in a lot of ways. I admired my daddy, but my daddy never gave me love. Likewise, I admired Joe Gibbs, but he never gave me praise.

I don't know why it took so long for him to call me. I imagine he was pissed at me for messing up, but I can't answer for sure.

When he finally did call, he wanted to rendezvous the next day. He suggested I come to Redskin Park, but I said, "I don't want to go there. Let's meet at the Dulles Marriott." Why did he call? I was gonna be reinstated the following Monday, and I assumed he wanted to tell me face-to-face beforehand that he was going to release me and explain why.

Then he called to cancel our meeting. He said we were jumping the gun and he wanted to wait. The Redskins were playing New Orleans that Sunday, and I figured he wanted to wait until Monday to make sure none of his defensive ends went down. He didn't want to cut me prematurely and then need my ass if a starter got injured.

But I never heard from Gibbs again. They walloped New Orleans, and no one got injured. After Paul Tagliabue reinstated me that Monday, Gibbs took about ten seconds to cut me.

When the TV crews knocked on my door, I granted them interviews. The I broke down in front of them and—what else—cried.

The finality of the cut made me sad. I remembered my last game at Oklahoma State, standing there before introductions, crying while they played this beautiful song. It was like, You will never wear this Oklahoma State uniform again. This is over.

Well, I had the same feeling when the Redskins cut me. Normally, the Redskins bring players back and forth. For instance, Terry Orr has been cut a trillion times and has come back a trillion times. But I was one player they would never bring back. It hit me like an anvil that day that playing for the Redskins was over.

I kept thinking that I'd never wear the burgundy and gold again. I loved playing in that city. I'm the type who loves glamour, and that's what Washington, D.C., is. I just like what Washington stands for: our nation's capital. It has a lot of nationalities; it has money. All the citizens of the United States could go broke, but Washington wouldn't. There's no other city like Washington. Of course, Washington also has a lot of cocaine. Too bad about that one.

Glinda was just as manic about my being cut as I was:

When Dexter got cut, he sort of lost his family. He still had me and his two kids who loved him, but not the Redskins anymore. He had felt safe with them.

Why couldn't they understand drugs were a disease? Drugs weren't something he wanted to do. He didn't want to hurt his family, meaning the Redskins. Drugs are a cancer.

It hurts me that he isn't a part of that family any longer. Fifty percent of me says they should've brought him back, and 50 percent says I understand. It's just they turned on their brother.

I don't think it was Jack Kent Cooke's decision to cut him. I don't think he cared. I think he lets Gibbs make the decisions on who to play and who not to. It's Gibbs's team. Gibbs didn't want egg on his face if Dexter screwed up again; and when it came time for Dexter to be reinstated, the team was doing all right without him. Gibbs probably worried about the morale of the team if they brought him back. Players would've said, "You're moving us around for him?" But the bottom line is they knew he could still play well, and they should've known after ten years that Dexter had a heart the size of a mountain.

They could've said, "Dexter, one false move, and you're out of there." He'd have been so appreciative, he'd probably have kicked butt more than ever.

I guess Gibbs felt he'd already given me a zillion chances, and he thought other players would've resented it if I came back.

Hell, they'd always resented me. I never really wanted any of them to be my friends anyway. I was better than them; I was a frickin' great player, and I didn't want to run around with them.

In my early days, I got all the TV exposure, and the other guys got nothing. I probably also got away with a lot of crap. Donnie Warren once said, "The crap you get away with I never could." Because I was a great player.

We didn't have that much talent early on in Washington. I was probably the most talented, and some of my teammates were jealous. Even half the black guys weren't talented. Art Monk is; Darrell Green is; Charles Mann wasn't early on; Dave Butz wasn't; Joe Jacoby and Russ Grimm were. I'm sure guys resented me, and then I'd predict what I was going to do in the game, like when I said I was going to ring Joe Montana's clock in 1986.

Well, Grant still was on the team when Gibbs cut me. I wonder if he thought the guys would've welcomed be back or not:

I think they would've. As long as he was performing. But Dexter, he was the luckiest guy I'd ever seen. He had nine lives as a football player. For him to be able to come back after doing all those things? The Redskins were trying to replace him for years because Gibbs didn't like guys mouthing off, but they always took him back. Until 1990.

Gibbs could have been my idol if he'd shown emotion, but he did not. There was a twenty-four-hour period for teams to claim me after Gibbs cut me loose, and the one coach who showed compassion toward me was my old partner Joe Bugel, who was then head coach of the Phoenix Cardinals.

Bugel called me at home the day I was cut and asked me what I'd been doing; I told him I was strong enough to lift a house. His Phoenix Cardinals plucked me right off the waiver wire, and I was a Phoenix Cardinal. Can you believe it?

Comparing Joe Gibbs and Joe Bugel is like comparing apples and oranges. Gibbs is more standoffish, more plastic. Plastic, that's the word. You never know what he's feeling. Joe Bugel has paid me compliments, whereas Joe Gibbs would not do that in his wildest dreams. Perhaps he believed my head was too large already, and he didn't want to stroke me, but I believed I needed a little stroking from time to time. Just like I needed it from my daddy.

What I'm saying is that Gibbs played me down. I imagine it's because I have a different personality from an Art Monk. I was looking for approval, and they thought if they praised me I might go overboard. Keeping quiet about me was their way of controlling me.

Maybe by 1989 Gibbs had had enough and had given up on me. In 1987 he had tried to get me to admit to drugs, and I wouldn't; he'd talked about life and doing the right thing. In those cases, I guess Gibbs didn't hold back his emotions, because I think he genuinely cared about me. I'm not saying I didn't like Joe Gibbs. I always did, and I still do. I'm not bitter that he cut me either. Why should I be bitter? I snorted the coke; he didn't. Can you imagine Joe Gibbs on coke?

It's just that in the end I needed attention from him, and you'd just have to say he was plastic instead.

Yet, when I got the phone call from Bugel, he was so positive. He didn't call me to ask, "Are you sober?" He made me remember all the good things I'd done. When I first reported to the Cardinals in late November, he invited me over to his house for Thanksgiving. I owed the man.

I've only seen Gibbs once in person since he axed me. After the 1990 season we bumped into each other at my tennis club in Virginia, and we rambled on about the time I knocked a bunch of Gatorade on his son, Coy. After nine years of going to war together, this is what we had to talk about? Me spilling Gatorade on his son? Gibbs didn't know what to say. I guess I didn't know what to say either. I think I said, "I can't wait to play you." I was still with Phoenix at the time, and we talked a little about the Cardinals.

Then I told him I'd smashed some cups in Dallas during my second game with Phoenix, and that's what made Gibbs reminisce about the time I smashed cups on Coy. Eventually, the conversation just fizzled. I think he asked about my family, and that was it.

Maybe something *is* going on inside of me about Joe Gibbs. I want to be hard on him, I guess. When I think of him, I think of a lot of great things, but I want to look at a lot of negatives, too.

Certainly, Gibbs had concern for me. We sat in his office in the middle of my drug binges, and he wanted to read the Bible with me, wanted to meet with me every Friday and go over Scriptures. When I crashed my truck outside Redskin Park, he told me to get some sleep. He looked out for me.

He later cut me, but I did that to myself. I don't blame him, nor should I be mad at him for that. I looked up to him. Gibbs had his bad moments with a lot of players, not just me. There were times, for instance, when he was pissed at Charles Mann, too, pissed that Charles was hurt. So I wasn't the only one who got him riled.

Hell, Gibbs got me riled, too. In 1989, my last season in Washington, Gibbs came to me one day when I was stretching before practice and said, "I'm taking up for you."

"What?" I asked.

"They say you're getting slow and you're not as strong," he said. "I went to check with Dan Riley about it, but he says you're stronger and faster than ever. But everyone else says you're getting slower and weaker."

I snapped, "You don't have to take up for me 'cause I don't give a shit what anybody says."

"You don't care about winning?" he snapped. And then he walked away.

Gibbs was trying to turn it into a winning thing. Hell, I was benching 500 pounds at the time and was using 155-pound dumbbells. But suddenly Gibbs is accusing me of slowing down, and here was Don Breaux saying, "You're not flying around like you used to in practice."

Well, that was *true* about practice. I was older and wiser. I had grown up, and I don't think the Redskins want their athletes to grow up. So when Gibbs came up to me that day, he was obviously trying to get under my skin and motivate me. He and the other coaches probably saw I wasn't hustling in practice, and what Gibbs was doing was all psychology. I was taking care of my body, but they wanted me to kamikaze it all the time. But you won't last four years in the NFL if you do that.

We had this guy, Otis Wonsley, who was the greatest special teams player I've ever seen. But when Otis got hurt, the Redskins turned their backs on him. Otis Wonsley was one beat-up dude at the end, and I remember how Gibbs used to praise him. He would say, "Otis is like a son to me." He lauded Otis on a daily basis, but he wanted Otis to give everything because they know there'll be more meat coming along later. When Otis got hurt, they started praising Greg Williams. He was the new Otis, and Otis got cut. Then Greg got cut. And so on.

Don't get me wrong; Gibbs is a great coach. He's got an excellent offensive mind, the best. He couldn't play the game, but he understands it better than anybody.

Am I mad at Gibbs today? No. I *wish* he would have cut me in person. After nine years, all I deserved was a phone call? That hurt me. Not that I was angry with his decision; I was the one who screwed up by using drugs. I let people down, and people had no trust in me. I am responsible for that. Gibbs helped me many times, but it is upsetting that he didn't meet me at the Dulles Marriott as he said he would. I would've loved to have listened to him. I respected the man.

So, inside, I just feel he let me down a bit. When he called me as I was about to come back from my 1989 suspension, he said, "I've been trying to call you." I thought, Oh, come on. Don't snow job me. You're insulting my intelligence. I mean, I busted my butt for him, and he wasn't being real with me. That's why people want to bust their butts for Buddy Ryan and Bum Phillips, but you never hear people say they want to bust their butts for Gibbs.

To this day, there's only one thing I'm still pissed at Gibbs for: him taking me out in 1989 on second-and-long situations to go to a 3–4 defense. One day I was angry, and I probably would have gotten into a shouting match with Gibbs or walked out on him. One of my player representatives, Randy Vataha, calmed me down and told me to approach the subject with a "we" mentality instead of an "I" mentality. He told me to say my coming out on second and long "was bad for the team." Randy saved me.

So it was just an awkward day when I bumped into Gibbs at the tennis club in 1990. We stammered, trying to talk, and went our separate ways. It was at about that time I finally got over my Redskin worship.

In fact, I told a friend of mine, "Hey, if the Cardinals give me the $1.6 million contract I want, I'll have my ashes sprinkled over Sun Devil Stadium."

AN IDLE THOUGHT

My Redskin teammates never knew what to make of me. On the last day of my last minicamp in Washington, the front office had a cookout for players, complete with kegs and cases of beer. I guess some of the guys thought it would freak me out to be around alcohol.

Ravin Caldwell, a linebacker, actually walked up to me and waved a beer in my face. He said, "Nah nah nuh nah nah, you can't have one of these."

I guess he thought I'd be foaming, like I was dying for one and couldn't have one.

It didn't faze me when he did that. I've never been an alcoholic. I didn't even think twice. Actually, I thought it was kind of cute. He was the one poisoning his brain with beer and wine, and my system was clean of that stuff.

There were guys there that day pounding it and boozing it, and the Redskins paid for the beer!

I think it's a double standard, in a way. I admit I did drugs, but, for years, a bunch of those Hogs have met in a Redskin Park shack after practice, drinking like winos. *On Redskins property!* They call themselves the Five O'Clock Club and wear hats and jackets publicizing it. Yet I'm the one who got in trouble for being a member of my own five o'clock Club, 5:00 A.M., that is.

I had a different method to my madness. But we were all *mad*, if you know what I mean.

C H A P T E R   36

Bugel Boy

JOE BUGEL IS MY MAN, BUT I WISH HE HADN'T claimed me off waivers. I would've felt more comfortable with another coach who also claimed me. But he couldn't get my rights because his team had a better record than the Cardinals.

I'm talking about Philadelphia's Buddy Ryan.

If I'd been Buddy's property, I would have been an impact player again. Buddy believes in a 4–3 defense that emphasizes the pass rush, but the Cardinals played a more passive 3–4 scheme that emphasized linebackers. From day one, the Cardinals had me lining up over guards and centers, and all they wanted me to do was push like a sumo wrestler. Hell, you need a beer belly to play that style.

If I'd weighed 300 pounds, the idea might've worked. But I'm 260 with Carl Lewis legs, and I don't want to weigh 300 pounds because then I couldn't wear Ralph Lauren. You ever seen a 300-pounder on the cover of GQ? No, and you ain't ever gonna see the Fridge on the cover of that magazine, I promise.

My first day in Phoenix—in November 1990—I knew it was the wrong place for me. Bob Woolf had nearly called the Cardinals beforehand and asked them to pass on me. I sort of wish he had.

The Phoenix fans were great to me; there just weren't enough of them. I didn't suit up for my first two games out there, and when I tried to sit in the stands during the first one, I got mobbed so much for autographs I had to leave.

The problem was they only drew about 30,000 a game. I cannot play to the best of my abilities unless there are 60,000 fans in the stands. I told the Phoenix coaches one day I wasn't playing unless at least 50,000 showed up for one of our 1991 preseason games.

Hell, I wouldn't play football if it wasn't on TV. I swear, if football was only on radio, I'd just as soon play soccer.

Another problem with the Cardinals was they were clearly a low

312

self-esteem team. I ended up talking my way out of there because of that. I couldn't handle playing in a 3–4 scheme unless they used me as an outside pass rusher, and when I told the media, "If anyone's in need of a great defensive end, please call 602-379-0101 [the Cardinal office number]," Phoenix management grew very sensitive.

Speaking of Cardinal management, you had to love ole Mr. Bidwill, the owner. Mr. Bidwill has the reputation of being slightly cheap; but he took care of me, so I have no complaint. He's simply an 180-degree turn from the Redskin owner, Jack Kent Cooke. I mean, Mr. Bidwill used to eat in our training camp cafeteria and would hang around like a floppy-eared dog. Cooke would *never* eat in a Redskins cafeteria unless it had caviar.

Bidwill reminded me of a custodian sitting on a tractor-trailer. I don't mean that to sound derogatory; it's just the way he dressed and carried himself. He was much more down to earth than Mr. Cooke, who had a new car and wife practically every day.

I used to mess with Mr. Bidwill—all in fun, of course. I wanted him to loosen up a little. He's much too serious, and his lips are always furled downward. It seems nobody ever confronts him or interacts with him or even holds a conversation with him.

So one day as he walked by while we were scrimmaging, I called out, "Hey, Mr. Bidwill, let's trade jobs."

"Oh, no, Dexter," he answered.

A little bit later, we were in the locker room, and he found two quarters lying on the ground. He picked them up and asked, "Whose quarters?" I said, "Those are my quarters, Mr. B." I reached out my hand, but then I said, "No, no, no. They're not mine." He urged, "Oh no, take them, Dexter. You'll need them for your flight home."

Another day, he was walking around in his tight-ass coat that looked like it didn't fit him. Here I was about to leave in my steamy-hot truck, so I said "Mr. Bidwill, would you like a ride?"

He declined, "Oh, no, Dexter. I have a ride."

And he went to hop in his big old long Cadillac.

One time he was leaving our training complex in Flagstaff to drive back to Phoenix, and I commented, "Mr. Bidwill, I thought you would be flying back in a helicopter. I thought you'd be like Donald Trump."

He said, "Oh, no, Dexter. I heard you were a bullshitter in Washington, and now you're our bullshitter."

I said, "Oh, OK, Mr. Bidwill."

I swear, with his brown shirts and khaki pants, he looked like a custodian. It looked like he was in uniform.

* * *

I changed my jersey number from 72 to 92—92 is closer to God—and suited up for my first game with the Cardinals on December 9, 1990, in Atlanta. In pregame I went into my usual sweat, as in Washington, and I think I broke a chair. Knowing my ritual, Bugel did not bat an eye.

A week later in Dallas, I turned over a water table on the field because I was pissed from riding the bench. The Cardinals had never seen such a thing, and they all looked at me as if I were on drugs. What, me on drugs?

It still wasn't my worst attack on a football stadium. When I was with Washington, I once tore up a Texas Stadium cabinet that had been built to hold the yellows pages for a pay phone. In Giants Stadium I kicked a phone off the wall. I got so riled, I went "Arrrrrrgh," and just booted it.

Well, I didn't record a sack or tackle in my four Phoenix games of 1990, but, they hardly played me until the season ender against Philadelphia. I played exactly one play of the Giants game, and I swear I nearly tackled the coach. I nearly decapitated him. When they played me, I was lining up *inside!*

Obviously, the Cardinals were featuring their outside linebacker, Kenny Harvey, but if they had been smart coaches, they would have gotten creative and figured out a way to utilize me, the best pass rusher in football.

The only thing that kept me sane was the team drug counselor, Gary Mack, who also worked with the Chicago Cubs and Seattle Mariners. During my entire stay in Phoenix, I could call Gary as I did Pham in Washington. When something came up that irritated me or made me sad, I could dial Gary. There isn't anything like having someone close to listen to you. If you've got a problem, you can't solve anything if you don't talk about it.

I used to stay to myself. In my Redskins drug days, I internalized. But in Phoenix I would go to a meeting or call Gary. I was reaching out. Wasn't I mature?

When the 1990 season ended, I hauled it back to D.C. I have to admit I hard urges to relapse. I was thinking about drugs, and I had no desire to go to AA meetings. One night I started putting on what Glinda calls my "get-high clothes." I knew I had to work the telephone to overcome my urge, and I called Pham (no answer) and three or four other people (no answers). My last call was to Jim Vance, the anchorman at the NBC affiliate in town. (He answered).

Jim and I met at a club in Georgetown—Paolo's—and you know

what? The urge left again. I guess that was what AA was about. I would never call up a soul in the old days because I didn't want anyone to talk me out of it.

The worst day of my off-season was my birthday, February 2. That's when my best friend in the world died.

Lester had been to the doctor several times, and they had warned him about his cholesterol. But he still worked himself to the bone—detailing and repairing cars—because he had a family to support.

I never thought he was in danger. Glinda, looking back, had an inkling Lester knew he was on his way out:

*W*e had seen Lester the same day he died. He had washed my car, and he washed it better than he had ever done. When we went to pick up the car, Lester kept saying, "Glinda, do you like it?" He needed to know. I said, "Lester, I love it." He went, "Are you sure you like it? If you see anything wrong, I'll do it over."

It's funny, I hadn't seen Lester in maybe a week before that. But he called me three times saying, "Get your car over here; I've got to wash your car." Usually he'd be around our house more often.

He didn't look sick. But starting about a month before he died, he'd drop in to see how I was doing, and when he'd kiss me, he'd give me the biggest squeeze like it was the squeeze of death almost. He would hug me so hard, it would literally take the air out of me. He'd say, "I just love you and Dexter so much," and he'd kiss me.

Looking back, it was as if he kind of knew. In fact, six months earlier he'd sat and told me, "I don't think I have too much longer for this world." I said, "Lester, don't say that."

Well, the phone call came at like two in the morning. I could hear Dexter talking, "OK, all right. Are they there yet? OK. Call me back and let me know what happens."

I'd fallen asleep in Dalis's room, and I came in and asked, "Who was that? Who's sick?"

"Oh, that was Odessa," Dexter answered. "She said Lester passed out, and she can't revive him. The ambulance is there, and they're taking him in . . ."

I said, "Why did you tell her to call you back, Dexter? For her to call you in the middle of the night, it must be pretty scary for them, and that's your best friend. You ought to get up and go to the hospital."

But Dexter kept saying it was nothing. Probably ulcers, he said, because Lester was always sick.

Dexter finally agreed to go to the hospital to support the family while they waited. He walked in there like a big shot. "Move out of the way," he demanded. "Where's Lester Townsend?" One of the orderlies pointed to a room and said, "He's in there."

"How is he?" Dexter asked.

"Uh, he died," they answered.

"No, I'm talking about Lester Townsend."

"Well, he's passed on."

Dexter said, "Where is he? I want to see him. Now!" Dexter just walked straight into the room and must've stayed in there ten minutes by himself. He said it looked like Lester was asleep, and he just touched him.

You won't believe what Dexter did at the funeral. Before the viewing of the body, he took his camera in there to get pictures of Lester in the casket. I've heard of people taking maybe one picture—I still think that's a little creepy—but Dexter took lots of shots. It was the weirdest thing. It's probably most of the pictures we have of Lester, and it's all of him in the casket.

The first picture Dexter wanted me to take was of him and Lester together! Dexter was leaning down next to Lester in the closet, giving the thumbs up sign and smiling. I said, "Dexter, you're much too happy."

He had his arm around Lester's head, and he was leaning down to Lester's head with the thumbs up sign. That was his buddy.

Do you know what they buried with Lester in his casket? My nameplate from Redskins Park and a football with my signature on it. It was a football I'd given him after we won a Super Bowl, and he'd always wanted to be buried with it.

I loved Lester—my one friend—and I miss him. There'll never be another Lester. Lester would've kicked Joe Bugel's ass for me if he'd been alive for the 1991 season.

First of all, I was a free agent in 1991 and had to negotiate my first contract since 1986, back when I called Cooke a miser. It was obvious I wouldn't be signed by the first day of training camp, and a Phoenix reporter, Lloyd Herberg, called and asked, "Do you think you'll be a holdout?"

I answered, "When's the first day of camp?" I knew when it was, but I was playing dumb. He told me, and I said, "Oh, no. I won't be there. I'm planning to be in Aruba belly dancing that day."

The Cardinals had never seen anything like me, boy. I called up Larry Wilson, their general manager who happens to be in the Hall of Fame, and I let him know I wanted $1.6 million. He said, "I can't pay that. I've got to pay the people protecting the franchise."

"What?" I asked.

"Rosie [quarterback Timm Rosenbach] is the franchise," he said.

"Who?" I was incredulous. "I thought when you said franchise, Mr. Wilson, you were talking about me."

"No, not you," he said.

"No, Mr. Wilson." I said. "*I* am the franchise."

Pretty soon that became my rallying cry. I'd call Larry Wilson and tell his secretary, "Tell Mr. Wilson the franchise is on the phone."

Well, I didn't get my $1.6 million. I actually got $600,000 for 1991, with a $50,000 roster bonus and $25,000 more as soon as I collected my first sack. That's the biggest base salary I'd ever had in my career, and it came after a year's suspension for drugs. You just know I was a bad-ass player to be able to get that.

When I got to training camp, I urged everyone to call me Franchise. I'd answer my telephone, "Franchise speaking," One day, I told the trainer to call me Franchise, and he said, "Did you say French Fry?" "I could've sworn you said French Fry." So that's what everyone started calling me: French Fry.

All this time I was getting some bad vibes from the Cardinals, as if they knew I wouldn't be around. During an evening training camp practice, quarterback Rosenbach tore up his knee. It was so tense out there that night I figured I'd loosen things up. I saw Bill Bidwill, Jr.— one of the owner's many sons who worked for the team as a scout—and he said, "What's up, French Fry?"

"Babe, I'm the Franchise," I countered.

"You're not a franchise player," he snapped. "There's not one guy on this team who's a defensive franchise player."

I said to myself, That's why this guy is scouting for the Cardinals. He don't even know how to throw a football, and I didn't care if his daddy owned the team.

I knew right then I wasn't long for that place. They first started using me as a nickel pass rusher—lining me up over the guard—then they finally wised up and lined me up outside, where I could use my Leroy Burrell speed. The only problem was, they already had Ken Harvey as their right outside pass rusher. So here I was, the best pass rusher in pro football being used as a second stringer on nickel downs. I was playing with a bunch of scrubs, and I wanted out.

Another of Bidwill's sons, a nineteen-year-old, actually did bed checks during training camp. Imagine a nineteen-year-old doing bed checks on grown athletes! Hell, bed check was past the kid's bedtime.

One time I went up to that nineteen-year-old Bidwell and told him, "I've seen you driving your Porsche. You're spoiled, aren't you?"

Early in training camp at Flagstaff, Arizona, we scrimmaged the Chargers, which was where Bobby Beathard, Dan Henning, Dicky Daniels, and Billy Devaney—all former Redskins staffers—were working. It was like my little Super Bowl.

Beathard thought I was mad at him. When the Chargers first showed up, he came over to where the defensive lines were and looked at me. He thought I wasn't gonna speak to him, but I turned the tables and said, "Hi, Bobby."

But I was into the scrimmage. As we were lining up, I shouted, "Let's knock their balls off." Dan Henning, who was the Charger's head coach and who I'd always liked in D.C., said, "Now Dexter, you don't have many friends, but I'm one of them. Cool it."

It was right after that scrimmage that I basically told the Cardinals to trade me. They had made it seem like I was fighting for a roster spot. I almost said, "I don't need to play for you mothers. You're the worst team in sports history." Jerry Rhome, who used to be with me in Washington and now was the Cardinals' offensive coordinator, told me to stay cool and that he'd find out what was going on.

My ego was involved. I felt like if I was fighting for a roster spot, I'd help them out. They could let me go. I decided that if it stayed like this after our preseason game against the Bears in Chicago, I would be out of there. I'd call my agents, Bob Woolf and Randy Vataha, and get them working on a trade or ask the Cardinals to cut me. I didn't need to be there. I didn't feel it was my team; I needed to be with my team. A bunch of other teams could use me, though I knew I couldn't go back to the Redskins or to the Chargers because in San Diego Beathard was still bitter at me:

Was I still bitter at Dexter? I thought I was. I went up to Flagstaff with the attitude, Hell, Dexter screwed us in Washington, so . . . But then when I got to talking to him, I really hoped he would do something. I wanted to think there was still a lot of good in Dexter, but just when you'd be nice to Dexter or try to get along with him, he'd kick you in the ass, and you'd think, Why did I do that? Why was I nice to him? So there was always that challenge: What approach do you take with Dexter? In Flagstaff I ended up being nice.

I got some much needed leverage on the Cardinals in that Bears preseason game when I sacked a quarterback and caused the fumble that led to our winning field goal.

That's when I went public with my demand to get out of there. I heard the Tampa Bay Bucs had a scout at the game watching me, and I said to reporters, "I hope the Bucs saw that sack."

Bugel called me in and warned, "French Fry, watch your mouth. Here we go again with you." He kept saying I would not be traded. "You think we're stupid and will just give you away?"

But Larry Wilson told me, "Pal, I think you're right. This isn't the place for you." Larry always calls people "Pal."

They were giving mixed signals, but I never believed they'd cut me. I used to go up to guys saying, "Look here, man. You're goin' home next week." I once let a guy borrow my hair-cutting shears, but I continued, "Bring 'em back soon, 'cause you may not be around long." I'd tell guys, "If I don't see you tomorrow, good luck." I remember one guy said to me, "Looks like you're gonna make the last cut, Dexter." And I said, "Hell! The only way I'm getting cut is if they sell the team or something. I ain't goin' nowhere."

In a way, I was feeling comfortable on the Cardinals. For instance, we each had defensive stunts named after us, and I had my personal stunt called "Coke." Everyone thought that was humorous.

I believed Bugel when he said I was staying put, so I brought Glinda and the family out to Phoenix. We were gonna look for a house or a condo. I brought them to a preseason game.

Bugel said I'd stay in Phoenix, but they still weren't using me correctly on defense.

Apparently, the Cardinals had a chance to trade me to Tampa Bay after the next-to-last preseason game, but they waited. Then they hardly used me in the last preseason game against Denver, and when they asked me to enter the game in the fourth quarter, I said, "Hell, no. I'm not going in."

As I was leaving the field, I saw Broncos coach Dan Reeves and told him, "I love Denver." I was hoping he'd trade for me. I saw the owner, Pat Bowlan and said, "I want to play for you." He just looked at me weird.

Next thing I knew, the Cardinals cut me. They said they tried to trade me, but Tampa Bay figured they could get me free on waivers. So I was flat-out released. Bugel called me in to break the news, and I sneaked in a portable tape recorder in my lapel pocket. I wanted to have this speech for all time.

An excerpt:

Me: How ya doing, coach?

[He wouldn't look me in the eye; he kept his head down for a while.]

Bugel: OK, Dex. Have a seat . . . Well, we aren't going to be selfish and keep you here as a backup. Larry and Mr. Bidwill thought you had great charisma, but as long as Ken Harvey is healthy, you're not going to get much playing time.

Me: Sure.

Bugel: I just told them you're a tremendous player, and we don't want to hold you back.

Me: I hope the Rams don't claim me [I'm laughing]. 'Cause that's who you open your season with, and I'd sure hate to come back and play you.

Bugel: If that happens, stay in the locker room [he's laughing]. OK, Dexter?

Me: Well, I don't want to take too much of your time, coach.

Bugel: You won't get even with me now [he's laughing]. Will you?

Me: The best revenge is massive success.

Bugel: Good luck. I really wish you the best.

Me: Thank you for giving me this opportunity.

Bugel: I tell you what, I told my wife and kids about this, and there were some tears in the house. You know what I mean?

Me: OK.

Bugel: You've got a ton of friends.

Me: Thank you . . . I love you. I wish you the best.

Bugel: Love you, too, buddy.

I called a press conference after I left his office, and I told the media the Cardinals had better hope the Rams don't pick me up because the Rams open with the Cardinals, and I might roll up Bugel and Larry Wilson with a chop block on the sidelines.

Wilson called me later to say if I tried that, he'd kick my ass. Do you believe he said that? He said, "Pal, I'll kick your ass." That was funny.

He also said Bugel was upset I'd threatened him in the papers; so I called Bugel to apologize. I told him I was just kidding, that he should know better than that. He said he was planning on wearing knee pads, just in case.

The truth was, I was really on Bugel's side. The problem with that organization is at the top. I hear his job may be in jeopardy if the Cardinals lose big this year, but Joe Bugel is one of the great motivators, in my book. He, Wayne Sevier, and Woody Hayes are at the top of my list. When he'd give his emotional pep talks in Phoenix, I'd be foaming at the mouth, but I'd hear other players saying, "He oughta cut that shit out."

Well, they don't know anything except how to lose. Bugel came from a winning organization—the Redskins. That boy knows how to win. If the Cardinal players don't like it, it's because they're a bunch of losers who don't know anything else. They've had Gene Stallings, so they don't know winning. And they've had Larry Wilson smoking his four packs of cigarettes and calling me "Pal."

Let me tell you the difference between the Cardinals and the Redskins. The Cardinals cut me because of my big salary; and the Redskins kept Gerald Riggs, let him come in one down—short yardage—and paid his butt $600,000. So, you tell me where the commitment is: in Washington or Phoenix?

Anyway, after I got my ass cut, those twenty-four hours I waited to see if I got claimed were the longest of my life. I said the serenity prayer: "God, grant me the serenity to accept the things I cannot change, the courage to change the things I can, and the wisdom to know the difference." It was like a cloud was hanging over my head. For so long I'd led the great life of the NFL, and now I was seeing it from the perspective of a scrub.

Getting cut felt like the day I got suspended. Glinda and the kids were with me, and we went to a mall. I kept thinking to myself I shouldn't be here. I should be at practice. Malls are where players' wives should be, and now I don't know if I'll be able to support my family. It showed me that when you do drugs, even if you clean yourself up, things don't always come up roses. I was going on two years of sobriety when I got cut, and it was like I was still paying for my mistake.

I couldn't believe I'd been cut by the worst franchise in pro football history. I needed to go to an AA meeting to calm myself. I tried to rationalize the whole thing. I decided they didn't want to keep me because of my contract or because I talked too much or because of the 3–4 scheme. Basically, it was really the scheme, but they could have traded me and helped me save face. I asked their assistant general manager, Erik Whidmark, if they ever got a solid trade offer from the Bucs, and he said, "Yeah, we got offered a Johnny Mathis album, but that's it."

A Johnny Mathis album? You can imagine how my ego was doing. Everyone thought I'd have a coke relapse, but it's strange. I'm more liable to do coke when things are going great. Then my outside seems like a million bucks while my inside still feel like garbage, and I'll do coke to escape that garbage feeling inside. That's why I did coke after the illiteracy hearing. But when things are bad, my outside feels like garbage and my inside feels like garbage, and there's no feeling of falseness. So I don't use coke. My drug counselors might want to take notes on that.

However, I will admit the morning after I got cut, I woke up thinking, I can use cocaine. The league doesn't have jurisdiction over me anymore. It was only a fleeting thought, mind you.

Finally, after twenty-four hours, I got a call from Larry Wilson telling me the Buccaneers had picked up me and my $600,000 contract. When I hung up, I went, "Whuuuuuuuuuuuuuuuuuuuuuuuuuuuu!" I didn't feel like a peon anymore.

I felt Tampa Bay was a better place for me. At least Tampa Bay had fans at their games, and I wouldn't have to play in front of Yates High School-size crowds anymore.

AN IDLE THOUGHT

Two of my favorite people in the world to poke fun at are Dave Butz, the UPS courier, and Mr. Bidwill, the custodian.

Wouldn't you know it, those two were already linked for all time before I met them.

In 1975 the Redskins signed Butz away from Bidwill's St. Louis Cardinals, and Commissioner Rozelle ordered the Redskins to compensate the Cardinals with two number-one picks plus a number two— the largest compensation deal in league history.

For Dave Butz?

I approached Mr. Bidwill at training camp in 1991 and said, "Mr. B., Dave Butz wasn't even worth a number-one pick, was he?"

And Mr. Bidwill said something like, "Oh, no, Dexter. He wasn't."

CHAPTER 37

A Buc Stopped Here

BEFORE THE TAMPA BAY BUCS CLAIMED ME OFF the waiver wire—they were the only team brave enough to do so— they called John Lucas. John, who had supervised my most recent trip to drug rehab, gave the seal of approval; and the Bucs felt I was worth the gamble.

Their defensive coordinator, Floyd Peters, had particularly fought for me. He needed a left defensive end, and even though I'd always played the right side, he knew I was one pass-rushing SOB.

Little did I know that Floyd would nearly drive me to my relapse.

Initially, I was fired up to be in Tampa. One of the Bucs' secretaries called me in Phoenix to set up my travel arrangements, and I answered the phone, "Franchise speaking." She told me my flight number, and I asked, "Is that first class for a Buc?" She answered, No, that the Bucs couldn't fly me first class.

I should've known then, man.

Before I left Phoenix, my old TV station in D.C.—Channel 5— called me for an interview. It was my chance for a few parting shots. They asked if I wished the Redskins had picked me up, and I said, "I do not want to see Johnny Cakes, nor do I want to see his old man. I don't want to see Joe Gibbs. And I'm not craving drugs. Hallelujah! I know Gibbs would like it if he heard me say 'Hallelujah.'"

Unfortunately, Channel 5 never used those quotes on the air. They were probably afraid of upsetting Jack Kent Cooke.

Anyway, after I'd talked my way out of Phoenix, I figured I'd better hold it down in Tampa. I went in there acting like a lily-white boy, saying, "Yes sir, no sir." However, when some reporter asked me how long I thought it would take to beat out the starting left defensive end, Ray Seals, I asked, "Who is Ray Seals?"

"I'll be starting soon," I predicted. "Trust me."

323

I really had no idea who Ray Seals was, but it seemed the Bucs immediately thought I was an arrogant guy and that they had to humble me. For the next four months, that's all Floyd Peters did: humble me.

The season opener against the Jets in New York came five days after I arrived from Phoenix. Floyd didn't want to use me because I didn't know the defensive system yet. Hell, he expected me to sit on my hands and watch? I'm the type of guy who paces endlessly on the sidelines, sweating, heading for the oxygen tank. I'm supposed to sit and watch?

When Floyd gave his sideline instructions to the defense that day, I was always in his sight line. I'd be six inches away from him so he'd know I was rarin' to go. I'd be kneeling whenever he'd kneel. When he wouldn't put me in, I tugged on his sleeve. One time, I threatened to put my ass in the game myself. I think I got in for three plays at the most, and we lost.

The following week against Chicago, I was pumped up and in a wild mood. The morning of the game, I called room service and said, "Can you grill me a cat?"

The room service person said, "Excuse me?"

I said, "I'd like for you to go outside and catch me a cat and grill it."

The guy said, "Hold on."

He took so long to come back on the line, I hung up.

During the Bears game, Floyd sent me in early and I sacked Jim Harbaugh on my first play. I threw tackle Keith Van Horne away and sacked Harbaugh's behind. Floyd left me in for a while.

But I was clearly going through a transition. In Washington, I'd always been the big wheel on defense, but now I was being put down. Keith McCants, one of the Bucs' hotshot young players, had me over to his place and told his mother, "Mom, Dexter's older than you."

In a meeting one day, Floyd was talking about when he played, and I asked, "Did they wear facemasks back then?" Keith said, "Back then? Boy, that's when you played, too! You're the same age as Floyd."

I never thought I'd hear that. I was on the receiving end now. I was the senior guy on the team, and I felt like UPS courier Dave Butz.

I went home one Monday night, and the Redskins were on "Monday Night Football" against the Eagles. That was the *first* time I missed being a Redskin. They were playing at RFK Stadium, and all these memories rushed back to me. That was my field; I owned that place. If it weren't for those damn drugs, I still would have been there.

Back home, Glinda was going through similar agony. She was still living in Washington, while I was in Tampa:

Dexter didn't have to live in D.C. and be reminded of the old days. I did. In a sense, it felt like Dexter was dead, and I had to mourn his loss from the Redskin team the entire 1991 season. I had looked forward to football season so much for eleven years, and then to have it taken away; I wasn't a part of D.C. anymore. I know it sounds stupid and petty, but I kept thinking, How could Coach Gibbs do this to me? How could he cut Dexter? He knew we were good people and that the family would be split up once he cut him. It could've been so esay to take him back. They had always said, "This is a team, this is a Redskin family," but . . . Gibbs basically gave Dexter his death sentence.

It was just so hard to live in D.C. and see all the Redskins' wives. One day I ran into a Redskin player and his wife. He had just bought her a new diamond ring. They also have a magnificent home and a beautiful car, and we're still in our town house. I felt like, Damn, it could've been Dexter and me.

But Dexter didn't have to see this because he was in Tampa. I'd go driving with our kids, and we'd pass big houses in the neighborhood, and Little Dexter would say, "I guess we're poor and we can't afford that house. I wish we could have a house like that. Charles Mann does."

I couldn't even walk around saying "My husband's kicking butt." Before, I used to have a sense of pride about him, but now he was on this losing team in Tampa and he wasn't doing diddly. The great Dexter Manley was no more. He was on a lousy team that didn't care about him, and he was realizing his legend was gone. I told him he had to kiss his coaches' ass now the way a few players used to when he was a rookie. It was time for him to kiss butt.

I wanted to blame Dexter for screwing up our life. His little boy was more interested in football than ever, and he couldn't run to RFK and see his daddy play for the Redskins. He was finally at the age he liked to tell everybody who he is, "My daddy's a big football player. You've heard of him, he's Dexter Manley. I'm Dexter Manley, too."

The Buccaneers were on TV once, and Little Dexter kept asking, "Is Daddy on yet? Is Daddy on yet?" Big Dexter didn't play the first half, so Little Dexter left the room. He said, "I'm tired of waiting to see my daddy. If you see him go in the game, call me." I mean, he was starting to think his daddy was no good. And when Big Dexter would call home after games, Little Dexter would ask, "Daddy, did you get any sacks? No? Oh, you'll do better."

The Buccaneers just wouldn't start me. I knocked over some air blowers when they wouldn't put me in on pass rushing situations, and Floyd said, "Son, you better watch it. I'm evaluating you."

Floyd said I wasn't mastering the defense quickly enough. One day he asked me what my nickname was, and I said, "Franchise!" He suggested, "Uh, we better come up with a new nickname for you."

To be honest, I didn't understand his defense. I didn't tell him this, but it had to be my learning disability. I'm slightly dyslexic, and I'd always been used to playing the right side. When I played the left side for Floyd, I felt turned upside down.

In Phoenix I had had a training camp to learn the system, but Tampa picked me up five days before the season and expected me to be an Einstein. All the time I was with the Bucs, I felt my dyslexia was worse than ever. I wanted to prove to those people I was smart, but I couldn't get the system down pat.

They must have thought I was dumb. Early in the season, even the offensive coordinator came up to me and said, "Do you know your shit?" He kept asking me that. When I'd keep making mistakes, I'd think, What is it? Why am I making these errors? Why haven't I improved? It's got to be my learning disability.

In Washington, Torgy and the defensive coaches would review the game plan on the blackboard and would give us a piece of paper with the plan written on it for reinforcement. That made it easy. I'd look at the blackboard and at the paper, and I had it down pat. Visualizing off of a blackboard was always easy for me; my problem has been in understanding written words. The Redskins made it simple for me by handing me the paper during the blackboard session, so I could match the written word with the visual.

But Tampa gave us a blank piece of paper and had us *write* the game plan on it ourselves.

I guess that is why I wasn't starting ahead of Ray Seals. Floyd would say, "Are you gonna run you're *own* defense or are you gonna run *ours?*" That's how Floyd would talk. He had a booming voice and would pronounce words as if he was General Patton.

The whole defense would tease me. They'd say, "Oh no, we've got to help Dexter." It was the same with the Redskins my rookie year. It was that learning disability. I wasn't the only one who made mistakes. It's just that Floyd's pets were Broderick Thomas, a young linebacker, and McCants, whom he'd turned from a linebacker into a defensive end. To Floyd they could do nothing wrong. But with me it was "Dexter doesn't *know* the *defense.*"

They used to fine us a dollar for every mistake in practice, and Floyd would yell, "Get a dollar on *Manley*. Tell him what to *do*."

On the sidelines during games, Floyd would say to everyone around, *"Manley* makes me *nervous."*

He blamed everything on me. Once Ray Seals was injured on a third down play, came hobbling off, and said, "Get in there for me, Dexter!"

I ran in like Ray said, except it was fourth down and the other team was fixing to kick a field goal. So I had to sprint off real quick. Floyd was like, "What are you *doing? Come* here. *Goddamnit, Manley, come* here!

Floyd accosted Ray Seals, "Why are you telling *Manley* to run on the *field?"*

Ray answered, "Well, I didn't know," but Floyd still hounded me. He said, "Why is it always *you, Manley?"*

For some reason, I made fewer mental mistakes in practice than in games. I'd go in the games all hyper, and—bam!—the defense would just leave my head. Floyd would say, "That's the one bad thing about you, *Manley.* It's your *concentration."* I'd start thinking about it too much and would be a nervous wreck in the huddle. Everyone would be talking a mile a minute in the huddle. There was no organization on that team.

I tried to study my plays at home, but another of my learning problems is that I have an attention defecit disorder. I start studying, but I last about twenty minutes before I need to call somebody on the phone. I have a hard time focusing. I can't stick with one thing. It doesn't make any sense to me.

Little Dexter has the same problem. He's coming out of it lately, but he can't stick to anything for much more than two minutes. I remember standing on the Buccaneer practice field thinking about my learning problem. I'd think, Why me? And why are my kids like me? My daddy wasn't like that. I used to admire my daddy for sitting up and writing out all his bills. When I write out my bills, I believe it is the greatest accomplishment of all. I feel so successful when I do that.

But it saddens me that Little Dexter has my deficiencies. Glinda's noticed it:

Little Dexter is go, go, go. But you put him down in a lying position, and he's out like a light. He's asleep. Big and Little Dexter are like that. They go until they drop. They have that energy. Even when they're tired, they don't know it. They can't stop. But once they do sit, they're gone.

One time we were trying to diagnose Little Dexter to see if he is hyperactive, and we met with a child psychologist. Dexter and I were sitting with the doctor, and the doctor was talking in a monotone; next thing you know, Big Dexter is nodding off. The doctor kept talking as if he hadn't seen Dexter sleeping, but eventually we all started laughing. Big Dexter cannot keep his attention focused.

I decided to go back to school while I was in Tampa. I had told the Buccaneer public relations office I wanted to get involved in fighting illiteracy in the Tampa/St. Pete area, and when I gave a speech for them one night, I decided I should stay sharp and continue my education as well. I thought to myself, I don't need to mingle with these people. I still need to work on me.

I attended a workshop at a local elementary school. They tested me, and I graded out on a ninth-grade reading level and a ninth-grade vocabulary level. It had been five years since I'd started out on a second-grade level at the Lab School, so I'd made seven grades' worth of progress. It was wonderful.

Actually, I still was on a second-grade level in some areas; I believe reading comprehension was one. So I knew I had to continue going to Sara when I got home.

As for learning the Buccaneer plays, I was finally catching on. Big ole Ray Seals injured his ankle and had to go on injured reserve; so I was the starter by midseason.

In retrospect, that may have been bad.

I started experiencing some of that false glory again. First of all, I was already on TV all the time. The CBS affiliate in town had signed me as a regular contributor to their Sunday night sportscast, and when I became a starter, I again began believing I was larger than life.

I had my share of confrontations on the field. In practice one day, Broderick got into a fight with some guy; and when I tried breaking it up, Broderick ripped into me. He started hitting me in the head. Hell, I didn't retaliate. I was an old bull. I stood and took it.

Later in the year, I again faced off with Jim Dombrowski against the Saints. Dombrowski's the offensive guard from the Saints whom I spit/sneezed on back in 1988. This time I bulldozed him into the backfield, and he grabbed me. I said, "You're sorry; you can't block me," and then he said something, and then I almost spit on him. I started to, but didn't.

*   *   *

In the middle of the week, I would start hanging out at strip bars too much. I should've known then that something dastardly was going on inside of me because those strip bars always reminded me of drugs.

Tampa probably wasn't a good place for me. In Phoenix I never went into strip bars, and the players I hung out with there weren't into seedy things. But the Tampa players liked to *party,* and I'm so impressionable. Also, in Phoenix I had Gary Mack to call whenever I got urges. Gary had set me up with a black psychologist, too, whom I liked. In Tampa I saw a psychologist every Tuesday—Doc Kliene—but there just wasn't the same rapport.

I was developing some shaky tendencies, like I stopped going to AA meetings and quit going to school. Floyd was still all over my case. I tried to make him feel good one day and said, "You used to play with the Redskins, too. Didn't you?"

He answered, "*Yes,* I did. I *played* with them my last *year.* I was just like *you.* I was on the downside of my *career.*"

One of the other defensive coaches, Ray Hamilton, cautioned, "Floyd, lighten up. Put some sugar on it."

The beginning of the end for me was when I took a sip of champagne. I don't know if Floyd had contributed to my lower than normal self-esteem, but I believe so. I had been working on two years' sobriety, but one night I went to a club—which was stupid in the first place—and sneaked a sip of Dom Perignon when no one was looking.

Less than a month later, I did cocaine and lost the NFL forever.

It was just like Washington in 1989. Here I was, waiting for my drug test results to return, and it was like torture. Deep inside, I knew my career was over, but who could I tell? I stood away from my teammates during practice. I even told one of the tackles, Rob Taylor, to say a prayer for me, and he had no clue what I was talking about. I went up to hug the trainer goodbye, and he said, "Dexter, you've got two more games."

I was talking to tight end Ron Hall one day and asked, "How many more years are you gonna play, Ron?" He replied, "Oh, four or five more." I said, "Man, Ron. This is my last year. I'm going to Canada next year." He laughed and started calling me "Montreal" or "Ottawa."

You know who picked it up? Broderick Thomas, the best player on the team. In the defensive huddles, I kept repeating, "It's been great playing with you guys," and one day Broderick came to me with this look in his eyes and asked, "Dexter, what's wrong with you? Have you had a relapse?"

I kept saying, "Been nice knowing you guys." And Broderick said, "Come on, Dexter. You can play three more years. This is not the Dexter I remember who came in here saying, "'Who is Ray Seals?'"

When I eventually announced my retirement, which was a pathetically sad day, the Buccaneers were supportive of me. The owner, Hugh Culverhouse, wasn't able to make it, but his daughter, Gay Culverhouse, was there. Just like with Mr. Bidwill, I used to joke around with Mr. Culverhouse. One day I told him I saw he was listed in *Forbes* magazine as one of the four hundred richest men, and he said he wasn't *that* rich.

We started shooting the breeze, and he told me about a hunting trip he took to Africa. He asked, "Dexter, do you want to go on a hunting trip?"

"Mr. C," I answered, "every time I go in the inner city, I feel like I'm in Africa. They have shootings every day."

Mr. C liked me.

But then it was all over. I ruined twenty-plus years of football with one quick hit of cocaine. I didn't think that small an amount would stay in my system, but it lodged inside me like a termite.

So many things passed through my mind, like the day I'd met Culverhouse outside the NFL office when I was being reinstated. When I flunked my Tampa test, I was supposed to go back to New York to meet with Tagliabue one more time, but I retired before we ever scheduled it. Crap, I wish I'd had that meeting with Tagliabue. I would've gotten that one last crowd of New York media. Maybe I would've been a sellout.

In my heart of hearts, I believe if I'd stayed with the Cardinals and had had Gary Mack around me, there'd have been no relapse. Tampa is a seedy town, man. I keep thinking of when my aunt Melba died when I was a little boy. She had moved to Oakland, and everyone said if she hadn't moved there, she wouldn't have ever died. I feel that way about my move to Tampa. If I'd stayed in Phoenix, I wouldn't have died. My shit was so together there.

During my final days in Tampa, I was driving down Dale Mabry Boulevard remembering how good my life had been. I remembered how happy my family was when they visited me and how now my life was a disaster. Well, maybe not a disaster, but certainly I'd have no easy task ahead. In the blink of an eye, my life had changed.

The night of my retirement speech, Broderick Thomas visited me at my apartment, and so did another teammate, Eugene Marve. Ray Hamilton, my position coach, stopped by to pat me on the shoulder, too. It made me feel somewhat better. The Bucs were so supportive; the Redskins had only issued me athletic supporters, never real support.

It was about ten days before Christmas. My plan was to join Glinda and the kids at my in-laws' house in Chicago. I talked to little Dalis on the phone, and she said, "You did this so you could come home early for Christmas, right, Daddy?" Little Dexter said, "Were you bad again, Daddy?"

I'll never forget driving to the Tampa airport. It was a cloudy Sunday, and nobody was on the street. It was like a ghost town. It made me think of when I left Tampa after the Raiders blew us out of Super Bowl XVIII: hollowness. I drove by the Buc practice field and saw the goal posts. It was like, What now? What's my purpose?

AN IDLE THOUGHT

When I was in Tampa, I wrote a letter for the first time in my life. I mailed it to Glinda, and she nearly hit the roof:

Well, I'd been hurt because he didn't send me anything for our anniversary. Usually I get a gift or at least flowers, but this was the first year I didn't get a thing. We'd been through a lot, and I thought this was one year he needed to let me know how he felt. Especially with him being away and me taking care of the kids.

When I didn't even get flowers, I started feeling evil toward him. Finally I told him why I was mad. His response was, "Really? I was busy."

Then, about a week later, he sent me a nice card about how much he loved me and missed me. It put such a smile on my face.

It was the first letter from him in my life! He sent me a check and wrote, "How are you doing? I hope everything is fine, and thanks for a being a great mother to my children." And all the words were spelled right!

For the first time, I saw he appreciated me. You knew it took time for him to do that. It was a short note, but it was in letter form. I had to wait ten years, but . . .

I'm not a good writer, so what do you expect? When I write letters, it creates fear and makes me uncomfortable. It reminds me of what I've been through, all the struggle. So you think I'm gonna all of a sudden want to write a letter?

Those old feelings come back when I write, those old insecure thoughts. I can read, and it's no problem, but writing is so scary to me. It's like I'm still covering up and don't want to do it because it's like being a failure. It's something I can't do, so why should I do it and make myself feel bad? That's why I never write letters.

But I got over it and wrote Glinda. It wasn't perfect. For instance, I spelled *hope* like this: hOpe.

C H A P T E R 38

Bye, Big Bro'

AND YOU THOUGHT I HAD A BAD YEAR.

The last time I saw my brother Gregory—June 1991—I visited him in the Huntsville state penitentiary. He was due to complete a two-year sentence in September, and I brought him a *Sports Illustrated* and watched him play dominoes in the prison gym. Then we sat down and talked about life after prison. I suggested he get a job, maybe in grocery supply or in loading or driving trucks.

He said maybe he'd start some sort of janitorial service. Not long after that, he wrote me this letter from jail (he is a *great* writer):

July 7, 1991

Hello Li'l Bro:

What's going on in your world? It should go without saying because your world is the best.

Dexter, I want so much to be a part of it, too. I am doing okay, man. I've just been thinking since we last saw each other. You asked me what I was going to do when I got out, and I could not narrow it down to specifics. But now let me run something past you.

Dexter, I need you, man, because I went through my life spinning my wheels and have nothing to show for it. Is there something I can do for you as far as work? Maybe there's somebody you know that has a business and needs a good worker. One thing that I know I can do good—or maybe I should say, do well—is sell. I've had to sell myself all my life, and I've done a good job at it.

I also meet people well. As you know, I sold jewelry, and you know how good I was. Also, I've been in the car selling business. I didn't last long because I didn't have the attire for it, and also I didn't have the patience because I needed money. That was during the time when Pam and I broke up.

Dexter, I have no ties in Houston, other than my son, so there's nothing to keep me there. I want to get away, and it does not matter where, as long as I can get my life back on track. And I mean on track. There's a girl that I like there in Houston, but if she isn't right or if she doesn't have her stuff together or nothing on the ball, than c'est la vie to her, too. I don't need anything holding me down no more. It is time I live up to my real potential if my son is to be proud and is to want to be around me. I have not heard from him since you brought him to see me. But you know what Dexter? I'm not mad at him or his mother because it's my fault it's this way. I really want to change, man, and I need my brother's help. We can help each other be strong.

I can remember when all I did was work and work hard. But after Pam and I split up, I went bad. It is time that I come back up, and I can do it with a little help. I'll be taking this cabinet-makers course before I leave here, so I'll be able to remodel kitchens and bathrooms and build carriages and stuff like that. I can even sell a house.

Dexter, you said it is time you started thinking about what you are going to do after football. Well, start it now and let me keep it going for you. I have some management skills. I only need thirty hours to achieve my liberal arts degree.

Dexter, give me a chance to help you and help myself. I won't let you down. This way, I can save my money and put it back into whatever you want to do. Then we can become partners. I have a good sense for business, li'l brother. I just never had the chance to show what I can do. I've always wanted to talk to you concerning this opportunity, but was not stable enough and I knew you didn't have faith in me at the time. Now, it is time. I'll be forty by the time I'm out of here, and I'll be ready mentally.

Some way I get the feeling that you want to help me. I know that the past has stopped you from investing in me because of my lifestyle. But invest in me now, Dexter, and I'll bring you a good return. Let's work together. I see a lot of people here that are rotting away, and I don't want to be like they are. And I hope you don't want to see me here the rest of my life.

There is so much that I can do, man. If you want to set something up in Houston or wherever, it does not make any difference. Let's get something going. We need to put our heads together, or I'll let you decide what it should be and take it from there. This could be a good reunion for us, Dexter.

Things are fine. Everybody is asking bout you. There's a lot of fellows here that you were raised up with.

I know camp is getting ready to start, so do your thing, man, and show them what you're made of. Say, so y'all need an equipment man or anything? Do you still have a butler or chauffeur? Oh yeah, be sure and tell Glinda and the children hello and that I send love to all of them. Do you still have your Ford Bronco, or is it time for some new wheels? If so, I'd like to have the Bronco. I am going to need something to get around in.

If you have maybe $1,000 or $2,000 spare, I can get me an old piece of car or truck to get me by. I guess you say I'm sure asking for a lot (smile). Look at it this way, how can I look as sharp as you if I'm walking (smile)?

Say, Dexter. I'll close now, but never my love.

> Love Always,
> Big Brother, Greg

P.S. Write me, dog gonit. Be cool, I love you. Or maybe ask Glinda to write the letter for you.

I'll give a chronological rundown of what happened next:

Gregory was released from jail on September 14, and Cynthia was afraid he would hook up with the girl he wrote about in his letter. Cynthia said she's bad news and wanted Gregory to come stay with her instead.

On September 19 I talked to Gregory for the first time after he was out of jail. He was living with Cynthia, and he sounded all right, though he asked me for some cash. Cynthia's husband was to get back from a trip, and they were going to give Gregory a barbecue later in the day.

On September 26 Cynthia told me Gregory had stolen their car the previous day. Her mother-in-law had given her a car, and Gregory took off in it, and she had called the police. We agreed he'd probably show up and come up with some excuse, but I knew he wasn't getting any more money from me. I had wired him $300, but no more. It's called "tough love."

Cynthia found out where the car was five days after Gregory took it. The water pump had broken, and Greg just left it at a service station. Cynthia called the station to make sure they didn't give him the car keys when they got it fixed. He wouldn't have had any money to pay for repairs anyway.

Gregory then had the nerve to show up at Cynthia's house. He admitted, "I know I made a dumb move," and that was it. Cynthia said, "Gregory, you don't care about anyone but yourself. I needed to get to the store and couldn't even get the kids to the doctor.

A week later Gregory stole a $180 car payment from Cynthia.

He'd also pawned their lawn mower. Cynthia told me she'd never let him back in the house, not even to eat.

On November 5 Gregory's parole officer came by because he had skipped an appointment. Cynthia called Greg's girlfriend's house to let him know he had better call his parole officer because he had a warrant for his arrest.

By December 11 Gregory was back in jail. It only took him three months to find his way back behind bars. Isn't that ridiculous? Because he broke probation, they were looking for him; and they found him because he got arrested for stealing.

You know what I hear he stole? *Contact lenses!* He thought he could sell them and make some money.

If not for football, this could have been *my* story.

AN IDLE THOUGHT

I never did get to do a United Way commercial.

C H A P T E R 39

Fifth Down

A LOT OF PEOPLE WISH THEY COULD RETIRE BY the age of thirty-five. Well, I tried it, and all I can say is, Don't give up your day job.

For years, I had several visions of my life after retirement: homeless and losing teeth fast; pushing a Safeway shopping cart; using *The Washington Post* sports page as my blanket; holding an empty Campbell's cream of mushroom soup can and begging for nickels.

For this reason, I figured to be a tightwad upon leaving Tampa Bay, but I arrived in Chicago for Christmas and blew a wad of money instead. I was driving my rental car down the Loop—not a compact car, by the way—and had the urge to buy a full-length fur coat. I laid out four grand for a coat the clerk said retailed at eighteen grand. I must've still been a big name; my purchase was noted in the *Chicago Tribune* the next morning.

I admit shelling out that kind of cash was compulsive behavior. It was my disease talking, and it was something I had to explain to Glinda. It was like buying the Rolls-Royce all over again.

When I wore the coat in public, I began judging every person around me. I'd see a successful businessman, and I'd compare his outside to my inside. I may have been as dressed up as a CEO, but my outside did not match up with my inside, and I was kicking myself. I kept beating myself up.

Christmas night, Glinda and I took Little Dexter to the Bulls-Celtics game, and it was agonizing to watch other pro athletes and know I was no longer in the frat. I watched Joe Montana interviewed on "Monday Night Football," and I knew that old sucker was gonna get one more season. But myself, I couldn't even come out of retirement like Kareem Abdul-Jabbar says he wants to do every year.

At the Bulls-Celtics game, Little Dexter asked me, "Are you

stronger than Michael Jordan, Daddy?" He then wanted Jordan's auto-graph. After the game, Glinda saw Jordan's wife, introduced herself, and started making chit-chat. She then had Mrs. Jordan autograph Little Dexter's cap. I kept at a distance.

I admit it was comforting that so many people at the Bulls game tapped me on the shoulder, gave me a thumbs up, and said they were pulling for me. I guess people like me, maybe because I'm an underdog. But not only was I now an underdog, I was still worrying if I could afford underwear. Ain't I strange? I buy a full-length fur coat, but then I'm saying I've got to pinch pennies.

I thought I'd be more frugal than to buy a fur coat, but it just shows you how much I needed a quick fix. Darryl Grant can attest to my normal tightness:

Man, I've seen Dexter tip waiters a penny. I'd say, "Why, Dex?" and he'd say, "Darryl, they got jobs. Besides, my soup was cold."

I once tipped a bellcap at the Dulles Airport five dollars for lugging my bags, and he said, "Thanks, man. You're all right. Dexter Manley came through here not long ago with twenty Louis Vuitton bags and tipped two of us fifty cents each."

I'm not that low-down. I give cash to the homeless, and I keep a list of percentages in my wallet so I can calculate how much to tip. I admit I can be dirt cheap if I have to, though. One of my tricks is to carry around a lot of big bills—fifties and hundreds. That way when I go out with a buddy to eat, I can say, "Man, all I've got is big bills. Can you pick this one up?" I read where Muhammad Ali used to do that.

I just like to give myself perks, like the fur coat. I've spoiled myself too much over the years. I've treated myself to pedicures and facials. I mean, I'd always be the only black guy in the salon.

I've probably done the facial thing because I had the money and wanted to look like a million bucks, and I've doubted my looks. It's a carryover from childhood. I was this dark kid with a funny gap in his teeth, and it took me a long time to realize I was handsome. Now, I mean it when I say that scar on my cheek is sexy.

My fear is that I'll get a beer belly and go bald. I've already had a hair weave once—back when I played for the Redskins—and it didn't take. Actually, it was a hair transplant, and I had to wear a white turban on my head afterward, like Pham, so the plugs wouldn't infect.

I wore the turban for a whole day, and when I returned to the doc the next day to get my head washed, there was blood everywhere. I spent $2,500 for that crap.

See, I want to look upscale. Probably it's a façade thing. When the Bucs played the Vikings in Minnesota last year, I bought twelve different bow ties. I decided bow ties would be my new fad; they seem impressive on people. Come to think of it, Mr. Bidwill wears bow ties, and I've thought about calling him in Phoenix for instructions on how to tie one.

He'd probably say, "Oh, *no*, Dexter, I can't help you."

My latest quest before retirement had been to get braces for my teeth. I know I'm thirty-four, but it's never too late for braces. I have a slight underbite, and I want it corrected. Glinda can't believe it because she and everyone else likes my smile the way it is:

He's so phobic about his looks. I made the mistake of noticing his underbite a couple years ago. I said, "Dexter, you're beginning to look like my old dog, Heather," and he took me literally.

After New Year's, I took my bow ties and my fur coat home to D.C. for the first time since retirement. All those material things wouldn't help me now. The Redskins were about to make their Super Bowl run, and they were all over the news; and it made me envious and depressed and urgent to use drugs again.

I could hardly stand being in D.C. It wasn't as if I could walk around town with one of those William Kennedy Smith trial fuzzballs over my face. Everyone recognized me and knew I'd been a scoundrel again. I had such a fear of not having football adulation anymore. I needed publicity. I *need* it! I enjoyed being the talk of town when I was a Redskin, but now that I was retired, you think anyone would pay a nickel's worth of attention to me? No one runs up to Bobby Mitchell or Charley Taylor anymore, and they're Hall of Famers.

In the middle of all this Redskin mania, I hated that I'd never gotten the chance to return one more time to RFK Stadium as a member of an opposing team. Would they have booed me? I doubt it. I know that if I'd gotten a sack, I would've pointed over to Joe Gibbs and boned him.

As I sat in D.C., I missed so much about football. I missed being on "Monday Night Football." I used to love it when Hank Williams, Jr., sang "Are you ready?" before every Monday night game.

As the Redskins made their 1991 Super Bowl run without me, I was glued to the TV set. I rooted for them, darn it. I sat there like a glutton for punishment and watched every sportscast and player interview. It made me want to vomit and reminisce at the same time. I remembered the Sundays we'd leave for the Super Bowl. We would get a police escort to the airport for a big sendoff, and all the roads would be blocked off. And I'd have thirty or forty tickets to sell, which meant *big* money. Sitting at home watching it from a distance, though, I found myself feeling envious. That was supposed to be *me* out there.

I mean, I once owned D.C. Now that I wasn't a part of it, I felt like a retired player. I was watching Art Monk and Jim Lachey, and I said to myself, I belong out there. I realized—it's amazing it took me this long to realize it—drugs got me run out of Washington.

Only one Redskin called me to see how I was doing: Darrell Green again. I didn't expect anyone to call anyway. It was that way before, and why should it be different now?

It was agonizing to see all the Super Bowl hype. Charles Mann got interviewed live from his house on CBS by Greg Gumbel and Terry Bradshaw. As the Super Bowl approached and the more I thought about it, I knew I either had to find a job to get my mind off the Redskins or check into drug rehab somewhere. Maybe it was time to head back to Sierra Tucson and walk the serenity trail. Maybe it was time to listen to my drug counselors—*for once.*

As far as finding employment, I got a job offer a few days after retirement. Some guy telephoned Bob Woolf to say he'd hire me as a bounty hunter. I told Bob to forget it. That's not my gig. My kids are too important to me.

I'd prefer a job at the Ritz Carlton. Remember, I wanted to major in hotel/restaurant management? Well, it's never too late now that I can read. The Ritz Carlton is right up my alley. I want the best, and the Ritz, to me, is the best hotel in the world. I hope the Ritz would have me. Some companies might hold my relapse against me, which is a consequence I must live with.

It's like when I first came forward with my illiteracy. If I'd stayed sober, I could've taken the world by storm. Companies were knocking on my door, writing me letters. If I'd stayed clean and sober, I could've been another Bill Cosby. *Reader's Digest* was planning an in-depth piece on me, and I was expecting to do an interview with *Sports Illustrated for Kids.* I had that movie deal with Leonard Goldberg going, too. My name was making a comeback in a good, clean way. But that's gone—for now.

we don't address it now. It took her a long time just to spell her name. She'd have the D and A and the L and the I and the S, but not in order. She'd shout, "Well, I have it down on the paper!"

You just can't put her in a class with thirty kids, so I called Sara Hines, my tutor. I'm not overconcerned, but I'm going to get Dalis in specialized classes if I have to tip people *half* a cent. My kids are going to get it right; I'll make sure they get it. I'll make sure that I save enough money so they can learn to read and write and go to Europe by themselves some day and take trains to Italy and Germany like white middle-class kids do.

My kids mean much more to me than . . . fur coats. I'll never forget the day one of the Redskins' defensive coaches, Larry Peccaitello, asked me, "Do you tell your kids you love them? Do you hug them and kiss them?" I felt like saying, "Get the fuck out of my face." I took it like, Oh, I'm a black guy, and I don't know how to show that kind of compassion.

Hell, I kiss my kids so much, it's as if I'm Saudi Arabian. I want them to say, "He's a good daddy." I want them to be able to say that with conviction, so I give them the love I never got. I kiss them on one cheek and then the other, and tell them, "Your blood is precious. Your blood is royalty." And I really do think our blood is royalty.

No matter what Larry Peccaitello thinks, I tell my kids I love them, and I show them I love them by getting them the best education.

The irony is, if Joe Theismann had never broken his leg and if I hadn't had my *own* problem diagnosed at the Lab School, I could be sitting here with two learning-disabled children and not knowing what the hell to do.

With Little Dexter, we've had teachers say he is so brilliant, so manipulative, so cunning. Sounds like me, huh? He is not stupid, but you have to teach him differently. I ask Dexter to raise his right arm and he'll usually raise his left. I'm not saying my kids are dyslexic, but they can't learn at the same rate as other kids or the same way.

Thanks to the diagnosis of his learning disability, Little Dexter loves school. He literally hates weekends. On a Friday night, both he and Dalis will say, "Is it school tomorrow?" When Glinda says no, they go, "Ohhhhhh." Little Dexter's self-esteem is up, too. He looks at the clock and can't wait to run across the street to first grade.

We originally had Little Dexter in a school for gifted children when he was three. One day he was walking down the stairs for the school bus and started crying. He was praying, "Oh, Jesus, please give me a happy day today." Glinda had him out of that school the next day.

She said any time a three and one-half-year-old has to pray for a happy day in school, something's wrong. It was too much for him. Other kids were whizzing by him.

They say that most school dropouts in this country are learning-disabled children. They feel like failures when they're at school. So thank heavens we had the Lab School at our disposal to get Little Dexter diagnosed.

In the meantime, it was time for Little Dexter's daddy to go back to *Daddy School.*

A week before the Redskins–Bills Super Bowl in Minneapolis, I checked into Sierra Tucson for drug treatment. Thomas Henderson talked me into it:

I, Hollywood Henderson, predicted everything that happened to Dexter Manley. He didn't want to listen. See, if you play around with sobriety—if you slow down instead of stop or if you take a sip of champagne—you're done.

He took his sip of champagne, and you know what that led to. It does not matter if he says he's not a big drinker. If he drinks a glass of alcohol—one glass!—it has still altered his mind. I told him, "It's going to get you." All of my predictions were, "You're going to relapse. You're going to get banned." I told him, "The NFL'll give you a double-life sentence. They'll call it a life ban without possibility of reconsideration. The Dexter Manley Clause."

Now I just pray Dexter will be focused and will not sit there with a wish list that's impossible to reach. He wants to work in radio and TV, but he might as well forget the national network. He can probably work in local radio in D.C. That's realistic.

I've always been Dexter's reality check. He'll call me and say, "Hey, Thomas! It's Dexter here!" He'll do his pleasantries, and then I'll say, "What the heck have you done now?" When we finally get down to business, he can't stay on the phone too long. I'm too much reality for him.

The difference between Dexter Manley and me is that I found myself in a hell hole, in the joint, in jail. I'd never been banned by the NFL, but I'd been banned by myself to prison. Dexter doesn't have to hit that rock bottom, I hope.

Gary Mack dropped me at Sierra Tucson's front door, but I didn't exactly sprint in. I had fought every drug conselor I'd ever met.

I'd doubted their theories and conned them. Why would this trip be any different?

There were twenty or so patients in my unit, and I rebelled from the first moment. I was the only black person in there, and I was big and obviously stuck out like a sore thumb. They accused me of loitering in the detox area and reprimanded me. I'd gone there to get some tetracycline for my skin, and they said I was loitering. Other patients had hung out more than me, but everyone *knew* who I was, so I got shit on.

I wasn't helping matters because I complained immediately about not being able to use the phone. You know me and the phone. But so what if my vice is the phone. I've been in rehab centers where patients had sex and were drinking and drugging behind counselors' backs. *I've been places where they used drugs in treatment!*

All I did was sneak the use the phone. I saw an office door open and called Glinda.

The last straw was when my counselors assigned me to an AA meeting, and I wanted to attend an NA (Narcotics Anonymous) meeting instead. I said, "It seems like a mistake: I need to go to NA." My counselors got pissed. They wanted me to sign a contract that said I should go to the meetings I was assigned to, I should not loiter, and I should always have a phone pass when I used the phone. They said if I violated the contract there would be no second chances. I'd be booted out.

I did them a favor. I left.

I hadn't even completed five days of treatment, and I already was on a flight out of there. I wouldn't call to tell Glinda though. I realized that Glinda's role in my life had become like a mother's. She'd scold me, and I didn't want to be scolded.

As I was bolting Sierra Tucson, one of the counselors asked, "Are you about to use? Are you about to do drugs?" Hell, I only do drugs when I'm up. I had no desire to use. If Freddie had walked in the room with that Pennzoil can full of coke, I would have ignored him.

That night I sat in a Phoenix hotel room thinking about it. No, I didn't want to use drugs, but if I didn't listen to my disease, I would use them again eventually. I'll just do a little bit, I would convince myself.

Being in Sierra Tucson—even only for five days—was a reality check. It hurt so much to be back in treatment saying, "How? Why?" But I'd eased out of the program in Tampa, by no longer attending the meetings and staying in touch. I didn't take care of Dexter. I took care of my disease.

It hit me then. I said to myself in that sterile Phoenix hotel room, "Goddamnit, maybe I should go back to Sierra Tucson." I thought how powerful it would be for me to walk right back in that front door. I called them to tell them I was returning.

They said no.

I felt hurt, rejected. Two other patients from my group had left the program when I left, and my unit had been in disarray. Sierra Tucson didn't want me back because of that. They said I could come back with a new unit thirty days from then, but not now. I felt sad and humbled. I really *wanted* treatment, and I would've gone to any length to go back in. I was eager, but they flat-out rejected me.

When I finally broke the news to Glinda, she was pissed and wanted a separation from me. She finally was prepared to rename Little Dexter:

That's because I didn't want Little Dexter carrying around his father's prophecy. Little Dexter had the same name, looked like him, and had the same learning disability. Maybe he'd carry it all the way and use drugs, too.

So I asked Little Dexter, "How do you like your middle name, Keith?"
Little Dexter said, "No, I like the name Jason."

I flew from Phoenix to Houston to see my only sibling who wasn't in jail: Cynthia. I watched the Redskins win the Super Bowl with my son Derrick. Part of me didn't want to see the game. I said to myself, I can't watch this. It was difficult because it made me look at myself and think I was no good. But it's not me that's no good, it's my *disease* that's no good.

The Redskins won big, and I was sort of depressed. But then I thought, How does Dan Henning feel? Jay Schroeder? Buges? They weren't with the Skins anymore, either, and I bet those boys were envious, too. I talked to Darryl Grant, and he said he couldn't even watch the Super Bowl. I thought I was the only guy going through it, but that wasn't true.

I woke up the morning after the game and thought of George Rogers, another ex-Redskin who's been on drugs and can't find a job. I didn't want to be another him.

I should've bugged Jack Kent Cooke for a job. Hell, when I signed my contract in 1983, he wanted to act like my best friend and told me,

"I'll get you a job when your career is over." He's so full of it. I don't know what he had in mind; maybe he wanted me to be his chauffeur.

When I got home to D.C. the day of the Redskins victory parade, Glinda still hadn't left me. I took her and the family for granted, and I went out to use cocaine again. But my kids weren't tots any more. They were old enough to smell my disease a mile away. A friend came over, and Little Dexter and Dalis told him—when I wasn't in the room—"Did you hear? Daddy went and did drugs again."

At night, while I was dressing the master bedroom to go to a movie, I'd ask Glinda to go out with me. She'd snap, "No!" She wouldn't sleep with me and wouldn't touch me. It was me every night on the basement couch.

Like I said earlier, I was so fucked up I couldn't even read my kids a bedtime story.

I fled for Tucson again.

AN IDLE THOUGHT

I wonder who will show up at my funeral. I was thinking of this the other day when Glenn Brenner, the great Washington area sportscaster, died. Everyone showed up at his funeral. Everyone.

I daydream about who'll come to mine. I wonder who will be there, how many blocks and blocks of people will pay respect.

Or maybe nobody will show.

C H A P T E R   40

Reality Stroke

THE GOAL OF A TREATMENT CENTER IS TO separate your man from your boy. They want to know everything about your past, and they suspect there are issues from your youth—like being forced to eat all your string beans—that turned you into a troubled adult.

I have over and over doubted this. I have also doubted I belong in rehab—period. The last place I went to—Sierra Tucson—grouped me with victims of incest, with depressed people who were always yawning, and with people who had attempted to kill themselves by slitting their wrists. I could not see how somebody who liked cocaine from time to time fit in with them.

On one of my first days inside, a member of our primary group was giving vivid details of how his daddy beat him. Matter of fact, he was reliving it and cowered, "Stop! Stop!" As I eyed him, my body began to shake visibly, and I drifted into some sort of shock. I was remembering how my daddy whupped me for setting my neighbor's house on fire and how he banished me to a closet. I was going back some twenty-plus years.

The guy in my group kept saying how he'd needed love from his daddy, and I shrunk as I sat there, agreeing from my own experience. Then the guy fell to his hands and knees as if in a seizure. He hit the ground hollering and kicking, and instantly it took me back in time. I remembered my uncle—his name was Huey D, and he was my momma's brother—who used to have epileptic fits at our house in the Third Ward. He'd be in my bedroom and go into a seizure, and I'd run wildly out of the room. Momma would order me to get a spoon and towel to make sure he didn't swallow his tongue, and I'd be right in the middle of his fit.

I remembered other times when he was violent, once chasing us out of the house with a knife. His brain wasn't well. Another day, he

348

started cutting all the telephone wires in our house, and we had to run next door to call our daddy. By the time Daddy raced home from work, Huey D was gone. That Huey D was a mean sonofabitch. He later got shot and killed in a drive-by. Supposedly, some guy had made a mean comment to Huey D, who cut him up with knife. He was coming out of a grocery store not long after and got shot in retaliation.

Well, this guy in my primary group conjured up all this childhood trauma for me. The experience brought back a lot of issues, and I started shaking and crying and my body went into shock. I froze, and I began kicking. I don't believe I had a seizure, but I was experiencing a lot of powerful emotion.

I naturally wanted to know why my body freaked out like that. Back in 1986, you'll recall, I passed out in Georgetown. What I didn't tell anybody is that I banged my head while falling, and an MRI (Magnetic Resonance Imaging) showed a little spot—smaller than a penny—in my brain. I guess you could call it a tumor, and the doctors were fairly sure I was born with it. They said it was of little concern unless it grew, but they suggested I monitor it every six months or so. However, I've been sloppy with my MRI appointments, and after my episode at Sierra Tucson, I wanted to know if the tumor was the cause. I will undergo more tests soon.

In the days following my outburst, my counselors sensed I was still fighting their program and denying, for the most part, the severity of my addictions. One of them pinpointed me and said, "You haven't lost anything. You lost your job, but you still have money and your family." He then asked me a question: "What can cocaine do to you?"

"Kill you," I answered.

He agreed and mentioned Len Bias, but then I said, "Yeah, but Len Bias was smoking coke. I don't free-base. I wasn't smoking it, so it's not as likely I'll die."

Then he asked, "Do you know cocaine can cause a stroke, too?"

That got my attention. I know strokes are one of the nastiest things someone can have. I'd rather be dead than have a stroke, or I'd rather have a heart attack.

When I related that to my counselor, he gave me an assignment. He ordered me to have a "reality stroke." He said, "I want you in a wheelchair."

"What?" I wanted to know.

"You take pride in your body," he said. "You're strong and look good, but what if cocaine gave you a stroke? Then you'd know what it's like to lose something."

I had to stay in a wheelchair for five days with one of my arms in a sling. In treatment you often find people walking around with a blindfold and cane, guided wherever they need to go by members of their primary group. They are sentenced to this blindness because they must learn how to trust, and in blindness they have no choice but to try.

Well, my "reality stroke" was similar. I was told not to leave the wheelchair—up until bedtime—and every time I wanted the hell out of that chair, for some reason, I always thought of cocaine. I thought of Mike Utley, the Detroit Lions player who was paralyzed last season making a block; and I thought of Darryl Stingly, the former New England Patriot who was paralyzed diving for a ball; and I thought of Jack Tatum, the Oakland Raider who hit the diving Stingley. I'd look at myself in the mirror at night and see this big body of mine plopped in this chair, and I'd think, This is awful. I'd think of drugs and of having a real stroke. The truth is, I was in awful pain those five days.

You don't know how glad I was to walk up a staircase finally. I was thrilled to jog up steps when it was over, although I found myself running up the ramps at first because I was so conditioned to using them.

My first few days in the wheelchair, I was still in my disease and mumbling, "What they're doing to me is abusive. My knees hurt from being cramped, and my butt hurts; and I'm not paying all this money to get my butt kicked." I almost started to walk out of the chair, but I caught myself and really, truly said to myself, This is what can happen from cocaine.

The hardest parts were not being able to get up from the chair on those nice, sunny days and having to ask people to roll me around. Every time I wanted up, I thought of cocaine, though. Hell, I could've gotten up. No one could have stopped me, but I pondered my commitment and stuck to it. It's like they say in the Big Book of AA: You have to be willing to go to any length. Well, I tried—for once.

The other thing my counselors started drumming into me was their belief I was a sex addict. I doubted them, but they made me wear a badge, nonetheless, that said, "Male Contact Only." That was their method. I said I wasn't a sex addict, and they promised I was; so they said, "OK, fine, you don't think you are, but wear this badge that says, Male Contact Only. If you say you're not, then it's no big deal."

So here I was with this label. It was as if you had to hide the women and children, as if I were a Los Angeles Raider.

This is how my wife and kids found me three weeks into my thirty-day stay when they flew to Arizona for Family Week. Family Week can be a frightening experience, but I guess it's also necessary. Members of your immediate family—from your parents to your kids—are invited. The purpose is to confront and settle issues between you and each one of them. It is supposed to help delve into your past and to put your secrets right out into the fray.

Glinda, Derrick, Little Dexter, Dalis, and my uncle Wilbur Hewitt—my momma's brother—made the trip. My sister Cynthia had a baby to look after and was absent.

The first day, I was allowed to speak with my family members and eat dinner with them, but after that dinner all contact was prohibited. The rule was that I could not speak to them or even correspond indirectly with them—via notes or cards—until the fourth day, other than in therapy. This was slightly horrifying to my younger kids, Dexter and Dalis, who would point at me when I walked by or wave or tug on their mommy's sleeve. I had no choice but to ignore them.

I guess the purpose of this was to reinforce the serious mood of the week. On the second day of Family Week, the members of my family were required to "list" me. It is actually called a "Tough Love List," where they write down what has bothered them about me. They would cite a specific behavior of mine and then say how it made them feel, such as, "When you went back on drugs, I felt sad and angry."

The counselors stressed that when we all relate our feelings, we should choose among the following words: *angry, sad, afraid, lonely, ashamed, hurt,* and *guilty.* Only those words.

The first person to list me was my oldest son, Derrick, who is fifteen. He is not very open with his feelings, so the process forced him to get some things off his chest. As it turned out, this was a great gift for Derrick, a forum for him to look me in the eye and unload on me. Considering he's been called "Dumb Dexter" in school because of me, he had much to relay.

The counselors had us move face-to-face in the middle of the room; we were circled by the other family members, the counselors, and the members of my primary group. Derrick seemed a bit uptight, but his main complaint with me was the following:

"When we were in Tampa for Thanksgiving and we were in your truck and you told me there was a positive drug test but you promised you hadn't used drugs . . . and then I got back to Houston and saw you admit on TV and you *had* used drugs, I felt angry and hurt."

Derrick broke down telling me this. I had lied to him, and it confounded him. Later, the counselors asked him what kind of relationship he'd like between me and him in the future, and Derrick took a long gulp, broke down again, and said, "Live . . . with . . . my . . . dad." The sadness in him was something I cannot describe. Looking back, I got in a fight the night Derrick was born, his mom and I split up when he was three, and I've been a telephone daddy pretty much since. Life has not been simple for him.

My other kids, the younger ones, did not "list" me. Instead, they drew pictures, under the direction of a child counselor, to depict their feelings. Little Dexter's picture was of me getting dressed to go out at night and going into a restaurant to use drugs. On the back, he was to draw a picture of how it made him feel, and his drawing showed tears down his cheek. He went on to say my drug use made him feel "sad and angry."

Dalis's picture was similar, especially the tears; but she would not look at me, and this made me cry. The only time she looked at me was when the child counselor asked how my drug use had made her feel. At that moment, she finally batted her beautiful eyes at me and said, "I felt mad."

Glinda was to "list" me the next day. The day before, I had tried to pass a card to her to tell that I loved her. But she rejected it, knowing cards were against the rules:

I felt scared when he tried getting that card to me, for it meant he was still in his disease. He knew he wasn't supposed to write me, and he had no regard for the rule. Same as before.

When she finally "listed" me, Glinda brought up her feelings about our marriage and about my phone calls to other women. There were tears, too, and she mentioned that she might leave me.

The next day, I was to "list" everyone back, to say what bothered me about them. Derrick was first again, and I said, "When we played tennis one time and you didn't hustle when I asked you to hustle, I felt hurt, sad, and angry."

I meant that. I expect him to show pride in his athletics. I then "listed" him for his poor schoolwork and for talking back to his grandmother and his mom (Miss Baker and Stephanye). I guess I have high expectations for Derrick, and Derrick usually doesn't meet them. I told the counselors I do not want my son "flipping hamburgers" someday and that he had to get on the ball. One of the counselors said flipping hamburgers is reality, but it ain't reality for my son. I try to put pressure on my kids. The Japanese believe in education, and I believe in education, and I said I did not want a kid of mine flipping burgers. I know that's part of life for some, and I'm sure my counselors thought I was arrogant to believe my son was too special to flip burgers. They probably felt I put my kids on some pedestal. But, darnit, most wealthy or upper-middle-class families don't have their sons flipping burgers.

I have to pull feelings out of Derrick; he does not volunteer them. A couple of weeks after I listed him in Tucson, I visited him in Houston and asked, "Are you mad at me?" He said, "I don't know" and hunched his shoulders. I believe it was great that in Tucson Derrick was forced to expound on things, but when I still saw him hunching his shoulders and saying "I don't know" in Houston, I felt sad. Something's not clicking.

But I love Derrick, and I still feel the Tucson experience and the "listing" experience were probably more valuable for Derrick than for anyone else. He's in the ninth grade, and he has four years left until he's out of high school. He has to take advantage of opportunities and get out of his shell and apply himself. I keep telling him if he doesn't, he'll end up flipping those burgers, and there'll be no one to blame but Derrick. I believe he is at a crossroads. One day we drove to see my brother Gregory in jail, and we saw a derelict pushing a cart full of empty cans, I cautioned, "Derrick, if you don't get busy, if you don't get your education, that's what will happen to you."

"It didn't happen to you," he said, "and you couldn't read or write."

I snapped. "Derrick, you don't understand. I had football. I worked diligently at it. But I don't see any of that [diligence] in you."

Because of Derrick's comment during that ride, I realize he has a lot of issues to deal with regarding me. Since his bad grades coincided with my latest drug relapse, it may have brought him down. I've seen him get As and Bs, and that's why I push him. But Sierra Tucson can give him an opportunity in life, give him values and a way to express himself. Hell yes, my behavior over the years has affected him. He catches abuse in school about me, and he doesn't feel like he has his dad because I'm not with him. But I have to accept my behavior, and he has to, too.

The great thing is since Tucson his teacher has called to say Derrick's grades have drastically improved.

Derrick is undergoing therapy now, like all my kids are. I want him to *know* I give a hoot about him, and I even left training camp in Ottawa to visit him in Houston and support him.

As for my two other kids, it was difficult to "list" them because they are so young. But with Little Dexter, I said, "When we went to the skating rink and I told you we had to leave and you called me a bad daddy, I felt sad, hurt, and angry."

Little Dexter nodded, and I believe he heard me loud and clear.

With Dalis, I said, "When you have not cleaned up your room, I felt sad and angry." She still couldn't force herself to look at me.

When it came to Glinda, I admitted some things to her that seemed to turn around her state of mind:

I *went in there with no hope of a marriage, but I left with hope. I set some boundaries and he made some commitments to me.*

Once upon a time, I was a great husband. But because of my chemical dependency and my disease . . .

Listen, people always call Glinda "Saint Glinda" for sticking by me, and I am surprised she has stayed with me this long. The thing about it is, black women are strong. Not that Glinda's a fool for staying, it's just that women are the backbone, so I had a strong backbone.

Right now, she and I are at a tough stage. We're building trust, or shall I say, I am. Glinda's been an integral part of my success. She's critiqued me on my football, and she's stood by me. She knows I'm a dedicated guy and will pay the price, and she tells it to me straight.

But the most important thing I want is to be a positive force for my family. There are times I have been one and—because of drugs— times I haven't. So if I had it to do again, I would do it differently. I wouldn't have associated with some people she didn't want me to, like Freddie.

So I want to be more positive for her and for my kids. I want her and them to see me do constructive things. When my father was at Tenneco Oil Company, he invested in stock; I want to leave that kind of legacy and be something they can be proud of.

Up until now, it's been frighteningly difficult for my family, but one thing I have to say about my wife is: Tough times never last, but tough people do. That's my wife. She's been stronger than me.

She's also been compassionate, warm, gentle, and a pleasure to talk with. When Glinda and I first met—March 31, 1982—we stayed together every day for a year. I had never experienced anything like that. Man, I truly love my wife, and I've done a lot of crap she doesn't approve of. At times, she'll say mean things to me because she's angry, and she has every right to be angry. When she gets that acid tongue, you wonder if there's love there; but I have a lot of respect for Glinda. My hat goes off to her that she's stood by me because I'm not an easy guy to live with. I'll love her to the end.

*W*hen *Dexter loses everything, maybe he'll get real. I'm just not sure that going to Sierra Tucson and to AA meetings back in D.C. are enough. I mean, he used to buy dope from a guy in AA meetings; so don't tell me just going to meetings is the cure-all. What's Dexter lost?*

I've had my son say to me, "Mom, why don't you find a man that doesn't use drugs?" My kid just wants somebody he can depend on and will be there for him. I tell Little Dexter that when you use drugs, you lose your job and your family. Of course, I've yet to prove the last one because I haven't left Big Dexter. You know what? I should put survived *on my license plates.*

The last day of Family Week was Reconcilation Day, where you ask for forgiveness and list what you love and like about everyone. You get a lot of hugs on Reconcilation Day.

The whole thing was an illuminating experience. I can't tell you I benefited from Sierra Tucson's lectures about drug abuse because I've heard every lecture there ever was about drugs. Let's face it: I've been to four treatment centers. But what I *did* learn in Tucson was that I don't have to hold secrets. For once, I got something out of rehab. When I get bored and restless—and it happens a lot—I realize that's my disease kicking in. It makes me impulsive, gets me on the phone.

I also know sex is a problem, but I'm not ready to go to sex addiction meetings yet. It's something I must work on.

Most of all, I believe there's an inner child in me, an inner child I carry with me wherever I go. Drugs must be hereditary. They *must* be. I've learned that much, and I've learned my past had *something* to do with it. I learned I must grieve the loss of my job in the NFL. I feel angry; but I must do more anger work, whether it's running to a parking lot and hollering, or whatever.

I cannot blame Yates High School, Oklahoma State, the Redskins, Joe Gibbs, or anything else for my illiteracy and my drug problem. I cannot blame my momma and daddy. I've got to blame myself. My momma and daddy didn't have the money to send me to a special school, and I can say I'm angry because they didn't pay enough attention to me or because the school system didn't help me. I'm allowed to be angry, just like my kids have a right to be angry with me. Anger is OK. My kids have a right, for instance, to their own bodies, and I shouldn't spank them. That's another thing I learned in Tucson. Hell, I caught some spankings as a child, and I can finally see that was abuse. My daddy never hit me with his hands or his fists, but I had two or three hellacious spankings from him, like the one after I set that neighbor's house on fire. That's when he also made me sit in a closet two or three times after school. I didn't sit in there long, but that was Daddy's way of making sure I never flicked a match again. He was trying to break me. Well, when that happened to me, I felt like my body didn't count. Now I've learned that every human being has a right to his or her body. If I don't want to be spanked, then getting spanked is going against my will. Same goes for my kids.

But can I blame my daddy for my adult problems? No. When I was a kid, I was born without the ability to read or write, and I thought it was impossible for someone to teach me how. Who did I blame? I blamed God because I felt, Why was I born this way? But now that I'm older and have been successful financially, I'm able to pay for the right education for myself. Imagine the people who can't pay for that? It isn't free, you know. So I feel fortunate.

Can I change my drug ways now? It's not easy to change. They say you have to go to Twelve-step meetings every day, but I was never willing to go to any length to change. I was satisfied just being sober, and I didn't want to go that extra mile. Now I know I can't go to a club or run out to some bar. Before, I felt I could. I was influenced by Ray Charles and Sammy Davis, Jr., both of whom had been on chemicals and then stayed sober without going to meetings. I put myself with them and said, "I don't have to go to meetings because *they* didn't go. The only thing I have to do is stay sober."

What I'm saying is, I began to take *their* inventory, not mine. You hear so many theories from old black people who say beating chemical dependency is just a matter of will power, and those tapes kept playing in my head. I believed I could do it on my own.

But hell, no, I couldn't. When I left Tampa last December, I met two Italian guys at the airport who said they used to be on coke. I asked them, "Did you go to meetings?" They said they just looked in the mirror, didn't like what they saw, and quit. They said they'd been sober seven years, and I began to remember Ray Charles. He just quit on his own, too. Why couldn't I?

Well, today I know I've got to go to meetings. I know if I don't, I'll be on drugs and coke. What will that mean? It will mean that all the yets are still there: I've yet to go to jail, yet to lose my family, yet to go broke, yet to be homeless, yet to kill someone. If I go back to drugs, the yets are possible. And it's tempting to go back, even knowing all the yets.

Today I also know *I am not my disease*. The Dexter in me is a good guy, but my disease wants me to think I'm no good, that I can't be trusted, that I create bad things and destroy other lives, that I inflict pain on others, that I'm destructive. Just last May Dalis was sleeping with Glinda and me, and I accidentally fell on her and broke the tibia bone in her leg again. I began beating myself up over it, like I always do. It brought back that old feeling that I'm no good.

But the real Dexter in me is loving and supportive of my family. I *must* remember that. I used to think I was a bad guy, that I couldn't be responsible; but what I understand now—through Sierra Tucson—is that my disease sits next to me, sort of on my shoulder, but it's not me. If I think I am my disease, then I am making more trouble for myself.

Understanding this difference helps me feel more positive about Dexter. No question, Dexter is a good guy, a giving guy, a sensitive guy. I care for others. I'm not trying to blow my own horn, but I think I can share with you that whenever the Redskins asked me to make appearances—for free—I did them enthusiastically. The Redskins have told me I was more open to doing things than most guys. I know the *real* Dexter is dignified.

So, for my sanity, I have to keep on believing I am not part of my disease. My disease is like a computer that wants to talk to me and make me think it's a close personal friend. But somewhere this friend betrayed me; it told me, "You need me, you can't live without me." That disease has been there a long time, and that's why I am out of football.

Let me tell you, it's a fight to stay with the program. Right after I left Tucson, I went to an AA meeting and fell asleep. The meeting was slow, and when I woke up, I wanted to leave. *But I didn't walk out.* That's a change for me. I know that if I fall asleep, that's a relapse symptom; so I went to another meeting in the next room, a meeting that captivated me.

I am so glad I am off drugs. So glad. Any day off of drugs is so great. I'm able to read a lot and finish things I set out to do.

I was off of drugs when I left Tucson, and guess who I ran into at the airport coming home? Charley Casserly, the Redskins' general manager. He seemed surprised at how good I looked and how healthy I sounded. He probably expected some bum. As we stood there, thousands of miles away from D.C., people kept coming up to me asking for my autograph and saying, "We're rooting for you, Dexter." Charley thought that was just unbelievable. It shocked him how many people knew me.

So here I am, still with my image somewhat intact, still with people patting me on the back. I've turned a corner. I realized that maybe it was my upbringing, maybe it was my childhood, maybe I was from a dysfunctional family, maybe it wasn't all right that my daddy took a dump in our dresser drawer.

The point is, I've got to realize I am not a garbage truck inside. I am a person who understands his past, and I need to stay sober for me. But if staying sober for *me* is not enough motivation, maybe I can stay sober for my kids.

I drove Little Dexter to the dentist last summer, and it was like déjà vu. It made me think of the day my own daddy took me to the dentist, which ranks as one of my most thrilling memories of him. *He'd paid attention to me!* Well, *my* kids are going to have many wonderful memories of me, and not just the times I took them to get their teeth cleaned.

So you think I want to slip back to drugs? You think I want to go broke and take my kids into poverty with me? You think I want them to be running around shirtless in the Third Ward? Even if Glinda leaves me and takes the kids, I'll still be responsible for them. When Derrick and Little Dexter and Dalis reach twenty-one years old, they'll still need a daddy. When they reach thirty-one, they'll still need a daddy. When they reach forty-one, they'll still need a daddy.

Hell, I need a daddy.

AN IDLE THOUGHT

I'd like to find me a plastic surgeon and have my face redone. I'd play a year in college, get drafted number two overall in the NFL draft, take the league's money, put it in the bank, and then have the plastic surgeon restore my original face.

And then Paul Tagliabue would go, "Oh, my gosh. It's Dexter Manley!"